INVENTING THE SCHL

Terence Zuber is a retired United States Army Officer, who received his Ph.D. from the University of Würzburg. His publications include *German War Planning, 1891–1914: Sources and Interpretations* (2004), *The Moltke Myth: Prussian War Planning 1857–1871* (2008), *The Battle of the Frontiers: Ardennes 1914* (2008), *The Mons Myth* (2010), and *The Real German War Plan 1904–1914* (2011).

'All the older literature now needs to be revised in the light of Zuber'
Sir Hew Strachan, author of *The First World War: To Arms*

'Zuber's scholarly work will play an important role in the continuing debates on military planning and on its relationship to the coming of World War One'
Journal of European Studies

'Zuber has produced an important work that throws much light on war planning and also on the process by which strategic interpretations become part of historiography'
Journal of European Studies

'Zuber's new work is undoubtedly intellectually exciting, and has opened up new fronts in military and diplomatic history'
Gary Sheffield, *Times Literary Supplement*

'the most important book on World War I in decades'
Robert Citino, author of *The German Way of War*

Inventing the Schlieffen Plan

German War Planning,
1871–1914

TERENCE ZUBER

OXFORD
UNIVERSITY PRESS

OXFORD
UNIVERSITY PRESS

Great Clarendon Street, Oxford, OX2 6DP,
United Kingdom

Oxford University Press is a department of the University of Oxford.
It furthers the University's objective of excellence in research, scholarship,
and education by publishing worldwide. Oxford is a registered trade mark of
Oxford University Press in the UK and in certain other countries

First published 2002
First published in paperback 2014

Published in the United States of America by Oxford University Press
198 Madison Avenue, New York, NY 10016, United States of America

British Library Cataloguing in Publication Data
Data available

Library of Congress Cataloging in Publication Data
Data available

ISBN 978-0-19-925016-5 (Hbk)
ISBN 978-0-19-871805-5 (Pbk)

For my wife

TINA NEIL

Acknowledgements

THIS BOOK WOULD never have been completed without the support and encouragement of two exceptional historians, my *Doktorvater*, Professor Wolfgang Altgeld of the University of Würzburg, and Professor Hew Strachan of Oxford University. It was clear that my thesis—that there never was a Schlieffen plan—would not be popular among many historians. Nevertheless, Professor Altgeld approved my dissertation topic and gave me far more latitude to pursue my research than is customary for a doctoral candidate in Germany. No student has ever had a better *Doktorvater*. Professor Strachan, in his capacity as co-editor of *War in History*, received my journal submission, 'The Schlieffen Plan Reconsidered', after it had been rejected by another military history publication because of the reviewers' dislike of my thesis. Professor Strachan took it upon himself to insure that both the article and this book saw the light of day. Professor Strachan, the senior expert in the history of the Great War, also submitted my dissertation to a most thorough critique. Neither Professor Altgeld nor Professor Strachan can be accused of assisting me because they agreed with my thesis; rather, both acted purely in the spirit of non-partisan support for historical research and debate. Ruth Parr and her team at Oxford University Press were exceptionally helpful, as was Herr Klaus Schinagl, who prepared the maps and my copy editor, Nigel Hope, saved me from numerous errors in three languages and did his best to transform my military English into something readable.

I also owe a debt of thanks to Professor Harm-Hinrich Brandt, under whose guidance my initial research was conducted. Professor Rainer Schmidt has been a friend as well as a source of assistance and inspiration for over ten years. Through Professor Schmidt I learned about research in Germany and developed an interest in the wars of 1866 and 1870/71 which has become a passion. I owe a debt of gratitude to the faculty of the department of history of the University of Würzburg for their old-fashioned insistence on observing Leopold von Ranke's principles of *Quellenkritik* and non-ideological history. Research in German archives was always a joy. I would like to thank the staff of the Kriegsarchiv in Munich, the Bundesarchiv-Militärarchiv in Freiburg, the Hauptstaatsarchiv Stuttgart, the Generallandesarchiv Karlsruhe, and Hauptstaatsarchiv Dresden for their assistance. Last but not least I am deeply indebted to the library staff of the University of Würzburg, in particular the patient people in the inter-library loan section.

Although it is hardly customary in an academic book, I must acknowledge my debt to the soldiers with whom I have served. This history is as much a product of the things I learned as an infantry officer as it is the result of the study of history and research in the archives. The three years I spent on the staff of the 12th Panzer Division as the VII (US) Corps liaison officer were the most interesting of my military career. I learned more about operations, tactics, and leadership from Colonel i.G. Klaus Kleffner, the Division Chief of Staff, and Lieutenant-Colonel i.G. Heinz Eilers, the Division G-3, than at any other time in my military service. I was fortunate to command companies in the 3rd Infantry Division for over three years, first the 3rd AG Company and immediately thereafter B Company, 2nd Battalion, 30th Infantry. I am deeply indebted to the patriotism, dedication, knowledge, and enthusiasm of the officers, non-commissioned officers, and soldiers in both companies. I would also like to express my appreciation to Captain Peter Herrly (Commander, A Company, 1st Battalion, 12th Infantry), Lieutenant-Colonel Eldon K. Schroeder (Commander, 2nd Battalion, 2nd Infantry), Lieutenant-Colonel James Ogle (Inspector General, 3rd Infantry Division), and Lieutenant-Colonel William Tredennick (Chief, Combined Arms Department, Ft. Benjamin Harrison), who taught me a great deal about tactics, training, and leadership. I would also like to thank J for years of supporting a difficult subordinate under stressful conditions.

Würzburg
July 2002

Contents

List of Maps

Abbreviations

AHR	*American Historical Review*
APG	*Archiv für Politik und Geschichte*
BA-MA	Bundesarchiv-Militärarchiv Freiburg im Breisgau
BM	*Berliner Monatshefte*
BTH	*Berliner Tageblatt und Handelszeitung*
DAZ	*Deutsche Allgemeine Zeitung*
DOB	*Deutscher Offizier Bund*
DOBl	*Deutsches Offizierblatt*
DR	*Deutsche Review*
DSZ	*Deutsche Soldatenzeitung*
DW	*Deutsche Wehr*
DWS	*Deutsche Wochenschau*
EEQ	*East European Quarterly*
GLA	General Landes-Archiv Karlsruhe
GP	*Die Große Politik der Europäischen Mächte*
HJ	*Historical Journal*
HZ	*Historische Zeitschrift*
JCH	*Journal of Contemporary History*
JEH	*Journal of Economic History*
JMH	*Journal of Military History*
JRUSI	*Journal of the United Royal Services Institution*
JSM	*Journal des Sciences Militaires*
KSF	*Kriegsschuldfrage*
KZ	*Kreuzzeitung*
LV	*Ludendorffs Volkswarte*
MG	*Militärgeschichte*
MM	*Militärgeschichtliche Mitteilungen*
MPW	*Monatshefte für Politik und Wehrmacht*
MW	*Militärwochenblatt*
MWR	*Militärwissenschaftliche Rundschau*
PJ	*Preußische Jahrbücher*
RDM	*Revue des Deux Mondes*
SF	Schriftenreihe Festungsforschung
SM	*Süddeutsche Monatshefte*
Streuffleur's	*Streuffleur's Österreichische Militärische Zeitschrift*
TR	*Tägliche Rundschau*
VTfHk	*Vierteljahresheft für Truppenführung und Heereskunde*
WH	*War in History*
WR	*Wehrwissenschaftliche Rundschau*

WW	*Wissen und Wehr*
ZMG	*Zeitschrift für Militärgeschichte*
ZP	*Zeitschrift für Politik*

Preface to the Paperback Edition

INCORPORATING THE CONTROVERSY generated by *Inventing the Schlieffen Plan* into an expanded edition of this book was clearly out of the question. The paperback edition is identical with the hardbound: we have only corrected two typographical errors.

Inventing the Schlieffen Plan and my 1999 article in *War in History*, 'The Schlieffen Plan Reconsidered', set off an unprecedented "Schlieffen Plan" debate:

> T. Zuber, 'The Schlieffen Plan Reconsidered' in: *War in History*, 1999; 3: pp. 262–305.
>
> T. Holmes, 'A Reluctant March on Paris', in: *War in History*, 2001; 2: pp. 208–32.
>
> T. Zuber, 'Terence Holmes Reinvents the Schlieffen Plan' in: *War in History* 2001; 4, pp. 468–76.
>
> T. Holmes, 'The Real Thing' in: *War in History*, 2002, 1, pp. 111–20.
>
> T. Zuber, 'Terence Holmes Reinvents the Schlieffen Plan – Again' in: *War in History* 2003; 1, pp. 92–101.
>
> R. Foley, 'The Origins of the Schlieffen Plan' in: *War in History*, 2003; 2 pp. 222–32.
>
> T. Holmes, 'Asking Schlieffen: A Further Reply to Terence Zuber' in: *War in History* 2003; 4, pp. 464–79.
>
> T. Zuber, 'The Schlieffen Plan was an Orphan' in: *War in History*, 2004; 2 pp. 220–5.
>
> R. Foley, 'The Real Schlieffen Plan' in: *War in History*, 2006; 1, pp. 91–115.
>
> T. Zuber, 'The 'Schlieffen Plan' and German War Guilt' in: *War in History* 2007; 1, pp. 96–108.
>
> A. Mombauer, 'Of War Plans and War Guilt: The Debate Surrounding the Schlieffen Plan' in: *Journal of Strategic Studies* XXVIII, 2005.
>
> T. Zuber, 'Everybody Knows There Was a "Schlieffen Plan": A Reply to Annika Mombauer' in *War in History* 2008; 1. pp. 92–101.
>
> G. Gross, 'There Was a Schlieffen Plan: New Sources on the History of German War Planning' in: *War in History* 2008; 4, pp. 389–431.
>
> T. Holmes, 'All Present and Correct: The Verifiable Army of the Schlieffen Plan', in: *War in History* 2009, 16 (1) pp. 98–115.
>
> T. Zuber, 'There Never was a "Schlieffen Plan": A Reply to Gerhard Gross' in: *War in History* 17 (2) 2010 pp. 231–49.
>
> T. Zuber, 'The Schlieffen Plan's "Ghost Divisions" March Again: A Reply to Terence Holmes' in: *War in History* 17 (4) 2010 pp. 1–14.

A summary of these debate articles is available on my website, terencezuber.com:

Immediately after publication of *Inventing the Schlieffen Plan* in 2002, Sir Hew Strachan asked me to publish translations of the most important documents, which I did in *German War Planning 1891–1914. Sources and Interpretations* (Boydell and Brewer, 2004). These included Helmuth Greiner's Reichsarchiv study, "The German Intelligence Estimate in the West" (from 1885 to 1914), Wilhelm Dieckmann's Reichsarchiv study "Der Schlieffenplan", five of Schlieffen's General Staff rides, Schlieffen's great 1905 wargame, the 1906 "Schlieffen Plan" *Denkschrift*, the younger Moltke's 1908 General Staff ride, the actual German 1914 deployment order, and six articles from the 1920s Schlieffen Plan debate.

I was approached in the spring of 2004 by Lieutenant-colonel Gerhard Gross of the German Army Historical Section (Militärgeschichtliches Forschungsamt – MGFA), with a proposal for a conference at Potsdam to debate my Schlieffen plan thesis. It would be organized by the MGFA and Dr. Michael Epkenhans of the (German government funded) Otto von Bismarck Foundation and held on 30 September – 1 October 2004. On the first day the participants were to present their positions, and on the second day there was to be a general debate. To facilitate this debate the MGFA was to assemble all the original documents and the original Schlieffen plan map would be posted on the wall. I was fully in favor of this concept and planned my presentation around it.

When I arrived in Potsdam, I discovered that instead of a two-day debate, Gross and Epkenhans had organized a "Schlieffen Plan" ambush. The German Socialist Party, which was in power in 2002, has always emphasized the evils of "German militarism", which most assuredly includes the "Schlieffen plan". The intent of the German Army Historical Section and the government-run Otto von Bismarck Foundation was to stifle my criticism of the "Schlieffen plan" dogma.

Therefore, my argument was to be presented first, in 45 minutes. The next two speakers, Thomas Foley and Annika Mombauer, were each given 45 minutes to present their arguments in favor of the Schlieffen plan. Gross, ostensibly the moderator, was supposed to give an even-handed summary of these arguments, but instead took the next 45 minutes to present his own argument in favor of the Schlieffen plan. This is obviously not how an honest debate is organized. There was no debate. Foley, Mombauer and Gross were able to rebut my arguments, I could not rebut theirs. My opponents were given triple the time I was to state their arguments. The original documents and the Schlieffen plan map were nowhere to be seen. (The rest of the conference, in spite of its title, concerned matters extraneous to the Schlieffen

Plan). The German press had been invited in order to announce that the existence of the Schlieffen Plan had been proven.

The only positive thing to come out of the 2004 Potsdam "Schlieffen Plan" conference was the discovery of document RH61/v.96 in the Bundesarchiv-Militärarchiv in Freiburg im Breisgau, Germany, a summary of German deployment plans from 1893/94 to 1914. Document RH61/v.96 conclusively confirmed, in detail, the central argument that I had made in *Inventing the Schlieffen Plan*: there had never been an operational "Schlieffen Plan", because the German army never had nearly enough troops to execute it. I published a summary and analysis of this document, and other newly discovered documents, in *The Real German War Plan 1904–1914* (History Press, 2011).

CHAPTER ONE

Inventing the Schlieffen plan

The history of German war planning prior to the First World War has been dominated by the 'Schlieffen plan', which was developed in a *Denkschrift* (study) written in early 1906 by the recently retired Chief of the German General Staff, Count Alfred von Schlieffen. The intent of the Schlieffen plan was to annihilate the French army in one quick enormous battle (*Vernichtungsschlacht*). The concept was to deploy seven-eighths of the German army between Metz and Aachen, on the right wing of the German front, leaving one-eighth of the army to guard the left flank in Lorraine against a French attack. No forces would be sent to protect East Prussia against the Russians. The right wing would sweep through Belgium and northern France, if necessary swinging to the west of Paris, continually turning the French left flank, eventually pushing the French army into Switzerland. If the French attacked the German left, in Lorraine, they would be doing the Germans a favor, for the attack would accomplish nothing and the French forces in the north would be that much weaker. Beginning in 1920, semi-official histories written by retired First World War German army officers such as Lieutenant Colonel Wolfgang Foerster, General Hermann von Kuhl, and General Wilhelm Groener, as well as the first volume of the official history of the war produced by the Reichsarchiv in 1925, maintained that this *Denkschrift* represented the culmination of Schlieffen's military thought, and provided Germany with a nearly infallible war plan: all that Schlieffen's successor, Helmuth von Moltke, had needed to do was to execute the Schlieffen plan, and Germany would have been practically assured of victory in August 1914. They contended that Moltke did not understand the concept of the Schlieffen plan, and modified it—'watered it down'—by strengthening the forces on the left wing at the expense of the main attack on the right. For this reason, the German army failed to destroy the French army in the initial campaign in the west in 1914.

The German historian and publicist Hans Delbrück had another explanation for the German defeat: he said that Germany had used the wrong war plan. The Germans should have stayed on the defensive in the west and attacked in the east. That was, after all, the plan of the

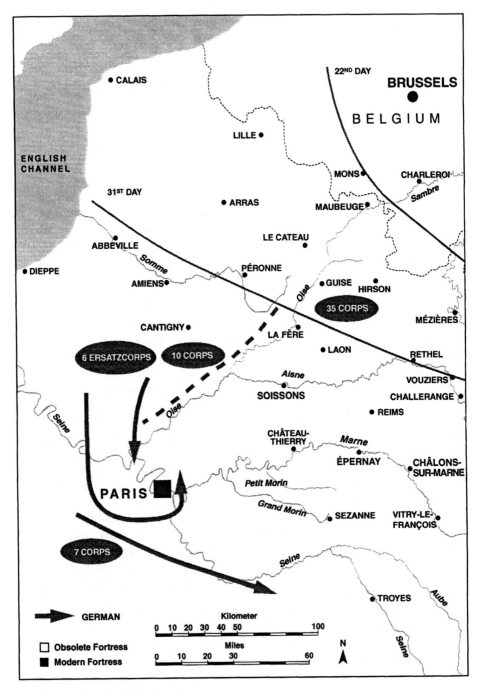

MAP 1. Ritter's Schlieffen Plan

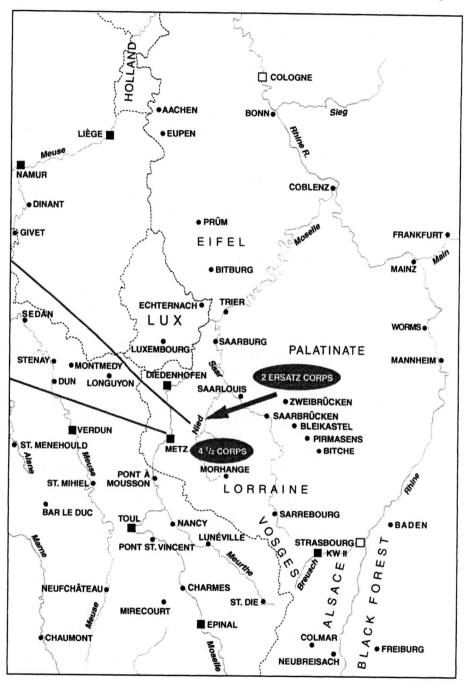

great Field Marshal von Moltke in the 1870s and 1880s. Such an eastern
offensive would have allowed Germany to respect Belgian neutrality
and have led to a negotiated peace. A complete German victory in the
west was in any case impossible. The General Staff replied that an eastern offensive would have led directly to a repetition of 1812 and that the
only solution to Germany's strategic problem was to defeat France and
Britain first. This debate between the 'Delbrück school' and the
'Schlieffen school' continued throughout the 1920s and 1930s in books,
periodicals, and newspapers.

In 1956 Gerhard Ritter took Delbrück's thesis one step further. The
Schlieffen plan, Ritter maintained, was the apotheosis of German militarism. It was the 'militarily perfect' plan which had no room for considerations of diplomacy, politics or international law. Ritter's view quickly
became canonical. Indeed, to Ritter's horror, it became the basis of a
criticism of German history that went far beyond his own. The
Schlieffen plan was transformed into the most visible symbol of
Wilhelmine Germany as a whole: arrogant, unbalanced, and militaristic.

After the Great War the Reichsarchiv in Potsdam, which was the
custodian of the pre-war German plans, treated them as classified docu-
ments. Access to them was essentially restricted to reliable retired offi-
cers, such as Foerster, Kuhl, and Groener. These men emphasized the
Schlieffen plan *Denkschrift* and revealed practically nothing of
Schlieffen's other war plans written between 1891 and 1905. The
Reichsarchiv never did publish the texts of these war plans, as it did for
the war plans written between 1871 and 1888 by Field Marshal von
Moltke. Only in the late 1930s did the General Staff publish some of
Schlieffen's exercises: *Die taktisch-strategischen Aufgaben* (Problems in
Tactics and Strategy; that is, test problems for General Staff officers) in
1937 and in 1938 the *Große Generalstabsreisen Ost 1891–1905* (General Staff
Rides in the East 1891–1905) as well as a 56-page article written by retired
Generalleutnant von Zoellner and published in the *Militärwissen-
schaftliche Rundschau.* Zoellner's article is one of the few which discusses
Schlieffen's pre-1906 planning in any detail, and it too emphasized the
importance of the Schlieffen plan.[1] The Reichsarchiv also pronounced
the *damnatio memoriae* on the failed Chief of Staff of 1914, Helmuth von
Moltke: all that we know of his planning is that around 1909 he made
the fatal modification to the Schlieffen plan. The Reichsarchiv, and
with it all of Schlieffen's and Moltke's war plans, was destroyed by
British incendiary bombs on the night of 14 April 1945. By a miracle, the
original copies of Schlieffen's *Denkschrift* had been among the few documents to be transferred out of the Reichsarchiv beforehand and there-

---

[1] Generalleutnant Zoellner, 'Schlieffens Vermächtnis', *MWR* 1938 *Sonderheft.*

fore survived. However, the *Denkschrift* was not made public until 1956, in Gerhard Ritter's *The Schlieffen Plan: Critique of a Myth*.[2] Although Ritter's book supplied details of the *Denkschrift* itself, it caused no fundamental change in the Schlieffen plan debate. Therefore, any analysis of German war planning prior to 1905, with unimportant exceptions, has had to be made largely on the basis of the fragments of information given by the official history and the retired officers.[3]

This book intends to prove that there never was a Schlieffen plan. It will present recently discovered documents from the Reichsarchiv, as well as previously neglected exercises from other German archives, to show that far from being the final expression of fifteen years of Schlieffen's military thought, the so-called 'Schlieffen plan' bore no resemblance to Schlieffen's war planning at all. Schlieffen's foremost concern was that the Austro-German armies were seriously outnumbered by those of the Franco-Russian alliance. To compensate for this numerical inferiority, Schlieffen intended to fight a *defensive* war using the mobility provided by the German rail net work to defeat each of the Entente armies in turn, in the immediate vicinity of the German border, and not throw the German army into a desperate invasion of central France. The 'Schlieffen plan' was invented by the General Staff to explain away their failure to win the 1914 Marne campaign. In fact, the German army never had nearly enough troops to execute an operation as ambitious as the 'Schlieffen plan', and Schlieffen himself said so. This has not been recognized because the 'Schlieffen plan' debate was in fact not really about military planning, but politics and 'militarism'.

There is no mention of the Schlieffen plan before 1920. Hermann Stegemann, the Swiss military historian, enjoyed cordial relations with the German army and the first volume of his history of the war, published in 1917, provided a very perceptive description and analysis of both German and Allied operations without mentioning the Schlieffen plan.[4] Although Stegemann did not have access to many of the details which became available later, his book remains one of the most important on the First World War precisely because he made his judgements

---

[2] G. Ritter, *The Schlieffen Plan: Critique of a Myth* (London, 1958); German edition *Der Schlieffenplan. Kritik eines Mythos* (Munich, 1956).

[3] The Reichsarchiv collected all of the planning and operations documents from the Baden, Württemberg, Saxon, and Bavarian state government archives. They were therefore also destroyed on 14 Apr. 1945. These archives currently have masses of non-operational documentation, but the Ia (operations), Ic (intelligence) files, and the *Kriegstagebücher* (war diaries) are almost all missing. Only the Bavarian War Archive (Bayerisches Kriegsarchiv) in Munich managed to retain some of their operational records.

[4] H. Stegemann, *Geschichte des Krieges Band I* (Stuttgart and Berlin, 1917).

on the basis of the immediate impressions, before the various participants could put their spin control on the narrative.[5] Stegemann noted
that the French deployed along the border with Germany and Belgium
in order to attack into Lorraine and the Ardennes.[6] He said that the
Triple Entente was confident that immediate Franco-Russian offensives
against Germany would be victorious, with the French attacking 'from
Maastricht to Basel,' and that a French victory in the initial campaign
would have 'brought them to the Ruhr.' Stegemann's evaluation was
that the French plan failed not in its conception but solely because of
the lack of offensive power of the French army.[7]

There was no question in Stegemann's mind that Germany had no
alternative but to seek a quick decision in the west and then transfer
forces east and therefore the Germans had to enter Belgium. He makes
it clear that this was the common evaluation of informed military opinion in pre-war Europe. The necessity to quickly defeat the French gave
the appearance that the German were the aggressors.[8] Stegemann was
accurately informed as to the German deployment and drew his conclusions concerning the concept of the German operation from both the
deployment and the conduct of the operation itself. He said that the
German left wing intended to draw the French out of their border fortifications on the Moselle into an attack in Lorraine and then engage the
French to hold them there, while the German right wing attacked the
French left.[9] He said that Schlieffen's contribution to the German army

---

[5] Even in 1915, however, spin control—as opposed to outright falsification—was
already at work. One of the issues that would later become central to the history of the
war was the question of whether the Russians mobilized first, and, if they did, whether
Russian mobilization meant war. The 1915 edition of the English Red Book (Collected
Documents relating to the outbreak of the European War, HMSO, London, 1915, pp.
ix–xii) performed spectacular mental gymnastics to prove the Russians were not guilty
on either count. Stegemann said the Russians were guilty on both counts. In the back of
his book Stegemann proudly reprinted his articles for the *Berner Bund* printed between
10 August and 16 September 1914, which demonstrate Stegemann's remarkable ability to
evaluate the military situation.

[6] The French General Staff released a communiqué on 25 March 1915 which
explained the French pre-war war plan. The communiqué presented essentially the
same description of the French war plan that was to appear in the French official history.
The French intent was to make it appear that the French deployed to enter Belgium only
after the Germans had violated Belgian neutrality. In fact, the French initiated the
'Belgian' variant before the Germans either had transmitted their ultimatum to the
Belgian government or had begun deploying troops. Ministère de la Guerre, État-Major
de l'armeé, Service Historique. *Les Armées Françaises dans la Grande Guerre*. Tome
Premier, Premiere Volume, 56, 86–7; Cartes, Maps 7 and 8; Annexes, 71–3. See pp. 256–7.

[7] Stegemann, *Geschichte*, 54, 87.

[8] Ibid. 70.

[9] Ibid. 107–8, 112, 124, 167: in concept, as we shall see, essentially the same conclusions
Schlieffen and Beseler arrived at between 1897 and 1902.

was that he had preserved the elder Moltke's legacy of a speedy and efficient mobilization.[10] The decisive factor during most of the campaign,
in Stegemann's opinion, was not strategy but the sheer offensive power
of the German army. The German army was completely victorious in all
the meeting engagements in Lorraine and in Belgium and defeated the
Anglo-French attempts to defend on the Sambre–Meuse. By 30 August
the French had broken contact and were conducting a general withdrawal with the Germans in hot pursuit.

Stegemann said that if the Germans were to destroy the French army
they would have to do so before the French were able to execute their old
plan to withdraw to the plateau of Langres. Once at Langres, the French
army was relatively secure: 'driving the French into Switzerland' was
clearly not as simple as it sounds. Stegemann said that the German
concept of the operation envisaged an advance between Paris and
Verdun, while the French defense was anchored on Verdun. The German
intent therefore was prevent the French escape to Langres by both
outflanking the French left to the east of Paris *and* breaking the French
center to the south-west of Verdun, between Sezanne and Bar-le-Duc.
Breaking the French center would also allow the Germans to attack the
French border fortifications from the rear and then link up the German
6th Army on the left, in Lorraine, with the German center. Whether the
Germans could have prevented the French from withdrawing to Langres
or not was questionable. When Kluck exposed the German 1st Army's
right flank and rear to the garrison of Paris he fundamentally changed
the strategic situation in favor of the French. Stegemann was unaware of
the debate within the German army concerning the role of Lieutenant-
Colonel Hentsch in ordering the German withdrawal from the Marne,
and instead ascribed this withdrawal to the logical consequence of the
changed German strategic position and stiffening French resistance.
Most important, Stegemann says that there was no possibility that the
Germans could have conducted a march to the west of Paris, and that the
French had built their defense around this fact.[11]

Stegemann's description of the campaign also identified the
mistakes made by various German commanders, which robbed the
Germans of opportunities to destroy large parts of the French army
prior to the battle of the Marne. He says that the Germans counterattacked too early in Lorraine[12] and that the German 3rd Army missed
golden opportunities to envelop entire French armies.[13] Moltke's
mistake was to send two corps to the east before the French had been
decisively defeated.[14] He said that it was the pressure of Kluck's 1st Army

---

[10] Ibid. 101.   [11] Ibid. 173.   [12] Ibid. 133
[13] Ibid. 145–7, 159.   [14] Ibid. 162, 168–9, 178–92, 238.

against the French left that forced the French withdrawal to the Marne and beyond, but it was also a grave error on Kluck's part to expose his right flank to a counter-attack from Paris.[15] It was already clear in 1917 that after the war a great many senior German officers were going to have a lot to answer for.

Practically the only major factors that are present in later histories of the war but are missing in Stegemann are the Schlieffen plan and the role of Lieutenant-Colonel Hentsch. The striking thing is that Stegemann's narrative is perfectly satisfactory, indeed even superior to the post-war histories precisely because it does not mention the Schlieffen plan. The chain of events and Stegemann's interpretation of the causes and effects are logical and plausible. The introduction of the Schlieffen plan to Stegemann's account would only add a counterfactual element: that the Schlieffen plan *should have been* the German war plan (but wasn't).

The person who provided the decisive influence in the genesis of the Schlieffen plan, if only indirectly, was Hans Delbrück. Before the war, Delbrück was the editor of the influential political journal the *Preußische Jahrbücher* as well as the author of the groundbreaking military history *Die Geschichte der Kriegskunst im Rahmen der politischen Geschichte* (The History of the Art of War within the Framework of Political History).[16] The title of the series was programmatic: Delbrück's interest was in the relationship between war and the political system of that period. Delbrück was also the first to utilize Leopold von Ranke's system of *Quellenkritik* in military history, which Delbrück called *Sachkritik*. His most important contribution to military history was his demonstration that in describing battles ancient historians wildly overstated the number of combatants. He completely rewrote the histories of the Persian campaigns in Greece and the battles of Alexander the Great on the basis of much smaller and more reasonably sized armies.

Less happily, Delbrück also attempted to reinterpret Carl von Clausewitz's book on military theory, *Vom Kriege* (On War). Delbrück maintained that Clausewitz had really wanted to divide all military strategy into two opposing types: either *Vernichtungsstrategie* (strategy of annihilation) or *Ermattungsstrategie* (strategy of attrition). He supported this assertion by maintaining that Clausewitz had mentioned such a division of strategy in a note written in 1827, but that he died in 1830 before he could revise *Vom Kriege*. Delbrück not only had a clear personal preference for *Ermattungsstrategie*, he also contended that the Prussian

---

[15] Stegemann, *Geschichte*, 168, 178–80.
[16] H. Delbrück, *Die Geschichte der Kriegskunst im Rahmen der politischen Geschichte* (4 vols., Berlin, 1900–20).

national hero Frederick the Great had pursued a strategy of attrition during the Seven Years War. Delbrück said that the era in which Frederick lived, with small, brittle, professional armies tied to magazines for resupply, did not provide him with the military means to conduct a strategy of annihilation. Delbrück thereby fell foul of the historical section of the Great General Staff. Prussian-German military doctrine in the nineteenth and twentieth centuries aimed at destroying the main enemy force in battles of annihilation. The first great Prussian practitioner of the *Vernichtungsschlacht* (battle of annihilation), the historical section of the General Staff maintained, was Frederick the Great, as demonstrated by the battles of Rossbach and Leuthen. The General Staff felt, correctly, that Delbrück was challenging the Army's monopoly in determining military strategy. The resulting polemical battle between Delbrück and his civilian supporters on one side and the General Staff historians on the other has become known as the *Strategiestreit* (strategy debate).[17]

Although Delbrück was not formally a member of any political party, he was a thoroughgoing supporter of the Prussian-German monarchial system and of the German chancellor from 1909 to 1917, Theobald von Bethmann Hollweg. It was this support for Bethmann Hollweg which provided the impetus for the articles he wrote in the *Preußische Jahrbücher* during the war in which he gave his opinion of the military-political situation. Delbrück's qualifications for the military side of such a task were non-existent. Volume III of his *Geschichte der Kriegskunst* was the last to be published before the war, and it stopped with the late middle ages. Delbrück says that volume IV was essentially complete in 1914, but even so, this volume deals mostly with professional armies in the early modern period. The culminating point of the book is the campaigns of Frederick the Great, with a cursory look at the French Revolution. Delbrück had not written anything about Napoleon, nor about the campaigns of Moltke in 1866 and 1870, nor the Boer War, the Russo-Japanese War, naval warfare, the American Revolution, or the American Civil War. In short, Delbrück was an expert on ancient and pre-modern European land warfare.

During the war, Delbrück maintained that in August 1914 Germany was faced with overwhelming enemy forces and had no alternative but to seek a swift victory in the west and then shift forces to the east, and that the German offensive, unfortunately, had to be conducted through Belgium.[18] In any case, Delbrück asserted, Russia was the real aggressor

[17] S. Lange, *Hans Delbrück und die 'Strategiestreit'* (Freiburg im Breisgau, 1995).

[18] H. Delbrück, *Krieg und Politik I. 1914–16* (Berlin, 1918); *II. Teil 1917* (Berlin, 1919); *III. Teil 1918* (Berlin, 1919).

and Russian aggression was the direct cause of the war. First, Russia had supported Serbian aggression against Austria. Then Russia had destroyed the last chance of a peaceful resolution to the July crisis. England and Germany had proposed that the Austrians would occupy Belgrade and then open negotiations with the Serbs—the famous 'Halt in Belgrade' plan. Delbrück contended that the Russians knew that a negotiated peace would have ruined Russian chances of dominating the Balkans and then of occupying Constantinople, which was the real objective of Russian policy. A peaceful resolution of the crisis might even have resulted in a revolution by outraged pan-Slavs in Russia itself. The Russians therefore torpedoed the Halt in Belgrade plan by ordering a general mobilization of the entire Russian army. The Russians were fully aware that such a mobilization meant world war—indeed, a world war was their intention. The French joined the Russians in order to regain Alsace-Lorraine. Britain, in Delbrück's view, played no part in the aggression against Germany. Nevertheless, Britain joined the Allies because Germany's rising naval power was poised to break Britain's naval hegemony.

Germany was therefore fighting a defensive war and Delbrück said that this determined German war aims. He said that by defeating Allied aggression, Germany would win the war: once defeated, the Allied coalition would never be formed again. Peace on the basis of the *status quo ante* would guarantee German security for the foreseeable future. The *status quo ante* obviously meant that Germany would retain Alsace-Lorraine. French hopes of *revanche* would have been destroyed and France would slowly decline to the status of a second-rate power. In September 1914 Delbrück established what he thought should be Germany's principal war aim: Germany should emerge from the war with her place in the sun, a great colonial empire in central Africa. This empire would put Germany on par with the other colonial powers, Britain, France, Russia, and the United States. This was the goal of the pre-war German *Weltpolitik* and *Weltpolitik* was the reason Britain had entered the war on the Allied side. The principal obstacle Germany faced to both attaining and retaining an overseas empire had always been British naval hegemony. This hegemony was soon shaken by spectacular U-Boat successes, such as the sinking of the armored cruisers *Aboukir*, *Hogue*, and *Cressey* on 22 September 1914. Delbrück was soon saying that the U-Boat was the revolutionary naval weapon that would surely break British naval hegemony: after the war Germany would be free to build so many U-Boats that in any future war both the British battle fleet and merchant navy could be swept from the seas in short order. Delbrück said that the balance of power at sea, which he called freedom of the seas, was practically assured. By this he meant that the security of both the post-war German colonial empire and German merchant shipping was certain. In October 1914 Delbrück said that Britain was in decline, whether she won the war or not. Throughout the war, he maintained that Britain was a weary giant crippled by colonial and political problems. If Germany could only gain a peace on the basis of the *status quo ante*, Delbrück predicted, in the post-war period Britain would be forced to share world power with Germany.

The *status quo ante* took a curious turn in the east, however. Shortly after the beginning of the war, Delbrück also said that the real loser in the war was going to be Russia, which would surely have to surrender Congress Poland, probably lose the other western provinces inhabited by foreign nationalities, and be pushed back into Asia. As German successes multiplied in the east, Delbrück transformed this prediction into his proposal for German policy. In 1915 the German offensive in the east overran Poland, and in 1916 the Germans attempted to establish a Polish satellite state. Delbrück supported this measure in the name of both national self-determination as well as German security. In 1915 Delbrück advocated that Germany establish a protectorate over Latvia and Estonia, where he proposed that the Volga Germans be resettled. By the summer of 1918 German forces were advancing practically unhindered through southern Russia, and Delbrück was advocating a renewed *Drang nach Osten*, including German presence in, if not outright control of, the south Russian provinces as far east as the Caucasus. Delbrück saw German control over western and southern Russia as providing Germany with an unassailable position in Europe, similar to the geo-strategic immunity enjoyed by the British Empire or the United States.

Delbrück expected a short war. As early as August 1914 Delbrück was doubting Allied staying power. Throughout 1914 and 1915 Delbrück denied that the British blockade was having any effect on the German war effort. At the same time, Delbrück also thought he saw signs of war-weariness among the Allies. Throughout the war, Delbrück would maintain that British and French collapse was always right around the corner. When the second Russian revolution took place in November 1917, Delbrück announced that Russia was finished as a Great Power and that the Russian threat to Germany's eastern border had disappeared for the foreseeable future.

Until the last months of the war, Delbrück contended that Germany had, in effect, won the war. Only one thing stood between Germany and a victorious negotiated peace and that was Belgium. As early as September 1914, prominent German politicians, industrialists, and intellectuals had come to the conclusion that post-war German security and economic development demanded that Germany either occupy or

at least retain economic and military control over Belgium. Delbrück
was adamantly opposed to such an idea. He felt that German desire to
control Belgium was an act of Napoleonic hubris which would signal to
Europe that Germany aimed at nothing less than continental hegemony. The Entente, he felt, would fight to the bitter end to prevent the
Germans from gaining control over Belgium. Even if Germany did win
the war and occupy Belgium, the only result would be the formation of
an overwhelming alliance against Germany, as Europe had united
against Napoleon in 1813–14.

The forces in favor of German control over Belgium formed the
Vaterlandspartei in 1917, and conducted a virulent propaganda
campaign to support their position. Delbrück became convinced that
the Vaterlandspartei was all that was standing between Germany and a
negotiated peace, a *Verständigungsfrieden,* which would result in German
gains in the east, an enormous African colonial empire, the destruction
of English naval hegemony, and world power for Germany. If the
German government would only make a clear promise renouncing
Belgium, he contended, the war governments in Britain and France
would fall and peace negotiations would begin.

In spite of his advocacy of German *Weltmacht,* Delbrück was unable to
see beyond central Europe. America remained a mystery to him. The
American Revolution could have provided him with a powerful demon-
stration of the effectiveness of *Ermattungsstrategie,* far more so than
Frederick in the Seven Years War, but he never considered it.
Throughout the war Delbrück was unable to understand why the
British blockade did not lead to a complete break between Britain and
America. After the United States entered the war in April 1917,
Delbrück acknowledged that the Entente strategy was to hold out until
the Americans could appear in force, which the Entente estimated
could happen in 1918 at the earliest, 1919 at the latest. Nevertheless,
throughout 1917 and until the American armies actually appeared on
the battlefield in the summer of 1918, Delbrück maintained that the
United States would be incapable of committing effective ground
forces to combat. He said repeatedly that American assistance would be
restricted to munitions, money, ships and aviation personnel.

Therefore, throughout 1917 and most of 1918, Delbrück continued to
maintain that only Belgium stood between Germany and a victorious
peace. He even went one step further. He acknowledged that the
British understood perfectly well that a peace on the basis of the *status
quo ante* was the equivalent of a British defeat. Nevertheless, from mid-
1917 to mid-1918 he said that, if the Germans would give up Belgium,
then the British were ready to throw out Lloyd George, bring Asquith
to power, abandon the French, and sue for peace.

Delbrück had not taken part in the pre-war discussion of tactics and operations conducted by military writers such as Theodor von Bernhardi and Schlieffen. However, in order to justify his wartime views on German grand strategy, Delbrück was drawn into presenting his opinions on strategy, operations and tactics. In December 1914 and January 1915 Delbrück stated that, in spite of the fact that field fortifications were stiffening up the situation in the west, it was still unnecessary for Germany to adopt an *Ermattungsstrategie*. In the summer of 1915 Delbrück was advocating strategic defense in the west and a giant offensive in the east directed at St Petersburg, Moscow, and Kiev. Such an offensive, he said, could easily be supplied by rail. At the end of 1915 Delbrück was optimistic: the German defense in the west and Austrian defense in the Alps had defeated Allied attacks with heavy losses, while the Austro-German armies had pushed the Russians out of Poland, Galicia and much of the Baltic coast. Delbrück became convinced that the German trench system in the west was impenetrable, an *idée fixe* that he would hold throughout 1917 and even into late 1918. Delbrück said that he had searched through world military history for a precedent to western front trench warfare and couldn't find one: he was apparently completely ignorant of the Petersburg campaign of 1864–1865 during the American Civil War. Delbrück failed to see that after 1916 geometric increases in the volume of Allied heavy artillery fire, the introduction of the tank, and the entry of large American forces into combat meant that the German trench systems could be broken.

When Falkenhayn launched his attack on Verdun on 21 February 1916, Delbrück saw the offensive as a justified application of the strategy of the war of attrition. Delbrück never acknowledged that attacking at Verdun meant that Germany had no forces for two of his pet strategic projects, offensives against Russia and Italy. His support was surely influenced by his faulty appreciation of the tactical situation at Verdun. Delbrück believed that since Verdun was a salient the French were vulnerable to converging German fire and that the German fire could also interdict French supply lines. The French could not afford to withdraw from this exposed position because surrendering Verdun would be an admission of weakness. Delbrück agreed with Falkenhayn that French rates of attrition at Verdun would surely be higher than German. Delbrück's assumptions were dangerously wrong. Owing to a lack of forces, the Germans were unable to extend their attack to the west of the Meuse until late in the battle. There was therefore no converging fire: in fact, German forces on the east bank suffered murderous enfilade fire from French artillery on the west bank. The Germans were also never able to interdict the French lines of communication. The Germans did not have enough artillery, ammunition or troops to win an attrition battle at Verdun. Nevertheless, on 29 April 1916 Delbrück wrote an article in the *Preußische Jahrbücher* proving that the French nation was being 'bled white'.[19] France had mobilized some 10 to 11 per cent of her population, said Delbrück, about 4 million men in total. Of those, 1½ million were already *hors de combat*, 1 million were rear echelon troops, leaving 1½ million combat troops, half of whom had already been through Verdun and were 'attrited'. Such attrition warfare has gotten an odious reputation as a repudiation of both strategy and simple humanity, and justifiably so. Even if successful against the French, such an analysis failed to fit the attrition battle at Verdun into German strategy as a whole. Delbrück did not even seem to be dimly aware of the disastrous effect that Verdun was having on the combat effectiveness of the German army. After an inauspicious start, the British began their own battle of attrition on the Somme, and on a scale the Germans could not hope to match. At the same time, the Austrian offensive in the Trentino in Italy failed and the Brusilov offensive was tearing the Austrian armies in Galicia to pieces. Delbrück drew no conclusions from this either. In fact, Verdun was a straightforward admission of intellectual bankruptcy in favor of brute force. Delbrück's advocacy of attrition warfare at Verdun should also be considered in context with Delbrück's later criticism of Ludendorff: none of Ludendorff's errors were as heinous as Verdun.

In 1916 the war had entered a new phase, true industrial mass warfare, which the Germans called the *Materialschlacht*, a term which Delbrück neither used nor understood. In the preceding two years the industries of Britain and France had completed the transition to mass munitions production. The Entente was also able to draw on production from the United States. Britain had raised and trained a mass army. The Anglo-French had so many heavy guns and so much ammunition that they could literally pulverize the hitherto invulnerable German field fortifications. German industry had lost the munitions production race, and the German artillery in 1916 often did not even have enough ammunition to be able to conduct serious counter-battery fire. As a consequence, in 1916 at Verdun and on the Somme the Anglo-French artillery began the gradual process of destroying the German infantry. The German army had entered the war relying on the high quality of its infantry battalions to bring it victory. Falkenhayn, with Delbrück's approval, was now tacitly allowing the Allied artillery to grind the last of these to powder. Delbrück was oblivious to all this: in his comments on the battles on the western front, Delbrück was satisfied to see that the Germans were not losing any terrain.

---

[19] Delbrück, *Krieg und Politik*, i. 256–7.

Most modern accounts of Delbrück's *Ermattungsstrategie* leave the impression that Delbrück fully considered all the factors of modern mass industrial warfare. In fact, economic factors were irrelevant to Delbrück's conception of *Ermattungsstrategie.* From August 1914 on, Delbrück continually downplayed the effectiveness of the British blockade. In September 1914, he maintained that Germany was in a better position to win an economic war than Britain. At no point in the war did Delbrück compare even the raw production capacities of the Entente, the United States, and Germany. Delbrück always remained a nineteenth-century intellectual (in 1917 he said that the foundation of a good education was still the study of Greek and Latin). Therefore, his defense of *Ermattungsstrategie* was not based on rational calculation of rates of production and wastage of forces, but rather in patriotic historical analogy: Delbrück repeatedly said, both during and after the war, that *Ermattungsstrategie* was appropriate for Germany during the World War because Frederick the Great employed an *Ermattungsstrategie* in the Seven Years War.[20]

In late 1917, Hugo, Freiherr von Freytag-Loringhoven, a senior General Staff officer, tried to lend some rational historical perspective to the World War in his book *Folgerungen aus dem Weltkriege* (Consequences of the World War).[21] Freytag was the German army's resident intellectual. He had written extensively before the war and his views on military history and current military developments were moderate and thoughtful. He was no knee-jerk opponent of Delbrück, but rather agreed that Germany must conserve her forces and that there were certain very general parallels between the Seven Years War and the World War. Freytag qualified that similarity by noting that this parallel could not be taken too far: the constitution of Frederick's Prussia and the economic system of the period were completely different from those of 1917 and therefore the military systems of the two periods were also different. Freytag said that the most fruitful parallel was between the World War and the American Civil War. Like the current war, the American Civil War was conducted by mass armies motivated by visceral hatreds. Somewhat alarmingly, Freytag drew the conclusion that in the American Civil War economic factors were of paramount importance. In spite of the operational and tactical superiority of the Army of Northern Virginia, the Confederacy was defeated by Union naval superiority and the Union blockade. Freytag went on quickly to say that history does not repeat itself.

[20] H. Delbrück, 'Die strategische Grundfrage des Weltkrieges', (PJ), 183 (Januar bis März 1921), 296 ff.

[21] Hugo, Freiherr von Freytag-Loringhoven, *Folgerungen aus dem Weltkriege* (Berlin, 1917).

Delbrück's reaction was that industrial factors made the American Civil War only mildly interesting. Delbrück's reply was that the most useful comparison was still between the World War and the Seven Years War and not between the World War and the wars of Moltke or Napoleon. To support this contention he cited the similarities in the increased number of artillery pieces Frederick employed during the course of his wars (19 guns at Mollwitz, 276 at Torgau) and the fact that for months at a time the armies sat in 'fortified' positions, which they even reinforced with the spade.[22] It is clear that this is neither a serious comparison nor analysis. Delbrück seemed to feel that the mere reference to the methods of the German national hero was sufficient to decide the debate on German strategy.

Delbrück's analysis of Prussia's strategic situation during the Seven Years War was in any case nearsighted. Prussia during the Seven Years War was not the independent great power Delbrück made her out to be. In fact, Prussia was one of the medium-sized allies of the greater of the two superpowers of the period, Britain. While Frederick was trying to hang on to Silesia, Britain was conducting complex sea–land campaigns over much of the globe, operations which would win her world naval supremacy, as well as North America and much of the Indian subcontinent. At the same time Britain fully occupied the forces of the other superpower, France, preventing French forces from effectively intervening on the continent, while paying Frederick the subsidies which alone kept Frederick's army in the field. Moreover, Frederick was only able to conduct his own strategy at all because the usual Austrian commander, Daun, was very cautious and almost never attacked. In any case, Frederick's *Ermattungsstrategie* failed and Frederick was losing the war, penned up in a fortified camp at Bunzelwitz in the Silesian mountains when he was saved by the 'Miracle of the House of Brandenburg': the death of the Russian Empress Elizabeth.

Delbrück had established his reputation as a military historian by asserting that warfare assumes its character from its historical environment. Specifically, he said that since Frederick lived in an era of brittle professional armies, the historical milieu itself prevented him from conducting a *Vernichtungsstrategie*. Employing Delbrück's own critical standard, few of the lessons from the Seven Years War would have been applicable to the World War. The Seven Years War was a *Kabinettskrieg* fought between absolute monarchs in a pre-industrial society, with professional armies using black-powder weapons. The World War was conducted by industrial societies and mass armies which were moved

---

[22] Delbrück, *Krieg und Politik*, ii. 313–14.

and supplied by rail and equipped with the entire panoply of modern weapons to include aircraft, tanks, high explosives, quick-firing artillery, machine guns, and poison gas. Any tactical or strategic similarities between the Seven Years War and the World War were practically accidental: Delbrück could just as well have cited Hannibal's old opponent during the Second Punic War, Fabius Cunctator (Fabius the Delayer).

In 1918 Delbrück supported the German offensives in the west, saying that they were fully consistent with *Ermattungsstrategie*. His only criticism was that the attack should have been coordinated with a peace offensive, that is, a clear German renunciation of Belgium. After the war, Delbrück changed his mind, and stated that the offensive aimed at winning a *Vernichtungsschlacht*, which on the western front was impossible. It would have been better to have knocked Italy out of the war with an offensive out of the Trentino.[23] To Delbrück's detractors, this proposal was a classic case of armchair strategy. On a small-scale map of Italy an attack from the Trentino salient appears to offer the prospect of an easy entry into the Po valley which could be exploited as far as Genoa or Florence. In fact, such an attack had been tried in 1916 and failed for two reasons. First, it was an obvious course of action, and the Italians were ready for it; second, the rail net in the Austrian Alps was too weak to support either a quick build-up or sufficient resupply. Moreover, the snow cover in the Alps required that such an attack be delayed until the late spring or early summer of 1918, at which point American troops would arrive in strength.

Delbrück's fondness for attacks on secondary theaters, which he said was the strategy Frederick the Great used late in the Seven Years War, indirectly points out a further weakness in his *Ermattungsstrategie*: the Allies, given their superior resources in men, material, and mobility, were in a far better position to fight on secondary theaters than the Germans were, and the Central Powers' secondary theaters—Austria-Hungary, Turkey, and Macedonia—were exceptionally weak. Even if Germany could have defended in the west until 1919, there was practically no prospect that Turkey or Bulgaria could have held out so long, and when they collapsed the back door of the Central Powers' position would be wide open.

In 1918 Delbrück continued to believe that a negotiated peace was right around the corner. He expected that the German army could hold out in the west indefinitely. Between August and November 1918 the German front in the west began to crumble, while Austria-Hungary disintegrated, the Bulgarians went home, and the British crushed the

---

[23] Delbrück, 'Die strategische Grundfrage', 302 ff.

Turkish armies in the Levant. The socialist revolution swept away
Germany's monarchial system, which Delbrück had supported with
heart and soul. The German revolution and the collapse of the German
army caught Delbrück completely by surprise. The revolution in particular was a bitter pill for Delbrück to swallow. He had become convinced
that the Social Democrats had dropped their anti-national and revolutionary dogma and been converted to German nationalism. Having
said during the war that the western front was invulnerable and the
socialists were reliable, both estimates now being quite obviously and
disastrously wrong, Delbrück became one of the first proponents of the
'stab in the back' theory: that the Social Democrats had chosen the
moment of Germany's greatest weakness and danger to launch their
revolution, thereby destroying both the German state and the German
army in the west and leaving Germany defenseless. Delbrück called the
revolution 'treason'.[24] 'There is no question', Delbrück wrote in 1920,
'that it was the revolution that rendered us completely defenseless, and
gave our enemies the means to enslave the German people.'[25] At the
same time, he placed equal blame on the Vaterlandspartei, maintaining
that Germany could have concluded a *Verständigungsfrieden* at practically any point in the war, if only the German nationalists had been willing to give up Belgium.

Delbrück's personal contribution to this disaster was his insistence
on the possibility of a negotiated peace on the basis of the *status quo
ante*. In the event, there were not even any negotiations at all: the Allies
merely imposed their conditions in the form of the Versailles *Diktat*.
None of the Allies showed any interest in a *Verständigungsfrieden*: the
French exploited the German defeat to establish French hegemony in
Europe, while the British eliminated the German battle fleet and
merchant marine. Wilson, the Fourteen Points notwithstanding,
supported every British and French peace condition except the
outright French annexation of the left bank of the Rhine. It was now
clear that the only way that Delbrück's *Ermattungsstrategie* would have
worked is if there had been a second 'Miracle of the House of
Brandenburg'. The German defeat meant the collapse of everything
that Delbrück had worked for and believed in. Delbrück had wanted
Germany to be a world power; instead, Germany was reduced to
complete powerlessness. The Versailles treaty confirmed what
Ludendorff and the Vaterlandspartei had contended all along, that the
Allied aim was the destruction of German power. Rather than gain a

---

[24] Delbrück, *Krieg und Politik*, iii, pp. v–vi: 'Waffenstillstand und Friede', *PJ, Band 175*
Januar bis März 1919, 424; 'Abschied' *PJ Band 178*, Oktober bis Dezember 1919, 371.
[25] H. Delbrück, 'Falkenhayn und Ludendorff', *PJ 180* (April bis Juni 1920), 279.

great colonial empire, as Delbrück had proposed, Germany lost her colonies altogether. Ludendorff's demand for border rectifications with Poland, which Delbrück had criticized, were minor compared to the massive blocks of German territory that Poland took in Silesia, Posen, and West Prussia. Delbrück's prediction that the Allies' Napoleonic peace merely laid the seeds for future war went unheeded in Washington, Paris, and London. A League of Nations, which Delbrück had ardently supported, was not going to include Germany and was clearly going to serve only as a guarantee for the Versailles peace treaty. The revolution and peace treaty were a total refutation of every policy that Delbrück had advocated during the war.

However, Delbrück never admitted he'd been wrong.[26] Delbrück explained the German disaster in the World War in two ways. First, in early 1919 Delbrück wrote that Germany had used the wrong war plan.[27] It would have been wiser to attack in the east and defend in the west: this was, Delbrück said, after all the plan of the great Field Marshal von Moltke between 1871 and 1888. It was commonly understood that Moltke's war plan during this period called for the Germans to attack from East Prussia to the south-east, with the Austrians attacking from Galicia to the north-east, the two armies linking up near Warsaw or perhaps Brest-Litovsk. Optimistically, the Russian forces in Poland would be caught between these pincers and annihilated. The Austro-German forces would in any case assume a defensive position in eastern Poland or White Russia and would not continue their attack into the interior of Russia. In the west, the German forces would defend along the Saar between Metz and Strasbourg. If necessary, the Germans would withdraw to the Rhine or the angle formed at Mainz by the Main and the Rhine. Once the Russians were defeated, forces would be transported from the east to the west.

Delbrück said that in 1914 an offensive in the east—an *Ostaufmarsch*—similar to Moltke's would have produced a quick, easy victory over the Russian armies in Poland. Germany could have also respected Belgian neutrality, which would have seriously weakened British enthusiasm for the Entente. Having made her conquests in the east, Germany could have defended in the west until the British and French were exhausted and sued for peace.

The *Ostaufmarsch* fitted practically all of Delbrück's wartime proposals perfectly: it avoided the Belgian issue entirely, permitted a defensive

---

[26] For two analyses where Delbrück can do no wrong, see A. Bucholz, *Hans Delbrück and the German Military Establishment* (Iowa City, 1985) and G. Craig, 'Delbrück, The Military Historian' in P. Paret (ed.), *Makers of Modern Strategy*, (Princeton, 1986), 326–53.

[27] H. Delbrück, 'Die deutsche Kriegserklärung 1914 und der Einmarsch in Belgien', *PJ* 175 (Januar bis März 1919), 271–80.

posture in the west under highly favorable conditions, promised significant gains in the east while crushing the Russian armies, and last not least would, in Delbrück's mind, surely have led to a negotiated peace. Indeed, the *Ostaufmarsch* proposal can be seen as merely a continuation of the *Strategiestreit* that had been going on since 1878: The *Westaufmarsch*—an offensive against France—was based on a *Vernichtungsstrategie*, the *Ostaufmarsch* on *Ermattungsstrategie* and *Verständigungsfrieden*.

Nevertheless, Delbrück was being wise after the fact. Delbrück himself had defended both the *Westaufmarsch* and the need to violate Belgian neutrality throughout the war. No one in 1914, or for many years previous to that, had expected anything but the deployment of the German *Schwerpunkt* (main point of effort) in the west. This was due to two factors: first, the example of Napoleon's 1812 invasion of Russia, and second, the fact that there were only two double-tracked rail lines across the Vistula into East Prussia. Deploying the main body of the German army to the east would have taken weeks, and even supplying the German forces while they were in East Prussia would have been difficult at best, while in the west the German armies would have been seriously outnumbered.

Delbrück's article in early 1919 was the first time that any serious military strategist had publicly proposed an initial German attack to the east. The long-term effects of this article have been immense. It set off the second round of the *Strategiestreit* between the General Staff and Delbrück which continues through their proxies even to this day. This debate defined the parameters for all subsequent analysis of the German war plan. It was the foundation on which the subsequent criticism of the Schlieffen plan has been built.

Few senior German officers, other than Falkenhayn, believed that Germany could have won a war of attrition or have attained a peace on any other basis than German victory. Delbrück's accusations were also a direct challenge to the professional officer corps at a critical juncture in German history. The old German state had collapsed, and a new one would have to be formed. Who would provide the officer corps for the new German army? In 1919, feelings against the old officer corps were running high. Delbrück's contention that the General Staff had used a faulty strategy was potentially fatal to their further employment and influence. In addition, after the draconian Versailles *Diktat* was imposed in mid-1919, many patriotic Germans expected that in the near future there would be a national rising *à la* 1813. The old officer corps wanted to be in a position to lead such a movement.

Indeed, the General Staff's concern with the post-war character of the German army is evident in Freytag-Loringhoven's *Folgerungen aus dem Weltkriege*, which was published in 1917, before the war had even ended. Freytag contended that the performance of the German army during the war demonstrated that the officer corps had prepared the army as well as possible beforehand: all that was needed after the war was to integrate the wartime lessons learned into the existing system.

Any defense of the officer corps in 1917 had to address the sole German failure to that point—the Marne campaign. Freytag said that the German army accomplished great things in August 1914 and that the German plan on the Marne in September was to finish the campaign with a double envelopment of the French army: the German left wing would break through the French border defenses on the Moselle while the German right wing outflanked the French left. Unfortunately, the German army was not strong enough for such an operation and in consequence the German right flank was itself turned by the attack from fortress Paris. What had been needed was another entire German army following the German right flank. The conclusion Freytag drew was that in the future Germany must prepare to use all of her available manpower and thereby have enough units to execute missions such as guarding critical flanks.

Freytag's explanation of Schlieffen's role in preparing the German army for the war was that he had trained the officer corps to be able to lead the mass army. In so doing, Schlieffen had further developed the principles laid down by Field Marshal von Moltke. 'For that reason', Freytag said, 'the beginning of the campaign in the west in August 1914 was conducted according to Schlieffen's ideas.'[28] Further, Schlieffen's operational thought was presented in his *Cannae* article. Here too, Schlieffen only developed further ideas already inherent in German military thought, in this case Clausewitz's observation (draft for Chapter 9, Book VIII) that decisive battle could only result from an envelopment or by forcing the enemy to fight with a reversed front (that is, with the enemy front line facing his own lines of communication, thereby cutting off the most likely path of retreat).

In 1917, Freytag discussed in detail the concept of the German elastic defense which had been put into effect in April of that year. He was therefore not shy about addressing the most important aspects of current operations. Nevertheless, he made no mention of the Schlieffen plan. Indeed, in Freytag's account Schlieffen's role in the pre-war preparation of the German army had more to do with training staff officers than with planning.

Immediately after the war, the General Staff was hit with a wave of critical books and articles. One of the first of these was Professor Georg

[28] Freytag, *Folgerungen*, 46.

Steinhausen's *Die Grundfehler des Krieges und der Generalstab* (Fundamental Errors in the War and the General Staff).[29] Steinhausen thought that Theodor von Bernhardi's aggressive *Weltanschauung* was representative of the pre-war attitude of the General Staff. He therefore assumed that during the July crisis the General Staff had argued for a preventive war. Quoting Freytag's description of the German war plan in *Folgerungen aus dem Weltkriege,* Steinhausen drew the conclusion only that Schlieffen's plan ('Der Schlieffensche Plan') had aimed at a quick victory in the west. Steinhausen said that the General Staff's most serious mistake had been that it had underestimated the military ability of Germany's enemies: in particular, the German attack failed because of the unexpected resistance of the Belgian army, the unexpected commitment of the British Expeditionary Force to the continent, and the unexpected defection of the Italians. The General Staff's cardinal error was to underestimate the political and military consequences of the violation of Belgian neutrality. Steinhausen was, however, no supporter of Delbrück's idea that a negotiated peace was possible at almost any time, noting that for such a peace to occur, both sides had to want it, and the Entente wanted victory, not a negotiated peace. Even though the General Staff had advocated a preventive war, Steinhausen said that the real cause of the war was Entente aggression, specifically the Russian general mobilization. In addition to the immediate effect of *Die Grundfehler des Krieges und der Generalstab,* Steinhausen's book had long-term influence: in the 1950s and 1960s Gerhard Ritter repeated most of Steinhausen's criticism of the General Staff practically verbatim.

Another early critic of the General Staff was retired Colonel Friedrich Immanuel, who had written extensively on military matters before the war. In his *Siege und Niederlagen im Weltkriege* (Victories and Defeats in the World War), Immanuel went one step further than Freytag in describing the war plan.[30] Immanuel said that the concept of Schlieffen's plan was contained in Schlieffen's *Cannae* article, and therefore Schlieffen had aimed at a double envelopment in the west. The German failure on the Marne was due solely to the failure of the *Oberste Heeresleitung* (OHL—the German headquarters) to correctly evaluate the situation. In particular, the OHL failed to retain a reserve army to support the right wing. Immanuel wasn't at all clear as to where these five or six corps were to come from. Immanuel's book also had long-term consequences: Ritter was especially fond of the idea that the German army should have retained a large reserve, and adopted it too as one of his criticisms of the General Staff.

[29] G. Steinhausen, *Die Grundfehler des Krieges und der Generalstab* (Gotha, 1919).
[30] F. Immanuel, *Siege und Niederlagen im Weltkriege* (Berlin, 1919).

2ilateral intended.

The General Staff's counterattack against Steinhausen, Immanuel and Delbrück (as well as against a host of less convincing criticisms, largely proposed by junior officers)[31] was not long in coming. In 1920, Hermann von Kuhl published *Der deutsche Generalstab in Vorbereitung und Durchführung des Weltkrieges* (The German General Staff in the Preparation and Conduct of the World War).[32] Kuhl had been one of Schlieffen's prize pupils. His last two assignments before the war were as chief of the western intelligence section and then as an *Oberquartiermeister* on the General Staff. On mobilization he was made chief of staff of the right-wing 1st Army. In *Der deutsche Generalstab* Kuhl was primarily concerned with countering Steinhausen's arguments that the General Staff had failed to correctly estimate the capabilities and intentions of the enemy armies, that is, he was defending the intelligence estimates that he had helped write. Kuhl also had to explain why the German army failed to win a decisive victory in the west in August 1914. In a small section in the middle of the book he provided the first detailed information about German war planning[33], while at the same time setting out the General Staff party line: Schlieffen had bequeathed a brilliant plan to his successor, who had failed to understand it.[34]

Kuhl said that Schlieffen initially adopted Moltke's *Ostaufmarsch*. In 1894 Schlieffen determined that the French were the more dangerous and aggressive enemy and he planned to attack them first. Schlieffen therefore decided to employ the mass of the German army in an offensive in the west. Between 1894 and 1899 the concept of the *Westaufmarsch* was to conduct shallow envelopment of the French left supported by a frontal attack on Nancy. In case of an Austro-German war against Russia, in which France had not yet become a belligerent, Schlieffen planned an *Ostaufmarsch* that was quite different from the old Moltke operation. The larger half of the German army would deploy to East Prussia. The main body would conduct a frontal attack on the Russian front on the Narew river while a smaller force conducted an outflanking operation to the north across the Niemen. The smaller half of the German army would wait in its mobilization stations until the French

---

[31] Particularly *Kritik des Weltkrieges, von einem Generalstäbler* (pseudonym for Captain G. Ritter) (Leipzig, 1920).

[32] H. von Kuhl, *Der deutsche Generalstab in Vorbereitung und Durchführung des Weltkrieges* (Berlin, 1920).

[33] Ibid. 164–70.

[34] As *WW* 1920 2. *Heft*, 233, noted: 'Zum ersten Male wird hier Schlieffens genialer Plan mit vielen Einzelheiten bekanntgegeben, gleichzeitig auch gezeigt, wie sein Nachfolger von der Bahn seines großen Vorgängers abwich und dadurch den Keim zum Mißerfolge legte.' (Here, for the first time, the details of Schlieffen's brilliant plan are revealed. At the same time, it is also made clear how his successor strayed from the path of his great predecessor and thereby created the basis for failure.)

commenced hostilities, and then conduct a rail deployment to mass against a part of the French army and destroy it. After 1899, Schlieffen further developed the *Westaufmarsch*. The attack on Nancy was dropped and the left-wing mission became completely defensive. Kuhl's description of Schlieffen's planning from 1891 to 1905 is accomplished in two pages. He then summarized what we now know to be the Schlieffen plan *Denkschrift*, saying that it was Schlieffen's final war plan. Kuhl explained that Schlieffen could employ the entire German army in the west because the Russians were occupied by the Russo-Japanese War. Kuhl's description of the deployment of forces and concept of the operation is short but an accurate summary of the *Denkschrift*: in particular, he emphasized the importance of a strong right wing. Kuhl said that Moltke retained the concept of Schlieffen's operation, but strengthened the left wing, with the intention of defeating the French in Alsace and Lorraine and then transferring forces, particularly the 7th Army, by rail to the right wing. During the actual campaign, however, these forces remained in Alsace and Lorraine, in order to conduct an attack to break through the French fortress line on the Moselle, which failed. The right wing, which was to carry out the decisive attack, was then too weak to execute its mission. Kuhl then went on to defend the concept of a *Westaufmarsch*. In particular, he emphasized the impossibility of attacking in the east: Germany simply did not have enough forces to attack in the east and defend in the west. Nor could Germany afford to defend on both fronts or wait until the western Allies violated Belgian neutrality: Germany had to utilize her interior position to make up for her numerical inferiority, defeating the French and then turning on the Russians.

In his article in the 21 December 1920 and 21 January 1921 issues of the *Deutsches Offzierblatt*, 'Warum mißlang der Marnefeldzug 1914?' ('Why did the Marne Campaign in 1914 Fail?'), Kuhl provided a condensed critique of Moltke's conduct of the campaign, emphasizing Moltke's inability to understand the Schlieffen plan. As we shall see, even during the war the principal German participants in the Battle of the Marne had written exculpatory papers to show that they had not been responsible for losing the battle. Kuhl's intention was to get his into print as early as possible.[35] Kuhl began by saying that 'I am of the opinion that it would have been possible to have arrived at a decision in the west in 1914 and that the campaign plan of Count Schlieffen would have succeeded, if only we had retained it and conducted it as

---

[35] Generalmajor Baumgarten-Crusius had even beaten Kuhl to the gun, publishing his defence of the Saxon 3rd Army on the Marne—*Die Marneschlacht, 1914*—in Leipzig in 1919.

Schlieffen intended.' Even in its altered form, however, the German war plan was superior to that of the French and the German army won great victories in the initial battles. A further victory on the Marne would have sealed the French defeat. The Germans lost on the Marne because in his initial deployment Moltke had reinforced the German left wing at the expense of the right. Moltke missed the last opportunity on about 23 August to make up for his initial mistake by not transferring forces from Lorraine to the right wing. Nevertheless, from Moltke's operations order of 27 August it appeared that he was still going to try to send the 1st Army to the west of Paris. The right wing proved too weak to execute this maneuver. The 1st Army alone took decisive action, swinging to the east of Paris and thereby forcing the entire French army to withdraw. The right wing was too weak, however, to continue turning the French flank and guard against a French attack from Paris at the same time, so the 1st Army boldly pressed on to the south. When the French did launch their offensive from Paris, the 1st Army replied with a highly successful counteroffensive. Then the commander of the German 2nd Army, Generaloberst Bülow, lost his nerve and ordered his Army to withdraw, while Lieutenant-Colonel Hentsch, a senior OHL staff officer and Moltke's personal representative, appeared at 1st Army headquarters and, citing the 2nd Army's withdrawal, ordered the 1st Army to retire as well. Kuhl contended that the loss of the battle of the Marne could not in any way be blamed on the leadership of the 1st Army.

Kuhl immediately followed this article in 1921 with a 266-page defense of the Schlieffen plan and 1st Army operations in *Der Marnefeldzug 1914* (The 1914 Marne Campaign).[36] Kuhl made it clear that the Schlieffen plan was the highest and most effective expression of the *Vernichtungsstrategie* and as such was diametrically opposed to Delbrück's *Ermattungsstrategie*. The Schlieffen plan had been the real war plan and surely would have produced a quick, decisive battle of annihilation had only Moltke executed it properly. Such an argument, Kuhl clearly felt, carried far more weight than Delbrück's defeatist, theoretical ruminations. The Schlieffen plan now became the central element of the post-war *Strategiestreit*.

In *Der Marnefeldzug* Kuhl also provided the first detailed description of the campaign in northern France, along with his excuses for the mistakes made by the 1st Army during the campaign. Throughout the campaign, relations between 1st Army and 2nd Army headquarters had been poor, primarily because the 1st Army resented being placed initially under the operational control of the 2nd Army. Kuhl continued

---

[36] H. von Kuhl, *Der Marnefeldzug 1914* (Berlin, 1921).

the feud into the post-war period, criticizing Bülow for cautious, uncertain and linear operations on the Sambre–Meuse, which, Kuhl maintained, cost the German army the chance to encircle the French 5th Army. He blamed Bülow for preventing the 1st Army from destroying the British at Mons. Kuhl also tried to explain away the 1st Army's inability to destroy one isolated British corps at Le Cateau.

Kuhl used every opportunity to argue that a second echelon of several corps should have followed the 1st Army, as provided in the Schlieffen plan *Denkschrift*, in order to guard the 1st Army's flank and rear.[37] This is one of the principal factors that made the Schlieffen plan so attractive to Kuhl. If the need for a second echelon were accepted then all of Kuhl's errors on the Marne would be satisfactorily explained. He maintained that the concept of the Schlieffen plan could still have been executed as late as 27–30 August by transferring forces from the German left wing to the right. Kuhl even said that he was uncertain as to whether or not Moltke was going to send a second wave of divisions behind the 1st Army. At this point Kuhl is stretching the lie a bit too far. If OHL really were sending reinforcements forward, they would have to pass through the 1st Army's own rear echelon and Kuhl would have surely have been informed of it, if only because of the supply problems involved. Kuhl, especially after the turn south on 31 August, wanted the 1st Army to deliver the decisive blow. Kuhl explained that when the 1st Army failed to execute its assigned mission in the OHL operations order of 5 September to guard the right flank against a sortie from Paris and instead pressed on to the south of the Marne, it did so because it was acting in accordance with the intent of the Schlieffen plan and the spirit, if not the letter, of Moltke's operations order, the concept for both being the envelopment of the French left wing. Kuhl then repeated his version of the battle of the Marne, again explaining that the 1st Army withdrew only because the 2nd Army had withdrawn and only after Hentsch issued an order in the name of the OHL for the 1st Army to withdraw. Kuhl's final conclusion was that the German Army system—troop training, officer corps, General Staff—had not failed on the Marne, rather 'leading personalities' had, by which he clearly meant Moltke, Bülow and, Hentsch.

After the war, senior German officers were presented with a practically insoluble problem. They maintained, with considerable justification, that the German army in 1914 was one of the best the world had

---

[37] For example, in the actual war plan 12 corps were deployed north of the Meuse. In his book *Bis zur Marne* the operations officer at that time, Tappen, argued that it was not physically possible to deploy more troops north of the Meuse. Kuhl devotes a large portion of his short review of Tappen's book contending that Tappen was wrong. *PJ* 185 (Juli bis September 1921), 407.

ever seen, and that the German infantry battalions were beyond all praise. Nevertheless, the German campaign in the west, in spite of forty years of preparation, was a failure. This failure could only be due to errors committed both by the General Staff as an institution and by individual senior officers. Kuhl, for one, had every prospect of going down in German military history alongside the Duke of Brunswick in 1806 or General Steinmetz in 1870. He would almost surely be held at least partially responsible for the 1st Army's failures on the Marne, at Le Cateau and at Mons. To avoid such a fate, Kuhl found three scapegoats, all of whom were conveniently dead in 1920: Moltke, Bülow, and Hentsch. The chief miscreant was Moltke, who, Kuhl maintained, had been given a brilliant plan by his predecessor and then was unable to execute it. Moltke's weakness of character was his, and Germany's, downfall. In Kuhl's scenario, Moltke maintained the concept of the Schlieffen plan—the right-wing envelopment—while being unwilling to take the risks in Lorraine which would alone ensure success. As the campaign progressed, Moltke lost touch with the battle and his orders became increasingly irrelevant. Moltke gradually let the operational control of the army slip completely from his grasp. In this environment, the 1st Army's headquarters alone followed the concept of the operation of the great Schlieffen plan, and their efforts would have been successful had only Bülow and Hentsch displayed a fraction of the 1st Army's determination.

The Schlieffen plan posed a challenge for Delbrück. He was forced to acknowledge in his article 'Falkenhayn und Ludendorff'[38] in early 1920 that the entire military establishment was unanimously of the opinion that the Schlieffen plan would have worked if only Moltke had executed it properly. Delbrück had to admit that the Schlieffen plan might have produced a decisive victory.[39] Delbrück's answer was that even if the Germans won a decisive victory, the Germans couldn't be sure that the French would sue for peace. Even if the Schlieffen plan had succeeded, the French army had been destroyed and Paris had been taken, the French would have continued to fight. The German people would have set the surrender conditions so high that a lasting peace could not have been attained. This argument has proven popular with opponents of the Schlieffen plan. Gordon Craig repeated it in his *Politics of the Prussian Army* in 1955.[40] Delbrück then went on to defend the standard-bearer of the *Ermattungsstrategie*, Falkenhayn,

---

[38] Delbrück, 'Falkenhayn und Ludendorff', 249–81.
[39] 'Eine solche 'Entscheidung' gab für uns im Weltkrieg (es sei denn vielleicht im ersten Monat) nicht.' (It was not possible for us to have won such a decisive victory in the World War—unless we did so in the first month), Ibid. 252.
[40] G. Craig, *The Politics of the Prussian Army* (2nd rev. edn., Oxford, 1964), 280.

including both Falkenhayn's inflexible defensive tactics in the west as well as his inability to accomplish his own mission of knocking the Russian army out of the war in 1915. In the latter case, Delbrück blamed Ludendorff, saying that Ludendorff had sabotaged Falkenhayn's plan. Amazingly, in 1920 Delbrück was still defending Falkenhayn's body-count strategy at Verdun. Finally, having made reference to Kuhl's *Der deutsche Generalstab*, Delbrück said that Germany should have begun the war with an *Ermattungsstrategie*, not the Schlieffen plan's *Vernichtungsstrategie*. This piece of *ex post facto* wisdom would be repeated by almost all the subsequent opponents of the Schlieffen plan.

Towards the end of the article, Delbrück made a curious and much overdue admission: he finally recognized that while attrition warfare may sound good in theory, it destroys the morale of the combat troops. The soldier may be willing to bleed for victory, Delbrück said, but he is unwilling to die for the cold-blooded calculation that the enemy units are being attrited faster than one's own. In the end, Delbrück acknowledged that Falkenhayn's *Ermattungsstrategie* cost him the confidence of the combat troops. Such an admission alone should have ended the *Vernichtungsstrategie–Ermattungsstrategie* debate.

Delbrück's other explanation for Germany's failure to win the war was to blame one person in particular for Germany's misfortunes, and that was Erich Ludendorff.[41] From 1908 to 1912 Ludendorff was the head of the deployment section (*Aufmarschabteilung*) under the younger Moltke, and had therefore helped to write the German war plan. Ludendorff, as Hindenburg's *Erster Generalquartiermeister* (chief of staff) had been the *de facto* head of the German army from August 1916 to October 1918. For Delbrück, Ludendorff became the personification of the *Vernichtungsstrategie*. In *Ludendorffs Selbstportrait* (Ludendorff's Self-Portrait) in 1922, Delbrück again advocated the *Ostaufmarsch* while he made Ludendorff personally responsible for the major features of the disastrous *Westaufmarsch*. In 1915 Moltke told the Center Party politician, Matthias Erzberger, that he, Moltke, had really wanted to conduct an *Ostaufmarsch*. From this, Delbrück concluded that Ludendorff, as the chief of the *Aufmarschabteilung* before the war, had been the moving force behind the adoption of the *Westaufmarsch*. Delbrück also said that there was no Schlieffen plan, only a Schlieffen idea. By strengthening the left wing in order to protect Lorraine and the Palatinate, Ludendorff had 'watered down' the Schlieffen idea. Delbrück maintained that Ludendorff, as the *Erster Generalquartiermeister*, had practi-

---

[41] H. Delbrück, 'Erich Ludendorff. Meine Kriegserinnerungen 1914–18', in: *PJ Band* 178 Oktober bis Dezember 1919, 83–101; 'Falkenhayn und Ludendorff', 249–81; *Ludendorffs Selbstportrait* (Berlin, 1920).

cally single-handedly blocked peace negotiations and continued the war in order to obtain territorial gains for Germany in Belgium and Poland. As far as Delbrück was concerned, throughout the entire war Ludendorff hadn't done anything right: even Ludendorff's contribution at Tannenberg was minimal.

Delbrück also contended that he was the first to demonstrate the 'Cannae idea'—that the double envelopment was the ultimate form of the battle of annihilation, the *Vernichtungsschlacht*—in his account of Hannibal's victory in 216 BC at the battle of Cannae in the first volume of *Die Geschichte der Kriegskunst*, which was published in 1900. Delbrück contended that Schlieffen adopted the *Cannae* concept in his articles which were published in the General Staff's *Vierteljahreshefte für Kriegführung und Politik* (Quarterly Journal of War and Politics) between 1906 and 1910. This piece of shameless self-promotion has been accepted as true by subsequent historians, because it would seem to show the intellectual origins of the Schlieffen plan. Delbrück even said that it was his *Cannae* concept which also provided the template for the German plan at the battle of Tannenberg. Delbrück's estimate of the importance of his description of the battle of Cannae is wrong on two counts. First, Livy's account of the battle of Cannae from Book XXII of his history of Rome was known to practically every schoolboy. Delbrück added nothing to what Livy had already said very well. Second, it is clear that Schlieffen's concept of the *Vernichtungsschlacht* was well formed before 1900, and that he drew his inspiration from Napoleon and Moltke, whose example was far more immediate than that of a Punic general in 216 BC. The tenor of *Ludendorffs Selbstportrait* is so immoderate that it damages Delbrück's credibility. Nevertheless, later summaries of the article have passed over its vitriolic tone in silence. Instead, *Ludendorffs Selbstportrait* has been cited to explain both the genesis of the Schlieffen plan and Ludendorff's role in 'watering it down'.

The General Staff's second volley in the post-war *Strategiestreit* was provided by Wolfgang Foerster. Before the war Foerster had written a military biography of Prince Friedrich Karl.[42] Foerster had been on the staff of several major commands during the war. He started the war as a captain, was promoted to major on 28 November 1914 and remained at that rank for the duration. In January 1919 he was transferred to the General Staff's historical section and in the autumn of that year he became an *Oberarchivrat* in the Reichsarchiv. There he was chief of the section which wrote the official history of the war in the west to the autumn of 1916, including the volumes which described the Schlieffen

---

[42] W. Foerster, *Prinz Friedrich Karl von Preußen, Denkwürdigkeiten aus seinem Leben* (2 vols., Berlin, 1910).

plan and the Marne campaign. He was not promoted to lieutenant-colonel until he officially left the army on 10 April 1920. In 1931 he became director of the historical section in the Reichsarchiv and in 1935 president of the military history section of the Army.[43]

In 1921 Foerster published *Graf Schlieffen und der Weltkrieg* (Count Schlieffen and the World War).[44] Whereas Kuhl used the Schlieffen plan largely to justify the actions of the 1st Army, Foerster used the Schlieffen plan to justify the conduct of the General Staff and the General Staff's doctrine of the *Vernichtungsschlacht*. At the same time, he attacked Falkenhayn's *Ermattungsstrategie*. In presenting his case, Foerster had to make public major portions of the Schlieffen plan *Denkschrift*. To illustrate this he published, for the first time, a map (map 3) from the Schlieffen's papers (*Nachlass*) which showed seven active army corps and six corps of replacement troops swinging to the west of Paris. While he did not print the entire text of the *Denkschrift*, neither did he try to gloss over its inconsistencies. Having explained the concept of the operation and the force deployment in some detail, Foerster then acknowledged that Schlieffen not only used the entire German army in the west, but that he also used eight non-existent ersatz corps. He explained this by saying that Schlieffen's legacy to Moltke was in two parts: first, the concept of the plan itself, the great right wheel through northern France, but also the requirement to build up the German force structure in order to carry out the plan.

Foerster, citing Moltke's *Große Generalstabsreisen West* (Great General Staff rides in the west) in 1906 and 1912, said that Moltke had decided that the French were going to launch a major offensive into Lorraine at the beginning of the war. He therefore retained the concept of the Schlieffen plan while doubling the number of German divisions in Lorraine. At the same time, Moltke created the option of modifying the German plan in order to be able to fight the main battle in Lorraine. Once the battle in Lorraine had been won, a regrouping of forces would presumably follow to allow the Germans to conduct the right-wing envelopment around the French fortress line. Moltke had therefore not entirely given up the concept of the Schlieffen plan. His changes to the plan, however, betrayed a lack of comprehension of the plan's intent. This was because Schlieffen had developed the plan through years of study, while Moltke had inherited it as a fully developed concept of the operation. Moltke was therefore equally uneasy

---

[43] M. Herrmann, *Das Reichsarchiv* (Berlin, 1993), 234. Excellent is M. Reymann, *Die Entstehung des Reichsarchivs und die Bearbeitung des amtlichen Kriegswerkes 1914–1918*, BA-MA MSg 131/7.

[44] W. Foerster, *Graf Schlieffen und der Weltkrieg* (1st edn., Berlin, 1921).

with the idea of launching the right wing through Belgium as he was of allowing superior French forces to attack into Lorraine.

In the event, Foerster said that Moltke tried to execute the Schlieffen plan's right-wing envelopment while defeating the French in Lorraine. As Schlieffen had foreseen, the French were defeated in Lorraine, but were not destroyed: they merely retreated to their fortress line. Moltke could have redeployed forces from Lorraine to the right wing as late as 27 August and successfully carried out the Schlieffen plan, but he did not, preferring to attack the French all along the front. He even withdrew two corps from the right wing and sent them to East Prussia. By 4 September the Schlieffen concept of a right-wing envelopment had to be abandoned and Moltke then tried to conduct a penetration of the French center to the west of Verdun. The French counterattack forestalled this plan. In summary, the Germans lost the campaign in the west owing to Moltke's weak leadership and his failure to follow the Schlieffen plan.

In 1921 Delbrück regained his confidence, which had been severely shaken by the loss of the war and the disclosure of the Schlieffen plan. In 'Die strategische Grundfrage des Weltkrieges' (Fundamental Strategic Questions of the War)[45] Delbrück renewed his attack on Ludendorff and the *Vernichtungsstrategie*. Delbrück said that the German army was not strong enough to win a decisive battle in the west, Schlieffen plan or no Schlieffen plan: Schlieffen's concept, after all, was for a one-front war. Delbrück then said that even Schlieffen found it necessary to keep six corps in East Prussia. This was not true of the 1905 *Denkschrift*, but this assumption was perfectly understandable. How could East Prussia be left entirely defenseless?

This is probably the first time that this most characteristic problem of the Schlieffen plan was recognized: in the *Denkschrift* Schlieffen used the entire German army in the west plus eight non-existent ersatz corps. One can use notional units—the ersatz corps—in an exercise, but that is hardly acceptable in the real war plan. The question therefore remained: What did the real war plan look like? Was the Schlieffen plan the basis of Schlieffen's last *Aufmarschplan*, which was effective from 1 April 1905 to 31 March 1906? Was it the concept of the 1906/7 plan? If so, what modifications were made to account for the fact that the real German army was considerably short of the force required in the *Denkschrift*? Did Schlieffen deploy units in the east in the real 1905/6 plan or not? If not, when did the war plan finally recognize that East Prussia needed to be defended? How was the plan for the west changed to accommodate the loss of these forces? As we shall see, Ludendorff

---

[45] Delbrück, 'Die strategische Grundfragen'. *PJ* 183 (Januar Bis März 1921) 289–308.

said that Schlieffen did deploy forces in East Prussia. Delbrück
contended that Ludendorff changed the actual war plan in 1909/10 by
deploying the 7th Army in Alsace and thereby moving the entire
Germany army to the south. Changed it from what? Delbrück didn't
provide a clear answer to this problem, and no one else has either. The
usual solution among historians is to ignore these questions altogether
or pass them over as an insoluble riddle.

Delbrück then went on to say that any attack in the west was doomed
to failure, because no *Westaufmarsch*, not even the Schlieffen plan,
could ever have been executed quickly enough to have stopped the
Russians. Anyway, even if the Germans had destroyed the French army
and taken Paris and Verdun, the French would have withdrawn behind
the Loire and continued the fight, the British would have immediately
instituted conscription, and the Americans would have declared war. In
a year giant Anglo-Saxon armies would have appeared in France. Such
overstrained arguments do not even win Delbrück debating points.

If a *Westaufmarsch* were really essential, Delbrück said, then the
concept of the operation should have been compatible with an
Ermattungsstrategie. Since it was impossible to destroy the Entente
armies in the west, the German army should have occupied northern
France as far as the Somme and then have assumed a defensive position
behind the river. Northern France would then be held for use in the
peace negotiations. This, Delbrück said, is exactly what Frederick the
Great did when he occupied Saxony at the beginning of the Seven Years
War.

In 1925 the first volume of the Reichsarchiv official history of the war
appeared.[46] It gave a short description the elder Moltke's defensive war
plans in the west and then said that in 1894 Schlieffen decided to begin
the campaign in the west with an attack on Nancy and the Meuse
fortresses. In the *Aufmarschplan* for 1898/99 Schlieffen intended to
maneuver to the north of Verdun by transiting south Belgium and
Luxembourg. He continually developed this plan until his
Westaufmarsch culminated in the 1905 *Denkschrift*. The official history
provided a six-page summary of the Schlieffen plan *Denkschrift*—the
longest so far.[47] It said that the Schlieffen plan was based on the
Westaufmarsch for 1905/6, in which the entire German army was
deployed in the west. The Reichsarchiv also said that there was an alternative plan in 1905/6 for a two-front war. This would also be called an
Ostaufmarsch. To reduce confusion Schlieffen's *Westaufmärsche* were
called *Aufmarsch* I, and his *Ostaufmärsche Aufmarsch* II. The *Ostaufmarsch*

[46] Reichsarchiv, *Der Weltkrieg, Band I, Die Grenzschlachten im Westen* (Berlin, 1925).
[47] Ibid. 55–61.

1905/6 deployed three corps and four reserve divisions—probably ten divisions in total—in East Prussia. The official history gave no details concerning the deployments either in the east or west for this plan, nor did it explain what the concept of the operation was on either front. This is truly surprising, for the 1905/6 *Ostaufmarsch* would have been based on a deployment that was far more similar to the German situation in 1914 than either the 1905/6 *Westaufmarsch* or the Schlieffen plan *Denkschrift*. The official history then goes on to acknowledge that in 1905 'a number' of the reserve corps had only one division,[48] whereas in the *Denkschrift* Schlieffen employed them as though they were full-strength two-division corps, and that there were also no provisions at all in 1905 for establishing the ersatz corps. The official history jumped to the 1908/9 plan to note that XIV Corps was given the mission of protecting the upper Rhine—an inconsequential change. The corps assembly area was not mentioned. There is no indication of what the real, operational war plan looked like in 1906/7 and 1907/8, that is, of how the Schlieffen plan *Denkschrift* was altered to fit the much smaller force actually available in the west. Nevertheless, implicitly some of the Schlieffen plan must have been employed, for the official history then says that as of the 1909/10 plan Moltke decisively changed the war plan: the 6th Army was deployed in Lorraine and the 7th in Alsace, each consisting of four corps (three active, one reserve). Moltke's concept of the operation emphasized a decisive battle in Lorraine. An attack by the 6th and 7th Armies on the Moselle north of Fort Frouard and against the Meurthe was also considered likely. In 1910 the rail transfer of the 7th Army to the right wing was fully planned out. After 1910 preparations were made to move the 7th Army by rail 'on order' to wherever it was needed. It is evident that the Reichsarchiv did everything possible to muddy the waters and avoided clarity like the plague.

The Reichsarchiv said that Schlieffen's intent was that under all circumstances the right wing, which must be made as strong as possible, should advance through Belgium and northern France until it gained the flank and rear of the French army. Any French attack would have to turn to meet this advance. In contrast, in the exercise critiques of General Staff rides Moltke had often said that the right-wing advance was unnecessary once the French had advanced out of their fortifications and into the open in Lorraine. In this case, the right wing must turn immediately south in order to take part in the main battle.[49]

---

[48] A German Reserve corps had practically none of the corps troops found in an active army corps: in particular, it had no corps artillery. Later, it would not have an aviation detachment as active army corps did. Therefore, a Reserve 'corps' with only one division was really just a reserve division with an unnecessary corps headquarters.

[49] Ibid. 64–5.

The official history established conclusively that the Schlieffen plan *Denkschrift* was the most important document in German war planning before the Great War. Subsequent historians, however critical of the plan itself, have accepted that this was true. The only debate has been as to whether it was brilliant or ill-conceived, bold or rash. Curiously, the official history did not publish a map showing the Schlieffen plan. The only map available was the rather general sketch Foerster provided in *Graf Schlieffen und der Weltkrieg*. This was widely reproduced. The great arrows sweeping across France exercised a strange, hypnotic power on civilians, academics, and Anglo-Saxon officers. This, they seemed to believe, was the way great strategy should look. Many appeared to derive a sense of satisfaction at having been initiated so easily into the mysteries of the great war plan of the General Staff. The concept of the Schlieffen plan was so simple that every commentator felt he understood it and was justified in passing an opinion on it.

Beginning in 1919, Ludendorff had published a series of books and articles in which he defended his conduct during the war and attacked Delbrück's strategy of attrition warfare and negotiated peace. In 1922 in *Kriegführung und Politik* (War Leadership and Politics), Ludendorff also defended Moltke's *Westaufmarsch*.[50] He said that Moltke maintained the concept of the Schlieffen plan, indeed he improved on it, for Schlieffen's left wing had been too weak. Moltke's failure was in executing the plan: he should have won a decisive victory in Lorraine and then transferred forces from the left to the right wing. In 1926 Ludendorff wrote that a good measure of the blame for losing the Marne campaign had to be assigned to the Reichstag, for failing to implement universal conscription. Schlieffen himself shared some of this blame, for he developed a plan which required a larger army yet failed to insist that his demands be met. Instead, Ludendorff said, Schlieffen played exercises using non-existent notional units.[51] The chancellor and war minister failed to demand a larger army out of fear of the Reichstag. He said that in the question of increasing the size of the army (*Heeresvermehrung*), Moltke was more dynamic than all of the others, because he pushed through the Army bills of 1912 and 1913. Moltke also recognized that the army was too small to execute the Schlieffen plan. The failure of the Schlieffen plan was due in the last analysis to the failure to increase the size of the army. There was only one way to compensate for Germany's numerical inferiority, and that was to use rail mobility as a 'force multiplier', concentrating a strong German army by rail to defeat an enemy army and then moving the

[50] E. Ludendorff, *Kriegführung und Politik* (Berlin, 1922).
[51] E. Ludendorff, 'Der Aufmarsch 1914', *DWS* 32(3) (8 Aug. 1926), 1–2.

victorious German army again by rail to engage a second enemy army. He said that the campaign in the east in 1914 (where Ludendorff was the chief of staff) provided a classic example of this concept, while in the west in 1914 it was not used at all. Ludendorff also criticized the concept for Schlieffen plan right wing. He said that because it had to maintain contact with Diedenhofen-Metz, the right wing was inflexible. In particular, the right wing could not be extended far enough toward the north to reach the coast and cover the right flank against envelopment. Ludendorff said that Schlieffen's epigones could only extol the plan as a recipe for victory (*Siegesrezept*) because the Schlieffen plan was never put to the test. Ludendorff reiterated that there is no such thing as a 'perfect plan' and that a soldier puts his faith in the perfect plan at his own peril. The decisive factor in war is the execution of the plan. The German army failed in the west because the leadership failed, not because the plan was inadequate.

In 1929 Kuhl published *Der Weltkrieg* (The World War), a collection of the pieces he had written during the preceding five years for the *Berliner Börsenzeitung*.[52] The first forty-five pages of the first volume of *Der Weltkrieg* restated in condensed form the description the of Schlieffen plan and the *apologia* for the 1st Army during the Marne campaign that Kuhl had first presented in 1921. The book had one significant if unanticipated consequence. To this point Ludendorff had remained largely aloof from the Schlieffen plan discussion. He now apparently felt that Kuhl's description of German war planning might be taken to reflect unfavorably on him: Ludendorff was, after all, the head of the *Aufmarschabteilung* when Schlieffen's great plan was altered. It was one thing for a civilian like Delbrück to cast aspersions: that a senior officer such as Kuhl might do so, even by indirection, could apparently not go unanswered.

In response to Kuhl's book, *Der Weltkrieg*, Ludendorff published two practically identical articles in December 1929 and January 1930 in which he defended the younger Moltke's war plan in 1914.[53] Ludendorff reiterated that Moltke followed the concept of the Schlieffen plan, but failed to execute the plan properly in 1914. Ludendorff supported his contention by comparing the number of divisions available in the various plans. He said that Schlieffen's *Denkschrift* called for the employment in the west of 80 infantry divisions and 16 ersatz divisions, whereas in 1905 the German army had available only 72 infantry divisions, that is, there was a shortage of 24 infantry and

[52] H. von Kuhl, *Der Weltkrieg 1914–1918*, i, (Berlin, 1929).
[53] E. Ludendorff, 'Der Aufmarsch 1914', in: *LV Folge* 31 vom 24. Dezember 1929 and also in *DW* (4 Januar 1930), 3–4.

ersatz divisions. In the real war plan for 1905/6, Ludendorff said Schlieffen deployed 10 infantry divisions in East Prussia and 62 in the West, with 54 infantry divisions allocated to the right wing, north of Metz, and 8 infantry divisions to the south of Metz, in Lorraine. (Ludendorff doesn't even consider that the Germans might not leave any troops at all in East Prussia, a strong indicator that this was never in fact a possibility.) In 1914, Moltke had available 79 infantry divisions and 6 ersatz divisions. He deployed 9 divisions in East Prussia, 16 in Lorraine and Alsace, and held the ersatz divisions in reserve, leaving 54 divisions for the right wing attack, which, Ludendorff said, was the same number as actually provided for in the 1905/6 war plan.

This is also an elaborate fraud. Ludendorff has shown only that, with 54 divisions, the right wing in the real plan in 1914 was no stronger than the right wing in the real plan in 1905/6. The true problem is that the right wing in the 'Schlieffen plan' *Denkschrift* contained 82 divisions (70 infantry divisions and 12 ersatz divisions) not 54. Ludendorff did not explain how 54 divisions were expected to do the job of 82, and no historian of German war planning has been able to explain this either. The Schlieffen *Denkschrift* required a German army of 96 divisions in the west, while there were only 62 available in the west in 1905/6 and only 76 in 1914 (including the ersatz divisions: in fact, Moltke planned until the last minute to send the ersatz divisions to East Prussia). The Reichsarchiv official history had brushed the problem aside with a general observation that Schlieffen was merely establishing a program for the future.[54] The necessary divisions were, however, never established. There was no possibility that the forces actually available were ever adequate to execute the 'Schlieffen plan', especially not the march around Paris. Nevertheless, all subsequent historians have accepted that the concept of the Schlieffen *Denkschrift*, including the march around Paris, provided the concept for the subsequent German war plans.

The last major participant in the Schlieffen plan project was General Wilhelm Groener, who as a lieutenant-colonel was chief of the railway section in 1914. Groener's entire wartime service was spent in the rear area, trying to increase the output of Germany's war industries and coordinating with political, industrial, and labor leaders. In October 1918 Groener was Ludendorff's successor as *Erster Generalquartiermeister*. After the war, Groener remained an ambitious man. From 1928 to 1932 he was sometimes war minister and minister of the interior and arguably the second most powerful man in the Brüning government. He wrote an article in the first quarterly issue for 1920 of the *Preußische*

---

[54] Reichsarchiv, *Der Weltkrieg Band I*, 55.

Jahrbücher which, simultaneously with Kuhl, presented the Schlieffen plan idea to the public.[55] He also wrote a review of Kuhl's *Der Generalstab* for the third 1920 issue of the *Preußische Jahrbücher*, reinforcing Kuhl's thesis that the Schlieffen plan had been the basis of the German war plan.[56] Groener was intimately involved in writing the official history of the war. He read the proof copies of all of the volumes of the official Reichsarchiv history of the war.[57] In 1925, Groener was appointed to the Historische Kommission which supervised the Reichsarchiv (Kuhl was appointed in 1926).[58]

Groener also wrote *Das Testament des Grafen Schlieffen* (The Testament of Count Schlieffen) in 1929 and *Der Feldherr wider Willen* (The Reluctant War Lord) in 1931.[59] Groener did not discuss the evolution of the Schlieffen plan, nor did he provide a map showing the concept of the 1905 *Denkschrift*. The *Leitmotiv* of both books was to show how Schlieffen would have successfully implemented the Schlieffen plan in 1914. Groener insisted that the Schlieffen plan was not merely a concept, but a working war plan. This is made explicit in a review of a book on the war by Professor Bredt. Groener stated that, 'The Schlieffen plan is not only to be understood as a "basic concept", but as an operations plan that had been worked out in all of its particulars. The plan is in fact contained in Count Schlieffen's *Denkschrift* of December 1905, after Schlieffen had worked out the principles of the *Aufmarsch* in years of study while on the General Staff.'[60] In *Der Feldherr wider Willen* Groener hammered home the point that none of the German senior commanders in 1914 understood Schlieffen's concept, in particular neither Moltke nor Bülow. Groener acknowledged that this was remarkable, considering the length of time that Schlieffen had been Chief of Staff; perhaps, he said, the psychologists would be able to explain it. Groener also maintained that Germany should have conducted a preventive war in 1905. The failure to take advantage of this favorable opportunity lay not with Schlieffen, but with the political leadership.

Groener was faced with the problem of making the Schlieffen plan order of battle match the forces available in 1905 and 1914.[61] Groener began by saying that it wasn't important that Schlieffen used more

[55] W. Groener, 'Die Liquidation des Weltkrieges', *PJ* 179 (Januar bis März 1920), 48.
[56] W. Groener, 'Der Generalstab', *PJ* 181 (Juli bis September 1920), 120–1.
[57] Herrmann, *Das Reichsarchiv*, 236–7.
[58] Ibid. 91.
[59] W. Groener, *Das Testament des Grafen Schlieffen* (2nd edn., Berlin, 1929); *Das Feldherr wider Willen* (Berlin, 1931). Groener provided a preview of these books in his review of the first two volumes of the Reichsarchivwerk: Das Kriegsgeschichtliche Werk des Reichsarchivs', *PJ* 199 (Januar bis März 1925), 47–56; 205 (Juli bis September 1926), 129–57.
[60] BA-MA, *Nachlaß* Groener N 46/40, 1–2.
[61] Groener, *Testament*, 202–3.

forces in the 1905 *Denkschrift* than were actually available in 1905, the only thing that mattered was the comparison between the force structure in the 1905 *Denkschrift* and the forces available in 1914. At one fell swoop, the question of what the real, operational Schlieffen plan looked like in 1905/6, 1906/7 and 1907/8—up to Moltke's changes of 1909—was brushed aside. Groener acknowledged that the Schlieffen plan required 'at least' 8 ersatz corps and that only 3 corps equivalents were available in 1914. His explanation was that a 'large difference appeared concerning the reinforcement of the field army that Schlieffen had wanted to obtain from the ersatz, Landwehr and Landsturm.' Having made this almost incomprehensible concession, Groener left the ersatz divisions out of his further calculations altogether. He said that the Schlieffen plan *Denkschrift* required a force of 26½ active corps and 14 reserve corps (conveniently leaving out the 8 ersatz corps). He then wrote that in 1914 the total German force included 26 active corps and 13½ reserve corps. The difference between the Schlieffen plan and the order of battle in 1914, according to Groener, was therefore not significant. Groener acknowledged, however, that in the actual 1905 war plan, Schlieffen deployed 5 corps in the east, so he *must* have done the same in the Schlieffen plan *Denkschrift*. The Schlieffen plan force in the west therefore contained 23½ active corps and 12 Reserve corps (35½ in total), which, Groener said, was essentially the same as the 35 that were really available in the west in 1914.

Groener's calculation was a patent repetition of Ludendorff's fraud, with embellishments. Groener was making maximum use of the fact that the Schlieffen plan *Denkschrift* had not been published in full to construct an outright lie. In fact, the Schlieffen plan *Denkschrift* was intended for a one-front war. The *Denkschrift* deployed 48 corps in the west, including all actually available active and reserve corps as well as imaginary reserve and ersatz corps. Groener came up with only 35 corps in the west in 1914. Even if one helped Groener out and added the 3 ersatz corps equivalents actually available in 1914, making 38 corps in the west total, by Groener's figures the German army in the west in 1914 was still 10 corps—two entire armies—short of what was required for the 'Schlieffen plan'. Nevertheless, all subsequent historians agreed with Groener that the Schlieffen plan provided the concept for the German plan in 1914.

Wolfgang Foerster tried a different fraud in 1931 in *Aus der Gedankenwerkstatt des Deutschen Generalstabes.*[62] First he tried to bring

---

[62] W. Foerster, *Aus der Gedankenwerkstatt des Deutschen Generalstabes* (Berlin, 1931), 36, 39–41.

Ludendorff over to the Schlieffen plan project by announcing that Ludendorff was Schlieffen's heir. Then he turned to the serious question of Schlieffen's use of imaginary units. In 1921 Foerster acknowledged that the Schlieffen plan required more troops than were actually available and that the requirement to raise these units was part of his legacy to his successor.[63] In 1931 Foerster said that he had misspoken: Schlieffen had *really* based the Schlieffen plan on the order of battle for the 1906/7 mobilization year, when the XX and XXI Corps and the Guard Reserve Corps became available, presumably bringing the Germany army closer to the (unstated) number of divisions needed. Unfortunately for Forester's theory, all three corps were *Kriegskorps*, mixtures of reserve and active army units, which had been created at Schlieffen's insistence in 1902.[64] Even Foerster had to acknowledge, in the vague and evasive manner that the Schlieffen school reserved for such things, that the necessary number of ersatz units did not exist.

The next step in the Schlieffen plan debate was taken in an article titled *West oder Ost-Offensive 1914?* written in 1941 by General Ludwig Beck. Beck had been appointed Chief of the General Staff on 1 July 1935. During the Sudeten crisis he predicted that the French would fight rather than submit to Hitler's demands. His resignation on 18 August 1938, in the middle of the crisis, found no support in the officer corps. Beck was a member of the Berlin *Mittwochsgesellschaft* (Wednesday Society) of prominent persons hostile to the Nazi regime which discussed Germany's political situation. *West oder Ost-Offensive 1914?* was presumably presented there. With Carl Goederler, Beck became the focus of the opposition to Hitler and would have been President of Germany had the 20 June Putsch succeeded. Instead, Beck was arrested and executed that day. *West oder Ost-Offensive 1914?* was not published until 1955.[65]

West oder Ost-Offensive 1914? was the culminating point of the military case against the Schlieffen plan. Gerhard Ritter, who was also a member

---

[63] W. Foerster, *Graf Schlieffen und der Weltkrieg* (2nd rev. edn., Berlin, 1925; 1st edn. 1921), 35. There is an undated note in Foerster's *Nachlaß* that shows that he knew full well that in 1905/6 and 1906/7 the German army had only 72 divisions and that XX and XXI Corps and the Guard Reserve Corps were already included in the order of battle. BA-MA *Nachlaß* Foerster N121/35.

[64] Reichsarchiv, *Kriegsrüstung und Kriegswirtschaft 1. Die militärische, wirtschaftliche und finanzielle Rüstung Deutschlands von der Reichsgründung bis zum Ausbruch des Weltkrieges* (Berlin, 1930), 66, 74–5; C. Jany, *Geschichte der Preußischen Armee vom 15. Jahrhundert bis 1914. Vierter Band. Die Königlich Preußische Armee und das Deutsche Reichsheer 1807 bis 1914 (Zweite ergänzte Auflage herausgegeben von Eberhard Jany*, Osnabrück, 1967), 296–7.

[65] L. Beck, 'West oder Ost-Offensive 1914?', in Hans Speidel (ed.), *Ludwig Beck, Studien*, (Stuttgart 1955), 139–89.

of the anti-Hitler opposition, probably became aware of it as early as 1941 and after the war adopted it outright and propagated it in his own works. It seems clear that when Beck wrote this article he did not have access to the Reichsarchiv, but based his arguments largely on those of the Delbrück school. Beck said that the elder Moltke had perfected the *Ostaufmarsch* in twenty years of work between 1871 and 1890. Moltke recognized that it was impossible to predict the length of the next European war because a Great Power could not be forced to sue for peace by inflicting one or two defeats on it. Moltke's strategy was to cripple Russia in an initial joint Austro-German offensive, and then turn on the French with the eastern front secure. Moltke also had the political wisdom to reject an offensive through Belgium.

Schlieffen, said Beck, adopted an offensive against France in a *Denkschrift* written in July 1894. At first, Schlieffen planned to conduct a frontal attack, and for that purpose he increased the *Westheer* from two-thirds of the total force, as it had been under Moltke, to four-fifths of the total force. Schlieffen also did not believe that it would be possible to cripple the Russian army with a double envelopment of Poland early in the war: the Russians would first defend the fortified Niemen–Narew line and then withdraw into their vast interior. In 1897 Schlieffen decided to attack through Luxembourg and Belgium. The decisive right-wing envelopment in the 1905 *Denkschrift* was the logical conclusion of Schlieffen's strategic thought. Schlieffen's 1912 *Denkschrift* was his last expression of his maneuver. The younger Moltke adopted the Schlieffen plan, but never fully made it his own, strengthening the left wing at the expense of the right.

Beck said that the most important factor in German military strategy should have been the preservation of Belgian neutrality. Had Germany done so, there was every reason to believe that Britain would have remained neutral. In addition the Germans would not have been able to defend in the east while attacking in the west. Since it was impossible to overthrow a Great Power in one or two campaigns, Germany should have prepared to wear her enemies down.

Beck said that Schlieffen developed an *Ostaufmarsch* for a war against Russia alone, with the French at least temporarily non-belligerent. He called this the *große Ostaufmarsch* (great *Ostaufmarsch*). The Germans would attack in the east with 16 corps and 7 reserve divisions, which Beck said was half the German army (it was really two-thirds of it). Beck acknowledged that this deployment would have taken a considerable time owing to the weak East Prussian rail net work. The main German attack would be directed against the Narew while one army secured the left flank against the Russian Niemen army. Beck said that Schlieffen himself did not rate the chances of this offensive very highly, and in 1913

the younger Moltke cancelled planning for the *große Ostaufmarsch* altogether. In Beck's mind, this was a mistake. A victory in a parallel battle
in the east, an 'ordinary victory' in Schlieffen's terms, was perfectly
acceptable to Beck. Even if the Russians could not have been decisively
defeated, the German army would have been able to occupy the
Bug–Narew line. This, Beck said, would have shortened the German
defensive line by half, that is, Beck maintained the elder Moltke's dubious theory that to defend in the east the Germans had to construct a
continuous defensive line along the entire border with Poland.

Beck said that the Germans estimated in 1914 that the total Russian
force included 117 divisions, 18 of which were in Siberia and Turkestan
and not immediately available. The Russians could assemble 63 of those
divisions in Poland by the 18th day of mobilization. The Austrians estimated that the Russians could assemble 60 divisions by the 20th day at
the earliest.

Beck's plan was to increase the forces in East Prussian from 9 divisions to 20, with the possibility of supplementing this with the 6 ersatz
divisions.[66] This left 59 divisions in the west. This was a return to the
Moltke/Waldersee plan of 1888. Beck called this his Plan A. In the west
he would have deployed three armies with a total of 32 divisions along
the border with Belgium and Luxembourg. One army (11 divisions?)
would defend Metz. Two armies with a total of 16 divisions would
defend between Metz and Strasbourg. Since neither the Belgians nor
the British would be belligerent, for all intents, Beck said, the German
army in the west was still as strong as the French.

Beck said the French had about 80 divisions, which in fact would
have been 21 more than the Germans had, a 36 percent French superiority. In the east, the odds initially would have been about even: 20
German divisions and a maximum of 40 Austrian against 60 Russian.
The Austro-German situation would steadily deteriorate as the Russians
deployed their remaining 57 divisions to the west. In short order, the
Germans would have been outnumbered on both fronts.

Beck apparently saw the weaknesses in Plan A, for he then developed
Plan B. This was essentially an attempt to resuscitate Moltke's plan of
1880 for a full-scale Austro-German attack in the east. Nevertheless,
even Beck would have sent only 28 divisions to the east. Eighteen to
twenty of those would deploy in East Prussia. Beck said that the East
Army, in eastern East Prussia, would be deployed and ready to attack
the Niemen by the 12th day of mobilization. The West Army, with its left
flank at Johannisburg, would conduct an attack on the Narew on the

---

[66] Beck's strength figures are not clearly stated and are difficult to put together
systematically. The following summary can at best be considered an approximation.

20th day. An army in Silesia with 8–10 divisions would advance on the 12th day and reach the Vistula by the 22nd day. In the west Beck had perhaps 51 divisions. He reduced his forces to the north of Metz from 32 divisions to 16. He said that he would only have been able to extend his right wing as far as Prüm. An army would continue to deploy behind Metz and two armies with 16 divisions in total between Metz and Strasbourg. There would also be a reserve army of 8 divisions. Beck said that the principal advantage of both Plans A and B was that they observed Belgian neutrality.

In Plan B, some 51 German divisions would have faced 80 French, a French superiority of 29 divisions, or 56 percent. In the east, the Germans would have initially had a considerable superiority. But even Beck himself admitted that the Russians would have been able to withdraw and avoid a decisive battle. The Russians would then have reappeared in a few weeks in overwhelming numbers. Given the obvious military weakness of Beck's *Ostaufmarsch*, it would have been incredible if the German Empire had based its strategy on Beck's unexamined assertion that Britain would have remained neutral had Germany not invaded Belgium. Nevertheless, Ritter was to make this the centerpiece of his critique of the Schlieffen plan.

From the First World War to the 1990s, only one group of original German war-planning documents has come to light, this being the original drafts and copies of Schlieffen's *Denkschrift*, which Gerhard Ritter found in Schlieffen's papers being held after the Second World War in the National Archives in the United States. Ritter was even less qualified to comment on the German war plan than Delbrück had been. Ritter was born in 1888. During the war he served as a junior artillery officer. From 1925 to 1957 he taught history at Freiburg, specializing in the late Middle Ages and Reformation, and wrote an important biography of Martin Luther. He shared Delbrück's interest in Frederick the Great and wrote a short biography of Frederick in 1936. Ritter was 68 years old when his *Schlieffenplan* book was published in 1956 and had done no previous work in military history. Though Ritter freely and often admitted his lack of military expertise, he was not deterred from making the most sweeping judgements concerning operations and strategy.

Delbrück had remained a German patriot. He argued mightily against German war guilt and the war guilt clause (Article 231) of the Treaty of Versailles. Russian general mobilization, Delbrück said, was principally responsible for starting the Great War, for everyone knew that Russian general mobilization meant war. Ritter, after 1933–45, did not have the luxury of patriotism. Like Friedrich Meinecke, Ritter was faced with explaining the German disaster in the twentieth century, a disaster for which Ritter's generation and most especially his social class were directly responsible. In the closing address to the German historical conference in Bremen on 19 September 1953 Ritter found his explanation for the German disaster: militarism.[67] Ritter defined militarism as the one-sided determination of national policy according to military calculations, and not according to *raison d'état* (*Staatsvernuft*), public morality, peace and the rule of law (*Rechts- und Freidensordnung*). In a long discussion of the nature of militarism, Ritter came down foursquare in favor of rational eighteenth-century *Kabinettskriege* conducted by professional armies, which did not disturb the middle class, and he opposed wars by conscript armies which inflamed the passions of the population. Frederick the Great and Bismarck were Ritter's ideal political types because, according to Ritter, they conducted only *Kabinettskriege*. Bismarck denied all influence in policy-making to both the military as well as democratic popular enthusiasms: national policy under Bismarck was purely a question of rational *raison d'état*. However, Ritter acknowledged that even Bismarck was not able to avoid being dragged into a nationalistic war with the French republic after the battle of Sedan. As a consequence, Bismarck was forced to accede to the demands of his generals to annex Lorraine and Metz, a step that he later recognized had been a mistake.

Ritter said that Moltke was also no militarist, that he had no political goals of his own and never allowed his military planning to impinge on the political sphere. Moltke did, however, advocate total war and opposed the imposition of political goals on his military planning: for Moltke, the conduct of war was a purely military matter. Moltke's attitude unfortunately represented the wave of the future. In the conduct of the Second World War the victory of the military technicians was complete: this war was a total war fought according to purely military calculations, which reached its apogee in 'the barbaric destruction from the air of all the works of European civilization'.

Ritter contended that it was the increasing supremacy of technology in war that characterized the modern problem of militarism. Technological war approached the Clausewitzian extreme of total war and could not be directed by political considerations. In Germany after 1871 the mass army militarized the lower class and the middle class alike. The Schlieffen plan represented the culmination point of militarism in Germany. To succeed, the Schlieffen plan required a great increase in the German army, that is, an even stronger military influence on German society and politics. Nevertheless, Ritter said that careful study of the 1905 Schlieffen plan *Denkschrift* and Schlieffen's 1912 supplement show that the plan, far from being a formula for victory, was really an

---

[67] G. Ritter, 'Das Problem des Militarismus in Deutschland', *HZ Band* 177 (1954), 21–48.

exceptionally risky and uncertain gamble, so much so that Schlieffen was unable to arrive at a plan for a two-front war. Ritter had to acknowledge that even the elder Moltke had been unable to find a satisfying solution to the problem of a two-front war.

Ritter maintained that by 1914 the victory of militarism in Germany was complete. National policy in the July crisis was determined not by politics but by the 'purely technical' considerations of the mobilization timetables. Rather than fall a few hours behind in the mobilization race, the German government was forced to take on the odium of being the aggressor and the destroyer of the European peace. Similar considerations were operative in Russia, indeed in all of Europe. It was not so much that the soldiers were the guilty parties in this development. Rather, the system was at fault, the general arms race brought on by the ever more radical development of universal conscription. This was the concrete expression of the competition between imperialistic powers, with their industrial bases and nationalistic populations. Ludendorff, owing to his one-sided military thinking and belligerent attitude, was the clearest expression of German militarism. He was not, however, alone. The Allied side was also dominated by men who pursued total war in order to destroy their enemies. After the war, Germany was divided into politicians seeking accommodation with the west and militarists. With Hitler's accession to power it was no longer the Army that was militaristic: quite the contrary. The Army (and here Ritter surely meant Beck) tried to moderate Hitler's policies by citing 'purely military' considerations. It was the political leader of Germany—Hitler— who was the militarist, and who led Germany into the abyss.

In the course of time Ritter hardened his position. Militarism became for Ritter less a European and more a specifically German problem. In *The Sword and the Scepter* (*Staatskunst und Kriegshandwerk*) he said that in the late nineteenth and the first half of the twentieth centuries Germany was perverted by militarism.[68] Militarism was responsible for diverting Germany onto her *Sonderweg* and away from development into a western liberal democracy. The Army and General Staff were two of the principal exponents of militarism, and the single document that most exemplified militarism was the Schlieffen plan.

Ritter published the original Schlieffen plan documents in 1956 in his book *The Schlieffen Plan*. Although Ritter acknowledged he had found the plan among Schlieffen's personal papers, he did not explain why the original text of the German war plan was, from 1906 (when

---

[68] G. Ritter, *Staatskunst und Kriegshandwerk* (2 vols., Munich, 1954–68); English edition: *The Sword and the Scepter* (2 vols., Miami, 1969–73), 265. All references are to the English edition.

Schlieffen retired) to 1913 (when Schlieffen died), in Schlieffen's personal possession and not locked in the General Staff's operations section vault with the rest of the war planning documents. Indeed, after Schlieffen's death the Schlieffen plan became the property of Schlieffen's daughters[69] and remained family property until 1931 when it was turned over to the Reichsarchiv.[70] If the 'Schlieffen plan' was actually the German war plan, then in August 1914 the original text of the most closely guarded secret in Europe was in the custody of two Prussian ladies of a certain age, who, according to the various inventories in the Schlieffen plan file, stored the Schlieffen plan with the family photos.

The original documents, now located in the Militärarchiv in Freiburg,[71] consist of Schlieffen's drafts and handwritten final copy (in German Standard style), and titled 'Krieg gegen Frankreich', (War against France). The final handwritten copy appears to have been grafted together from pieces of several different draft copies, written by at least two different hands, and perhaps more. This is not a fair copy, but rather contains numerous deletions and additions. It is dated December 1905 but was apparently written in January 1906, after Schlieffen had retired. There is also an untitled supplement dated February 1906. There are two typed versions of both documents, bearing the younger Moltke's marginal comments, which are dated B [Berlin] 1911. In comparison with Schlieffen's exercise critiques, the *Denkschrift* is poorly organized. Schlieffen discussed the complete operation in the first three-quarters of the *Denkschrift*, right down to the organization of the rear area, then in the last quarter picked up at the very beginning and went through the conduct of the operation again. In a General Staff where orders were short, crisp, and clear, such verbosity was extremely poor form. In February, Schlieffen found it necessary to write a supplement to cover the possibility of British intervention on the continent. He was already aware of this possibility when he wrote the *Denkschrift* in January 1906, for he had played British intervention during his November–December 1905 war game. The General

---

[69] The first sheet in the 'Schlieffen Plan' file N 43/137 at the Bundesarchiv-Militärarchiv proudly announces in a beautiful feminine hand that the plan is *Eigentum von Elisabeth von Hahnke geb. Gräfin Schlieffen und Gräfin Maria Schlieffen*, that is, the property of Elisabeth von Hahnke, née Countess Schlieffen and Countess Maria von Schlieffen.

[70] W. A. Mommsen (ed.), *Die Nachlässe in den deutschen Archiven 'mit Ergänzungen aus anderen Beständen' Teil 1: Verzeichnis der schriftlichen Nachlässe in den deutschen Archiven und Bibliotheken. Band 1: Schriften des Bundesarchivs 17* (Boppard am Rhein, 1971), 453. My thanks to Frau Kornelia Bobbe of the Geheimes Staatsarchiv Preußischer Kulturbesitz in Berlin (Dahlem) for pointing this out to me.

[71] *Nachlaß* Schlieffen BA-MA N 43/137 handwritten, N 43/138 typed (microfilm).

Staff officers had emphasized that Schlieffen contended that if the French conducted an attack into Lorraine they would be doing the Germans a favor (*Liebesdienst*). One of the few surprises revealed by the original *Denkschrift* is that Schlieffen was not at all clear about how he would deal with a French attack in Lorraine. At one point, he says that such an attack would be doing the Germans a *Liebesdienst* because the pressure exerted by the right-wing envelopment would force the French to pull all their forces to the north. The right-wing envelopment should proceed as originally planned. At another point he says that the Germans should react to a French attack in Lorraine by changing the right-wing attack as little as possible, but nevertheless shortening up the right wing and turning it south at La Fère.

To this day it has escaped notice that Schlieffen was not even sure what he could do with the ersatz corps. On the one hand Schlieffen was emphatic that they were needed on the far right wing to block the west and south sides of Fortress Paris, and subsequent descriptions of the plan regard this as the only possible employment for them. It therefore comes as a shock to read Schlieffen's acknowledgment that the rail system might not be in a fit state to transport the ersatz divisions to Paris. Schlieffen had obviously recognized that the ersatz divisions would need time to organize and that they could not possibly catch up with the right wing by foot marching. If they could not be sent to the right wing, Schlieffen said that they might be deployed on the Meuse between Verdun and Mézières. If that was not entirely possible, maybe the rest could be sent to Metz or the right bank of the Moselle! However, without the 12 ersatz divisions, the right wing envelopment would clearly be impossible. Once again, Schlieffen was forced to recognize that the German army was not strong enough to conduct the Schlieffen plan. The point of the *Denkschrift* was obviously to raise the largest number of units possible, not to come up with a new scheme of maneuver. Once the units were raised, Schlieffen would find something to do with them. All in all, as an operations order the Schlieffen plan is a horror.

Ritter tried to maintain that his discovery of the original text of the Schlieffen plan fundamentally altered the historical perception of German war planning: Ritter felt he had spoken the last word that needed to be said concerning the Schlieffen plan. However, as Wolfgang Foerster noted, Ritter's *The Schlieffen Plan* book added little except detail to what was by then (1956) accepted as common knowledge. Ritter failed to subject either the text or the maps to systematic analysis, limiting himself to a few comments concerning the drafts of the plan. The most important detail the *Denkschrift* did confirm—the full extent of the discrepancy between the *Denkschrift* order of battle and the forces actually available either in 1905 or in 1914—was passed over by Ritter and everyone else. Rather, Ritter's clear intent was to renew the old *Vernichtungsstrategie–Ermattungsstrategie* argument, using the original text of the Schlieffen plan *Denkschrift* in order to win final victory for Delbrück. Ritter repeated the arguments of Beck, Steinhausen, Immanuel, and Delbrück as though they were established facts; the General Staff's perspective is hardly mentioned. Ritter further developed this position in *The Sword and the Scepter.* The choice of the English title may be euphonious, but it fails to convey the intent of the German—*Staatskunst und Kriegshandwerk*—which was clearly programmatic: *Staatskunst* is the art of governing and diplomacy; *Kriegshandwerk* is the military craft. To Ritter, the relationship between the two was the same as that between architecture and bricklaying. For Ritter, strategy has little to do with the military craft, but rather is determined with reference to domestic and foreign policy and propaganda. On the other hand, *Staatskunst* had nothing to do with industrial production and economic warfare, which were hardly even mentioned.

At the very beginning of *Der Schlieffenplan*, Ritter said that Moltke's *Ostaufmarsch* was superior to the Schlieffen plan, a contention he renewed in *The Sword and the Scepter.*

If Germany were to accept the immense burdens and dangers of a two-front war for the sake of Austria-Hungary, everything had to be done to avoid expanding it into a three-front war, and above all to make it plain to the world that the war was purely one of defense, an action in the aid of Germany's ally. There would have been but one way to achieving that end—foregoing any breach of neutrality, remaining on the defensive in the west, with nothing more than tactical offensive sallies, and concentrating the strongest action on the eastern front. Germany, in other words, had to cling to the principle of Moltke's original war plan.[72]

The political and military advantages of the *Ostaufmarsch* were immense. Ritter asserted that the French alliance prevented the Russians from avoiding the German army by withdrawing to the east. That the French would have been overjoyed to see a major part of the German army disappear into the Russian wilderness did not occur to him. In the west, on the other hand, the Germany army could withdraw to the 'broad and deep river barrier of the Rhine if need be.'[73] Britain's sole strategic and political interest was in Belgian neutrality and the German challenge to British naval hegemony was not a factor in the British decision to fight: 'It is highly unlikely, moreover, that Sir Edward Grey would have succeeded—even if such had been his intention—in involving his fellow countrymen in a continental war which, in effect, would have revolved around nothing more than helping the French

---

[72] Ritter, *Sword and Scepter*, ii. 203.   [73] Ibid. 198.

reconquer Alsace-Lorraine.'[74] Even the French would have been unenthusiastic: 'Would the French people have taken the field with the patriotic fervor they displayed in 1914 if, instead of repelling a German
invasion, it had been merely a matter of reconquering the provinces
lost in 1871 or of helping the Russians destroy the Danubian Empire?
Not very likely.'[75]

For Ritter, there was no question that this *Denkschrift* was the culmination of Schlieffen's strategic thought and the template for all subsequent war plans. Ritter assumed that Schlieffen had developed the plan
since 1897, tested it in the *Generalstabsreisen West* in 1904 and 1905, and
passed it on as his legacy to his successor. Moltke and Ludendorff then
modified the great plan by reinforcing the left wing.

Ritter's criticism of the Schlieffen plan was scathing: 'The sum total
of his work—his great campaign plan of 1905—was even more baneful
to German political life than the excessively swollen German naval
program in the Tirpitz era.'[76] Nor did Ritter make any attempt to
resolve the inconsistencies in the Schlieffen plan. Instead, Ritter made
the Schlieffen plan the central piece of evidence in his indictment of
German militarism: the Schlieffen plan was war planning run amok,
the 'purely military' plan 'based on military theory rather than on the
realities of history and politics.' [77] Far from being a blueprint for victory
(*Siegesrezept*), the Schlieffen plan had little chance of succeeding, while
at the same time Schlieffen took foolhardy risks (*ein überkühnes
Wagnis*)[78] trying to make the plan work. Schlieffen did not even
consider alternative plans, by which Ritter meant the *Ostaufmarsch*
(obviously influenced by Beck, Ritter said that *Aufmarsch* II, Schlieffen's
Ostaufmarsch, was only applicable in a one-front war in the east). The
Schlieffen plan was also inflexible: as the apotheosis of the rigid military mind, Schlieffen had tried to determine the entire course of the
campaign in advance. Most important, the violation of Belgian neutrality was a catastrophe: 'The entire world criticized Germany for being
led and ruled by unscrupulous militarists—a reproach that attached
itself to the name of the German nation like a curse . . . seen from the
perspective of later events [the Second World War] the Schlieffen plan
appears to be the beginning of the German and European disaster.'[79]

Ritter was bothered by the fact that the Schlieffen plan required
more forces than were actually available, but failed to ask why this was
so. Instead, Ritter explained the lack of troops in terms of German
militarism: the army did not insist on universal conscription because it
was afraid of diluting the authority of the monarchial officer corps by

---

[74] Ritter, *Sword and Scepter*, ii. 203.   [75] Ibid. 204.   [76] Ibid. 194.
[77] Ibid. 201–2.   [78] Ritter, *Schlieffenplan*, 68.   [79] Ibid. 93.

drafting too many socialist conscripts or commissioning too many middle-class officers. This is a hackneyed view, practically all the evidence for which rests on a few overused statements by War Ministers von Gossler and von Einem, not Schlieffen. Ritter did not seriously address the opposition of the Social Democrats to the entire German army; the attitude of the bourgeois parties has never been investigated by Ritter or anyone else. As for Schlieffen, Ritter said that he was secure in his military ivory tower, largely unconcerned by practical matters such as force structure.

By 1961 Ritter's view of German war planning had taken its most simplified and extreme form in *Der Anteil des Militärs an der Kriegskatastrophe von 1914* (Military Responsibility for the Catastrophe of 1914).[80] All his doubts about the genius of the elder Moltke had disappeared. As early as April 1871, Ritter said, Moltke had seen that the next war would be a two-front war and devised the perfect plan to fight it. In 'almost all of his war plans Moltke deployed the larger part of his forces in the east . . . for a large-scale joint offensive with the Austrians' while in the west he would observe a strict defensive, fighting the decisive battle somewhere between Metz and the Rhine. Nevertheless, Moltke recognized that a military victory was impossible. Moltke's goal was to wear down Germany's enemies and create the conditions that would allow German diplomats to arrive at a *Verständigungsfrieden*. Bismarck was informed of the concept of Moltke's plan and approved of it.

Ritter reiterated his charge that the Schlieffen plan was too risky. He now said that the Schlieffen plan was based in any case on the politico-military situation which obtained in 1905, when Russia was fully occupied by the Russo-Japanese war. The younger Moltke had not abandoned the Schlieffen plan, but merely modified it to accommodate the changes in the military situation after 1905. The French had massively increased the size of their army and had adopted an offensive war plan. Moltke had to increase the number of troops in Lorraine in order to force the French to do the same: otherwise, the French would mass against Schlieffen's right wing, a course of action, Ritter said, that Schlieffen had not even considered.

For Ritter, the Schlieffen plan also bore a heavy responsibility for starting the Great War. Ritter resuscitated the Russian foreign minister Sazonov's argument that Russia wanted to use her mobilization merely as a means of exerting diplomatic pressure on Austria. He now said that Sazonov was being completely sincere when he asserted that for Russia mobilization did not mean war. Russia could mobilize and deploy while

---

[80] G. Ritter, 'Der Anteil der Militärs an der Kriegskatastrophe 1914', *HZ* 193 (1961), 72–91.

negotiating.[81] Ritter contended that the Schlieffen plan forced
Germany to respond to a Balkan crisis by invading neutral Belgium in
order to attack France. Germany needed time to force Austria to negotiate. The Schlieffen plan made it impossible for that to occur. Ritter
failed to mention that the General Staff response, both in 1914 and
later, was that Sazonov was merely putting up a smoke screen to allow
the Russians to steal a march on the Germans, giving the Russians the
time they needed to bring their overwhelming numerical superiority
into play. Ritter asserted that the Schlieffen plan forced Moltke to act
rashly, to attack at once, while the other European powers had no such
requirement. In particular, Moltke was afraid that, given time, the
French and Belgians could block his advance through Belgium. To
implement the Schlieffen plan Germany declared war on France and
Russia, which was a great political error. For purely military-technical
reasons Germany was forced to assume the role of the 'brutal aggressor'.

Subsequent historians have based their description of German war
planning on Kuhl, Foerster, Ludendorff, Groener, and above all, Ritter.
In a 1976 article Paul Kennedy repeated practically all of Ritter's argu-
ments.[82] Gordon Craig's *Politics of the Prussian Army* (1964),[83] Jehuda
Wallach's *The Dogma of the Battle of Annihilation* (1986),[84] L. C. F.
Turner's 'The Significance of the Schlieffen Plan' (1979),[85] Martin
Kitchen's *A Military History of Germany* (1975),[86] and recently Arden
Bucholz's *Moltke, Schlieffen, and Prussian War Planning* (1991),[87] as well as
Holger Herwig's *The First World War* (1997)[88] accept Ritter's assertion
that Schlieffen intended to swing the right wing of the German army to
the west and south of Paris in order to produce a great battle of annihilation—a modern 'Cannae'.[89] In the most recent of these, Herwig's
1997 book, the map on page 61, titled 'The French and German Plans
of War, 1914' shows the arrow representing the 1st Army passing to the
west of Paris. The key explains that this is the 'Advance of German

[81] See also Ritter, *Sword and Scepter*, ii. 265.

[82] Paul Kennedy, 'The Operational Plans of the Great Powers 1880–1914: Analysis of
Recent Literature', *MM 19* (1976), 189–206.

[83] Craig, *Politics*.

[84] J. L. Wallach, *The Dogma of the Battle of Annihilation* (Westport CT, 1986).

[85] L. C. F. Turner, 'The Significance of the Schlieffen Plan', in Paul Kennedy (ed.),
The War Plans of the Great Powers (London, 1979) 199–221.

[86] M. Kitchen, *A Military History of Germany* (Bloomington and London, 1975).

[87] A. Bucholz, *Moltke, Schlieffen and Prussian War Planning* (New York, 1991).

[88] H. Herwig, *The First World War. Germany and Austria-Hungary 1914–1918* (London,
1997).

[89] Craig, *Politics*, 279; Wallach, *Dogma*, 56–7; Turner, 'Significance', 201–2; Kitchen,
Military History, 174; Bucholz, *Moltke, Schlieffen*, 209; Herwig, *First World War*, 46–7.

Army according to the Schlieffen Plan'. Since the six ersatz corps are not available to cover the south and west sides of Paris, Herwig (and in fairness to Herwig, everyone else) apparently thought that the 1st Army would march around Paris with no protection for its flank, rear, or lines of communication.[90] None of these histories explain where the German army would have obtained the 82 divisions for the right wing required by the Schlieffen plan, or 96 divisions for the *Westheer*. Ritter's criticisms are repeated almost verbatim: all agree that the plan was both inflexible and too risky, was a principal cause of the World War, and forced on Germany the role of the aggressor. All agree that the younger Moltke significantly altered the great plan. Craig and Kitchen go one better than Ritter and assert that Schlieffen had intended the *Denkschrift* for a preventive war against France.[91] The Schlieffen plan has become one of the most widely known and accepted commonplaces in European history.

[90] Herwig, *First World War*, 47–8.
[91] Craig, *Politics*, 283; Kitchen, *Military History*, 174.

CHAPTER TWO

Moltke's *Ostaufmarsch*, 1871–1886

Moltke's *Ostaufmarsch* occupies a critical position in the Schlieffen plan debate. Nevertheless, Moltke's war planning is poorly understood. This is not so much because of a lack of information as perhaps because of an abundance of it. The General Staff published seven volumes on Moltke's war planning and exercises, covering well over a thousand pages and including hundreds of maps.[1] These books are even more invaluable since the original documents were lost in the destruction of the Reichsarchiv. While they present a mass of original documents, they are not correlated with each other and are very heavy going for the non-specialist. The General Staff also did not make public an analysis of Moltke's planning: having published the documents they thought were appropriate for historical and professional use, the General Staff clearly saw no need to explain the workings of Moltke's war planning either to the general public or to armchair strategists. As far as the General Staff was concerned, strategy was a professional military matter. The General Staff therefore said simply that Moltke's *Ostaufmarsch* was appropriate in Moltke's period and the *Westaufmarsch* was the proper response to a later changed strategic situation, which was in large part the result of

---

[1] Prior to the Great War the General Staff published a volume on Moltke's planning in 1859 (Großer Generalstab, *Moltkes Militärische Werke, I Militärische Korrespondenz 4. Theil, Aus den Dienstschriften des Jahres 1859* (Berlin, 1902); one on his planning before the Austrian war in 1866 (Großer Generalstab, *Moltkes Militärische Werke I. Militärische Korrespondenz 2. Theil, Aus den Dienstschriften des Krieges 1866* (Berlin, 1896), and one on his planning prior to 1870 (Großer Generalstab, *Moltke's Militärische Werke I Militärische Korrespondenz 3. Theil, Aus den Dienstschriften des Krieges 1870* (Berlin, 1896). They also brought out a volume on Moltke in the planning and execution of operations (Großer Generalstab, *Moltke in der Vorbereitung und Durchführung der Operationen.* (Kriegsgeschichtliche Einzelschriften Nr. 36 Zur Enthüllung des Moltke-Denkmals) (Berlin 1905), one on his General Staff rides (Großer Generalstab, *Moltkes Militärische Werke II Die Thätigkeit als Chef des Generalstabes der Armee im Frieden 3. Teil Generalstabsreisen* (Berlin, 1906), one on tactical exercises (Großer Generalstab, *Moltkes Militärische Werke II Die Thätigkeit als Chef des Generalstabes der Armee im Frieden 1. Theil Taktische Aufgaben aus den Jahren 1858 bis 1882* (Berlin, 1892), and one on his tactical-strategic writings (Großer Generalstab, *Moltkes Militärische Werke II Die Thätigkeit als Chef des Generalstabes der Armee im Frieden 2. Theil Taktisch-strategische Aufsätze* (Berlin, 1900). After the war more planning documents were published (*H. von Moltke. Ausgewählte Werke. Dritter Band. Feldherr und Staatsmann*, ed. F. von Schmerfeld (Berlin, 1925)).

the revival of the French army. The only official history to receive widespread attention was Schmerfeld's short summary of Moltke's planning between 1871 and 1890. Like the rest, it includes very little analysis.[2] The General Staff histories fall clearly within the realm of the 'purely military' so much disliked by Delbrück and Ritter. For all these reasons they were not used by Delbrück, hardly used by Ritter, and received little attention elsewhere.[3] Delbrück, Ritter, and their followers based their opinion of Moltke's planning in general and the *Ostaufmarsch* in particular on the 'halo effect' surrounding Moltke: the victor of the wars of German unification must have been a brilliant planner. Relying largely on hero-worship and patriotic German sentiment historians commonly assumed that after 1871 Moltke presciently prepared for the inevitable two-front war. If Moltke had advocated the *Ostaufmarsch* after 1871, then that was reason enough to accept it as correct. However, Moltke's war planning in fact bore no resemblance to the picture presented by the hagiographies of Hans Delbrück and Gerhard Ritter.

From 1859 until 1914 two factors would dominate military planning: rail deployment and the mass army. The distinguishing characteristic of rail deployment was the need for speed. Whoever deployed first could attack first. Whoever attacked first had the initiative and could determine the time and place of the first battle, which would probably be decisive. The army that deployed faster would probably win the first battle because, being ready first, it would outnumber its enemy. From 1859 on, first the Prussian General Staff, and then all the General Staffs of Europe, would work furiously to shorten the time required for mobilization and deployment. In 1914, just before the Great War broke out, Wilhelm Groener, the head of the German rail section, was still trying to shave four days off the German deployment. Speed in deployment also meant that it was necessary to initiate operations immediately once the deployment had been completed. In the very infancy of rail deployment planning, Moltke stated that mobilization must be followed immediately by deployment, and that the deployed army must attack. Mobilization meant war. 'It is nonsensical (*untunlich*) for a mobilized army to adopt a passive deployment which seeks to accommodate all possible eventualities' Moltke wrote on 7 February 1859. Three months later he wrote, 'A mobilized army which is passive will merely lose strength to no purpose, and give the enemy time to train replacement

[2] F. von Schmerfeld, *Die deutschen Aufmarschpläne 1871–1890* (Berlin, 1929).

[3] In spite of its title, Arden Bucholz's *Moltke, Schlieffen and Prussian War Planning* principally describes the changes in the staff procedures involved in rail mobilization and deployment. The central figure in the book is Wilhelm Groener in his capacity as head of the railway section and none of the General Staff histories of Moltke's war planning cited above are listed in Bucholz's bibliography.

MAP 2. Eastern Europe

LITHUANIA

Niemen

□ KOWNO

● VILNA

● STALLUPÖNEN

● GRAJEWO

●, GRODNO

Niemen

Biebrza

● BIALYSTOK

WHITE RUSSIA

Narew

□ BREST-LITOVSK

PRIPET SWAMP

● LUBLIN

KOWEL
●

UKRAINE

LUTZK
□

ROVNO □

□ DUBNO

LVOV
●

PRZEMYSL □

troops, organize new units and arm his fortresses.'[4] Gerhard Ritter and other historians would maintain that the Schlieffen plan bore special responsibility for causing the war because the plan called for an immediate offensive against France. This betrays a complete misunderstanding of the nature of war at this time, when every army would strive to increase the speed and effectiveness of its mobilization in order to keep up with, and if possible precede, its opponent. The goal was to be able to conduct an offensive at the earliest possible moment. Offensive military action was inherent in the nature of the system. Indeed, in 1914 the French and Russians were able to attack first. The *last* army to begin offensive operations in August 1914 was the German army.

FIRST WAR PLAN AGAINST A FRANCO-RUSSIAN ALLIANCE

In 1859 Austria was engaged in a war with Piedmont-Sardinia and France. Moltke felt that Prussia had a golden opportunity to intervene on the Austrian side and thereby unify Germany under the Hohenzollern dynasty. Prussia failed to do so, and as a consequence in the next two years Moltke drew up 'worst-case' scenarios for the eventuality that France would now turn her attention on Prussia. The worst of the worst cases was a Franco-Russian alliance against Prussia.[5] Moltke conjured up the spirit of Tilsit to show the degree of danger Prussia might soon be in. In a *Denkschrift* in October 1858 Moltke had already written that France needed to expand in Italy to prepare for the coming battle between the Latin west and the Teutonic center, which might even involve Britain.[6] In 1860 Moltke predicted that *Götterdämmerung* was coming: a battle of the Latin west and the Slavic east against the Teutonic center which would change the world. Such a battle would unite the German race. It would require that Germany's neighbors exert all their power to engage in such a battle of the titans (*Titanenkampf*). But the time was not yet at hand, Moltke wrote, for the Russians were not strong enough.[7]

Moltke's concept for his first two-front war plan in 1859 was to conduct a classic defense on interior lines:[8] 'The only possibility is to defend against one opponent with the minimum force, and with the strongest force possible quickly defeat the other opponent, and then win back what one has lost against the first enemy.' Moltke said that the most serious threat was in the west, but here Prussia could count on the assistance of Britain and possibly Belgium and the German states. In

---

[4] *Dienstschriften des Jahres 1859*, 29, 102.   [5] *Feldherr und Staatsmann*, 20–2.

[6] *Dienstschriften des Krieges 1870*, 11–12.   [7] Ibid. 19.

[8] *Feldherr und Staatsmann*, 20–2.

the east, he said that Austrian assistance was uncertain and therefore it was best to consider how Prussia alone could fight Russia. The Russians would throw their entire army against Prussia—a 'worst-case' scenario if there was one. The Russians could assemble 125,000 men in three months either to oppose a Prussian attack or to launch their own offensive. In six months the Russians could mass 272,000–300,000 troops against Prussia.

Moltke concluded that Prussia could not afford to wait for the Russians to complete their concentration but must attack immediately in the east. VII and VIII Corps would remain in the west. Seven corps could deploy to the eastern border in five weeks and in the eighth week of mobilization arrive at Warsaw. The Prussian offensive would not originate in East Prussia, but at Thorn on the Vistula, which was effectively the terminus of the Prussian rail net. From Thorn six Prussian corps would advance on three roads on the south side of the Vistula to Warsaw. Warsaw was the junction of the road net in central Poland. The Prussians would take the Warsaw citadel or cross the Vistula to the south between Warsaw and Ivangorod and then advance on Brest-Litovsk. Possession of Brest-Litovsk would make it impossible for the Russian army to concentrate. The Prussians had to get to Brest by the 12th week of mobilization. The best defense against Russia would always be the offensive, so long as the decision to attack was made early and the attack itself was conducted with 'ruthless speed'.

The Russians could assemble 31,000 troops at Kowno, which would be held in check by the I Corps. This would leave 46,000 Russians in Poland to try to stop 200,000 Prussians, which was of course impossible. The Russians would probably retreat into the fortresses in Poland and try to hold out until relief arrived. Even if the Prussians didn't show up at Warsaw until the 12th week of mobilization, the Russian field army in Poland (minus the fortress garrisons) would still number only 65,000 men and that would not change the strategic situation one bit.

Moltke coordinated his military campaign with his political objective. Prussia would give Poland her political independence, subject only to a personal union of the Polish and Prussian crowns under the Hohenzollern dynasty. Prussia could offer Poland much more than Russia could: constitutional freedom, national independence, access from the Vistula to the sea and 'connection to the civilized center of Europe'. Moltke understood that there were significant political problems associated with this course of action. Prussia would cease to be a purely German state and become a *Vielvölkerstaat* like Austria. The Poles had pretensions to Lithuania and Galicia and would be unhappy until the borders of 1772 were reestablished. Prussian relations with Austria would be strained. Politically, the Poles had always defined themselves in terms of the Insurrection, which did not bode well for settled domestic conditions.

It is difficult to overemphasize the importance of the eastern component of Moltke's 1859 two-front war plan: this plan was the template for the famous *Ostaufmarsch*. Indeed, the concept of the attack in the east probably changed very little before 1886, which was to exploit the slowness of the Russian mobilization and maximize the effect of the faster Prussian mobilization and deployment. It was all a matter of timetables and favorable force ratios. The political result would be the establishment of a glacis in the east against Russia.

1871: WAR WITH FRANCE AND RUSSIA—PREVENTIVE WAR IN THE EAST

In the spring of 1871, with France defeated and prostrate, while Paris was wracked by the Communard revolt and German troops still occupied the eastern part of the country, Moltke wrote a *Denkschrift* for a two-front war with France and Russia.[9] Ritter said that this showed that Moltke's 'foresight was remarkable'.[10] Delbrück, Ritter, and their followers maintained that in 1871 Moltke not only predicted that the next war would be a two-front war with France and Russia, but he also wrote a brilliant plan to fight it, the *Ostaufmarsch*. According to them, in this plan the Germans would launch a limited offensive in the east while staying on the defensive in the west. Ritter maintained that Moltke's *Ostaufmarsch* addressed all the problems that would be fatal for Germany in 1914. In the *Ostaufmarsch* there was no need for Germany to violate Belgian neutrality. The war would not be fought to the bloody end but could be brought to a diplomatic solution because Moltke's aim was not the destruction of the enemy but peace on the basis of the *status quo ante*. Schlieffen's mistake was to do exactly the opposite: the concept for the Schlieffen plan was to destroy the French army by marching through Belgium. The problem with this interpretation is that it views Moltke's planning from the perspective of 1914–18 and Schlieffen's planning solely on the basis of the Schlieffen plan *Denkschrift*. This chapter will show that Moltke was formulating a plan to further his own political objectives in the 1870s and 1880s, not for a war in 1914. Subsequent chapters will demonstrate that there is much more to Schlieffen's war planning than merely the 'Schlieffen plan'.

In his 1871 *Denkschrift* Moltke maintained that in the next war Russia would attempt to seize Constantinople. The Crimean War had shown

---

[9] Schmerfeld, *Aufmarschpläne 1871–1890*, 4–14.
[10] G. Ritter, *The Sword and the Scepter* (Miami, 1969), i. 229.

that the Russian army could not march on the city through the Balkans because of the Austrian *Flankenstellung*—a flanking position—in Transylvania. The Russians could not attack Turkey because of Austria and could not attack Austria because of Germany. In addition, there was nothing but enmity between the Russian and German peoples. Now the formation of the German Empire made fundamental changes in the geopolitical situation. Germany had an interest in preventing the breakup of the Austrian Empire; Austria needed German support to survive. Germany and Austria would come together, and for that reason Germany would become an enemy of Russia. Therefore, the Russians would make their main effort against Germany.

The entire Russian army consisted, Moltke said, of 34 divisions—400,000 men. Because of the vast size of the Empire and poor communications, only 20 divisions—240,000 men—would be available for an offensive in the west, while 27 divisions—325,000 men—could be assembled to defend Poland. This was not enough to launch a successful attack in the west so the Russians would need an ally, and that ally could only be France, once France had recovered from the 1870/71 war.

Austria could concentrate her entire army against Russia. Germany would have to fight on two fronts. In contrast to his 1859 plan, Moltke now said that the war with France had demonstrated that it took a very long time to force a modern state to sue for peace. Therefore it was impossible to conduct an operation based on interior lines, that is, concentrate on one enemy, defeat him, then concentrate on the other: it would take too long to defeat the first enemy. This statement has always been accepted without question to be both wise and true. It is the basis of Ritter's contention that Moltke foresaw that the First World War would be a long war and that the Germans could not defeat their enemies, but must negotiate with them. Moltke, however, was talking about 1870/71, not 1914. France had declared war on 19 July 1870. Paris fell six months and seven days later on 26 January 1871, at which point France surrendered. The war only lasted this long because the Germans insisted that the French give up Alsace-Lorraine. This six-month war clearly was a serious strain on the stamina of the 71-year-old Moltke, but was considered by everyone else to have been remarkably short. Nor did a war of this length place Germany in any strategic danger. In addition, Germany's position in the west after 1871 was much better than in 1870. Now the Germans held Metz. The distance from Metz to Paris was only about 280 kilometers: Metz is 190 kilometers closer to Paris than the Prussian assembly area at Mainz in 1870. Moltke acknowledged that the French would not be able to put an army in the field any larger than the one they had in 1870—300,000 men. The French would assemble 225,000 men at Vesoul (west of Belfort) to march on Strasbourg and leave an army of observation of 75,000 men at Verdun.

Moltke's plan was to split the German army in half. In the west Moltke would employ nine corps—300,000 men. Four corps would assemble at Strasbourg, four corps plus the Hessian Division would concentrate at Metz. These would all advance on Nancy. The 31st Infantry Division would deploy to Mühlhausen (Mulhouse) in the upper Alsace. Since the French only had 300,000 men too, there was no danger to Germany from this side. In the east, nine German corps and the Austrian army would overrun Poland, then take up a defensive position.

It was probably no accident that in this *Denkschrift* Moltke did not mention how long it would take the Russians to assemble their army at Warsaw. In 1859 he said that it would take six months. Moltke said that the most likely Russian course of action was to attack past Thorn on Berlin. It is about 450 kilometers from Warsaw to Berlin. Just marching from Warsaw to Berlin would take thirty days or more. It would therefore take the Russians seven months to mobilize and reach Berlin. It is not evident why Moltke would not want to mass superior forces (500,000 men at least) against 300,000 French, defeat them in less time than in 1870/1 (six months) and then turn on the Russians, who might very well still be trying to assemble 240,000 men at Warsaw.

On closer analysis, the contention that Moltke was conducting a defensive strategy is insupportable. He said the Russians could field 240,000 men in the offensive, 325,000 men in the defensive. The French had 300,000 men. Moltke said that the entire Austrian army could deploy in the east. Somehow Moltke failed to mention how many troops that would be, but in the 1866 war with Prussia it was approximately 375,000 men. The Germans had 18 corps available—about 600,000 men. Therefore the odds were at least 975,000 Austro-Germans versus 540,000 Russians and French, very nearly a 2 : 1 superiority. The Austrians alone outnumbered the Russians: together with nine German corps there were 675,000 Austro-Germans versus 325,000 Russians, a better than 2–1 superiority. The Russians and French would have to be insane to attack under such conditions, and Moltke would have to be a fool if he did not recognize this. Moltke was no fool, so this plan must have been exactly what it appears to be—a plan for a German–Austrian attack on Russia. An Austro-German alliance had a window of opportunity in which it could employ overwhelming numerical superiority to crush the Russians.

The object of this operation could only have been to take Poland away from Russia. Moltke acknowledged that German annexation of Poland was of 'doubtful value'. This has always been cited to show that

Moltke had no aggressive designs but wanted peace on the basis of the *status quo ante.* However, he then went on to say that the establishment of an independent Poland as a barrier against a 'half-Asiatic' Russia would be in the interest of all of Europe. If the Russians lost Poland, they would be thrust back into Asia. An independent Poland needed access to the sea; therefore, as in 1859, Moltke recommended that Poland be joined with Germany in personal union of the Hohenzollern dynasty. Alternatively, Poland's borders could be extended through the Ukraine to the Black Sea. In addition, between 1859 and 1888 Moltke advocated at regular intervals that in case of war the Germans should encourage a Polish revolt. The result of such a revolt could only have been to separate Poland from Russia.

Moltke's military analysis of the situation in the east was disingenuous if not mendacious. His demonstrably incorrect assertions have distorted the perception of Germany's military situation in the east ever since. First, Moltke contended that a Russian army at Warsaw was in danger of being encircled from the north by a German offensive out of East Prussia and from the south by an Austrian offensive out of Galicia. From a casual glance at the map, this looks quite plausible, as the salient of East Prussia extended to the east of Warsaw. Moltke's attack plan in the east provided for nine corps to line the East Prussian border between Thorn and Lyck. Seven corps would detrain east of the Vistula. Moltke did not say how many rail lines were available east of the Vistula, or how long it would take to conduct the rail deployment, and for a good reason. There was only one rail line over the Vistula in 1871, and deploying seven corps by this one rail line would have taken a considerable period. As late as 1888, the British general Sir John Maurice noted that the Germans only had one secure rail line in East Prussia.[11] Such a ponderous concentration could hardly have been kept secret from the Russians: the Russians would have had plenty of time to avoid the blow. Second, in serious war plans the German forces had to detrain west of the Vistula, at Thorn. A German advance from Thorn on Warsaw was a frontal attack, not an envelopment. Third, the Austrian rail net across the Carpathians was just as bad and their deployment would have been slow too. Moltke said that a decisive envelopment was possible in order to hold out the prospect that the Russians would be destroyed in Poland and not be able to withdraw to the interior and force the Germans to follow them.

Moltke also said that the Germans had to attack because it was impossible for the Germans to defend the Prussian border, which was 750

---

[11] J. F. Maurice. *The Balance of Military Power in Europe* (Edinburgh and London, 1888), 142.

kilometers long. Therefore it was necessary to deploy along the Prussian border and concentrate forward, as in 1866. This statement has also been accepted without question. In fact, Moltke was setting up a straw man. A bland statement that the border was 750 kilometers long does not constitute a serious terrain analysis, for it fails to consider the nature of the terrain and the lines of communications. If one of Moltke's General Staff officers had submitted him such a slipshod terrain analysis, Moltke surely would have given him the sack.

In 1879 Streffleur's *Österreichische Militärische Zeitschrift* did publish an analysis of East Prussia's military geography by one Captain Kirchhammer of the Austrian army.[12] Kirchhammer said that just because the terrain in East Prussia was flat did not mean that it was trafficable. The area was full of obstacles to movement, in particular swamps and the East Prussian chain of lakes. The road net was thin and disappeared in periods of bad weather into a sea of mud. Kirchhammer said that altogether movement in Prussia was so difficult that it should be compared to movement in high mountainous regions. The rivers Pregel, Vistula, Netze, Warthe, and Oder formed a barrier not equaled in the rest of Europe. Kirchhammer noted that since 1873 the Germans had spent large sums modernizing the fortresses of Königsberg, Thorn, and Posen. (This would have been odd if Germany's eastern borders were really indefensible, as Moltke contended.) A Russian attack on Breslau in Silesia was 'highly unlikely': the Russian logistic basis for this offensive was poor. Kirchhammer concluded by saying that in any Russian attack on Germany the Russians could not bypass East Prussia, but had to take it to secure their rear, and that Prussia itself was wonderfully suited for defense.

In 1879 a pamphlet titled *Die Befestigung und Vertheidigung der deutsch–russischen Grenze* (Fortifications and Defense on the Russo-German Border) was published anonymously (the third revision, in 1901, is discussed in Chapter 4). Mostly on the basis of this article, but also from the article by Kirchhammer, Lumley Graham published 'The Russo-German Frontier' in England in 1880.[13] Graham repeated Kirchhammer's grim assessment of the terrain on the Russo-German border. He added that the country was 'snow-clad and frozen for five months in the year'. In particular, the Masurian Lakes were a formidable barrier to a Russian attack. Graham said that there were only three German rail bridges over the Vistula. Two of these rail lines continued to the interior of East Prussia. A double-tracked line ran along the northern coast (Marienburg–Königsberg–Insterburg) and a single-

[12] Kirchhammer, 'Deutschland's Nordostgrenze', *Streuffleur's* 20(3–4) (1879), 229–39.
[13] L. Graham, 'The Russo-German Frontier in 1880', *JRUSI* xxiv (1880), 129–49.

tracked line ran through the centre of the province (Deutsch Eylau–Insterburg). Two single-tracked lines terminated on the west bank of the Vistula near Thorn. A rail line along the border connected Thorn and Breslau.

The Russians had three rail lines that terminated at Warsaw, one each from St Petersburg, Moscow, and Odessa/Kiev. Only one rail line proceeded from Warsaw to the west. All Russian rail lines were single-tracked. For 240 kilometers to the south of Thorn no rail line crossed the Russo-German border.

Graham said that the Russians had four possible avenues of approach into Germany: first, through East Prussia; second, along the Vistula; third, south of the Vistula on Posen; fourth, south-west against Silesia. The first two were the most favorable, and the Russians would probably use both simultaneously. An advance over Posen appeared tempting, as it led directly to Berlin. However, this avenue of approach would require the Russians to give up their rail communications and expose their rear to German counterattacks from East Prussia as well as Silesia. An advance to the south of Thorn would encounter very unfavorable terrain both there and around Posen. An attack between Thorn and Breslau would have no rail line to support it at all. An attack by the main Russian army on Silesia would lead away from the objective— Berlin—and would only be possible with assistance from Austria. This was highly unlikely. At most, the Russians could launch a supporting attack in this direction. A Russian attack would therefore have to proceed on two axes, one through East Prussia and one along the Vistula. Königsberg would have to be invested or attacked with a corps. The Germans had considerably strengthened Posen and Thorn. North of Thorn the Vistula provided a barrier 100 yards wide. The German frontier provinces could therefore be considered secured against Russia. The Germans would initially probably conduct a defense based on rail mobility. The Germans would then 'at once take that bold and active offensive so suitable to the German character'. Graham's analysis of the situation could serve in any of Schlieffen's *Generalstabsreisen Ost.*

On the other hand, Russian Poland was not prepared for defense. An Austro-German attack on Russian Poland would have been a walk-over. As Kirchhammer noted, even in 1879 the Russian fortifications were of little value. Nowo Georgiewsk (north-west of Warsaw) was obsolete, the fortifications of Warsaw were 'unimportant' and the fortification of Iwangorod had begun only in 1879. The backbone of the Russian defense would be at Brest-Litovsk. Kirchhammer noted that the Germans might try to attack the Russians before they were assembled and cut them off from the interior.

These published analyses of the military situation in the east were both more informative and more accurate than the one supplied by Moltke. It would have been easy to defend East Prussia, and unlikely that the Russians would have attempted to defend Poland. Moltke must have decided to attack in the east to serve his own purposes.

In 1871 Moltke insisted on taking Alsace-Lorraine as a strategic glacis. In the same year Moltke advocated an identical course of action in the east: breaking Poland off from Russia. Poland would thus become Germany's eastern buffer and Warsaw or Brest-Litovsk would become Germany's eastern Metz. There are also indications that Moltke thought Russia might also lose the Baltic states. The purpose of Moltke's *Ostaufmarsch* both in 1871 and later was to permanently push the Russians out of Poland.

In 1871 war against France resulted in the unification of Germany under Prussian leadership. A successful war against Russia would have similarly resulted in the *Großdeutsch* German /Austrian alliance that Moltke had always advocated as the ideal solution for all Germans. Such an alliance also meant *de facto* Germanic domination of *Mitteleuropa*. These considerations were the foundation of all of Moltke's later two-front war plans until 1887. With buffer zones and massive fortresses in the east and west and with a *Großdeutsch* alliance between Germany and Austria, Germany's position would have been unassailable.

It is well known that Moltke maintained that Germany needed a 'third War of Unification' to secure her position in Europe.[14] It has generally been assumed that this meant a second war against France. This seems unlikely. As we shall see, Moltke was never more than luke-warm at best about another war with France. Given the tenor of Moltke's post-1871 war plans, it is clear that this third war of unification was to be fought in the east, to bring Germany and Austria together and to assure security in the east by pushing Russia back into Asia where it belonged. Moltke probably had to temporarily abandon these plans in 1873: he personally signed the German–Russian military convention on 3 May 1873 and in June and October 1873 the Three Emperors' League was concluded. He would, however, quickly revive the *Ostaufmarsch* plan at the first available opportunity, during the Eastern Crisis of 1877–1878.

WAR WITH FRANCE, 1872–1875

In October 1872 Moltke began work on a plan for a one-front war against France.[15] He noted that the French 1870 railheads at Metz and Strasbourg were now in German hands. The French would therefore

[14] E. Kessel, *Moltke* (Stuttgart, 1957), 618.
[15] Schmerfeld, *Aufmarschpläne 1871–1890*, 18–21.

have to establish two armies, one at Verdun, the other at Langres, on the headwaters of the Marne.[16] Moltke said that the German army would concentrate with the center of mass at Metz. Moltke maintained that it was of decisive importance to mobilize and deploy as quickly as possible. If the French won the race to deploy first, then they could launch a concentric attack on the Germans; if the Germans deployed first, the Germans would launch a 'ruthless offensive' to the west to split up the French armies. The Germans should deploy quickly and then move to destroy the French armies while they were divided. To avoid this the French could surrender eastern France and unite their armies at Reims or Troyes. The Germans would then march on Paris to force the French army to fight.

Since Langres would be the French national redoubt for most of their war plans for the next forty years, it is important to note that Moltke recognized the significance of the place very early. Langres was a classic *Flankenstellung.* It lay to the south of any German advance on Paris. The Germans could not advance on Paris because a French army at Langres could move against the German rear. If the Germans advanced on the French at Langres, they would find the French in a strong position there and if necessary the French could always withdraw by rail to western France—the loss of Langres itself was unimportant.

In January 1873 Moltke made an observation that would be repeated by all of his successors.[17] The current French military measures—new fortifications, universal conscription, even French tactical doctrine—seemed to have a defensive character. But any war between France and Germany would be started by France. The French had the positive political objectives: reconquest of Alsace-Lorraine; conquest of the left bank of the Rhine; destruction of the German Empire. These objectives could not be attained by standing on the defensive. If there was going to be a war, then the French would attack.

In April 1875, during the *Krieg in Sicht* crisis, Moltke produced what can be considered his first serious west-front war plan since 1870.[18] This included a detailed intelligence estimate of the French army, which was truly alarming. Moltke said that the French were not only stronger than the Germans but they could also mobilize and deploy faster. Against 18 German corps the French could commit 19 corps and each French corps would be stronger than the German by 8 battalions. Moltke now said that the French could deploy on a 225-kilometer-long line Longuyon–Toul–Belfort in 12 to 15 days. As of the 13th day the French

[16] Moltke said that the Germans might meet the second group on the Doubs, which runs parallel to the Swiss border. Besançon is on the Doubs.

[17] Ibid. 21–31.

[18] Ibid. 46–52.

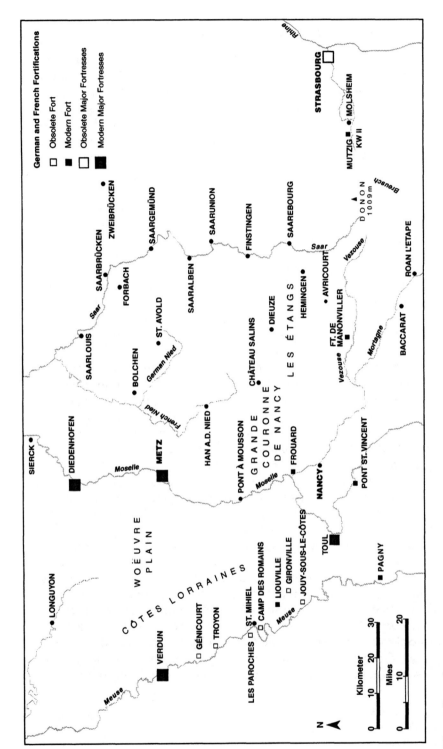

German and French Fortifications

☐ Obsolete Fort
■ Modern Fort
▢ Obsolete Major Fortresses
■ Modern Major Fortresses

STRASBOURG

MOLSHEIM
KW II
MUTZIG

Rhine

Breusch

DONON
1009 m

ROAN L'ETAPE

Vezouse

Vezouse

Mortagne

BACCARAT

AVRICOURT

FT. DE MANONVILLER

HEMINGEN

SAAREBOURG

Saar

FINSTINGEN

SAARUNION

SAARGEMÜND

ZWEIBRÜCKEN

SAARBRÜCKEN

FORBACH

ST. AVOLD

SAARALBEN

DIEUZE

CHÂTEAU SALINS

LES ÉTANGS

German Nied

BOLCHEN

SAARLOUIS

SIERCK

DIEDENHOFEN

Moselle

METZ

HAN A.D. NIED

French Nied

PONT À MOUSSON

GRANDE
COURONNE
DE NANCY

FROUARD

Moselle

NANCY

PONT ST. VINCENT

TOUL

PAGNY

WOËUVRE
PLAIN

CÔTES LORRAINES

LONGUYON

VERDUN

Meuse

GÉNICOURT

TROYON

LES PAROCHES

ST. MIHIEL

CAMP DES ROMAINS

LIOUVILLE

GIRONVILLE

JOUY-SOUS-LE-CÔTES

Meuse

N

Kilometer
0   10   20   30

Miles
0   10   20

MAP 3. Lorraine

could begin raids with detachments up to the size of cavalry divisions to break up the German deployment. Moltke's reply was to establish covering forces as of the 2nd day of mobilization. By the 15th day of mobilization the French could concentrate 13 corps at Toul. In successive *Denkschriften* since 1872 Moltke had been moving the French center of mass from Langres in the south to Nancy–Toul in the north. Now that movement was completed. The French, according to Moltke, could mass their main army opposite Lorraine and execute an immediate attack.

To oppose a French advance the Germans would have only 11 corps available on the 16th day of mobilization, 14 corps on the 18th day. It is not too much to say that in 1875 the Franco-German race to mobilize and deploy first began in earnest—at least in the minds of the Germans. Moltke's deployment was for three armies—15 corps—to mass on a 60 kilometer front to the south-east of Metz. A fourth army of three corps would assemble in the upper Alsace to block a French attack from Belfort. Moltke was expecting an immediate battle in Lorraine, a frontal slugging match, and wanted to concentrate the greatest masses possible to fight it.

Moltke felt that the most likely French course of action was to attack between Metz and Strasbourg and fight a battle in Lorraine. If the French won, they would mask Metz and Strasbourg, cross the Rhine at Mannheim and Worms and split south and north Germany: this was merely an updated version of his pre-1870 estimate of French intentions. In May 1875 Moltke said that the German right flank at Diedenhofen (Thionville) was not in danger. A shallow French envelopment of the German line to the north of Metz through Luxembourg was not worth the political complications, and a French attack through Belgium was even less likely. An attack on the left flank in the upper Alsace was also unimportant, since the decisive battle would be fought in Lorraine by the 17th day of mobilization.[19]

If the French didn't attack by the 17th day of mobilization, the Germans would advance on the Moselle and arrive there by the 19th day. This would produce the decisive battle, which might last several days. Eleven corps would be in the German first echelon, followed by three more. Moltke said that it was possible to employ such masses because the terrain in Lorraine and eastern France was relatively open and trafficable. Each forward corps, about 30,000 men, was formed in Moltke's favorite Gravelotte–St Privat phalanx formation on about a four-kilometer front. Moltke's intent was to swing to the south of Nancy–Toul and cross the Moselle. There was not even a hint of 'marching separately and

---

[19] Schmerfeld, *Aufmarschpläne 1871–1890*, 55–6.

uniting on the battlefield'. Most of the corps would have one road to march on. Concentrating 400,000 men in a 45-kilometer attack front would require that the advance be coordinated 'down to the last detail' by the army headquarters. To prove his point, Moltke selected two possible battlefields and designated corps battle positions for each.

By 1875 the French had, according to Moltke, fully recovered from the effects of the late war and were, if anything, militarily superior to the Germans. This was the military significance of the *Krieg in Sicht* crisis. It was only the first in a series of Moltke's increasingly pessimistic evaluations of Germany's strategic situation. This would have come as a surprise to the French themselves as well as to the rest of Europe.

RUSSIAN MILITARY WEAKNESS, 1877/1878

In 1871 Moltke had written that the Russians would not be able to attack Turkey because of Austria's *Flankenstellung* in Transylvania. Therefore, Russia would attack Austria's natural ally, Germany. Moltke's geopolitical reasoning was far from prescient. On 24 April 1877, Russia declared war on the Turks without attacking Germany and also without direct interference from Austria. The Russian performance in the Balkan war of 1877/8 established a real-world corrective to Moltke's Russian intelligence estimate. A good contemporary account of this war was provided by the American military attaché, Lieutenant F. V. Greene.[20]

The Russian army at this time consisted of 48 infantry divisions. A Russian corps usually contained two divisions. The peacetime strength of the Russian army was 560,000 men—about the same as the French and German armies. Although the Russians could theoretically call up 2,000,000 men, in reality the wartime Russian field army numbered at maximum 900,000 men and would probably be much smaller: it was still far too early to speak of a Russian steamroller. In peacetime, the Russian army was scattered over a vast area: eight divisions were garrisoned in the Warsaw military district, seven in Vilna, four in Kiev, six in St. Petersburg–Finland, six in Moscow, four in Kharkov, two in Kazan, four in Odessa, and seven in the Caucasus.[21] In 1877 Russia had 21,092 kilometers of railroad track, spread over European Russia and the Caucasus. By comparison, Germany, with a much smaller land mass, had 30,718 kilometers of track and France had 20,534.[22] The lack of speed of the Russian mobilization can be seen in the fact that the

[20] F. V. Greene, *Report on the Russian Army and its Campaigns in Turkey in 1877–1878* (Washington, 1879), 18–50. Greene was with the Russian headquarters in the field during the war.

[21] Ibid., Plate 1.

[22] M. Stürmer, *Das ruhelose Reich. Deutschland 1866–1918* (n.d.), 76.

Russians mobilized the six corps nearest the Romanian frontier in November 1876, well in advance of the expected start of the campaign the next summer. Otto Pflanze said that the Russians actually had *delayed* this mobilization in order to come up with the financial means to conduct it (and to prepare the international situation for war).[23] Four corps were deployed to the border at Kishinev in Bessarabia. Owing to the weakness of the Russian Black Sea fleet, X Corps at Odessa and VII in the Crimea were detailed for coast defense and never saw action. During the winter IV Corps (Warsaw military district), XIII and XIV Corps (Vilna military district) were also mobilized, but were retained in their mobilization stations. The Russians began moving IV, XIII, and XIV corps by rail on 8 May 1877. It took XIII Corps five weeks, until 13 June, to arrive at Galatz in Romania. XIV Corps arrived at Alexandria, 100 kilometers south of Bucharest, on 27 June; IV Corps came even later. The total force of seven corps numbered about 200,000 men. In the Caucasus the Russians mobilized the equivalent of about five infantry divisions. The Russians therefore mobilized in total 23 infantry divisions—slightly less than half their army—and deployed 19 of them. Only three corps had to be moved by rail, from Warsaw and Vilnius on the Odessa rail line. Nevertheless, this rail movement took about two months.[24]

The Turks could initially concentrate 165,000 troops for operations in Bulgaria. They were, however, well-armed. The infantry was equipped with American Peabody-Martini or British Enfield breech-loading rifles, both of which Greene said were superior to the Russian Krenk rifle. The Turkish artillery was equipped with Krupp steel breech-loaders, which were superior to the Russian bronze guns.[25]

The campaign itself was a disaster for the Russians. It took the Russians ten weeks, from 24 April to 3 July, to concentrate their forces in Romania, a friendly country, and cross the Danube. The Russians took a month—24 May to 24 June—to cross the Danube because of lack of bridging materials. It can be imagined how much success the Russians would have had in attacking into Brandenburg either across the Vistula or to the south of Thorn. The Russians quickly seized Shipka pass, but the Turkish commander, Osman Pasha, occupied a *Flankenstellung* at Plevna and dug in there. The Russians assaulted Plevna three times (20 and 30 July and 11 September) and failed all three times, losing about 30,000 men killed and wounded. They then laid formal siege to Plevna's field fortifications, which capitulated five

[23] O. Pflanze, *Bismarck and the Development of Germany* (Princeton, 1990), ii. 427–8.
[24] Greene, *Turkey 1877–1878*, 139–40, 380.
[25] Ibid. 140–1.

months later, on 11 December. One would have to assume that the Russians would never have been able to take a permanent German fortress by storm: any of the German eastern fortresses could have held out for months until forced by starvation to surrender.

After over eight months of operations, the Russian offensive, with Romanian assistance, finally got rolling. The Russians defeated the remaining Turkish army in the Balkans at Senova on 8–9 January 1878 and reached the defenses of Constantinople on 30 January. The Treaty of San Stefano was signed on 3 March.

It would appear that in a Russo-German war even modest German forces had every prospect of keeping the Russians on the east side of the Vistula indefinitely and could even hope to keep the Russians out of East Prussia entirely.

1877/1878: WAR WITH AUSTRIA AND FRANCE—DEFEAT AUSTRIA FIRST

Moltke's initial reaction was to assume that the Austrians, free of the threat of Russian intervention, would now ally themselves with the French and the two together would seek revenge for 1866 and 1870/1. Once again, Moltke's geopolitics led him astray. The inspiration for Moltke's concern was probably the same as Bismarck's: the *cauchemar de coalitions*, the alliance put together by the Austrian prime minister, Kaunitz, with France and Russia in 1763. There is no reason to believe that Bismarck communicated his fears to Moltke or ever told him to prepare a war plan on this basis. Bismarck explained his diplomatic policy in the face of this threat in his famous *Kissinger Diktat* of the summer of 1877 and his reply to the *cauchemar* was to be diplomatic, not military. In fact, in 1877/8 the policy of the Austro-Hungarian prime minister, Andrassy, was to intervene in the Balkans and he accepted the possibility that this would lead to war with Russia.[26] Moltke was also convinced that a Balkan war must lead to general war in Europe. This was something Bismarck was determined to prevent. There were in any case no real indicators that either Austria or France was preparing for war with Prussia. Nevertheless, Moltke wrote an initial *Denkschrift* for a war with Austria and France in February 1877 and expanded on it in December 1878 and January 1879.[27]

The February 1877 *Denkschrift* was not a war plan but rather presented Moltke's political appreciation of the situation. Moltke's concern was that it was still possible to revive the forces of German particularism and

---

[26] R. F. Schmidt, *Die gescheiterte Allianz* (Frankfurt, 1992), 274 ff.
[27] Schmerfeld, *Aufmarschpläne 1871–1890*, 62–5, 67–77.

break up the German Empire. There was no serious consideration of the enemy forces. The concept of the German operation was sketchy. Moltke said that the Germans should concentrate their main body in Bavaria and conduct a Napoleonic attack down the Danube, but he provided no details whatsoever on the execution of the operation.

In December 1878 Moltke said that not only would Austria seek to revise the verdict of 1866 and regain her position in Germany, but that she would also want to overturn the conquests of Frederick the Great and regain Silesia! The French objective would be the reconquest of Alsace-Lorraine. The French would advance as always between Metz and Strasbourg and cross the Rhine near Mannheim. The Austrians would probably advance through Silesia.

Moltke said that if the Germans divided their forces equally, they would then merely be outnumbered 2–1 on both fronts. Moltke therefore decided on a defense on interior lines. He said it was necessary to mass against one opponent and defeat him. He then took the defense on interior lines one step further, and maintained that it would be necessary to make the defeated enemy sue for peace. Then the Germans would turn with full force against the other opponent.

As Moltke saw it, the Germans should attack Austria and defend on the Rhine against France. Moltke was beginning to notice the effect that the French frontier fortifications and the refortification of Paris would have on any German attack into France: even if the Germans defeated the French, the French could withdraw safely behind their fortress line. In any case, the only thing that Germany could possibly want to take from France would be Belfort. Austria would be much easier to knock out of the war than France. Austria also had something Germany wanted: Germany would demand the German provinces of the Austrian Empire as the price of peace. This is surely the political purpose of the *Denkschrift*.

This strategy is the complete reversal of Moltke's 1869 plan for a war with Austria and France, when he decided to attack the French and defend against the Austrians, who would not pose an immediate threat. It is also the polar opposite of the strategy Moltke proposed in a two-front war against the French and Russians in 1871. At that time he said that the war against France had proved that a strategy based on interior lines was impossible: the modern state was too resilient to be knocked out of a war quickly. In 1878 he apparently thought that a strategy that would not work against the French would be successful against the Austrians.

Moltke said that in the west the Germans would abandon Lorraine and the Palatinate and defend along the Rhine with five and a half corps and three Reserve divisions (14 divisions in total). When the

French crossed the Rhine the Germans would fall back to Moltke's all-time favorite *Flankenstellung* on the Main. After subtracting fortress garrisons, the field army in the west would number 130,000 men. Though Moltke does not mention it, the French army by his own 1875 estimate would consist of at least 36 divisions: the French would outnumber the Germans better than 2–1. In the east, Moltke would establish two armies. Moltke was still uncertain of the Bavarians and said that 'for political purposes' the two Bavarian corps should not be left alone. With the addition of two Prussian corps they should be formed into a supporting army of 135,000 men and be deployed on the Danube between Regensburg and Fürth. The remaining nine corps, 350,000 men, would form the main army in Saxony, and would drive on Vienna. In a draft of this *Denkschrift*, Moltke said that he expected a decisive battle in Bohemia by the 23rd day of mobilization. Moltke said that by the 28th day the French would arrive at the Main *Flankenstellung*, at which time he could hope that German reinforcements would be *en route* from Bohemia.

This was obviously preposterous. In 1866 Königgrätz was fought on roughly the 57th day of Prussian mobilization. Moltke had proven only that the December 1878 plan was patently unworkable and that Germany could not, alone, fight two Great Powers. If there was to be a war with France, Austria needed to be placated.

1877: WAR WITH RUSSIA AND FRANCE—*WESTAUFMARSCH*

At the same time that Moltke was considering a war with France and Austria, he was also planning for a war with France and Russia. His first *Denkschrift* on the subject was written in February 1877, just as the Russians were mobilizing to begin their Balkan war. Moltke said that there didn't seem to be any grounds for a Franco-Russian alliance, which he called 'improbable'.[28] Only the acquisition of East Prussia could prove interesting to Russia. Nevertheless, Moltke said that the Russians would attack Germany. It appears that Moltke was reviving his 1871 idea that the Russians would start their Balkan war by attacking Germany.

Moltke's most important consideration was time. The French would be ready on the 12th day of mobilization. The French could march so quickly that even the 'arming' of Metz (putting the fortifications on a war footing) was in doubt. Although their army was already half-mobilized, the Russians would need until the 16th or 20th day of mobilization to assemble 200,000 men on a line Kowno–Radom, and from there it was 5–10 days' march to the German border. Implicit in this scenario is

[28] Schmerfeld, *Aufmarschpläne 1871–1890*, 65–7.

the assumption that the Russians would have to earmark a large force to watch the Austrians.

Moltke's conclusion was that Germany had to defeat France first. More than that, Moltke said that if the Germans were convinced that the Russians were going to attack, then it was certain that the French would attack Germany, too. Germany then could not mobilize soon enough, and regardless of the position France had taken, Germany needed to declare war on France and attack. 'A few day's head start against them [the French] is of incalculable value', Moltke said (shades of July 1914). The Germans would deploy 14 corps in the west (520,000 men) leaving only 4 corps (80,000 men) in the east. An immediate German offensive would crash head-on into the French offensive and the Germans could win a decisive battle in the 3rd week. In the east, the Germans would launch a raid with about 60,000 men on Plock before the Russians had time to deploy their main body. Thorn had to be held at all costs. Having defeated the French, Moltke would transfer 220,000 men to the east, leaving 250,000 to defend the line of the Rhine.[29]

While the aggressive nature of this plan is never mentioned, one paragraph from this *Denkschrift* is always repeated with approval by the advocates of the *Ostaufmarsch*. Moltke said that the Germans could not pursue the French to Paris. In the west 'It had to be left up to diplomacy to see whether we can obtain peace on this side at least, if only on the basis of the *status quo ante*.'[30] This was music to the ears of Delbrück and Ritter. Moltke had uttered the magic words, 'negotiated peace' and '*status quo ante*'.[31] Ritter and his followers then maintained that this was evidence that in the First World War Moltke would have approved of negotiated peace in the west on the basis of the *status quo ante*. They downplayed the fact that Moltke did so in the context of a very aggressive *Westaufmarsch*. Moltke, Delbrück, and Ritter may have been happy with the *status quo ante* but the French most emphatically were not. According to all of Moltke's post-1871 *Denkschriften* the French only would go to war in the first place in order to regain Alsace-Lorraine. The German Foreign Office would not have been able to sweet-talk the French into making peace. A peace on the basis of the *status quo ante* would only have only been possible after the French had been decisively defeated.[32]

---

[29] Moltke's figures don't add up. He started in the west with 520,000 men, then transferred 220,000 to the east, which should leave 300,000 in the west, not 250,000.

[30] This section was included in *Moltkes militärische Werke* published before the war.

[31] Ritter, *Sword and Scepter*, ii. 197.

[32] Moltke may also have considered a one-front war in the east. In 1877 he told the War Minister that the German army could deploy 16 (of a total of 18) corps to the east by the 21st day of mobilization. Schmerfeld, *Aufmarschpläne 1871–1890*, 109.

1879: WAR WITH RUSSIA AND FRANCE—*OSTAUFMARSCH*

In April 1879 Moltke revised his *Denkschrift* for a two-front war against France and Russia. Moltke maintained that Russia had been enraged by the lack of German support at the Congress of Berlin. If this antipathy should lead to a Russo-German war, the French would surely attack Germany too.[33]

Moltke now decided that the French border fortifications were so formidable that a quick decision was not possible in the west. Moltke's concept was to use the minimum forces—four corps and an infantry division plus 'very strong' fortress garrisons—to conduct a defense based on Metz, Strasbourg, and the Rhine. That was all that Moltke has to say about the defense in the west. That is not an oversight. In fact, according to Moltke's 1875 estimate 36 French divisions would be attacking Moltke's nine. The only hope for the Germans would have been to withdraw before making contact, avoiding a decisive engagement with the French at all costs. According to Moltke's December 1878 *Denkschrift* for a war with a Franco-Austrian alliance, the French would cross the Rhine on the 23rd day of mobilization and reach the Main on the 28th day. There would be no possibility that the Germans could hold the Main *Flankenstellung*. Moltke would have to transfer forces from the east at this time, regardless of whether the Russians had been defeated or not.

Moltke said that by the 21st day of mobilization at the earliest, perhaps later, the Russians could assemble 200,000 men opposite East Prussia. The center of mass of this force would be at Warsaw, with 51,000 troops in the city and a further 67,000 to the south at Radom. The line of the Niemen to the north was to be held by 37,000 troops at Kowno and 18,000 at Grodno, while to the west of Warsaw would be an advance guard of 25,000 men. By the 29th day of mobilization the Russians could increase this force to 348,000 men. Further Russian deployment would depend on the conduct of Austria. Moltke assumed that Austria would be at least an armed neutral, which would require the Russians to establish an army of observation to watch the Austrian border.

Moltke's estimate of Russian strength is short and vague. From Greene we know that the wartime strength of the entire Russian army was 900,000 men, organized in 48 divisions, of which 17 were in the Caucasus, Odessa, Kazan, and Kharkow military districts and were unavailable for immediate operations in the west. That would leave 31 divisions—about 581,000 troops. Fifteen divisions—perhaps 281,000 troops—had their garrisons in the Warsaw and Vilna military districts

---

[33] Schmerfeld, *Aufmarschpläne 1871–1890*, 77–81.

and would be available as soon as they were mobilized. The four Kiev
divisions, and probably the four in Odessa, would watch the Austrians.
That left six divisions in Moscow and six in St. Petersburg—225,000
troops. According to Moltke's figures, about four of those divisions
would be deployed against Germany. Whether the other eight would be
deployed against Austria or just had not deployed at all is unclear. The
Russians would have been in no hurry to mass against Austria, whose
deployment was as slow as their own. Therefore, by the 29th day of
mobilization Moltke expected to be opposed by 19 of the total of 48
Russian divisions. That the Russians could mobilize and deploy these
divisions by the 29th day might have been mathematically possible, but
given their performance in 1877, highly unlikely. Moltke gave no estimate at all of Russian intentions. That is not surprising. On the 29th day
the Russians still had up to 21 undeployed divisions, echelonned from
Moscow and St. Petersburg to the Caucasus. The Russians could have
little interest in accepting battle and no interest at all in attacking until
at least part of these forces had arrived, and that would take months.

According to Moltke's *Denkschrift* the Germans would deploy 14 corps
in four armies in the east, which would be operational sometime
between the 20th and 23rd day of mobilization. The 1st Army with three
corps (100,000 men) would be at Rastenburg, the 2nd Army with three
corps (100,000 men) at Soldau, the 3rd Army with four corps at Thorn
(including the two Bavarian corps, which Moltke didn't trust to leave at
home, totaling 120,000 men), and the 4th Army with four corps (130,000
men) at Gnesen. Moltke took special care to establish a covering force
to block Russian cavalry raids at the start of mobilization. The four
German armies would advance on Warsaw, with three armies to the
north of the Vistula and the 4th to the south. The odds on the 29th day
would be 450,000 Germans to 348,000 Russians. The Germans would
occupy Poland but not advance into 'the interior of Russia'. A victory
in Poland would allow the Germans to transfer forces to the west.

This plan demonstrates the weakness of the East Prussian railway net.
By the 23rd day of mobilization the easternmost 1st Army consisted of
three corps, only two of which arrived by rail march. The center of mass
of the 2nd army was at Soldau, only 70 kilometers east of the railhead at
Thorn. More than half of the German army—250,000 troops—was
deployed west of the Vistula. From there it faced a long foot-march to
Warsaw. Every step brought the Germans further from their railheads.
The mass of the German army would also be faced with crossing the
Narew.

Moltke's concept of the operation is spare in the extreme. Given a
more detailed consideration of the situation, it is easy to come to worri-
some conclusions. The Germans would complete their deployment to

the east about the 23rd day, the same time that the French would reach
the Rhine. The mass of the German army would be near Warsaw on the
29th day, about the same time that the French reached the Main. Even
under the 'best-case' scenario—a decisive battle in the east on the 29th
day—the Germans still faced at least a six-day foot-march back to the
railhead at Thorn, followed by a rail-march to west Germany. By this
time the French would be in Würzburg. The Bavarians would have been
aghast. Moltke then had to defeat the French and relieve Metz and
Strasbourg. The question still remains, how many corps could the
Germans shift west? The Russians had up to 21 uncommitted divisions,
plus the remaining forces in Poland or White Russia. The 'worst-case'
scenario was catastrophic: the Russians wouldn't fight at Warsaw but
would withdraw east to wait for the entire army to mass. The Germans
would then take Warsaw and transfer forces to the west, but they would
now have the long-term prospect of having to deal eventually with up to
36 Russian divisions—675,000 men—in the east and as large a French
army in the west.

Moltke said at the beginning of the *Denkschrift* that there would be a
Russo-German war because the Russians would attack. Nevertheless, he
did not discuss the Russian offensive. It would seem hardly credible that
the Russians would attack with only 19 divisions—348,000 men—on the
29th day against a numerically superior German army in view of the fact
that they might wait to reinforce the attack with up to another 21 divisions. Nor, given the Russian performance against Turkey in 1877 would
it seem that even a small German force, supported by the fortresses at
Königsberg and Thorn, the barrier of the Vistula and the German rail
net, should have had any difficulty defending against an immediate
Russian attack. Nineteen divisions (nine corps) is essentially the same-
sized force that the Russians sent into Bulgaria (seven corps). One
would expect that the Germans would do at least as well against such a
Russian force as the Turks had. Therefore, the only hope for the
Russian attack would have been to deploy as large a mass as possible.
Given the performance of the Russian railroads in 1877—and not mathematical models—assembling the maximum-sized force would have
taken months. It would appear that Moltke did not mention the
Russian offensive for fear that it would contradict his conclusions and
proposed course of action.

MOLTKE ADVOCATES AN AUSTRO-GERMAN ALLIANCE

Historians have had great difficulty making sense of these war plans.
Ritter called the plans for a war with a Franco-Austrian alliance
'unlikely and thoroughly preposterous eventualities' and found a

psychological explanation for them: they were intellectual exercises, Moltke's 'way of self-identification'.[34] In fact, there is good reason to doubt that the *Denkschriften* written between 1877 and 1879 were ever war plans at all. Since Moltke did not conduct strategic war games, at best these *Denkschriften* may be considered as a form of war game in which Moltke tested various strategic possibilities. As such, these *Denkschriften* show only one thing: that Germany could not fight a two-front war. In the *Westaufmarsch* the most Moltke could do was hope for a diplomatic solution with France in order to return a two-front war back to a one-front war. The consequence of an *Ostaufmarsch* against Austria or Russia was that the Germans would soon be faced with a French army on the right bank of the Rhine or even in central Germany.

These *Denkschriften* were written not primarily as war plans, but to support Moltke's political policy, which was to conclude an Austro-German military alliance. Since the very beginning of his tenure as Chief of Staff, Moltke maintained that the best guarantee of pan-German security and peace in Europe was through an alliance of 'the two German Powers'.[35]

Russian dissatisfaction with the lack of German support at the Congress of Berlin in June–July 1878 became quickly evident in August.[36] In September 1879, Bismarck told Moltke to brief Kaiser Wilhelm on the Russian troop build-up in Poland. This 'build-up' in fact consisted mainly of cavalry, which would have been useful in conducting raids into Prussia to disrupt the German deployment and little else. Moltke apparently went one step further and presented his 1877–9 *Denkschriften* to Wilhelm. Moltke told Wilhelm that the French army alone was at least equal to the German army. The French fortress line was impenetrable and the French peacetime army was 100,000 men and 160 guns stronger than the German. If the Germans lost a battle, they would have to fall back to the Rhine. Moltke's conclusion was that in a war with France, Germany might need the support of an Austrian alliance. He said that Germany could fight Russia alone, but the French would probably intervene in such a war. Again, Germany would need an alliance with Austria. Moltke told the Emperor that he had worked out two war plans in complete detail, 'even the deployment plan'. The first, and probably primary, plan was for a German war with Russia, the second for a war with Russia in which the French intervened, at which point Moltke said euphemistically that the German situation became 'extraordinarily complicated'. Moltke's intent in the latter case was to fight on interior lines with the minimum of forces on one front,

[34] Ritter, *Sword and Scepter*, i. 237.   [35] *Feldherr und Staatsmann*, 13.
[36] *GP*, vol. 3, nos. 446 and 447.

presumably in the west, while conducting the most powerful offensive possible on the other, in order to quickly win a decisive victory. The 1879 *Denkschrift* for an *Ostaufmarsch* was surely the basis of this plan. This *Denkschrift*, as we have seen, demonstrated that such a strategy for Germany alone was very dangerous and difficult and that the only reasonable conclusion one could draw from it was that Germany needed Austrian support. Moltke then said that Germany should support Austria 'with all her power' against Russia. Therefore, the recommendation Moltke presented to the Kaiser was for an Austro-German military alliance, directed primarily against Russia.[37]

On 10 October 1879 Moltke briefed the Kaiser on French military strength. He again used the opportunity to renew his arguments for an Austro-German military alliance.[38] Germany should be able to fight the French successfully, Moltke said. Even if the Germans lost the first battle, the French would have to commit 240,000 men to besiege Metz and Strasbourg: by defending on their own territory, the Germans would regain numerical superiority. In addition, the Rhine offered one of the strongest defensive lines in Europe.[39] The danger was that the Russians would intervene. This is the opposite of the argument Moltke made in the preceding September, when he pointed out the danger of France intervening in a Russo-German war.

Wilhelm was opposed to an Austrian alliance. He saw the threat as coming from France, not Russia. Bismarck had wanted a defensive alliance with Austria too, but was interested in it solely as a political instrument. Bismarck said that the purpose of the alliance was to prevent a war. If Russia knew the Austrians and Germans would support each other, then the Russians wouldn't start a war at all. Moreover, if the Russians did attack, then England might join the Austro-German alliance, which in turn would discourage a French attack on Germany.[40] Bismarck's ultimate goal, as in 1873, was a conservative alliance of the Three Emperors. Wilhelm reluctantly agreed with Bismarck and a defensive alliance with Austria was concluded in October 1879. When Moltke asked on 8 November and again on 2 December for permission to conduct detailed military planning with the Austrians, Bismarck was uninterested.[41]

---

37 Schmerfeld, *Aufmarschpläne 1871–1890*, 80–1.

38 Ibid. 82–4. *GP*, vol. 3, no. 505.

39 Wilhelm wasn't convinced. He said that holding Metz, Strasbourg, and the Rhine fortresses would require 200,000 German troops, and that Moltke was overrating the effectiveness of the Rhine as a military obstacle.

40 *GP*, vol. 3, no. 455.

41 Kessel, *Moltke*, 671.

PUBLIC EVALUATIONS OF THE EUROPEAN MILITARY SITUATION

The rise in European tensions in 1878/9 led to a renewed public interest in the European military situation. Articles published in the professional military journals in France and Germany furnish a useful contrast to Moltke's short and tendentious analysis of enemy capabilities. In France, a Major X (the pseudonym for Major, later General, Ferron) published an article on the Franco-German military situation in the *Journal des Sciences Militaires* in 1879 and a second article in 1880. The first was titled 'Les chemins de fer allemandes et les chemins de fer français au point de vue de la concentration des armées' (The German and French Railways with Respect to the Deployment of their Armies).[42] Ferron said that the German rail system was far more effective than the French. In particular, he cited the capacity of the German lines which led directly from Berlin to Thionville (Diedenhofen) and from Frankfurt to Metz. Ferron said that the French had only begun to build up their fortress and rail system in 1875.

Ferron said that the French frontier fortifications would force the Germans to attack through the Belgian Ardennes with one army, consisting of five corps. This army would probably cross the Meuse between Stenay and Sedan. He said that the Germans did not do so in 1870/1 in order to avoid adding the Belgian army to their enemies. If invaded, the Belgians would fall back on Antwerp and the support of the British fleet. Ferron said that the French General Staff had not given this possibility enough consideration. In particular, Mézières needed to be provided with modern fortifications.

Ferron also said that seven German corps would deploy at Metz–Thionville. These would form two armies, one which would advance through Luxembourg and one which would threaten the French fortress line. One army of five corps would concentrate at Strasbourg–Saarebourg.

The German intent would be to deploy as quickly as possible and attack before the French had completed their deployment. Therefore, whatever it costs, said Ferron, it was necessary for the French to match the speed of the German rail deployment. The first objective of the German army would be to take Nancy. The Germans would not attack Toul because it was too strong. They would then cross the Moselle to the south of Nancy: the Germans would be attempting a double envelopment of the Verdun–Toul fortified zone. Therefore, the French also needed to develop their rail net to allow forces to be concentrated

---

[42] X, 'Les chemins de fer allemandes et les chemins de fer français au point de vue de la concentration des armees', *JSM* (Mai 1879), 5–16; Juillet 1879, 357–380.

quickly on both flanks. Particularly effective would be a French counterattack from Verdun against the left flank of the German forces crossing the Meuse between Dun and Stenay.

To deploy 14 corps, the French needed 10 double-tracked rail lines.
Single-track routes did not count for deployment. Most of the French
rail construction at that time consisted of double-tracking existing
single-track lines. With 10 lines the French would be able to match the
German deployment. The French would deploy, as Ferron said many
military writers had already anticipated, with one army on the left at
Verdun, one in the center on the heights of the Meuse, and one in the
south between Pont St. Vincent and Epinal covering the 'Trouée de
Charmes'. Reserves would be positioned in depth, especially to the
north. Nancy was indefensible unless permanently fortified.

In Ferron's opinion the German army was superior in quality and
speed of deployment to all of its possible opponents and the French
might lose the initial battles. For that reason the French were preparing to defend in depth. In spite of their slower mobilization, the French
should be able to hold the Moselle and 150,000 French troops could
hold the 'Trouée de Charmes' against 250,000 Germans.

The French could not attack and they needed to delay their counter-
offensive for as long as possible. Ferron wanted fortifications practically
everywhere, but especially against a German attack through the
Ardennes. The Meuse at Dun should be fortified, as should Hirson,
Maubeuge, and the Somme at Amiens and Peronne. Only the area
north of Maubeuge could not be fortified, for the terrain was too open
and contained too many rail lines. Last, Ferron said that the war would
be fought inside the area Maubeuge–Paris–Dijon. Everything possible
must be done to prepare this battlefield.

In the following six months, Ferron gave the matter more thought
and then published the second article.[43] He said that the French rail
system was not complete, and that the Germans would have the initiative and would get to the Meusc first. Ferron saw three possible German
courses of action. First, the Germans could attack straight ahead against
the French centre and left. They would penetrate the French center,
between Verdun and Toul, while a second force attacked through
Belgium and Luxembourg against the French left between Dun and
Verdun. In the best case scenario, the German attack on the center
would be stopped on the *côtes Lorraines*, the Meuse heights. Therefore,
the French must guard against a German offensive on mobilization, an
attaque brusquée, to take the high ground there. Against the German
attack through the Ardennes, the French would try to hold the line

---

[43] X, 'Etude stratégique sur la Frontière du Nord-Est', *JSM* (Janvier 1880), 49–68.

between Reims and La Fère. In the worst case, Mézières, Verdun, and Toul would be isolated. The French should not fall back to the west, but to the south and adopt a *Flankenstellung* based on Neufchâteau and Epinal. Second, the Germans could attack through the 'Trouée de Charmes'. Again, if defeated, the French should retreat to the south.

The third German course of action was the easiest and the most likely. The Germans would deploy their mass of maneuver in the north, attack through the Ardennes, and seek to turn the French left. However, such an attack would not cut off the French from their line of retreat to the south. At the same time, the German armies were divided by Verdun, while the French army there held a central position between them. The French defense was also assisted by the mobility provided by the French rail net. The most promising French counterattack was out of Verdun and across the Woëuvre plain against the left flank of the German right wing, in order to cut their lines of communications with Luxembourg and the Rhine. If the German right wing was stopped, the French should then attack against the German center on the Saar in Lorraine. Once again, the French should retreat not to the west but along successive *Flankenstellungen* to the south, their right protected first by Toul, then by the Moselle fortress line, and finally Epinal, the keystone of the French defense. The French would attrit the German armies and threaten the German right with reserve armies assembled on the Seine and Marne.

In 1880, Ferron had described, in public, practically the entire German strategic problem in the west, as well as the most probable French defensive course of action. His estimates were to prove accurate until 1910. He did not foresee Plan XVII, an outright French offensive, but when Plan XVII failed, his calculations were just as applicable as they had been in 1880. The German strategic problem was no great mystery.

In 1879 a retired German officer, Captain Fritz Hoenig, published a book in which he presented the current state of the French army and stated, accurately as it turned out, that the French would only be ready for war in 1885.[44] Hoenig illustrated the current state of the French army by noting that the French IV Corps maneuver in 1878, which was modeled on the annual German corps-on-corps exercise, the *Kaisermanöver*, was the first large-scale French exercise since before 1870. The maneuver showed that the French still had far to go and that many of the problems of 1870 had not been solved. The French were able for the first time to test their mobilization procedures, and found them not entirely satisfactory. Reservists reported in up to a day late

---

[44] F. Hoenig, *Die Wehrkraft Frankreichs im Jahre 1885* (Berlin, 1879).

and often drunk. There were difficulties in equipping the mobilized personnel. Though things would have been better had war actually threatened, there was obviously still a lot of work to be done. The exercise itself was choreographed and schematic and the infantry was rigid, though the artillery at battery level performed well. Good staff work would correct these deficiencies, but only in 1878 did the French open the École militaire supérieure de Guerre, their equivalent of the German Kriegsakademie.

The structure of the French army would be the same in 1879 and in 1885: 19 active corps and five reserve corps. In 1885 the army would have a field strength of 845,000 men. The reserve corps would produce a field force of 133,000 men of the older age groups (which were of dubious military value). In addition, there would be five year-groups of territorials—700,000 men—and the six oldest year-groups of the territorial reserve. The 1885 total strength of 2,000,000 plus (the numbers varied) looked impressive on paper, but none of the territorials were organized into units. The field trains (supply units) probably wouldn't be combat-ready until 1885.

Hoenig said that the French rail deployment system would not be completed until 1885 either. Using that as a basis, he compared the French and German deployment possibilities. The French mobilization in 1885 would take eight days. Hoenig said that if both sides deployed in order to march into Belgium, the French had the advantage because they possessed one or two more rail lines and had more double-tracked lines available. Using nine rail lines, the French could deploy 650,000 men to the north Belgian border (Lille–Mézières) by the 16th day of mobilization. The French could deploy the same force to their eastern border (Verdun–Epinal–Belfort) with seven rail lines by the 18th day of mobilization.

Hoenig was fully aware of the importance of Belgium as an avenue of approach for both sides. He said that the British interest was to insure that Antwerp fell neither to the Germans nor to the French. Since the French could deploy to the north Belgian border more quickly, an advance through Belgium offered the French the prospect of fighting a decisive battle there while enjoying numerical superiority.

By 1885, Hoenig said, the eastern border of France would be completely fortified. The fortifications of Paris were already finished: the fort line covered a trace 135 kilometers long. Like many other German officers at the time, Hoenig considered what the German army would have to do to reduce Paris a second time. He said that a close and continuous blockade as in 1870 would require an army of 350,000 men holding a line 200 kilometers long. This was impractical. A better solution was a distant blockade with three armies: one with 180,000 men to the south-west of Paris; one with 150,000 between the Seine and the Marne to the north-west; a third with 150,000 men between the Seine and the Marne to the south. The German armies could thus preserve freedom of action against sorties from Paris as well as attempts to relieve the city. It was hardly possible to starve Paris out by this method. The best that could be hoped for was that the French would tire of the German occupation of the eastern half of their country and sue for peace. The 'Schlieffen plan' solution of conducting a close blockade with 180,000 *Ersatztruppen* seems lame compared to more realistic evaluations such as that by Hoenig.

Hoenig did not rate the French border fortification system highly, mainly because garrisoning it consumed a large number of troops. It was hardly invulnerable, and at best could delay the German attack. Once the fortress line was penetrated, the mass of the fortresses could be bypassed and their garrisons reduced to impotence. The French would have been better off relying on field fortifications. Hoenig then repeated the common evaluation of fortifications in the German army—that permanent fortifications have value only insofar as they supported the operations of the field army. This meant that the field army used the permanent fortifications primarily to assist it in maneuver. This is quite different from Moltke's policy of allowing the enemy to besiege strongly garrisoned fortresses in the hope that this would tie down large numbers of enemy troops.

Having said that the French would be ready in 1885, Hoenig showed that even then the French army would still have problems. The weakest branch of the French army was the artillery, which had guns but lacked trained gunners and horses: in case of mobilization the French would have to leave guns in depot for lack of crews and horse teams.

Hoenig's evaluation was that the new French conscript army had been in existence for only six years and was still an experiment. The French army was not yet fully organized and presented no threat to Germany. An isolated France was in any case powerless.

In 1879 F. M. von Donat published anonymously his pamphlet *Die Befestigung und Vertheidigung der deutsch–französischen Grenze* (The Fortification and Defense of the Franco-German Border) which he would update three times by 1894.[45] Donat was as concerned with a French attack as he was with a German one. He said that the only worthwhile avenue of approach between France and Germany was through Lorraine. This lay nearly on the principal line of communications between Berlin and Paris. In Alsace the space between the Rhine and

---

[45] F. M. von Donat, *Die Befestigung und Vertheidigung der deutsch–französischen Grenze* (1st edn., Berlin, 1879).

the Vosges was only 40 kilometers wide and useful only for secondary operations. The Vosges themselves, including the avenue of approach from Belfort to Alsace, were unsuited to the movement of large bodies of troops. A serious French invasion of the upper Alsace and Baden was pointless and unlikely. A French attack here would be a diversion. French military writers, noted Donat, were already saying that the Germans would attack from Cologne through Belgium on Paris. Donat did not believe a German violation of Belgian neutrality to be likely.

Donat said that Germany had at least ten continual rail lines from the interior to the Rhine. Soon Germany would have eleven Rhine bridges. Between Cologne and Strasbourg eight German rail lines led to Lorraine, terminating at Diedenhofen, Metz, and Avricourt. On the other hand, the French were not so well equipped, a fact which had been the source of a lively discussion in the French military press between 1872 and 1874. In 1879 the French had a total of seven lines to the German border, but only four led to Lorraine, while two went to Belfort. Therefore, the French rail situation was only marginally better than in 1870, when the Germans had eight rail lines to four for the French. From Donat's description, it would be difficult to see how Moltke arrived at the idea that the French could deploy to Lorraine more quickly than the Germans.

A French attack on Lorraine would first have to contend with Metz. Any force attacking Metz would have to be two to three times the size of Metz's garrison. The fortifications of Strasbourg had also been modernized. The Rhine was relatively easy to cross between the Swiss border and Mainz. Downstream from Mainz the Rhine was hemmed in by cliffs and difficult to cross. Only below Bonn did the terrain flatten out again. In order to cross the Rhine, the French would have to take one of the German fortresses, which Donat said were all ultra-modern and capable of sustained resistance. The French attack would come to a stop on the Rhine. Donat was reflecting Moltke's concept of basing the defense in the west on the German fortresses.

French military literature, said Donat, maintained that the Germans would deploy more quickly and would enjoy the strategic initiative. Therefore, the French expected to have to conduct a strategic defensive operation. Donat observed that the tactical defensive seemed to have many adherents in France. French officers said that modern firepower could be best exploited in the defensive and therefore concerned themselves with choosing good defensive positions. A successful defensive battle was usually to be followed by a counterattack.

The French would deploy along the line Toul–Belfort. Donat said that breaking this line would present considerable difficulty. On the other hand, Nancy was vulnerable since any fortification of Nancy was unlikely because of the size of the required works. The French would not, however, fight to destruction on this line. If defeated, the French main body would withdraw not west to Paris but south to Langres. One French army would garrison Paris and a new French army would be organized to cover the Loire. The configuration of the Parisian fortifications made sense only if they served as a base for a field army which would conduct offensive operations. The French expected that the Germans would blockade Paris, but would not attempt to conduct a formal siege.

The British army was also interested in military developments on the Continent. In 1880 Captain G. Macdonald published an article on French and German war plans based on the articles by Ferron and F. M. von Donat.[46] Macdonald said that the French assumed that the Germans would mobilize and deploy more quickly than they could. The French also assumed that the Germans would transit southern Belgium (although the French had not fortified the lower Meuse). Macdonald felt that the German march would be made as far to the south as possible, and not extend to Maubeuge–Givet in the north.

Macdonald said that the Germans were convinced that 'superior rapidity of mobilization and of concentration will be an almost certain guarantee of final success'. The Germans would deploy their entire army in the west. Five corps would move through southern Belgium and Luxembourg, eight corps would deploy on Metz, and five around Saarebourg–Strasbourg. This last army would cut the French off from the south of France. The German concept was to mobilize, deploy, and attack so quickly that they would catch the French in a disorganized state, before they had completed their deployment.

According to European military opinion, Moltke's evaluation of the French capabilities and intentions in 1879 was completely erroneous. European opinion recognized that the French build-up was only 5 years old, and the French would not be fully combat capable until 1885. The European experts calculated that the German mobilization and deployment was at least a week faster than the French, perhaps more. This offered the Germans an enormous advantage if they took the offensive. By and large, the publicly printed evaluations of French and German capabilities seem to have been accurate.

On the other hand, Moltke was giving the French credit for capabilities that they would not have until much later, and offensive intentions

---

[46] G. Macdonald, 'The Railways of France and Germany, Considered with Reference to the Concentration of Armies on the Franco-German Frontier', *JRUSI* xxiv (1880), 725–37. Until 1914, the British would get their military analysis second-hand. F. M. von Donat's book *Die Befestigung und Vertheidigung der deutsch–französischen Grenze* is discussed in Ch. 3.

that they did not have until 1911. By the 23rd day of mobilization, Moltke expected that the French could be on the Rhine when they really would probably have been behind the Moselle. Neither the development of the French army nor the French railroad net allowed the French to think of taking the offensive. Assuming that the French did intervene in a Russo-German war, that intervention would neither have been coordinated with the Russians nor planned in advance, but would have had to be developed extemporaneously. It would therefore have been poorly thought-out and inadequately prepared. The German army was a lot closer to being able to conduct a two-front war on its own than Moltke stated. The Austrian alliance was not as necessary as Moltke made it seem. It seems safe to say that Moltke was not unaware of the real state of the French army, but emphasized his 'worst-case' scenario in the west in order to support his contention that Germany needed an Austrian alliance.

1880: TWO-FRONT WAR—PREVENTIVE WAR IN THE EAST

Once the political alliance with Austria had been concluded, Moltke did his utmost to transform it into an effective military alliance. In January 1880 he wrote a plan for a general European war between the Austro-German alliance on the one side and France and Russia on the other side.[47] Moltke planned to deploy three armies in the west, including nine corps or 322,000 troops. The 1st Army, with three corps and a reserve division, and the 2nd Army, with four corps and two reserve divisions, would hold a defensive position on the Saar, from Forbach to Saarunion. Later commentators on Moltke's plan lead one to believe that Moltke's defense on the Saar anticipated trench warfare. Nothing could be further from the truth. Moltke did not ascribe any special value to field fortifications. Only four corps—eight divisions—would be deployed on the front line. The four forward corps would hold a position whose straight-line length was 30 kilometers and whose actual length on the ground was far greater. Each division therefore had to defend a front 4 kilometers long or more, which was twice as long as usual. Moltke said that these four corps on the front line could surely defeat any French frontal attack, at which point the remaining three corps, held in reserve, would counterattack. The 3rd Army, with two corps and a reserve division, would deploy to the south of Colmar. If necessary, it would withdraw to Strasbourg.

The situation in the west was dealt with in summary fashion. There was no estimate of French strength, mobilization speed, deployment, or

---

47 Schmerfeld, *Aufmarschpläne 1871–1890*, 86–97, 111.

intentions. This was surely not accidental. Such an analysis of French capabilities would have called into question the basis of Moltke's plan. First, the 9 German army corps in the west would be outnumbered 2 : 1 by the 19 corps of the French army. Indeed, if the French left two corps to watch the two German corps in the upper Alsace, then the French could have fought the decisive battle in Lorraine with 17 corps against seven German. Moltke hoped that the French would have to significantly weaken their field army to watch Metz. He proposed leaving all the troops that had their peacetime garrisons in Metz as part of the fortress garrison, plus the 13th and 16th Infantry Divisions from the VII and VIII corps. Moltke was willing to lock up over 10 percent of his field army in the west to garrison just one fortress. These divisions would be replaced in the 'active army' VII and VIII Corps by reserve divisions— in 1880 an almost revolutionary step. In return, Moltke expected that the French would have to deploy two corps to watch Metz. Moltke was obviously very proud of this disproportionate expenditure of French strength. Nevertheless, this still might leave 15 French corps in Lorraine against seven German corps. The Forbach–Saarunion position also covered less than half of the maneuver area available to the French. Even at the narrowest point there was a 30-kilometer gap to the north between Forbach and the border with Luxembourg at Sierck. Moltke brushed this problem aside with the observation that the French could not march past the German position but must attack it frontally. With the numerical superiority that the French enjoyed, it is hard to see why they could not have done both.

Nevertheless, although Moltke was far more optimistic than the situation warranted, he did recognize weaknesses in the German position. First, he said that the French might attack so quickly that Metz might not be provisioned. He could also have added that it might not have even been 'armed', that is, put in a proper state of defense. Second, he acknowledged that given the French numerical superiority (which he never explicitly enumerated) the Germans might well be forced to retreat to the Rhine. In fact, since the Germans were outnumbered 2–1, withdrawal to the Rhine would appear to have been unavoidable and would have to be made quickly to save the German army in the west from destruction. Indeed, once the French advanced beyond the narrow neck at Sierck–Saarunion, the terrain opens up like a fan and the Germans had no hope of holding another position in front of the Rhine. Moltke still believed that in advancing to the Rhine the French would have to detail such large forces to watch the German fortresses of Metz, Strasbourg, and Mainz that the French field army would be fatally weakened. In a frequently quoted passage, Moltke said that the Germans were therefore in a position to fight the decisive battle on the

Main to its conclusion. Moltke was merely restating his faith in permanent fortifications and the defensive *Flankenstellung* on the Main.

To support his case for the necessity of an attack in the east, Moltke painted a terrifying picture of the speed and size of the Russian mobilization and deployment. The Russian attack could come as a 'bolt from the blue' without warning: the omniscient tsar had merely to sign the mobilization orders. On the first day of mobilization great masses of Russian cavalry could conduct raids on vital installations, such as the bridge at Tilsit or the stud at Trakhener. By the 60th day of mobilization, Moltke said, the Russians could deploy 1,173,400 men in Lithuania, around Warsaw, and in the Ukraine. This number wildly exceeds both the estimate of the American military attaché as well as actual Russian performance in 1877/8. Moltke said that the Austro-Germans had one advantage—their faster rate of mobilization and deployment. To support this contention he conducted an elaborate comparison of the relative rates of deployment—something he had significantly failed to do in the west.

The German army would mobilize and deploy almost at once. By the 13th day of mobilization the Germans could assemble nine corps in the east, 360,000 men in all. Nevertheless, only three single-tracked rail lines crossed the Vistula. Only the 1st Army, with a paltry force of two corps and a reserve division, would deploy to East Prussia (and one of those corps and the reserve division were permanently garrisoned there). The 2nd army, with four corps and two reserve divisions, and the 3rd Army with three corps and two reserve divisions, would assemble on the west bank of the Vistula near Thorn (the 2nd Army still included the entire Bavarian Army). The 2nd Army would advance on the north side of the Vistula and reach Plock by the 20th day of mobilization. Behind it the 3rd Army would cross from the south to the north bank of the Vistula. Clearly East Prussia was incapable of serving as the base for a great pincer attack on Poland. The Germans had a long approach march over difficult terrain in order to conduct a frontal attack on Warsaw.

Moltke assumed that the Russians would attack immediately led by their army at Kowno. In order to cover the left flank of the Kowno army, the Warsaw army would advance forward of the Bug and accept battle in the open field. The German and Russian armies would crash into each other somewhere just west of the Narew. There was nothing sophisticated about this plan: Moltke intended to meet the Russians head-on and crush them with superior numbers. The other possible Russian course of action was to remain on the defensive at Kowno and Warsaw and await the arrival of more Russian forces. In that case the German armies would enjoy an interior position between the Russian armies and could presumably defeat them in detail. Moltke did not consider the possibility that the Russians would respond to a German advance on the Niemen–Narew position by withdrawing further to the interior, for example to Brest-Litovsk.

Operationally, Moltke saw only one possible course of action for the Austro-Germans: the situation in the east in 1880 was a carbon copy of the Prussian situation in 1866: the Austro-Germans needed to maximize the advantage provided by their faster mobilization and concentrate forward on Warsaw. The German offensive from Thorn to the Narew and then on Warsaw should enjoy numerical superiority. If the Russians tried to defend the Narew, 300,000 Germans would engage 216,000 Russians. Even by the 40th day the Russians would be able to assemble only 267,000 troops at Warsaw. Only on the 60th day, when Russian strength would rise to 400,000 men, would the Russians attain numerical superiority.

The real race was between the Russian and Austrian mobilizations, and here the odds did not look good for the Austro-Germans. On the 16th day of mobilization the Russians would have 101,000 men in Lithuania at Kowno-Vilna, 110,100 at Warsaw, and 103,000 in the Ukraine at Kowel—314,100 in total. The Austrians would be able to deploy 393,100 men, with 222,300 at Cracow and 171,000 at Lvov. The odds were therefore 753,000 Austro-Germans versus 315,000 Russians.

By the 24th day the Austrian deployment would be completed.[48] The Austrians would have 590,000 troops: 285,000 at Cracow and 305,000 at Lvov. The Russians would have 645,000 troops—176,000 in Lithuania, 181,500 at Warsaw, 287,500 in the western Ukraine: 950,000 Austro-Germans versus 644,000 Russians. This was the point of greatest Austro-German advantage, this was the time at which the Austro-Germans should try to fight the decisive battle. By the 36th day of mobilization, the Russian forces would increase to 911,800 men and would be for all intents and purposes numerically equal to the Austro-Germans. By the 60th day the Russians would complete their deployment and, at 1,173,400 men, would have 223,400 more troops than the Austro-Germans.

Moltke's plan rested on a narrow window of opportunity, which had to be ruthlessly exploited. This window of opportunity was most advantageous at the 24th day of mobilization and disappeared on the 36th day. The situation became favorable for the Russians by the 60th day.

---

[48] Moltke's calculations were optimistic. In 1882 the Austrian Chief of Staff, Beck, did not think that his army would complete its deployment until the 45th day of mobilization. However, in 1882 Beck told Waldersee that he would be ready in three weeks. E. Heller, 'Bismarcks Stellung zur Führüng des Zweifronten-Krieges', *APG*, (1926), Heft 12, 681.

There were two additional complications. First, there was the problem of coordinating with the Austrian government and army: Bismarck was not going to permit this in peacetime. Second, the Austro-German alliance was, at Bismarck's insistence, a defensive alliance. Moltke's plan, however, would have succeeded only as an immediate full-scale offensive, a coordinated Austro-German preventive war against Russia. If the battle in the east were fought on about the 50th–60th day of mobilization, then the Austro-Germans would meet a numerically superior Russian army in the east, while the French could very well be across the Rhine in the west. The point is, however, probably moot. Bismarck forbade any detailed military planning with Austria, and Moltke was unsure if the Austrians were willing to attack at all—an operation which he said did not square with Austrian military tradition. Moltke was afraid that the Austrians would prefer to stand on the defensive—a concern that was shared by his nephew thirty years later. Far from being wise, Moltke's *Ostaufmarsch* was rash to the point of being foolhardy.

1881: GENUINE PLAN FOR WAR WITH FRANCE

In January 1881 Moltke wrote a *Denkschrift* for a general German war plan (Moltke called it the *Grundzüge*—basic outline—for a war with France).[49] This plan included annexes for border security, fortress security, and 'arming' the fortresses. It would seem from these provisions alone that finally and at long last we are dealing with a genuine peacetime war plan and not a policy paper advocating a strategic course of action. In all cases the Germans would conduct a deployment with half the army to the east and half to the west. If it later proved that the Germans would have to fight only on one front, the prepared deployment would be conducted nevertheless and at its conclusion troops from the unengaged front would be transferred to the active front.

The elder Moltke's provisions for a one-front war should also be remembered in light of the events of 1 August 1914. At that time the German ambassador in London, Lichnowsky, in an attempt to get Berlin to guarantee Belgian neutrality, led Bethmann Hollweg to believe (incorrectly) that the British would remain neutral, and guarantee French neutrality, if the Germans would respect Belgian neutrality in return. Kaiser Wilhelm II jumped to the conclusion that Germany could now conduct a one-front war against Russia and told the younger Moltke to redirect the deployment to the east. Moltke said that that was impossible: the result would have been chaos. The Kaiser then said that 'his uncle would have given him a different answer'. The Kaiser's state-

---

[49] Schmerfeld, *Aufmarschpläne 1871–1890*, 97–107.

ment has been accepted by subsequent historians as accurate, and Moltke's inability to spin the German army 180 degrees has been taken as evidence of his 'militaristic rigidity'. In fact, the Kaiser was wrong: the elder Moltke would have given him the same answer that his nephew did.

Having dealt with the war plan in the east in detail in 1880, the 1881 plan considered the situation in the west only. The plan included—for the first time since 1870—a realistic and detailed analysis of French strength. The mobilized French army—without reserve divisions and new formations—was now estimated to include 19 corps, numbering only 475,000 men. When fortress garrisons were subtracted, the reserve (4th) battalions could be formed into an additional 3 corps, or about 75,000 more field troops. The total French field army of 550,000 men was far inferior to the total German force of 682,000 men. The 1881 estimate therefore bore no relationship to Moltke's estimate made during the *Krieg in Sicht* crisis just six years before, in which he had said that the French enjoyed numerical superiority over the entire German army. Moltke still maintained that the French could deploy more quickly than the Germans. The French had seven rail lines, could deploy the combat elements of their army by the 11th day of mobilization, and be completely deployed by the 13th day. It was assumed that the French would deploy five corps at Verdun, four corps at Toul, six corps at Nancy, and four at Belfort. Aside from the assertion that the French would have to conduct a frontal attack on the German position in Lorraine, Moltke made no estimate of the French concept of the operation. He did, however, express concern that the French border cavalry and artillery was fully supplied with horses and could launch raids as of the first day of mobilization to disrupt the German deployment.

Moltke said that the Germans could once again deploy only nine corps in the west, numbering in total 335,000 troops, including reserve divisions. The main force of seven corps (233,000 men) in Lorraine would occupy an entirely new position far forward of the Saar, from St Avold to Saaralben. The front line of this position would be only 19 kilometers long and would be held by four corps. One corps would be stationed at the right rear, at Forbach. One would be deployed on the left rear and one isolated far to the left at Saarunion. The position had no obstacles to its front. Moltke did not mention field fortifications. The position occupied less than one-third of the 60 kilometers of maneuver space available to the French in Lorraine, and the flanks were completely in the air. The plan was based on the assumption that if the French wanted to regain Alsace-Lorraine, then they would have to attack. Moltke was still convinced that the French, who by his estimate had at least 15 corps in Lorraine—392,000 troops, or 159,000 more than the Germans—could not outflank the position but would have to attack it frontally. If that were true, the new St Avold–Saaralben position had one advantage over the old Forbach–Saarunion position: it was 10 kilometers shorter. Moltke specified the deployment in this position in great detail, down to the location of the advance guards and the reserve divisions. With each of eight front-line divisions occupying 2½ kilometers of front, Moltke felt sure that his phalanx would defeat the French frontal attack with firepower alone. He could then counterattack, capture one of the French border forts, and break through the French fortress line. Once again, this was a classic Moltke defensive–offensive. In the upper Alsace the 3rd Army would presumably be able to amuse a French force twice its size, withdrawing on Strasbourg if necessary.

In case of a one-front war against France, Moltke reiterated that the eastern troops would have to complete their initial deployment and then redeploy to the west. Moltke made the somewhat unrealistic assumption that the situation in the west would be quiet and the redeployment from the east would proceed undisturbed. Moltke still concentrated the mass of the German army in Lorraine. He would position three armies—16 corps—extending the line north along the German Nied. Moltke prescribed the positions to be occupied down to divisional level. He said that such a line was difficult to envelop to the south through the Vosges and a French envelopment to the north through Luxembourg and Belgium was unlikely because a German counterattack could cut it off from France. One army with three corps would be stationed in the upper Alsace near Neubreisach. The combat troops would complete their deployment by the 13th day, the trains by the 18th day.

Moltke expected that a decisive battle would immediately follow the deployment. If the French did not attack, then (presumably on the 18th day) the German 3rd Army (6 corps—200,000 men) on the left wing would advance on Lunéville and Raon l'Etape. The fort at Manonviller could be reduced in a few days. On the 4th day of the offensive the 3rd Army would attack Lunéville and advance on the Mortagne. Moltke intended this attack to force a French reaction and bring on a battle. Considering the seemingly obvious purpose of the French fortress line as well as articles such as Ferron's, it is not at all clear why Moltke expected that the French might advance beyond their border fortifications and then fight the decisive battle at Nancy–Lunéville.

In 1880 the French completed their first war plan—Plan I.[50] The French expected that the Germans intended to repeat the campaign of 1870, with a rapid rail deployment followed by a violent attack, probably directed on Nancy. The plan was purely defensive: the mass of the

[50] A. Marchand, *Plans de concentration de 1871 à 1914* (Paris, 1926), 15–24.

French army was positioned far to the south-west in order to reduce its vulnerability to a German attack while their armies were still assembling. The 1st Army was deployed to the north-west of Belfort, the 2nd at Langres, the 3rd to the east of Troyes, and the 5th in reserve to the south of Troyes. The 4th Army was separated far to the left flank to the south-east of Reims. The 5th Army would not complete its concentration until the 25th day of mobilization. The French had made no provisions for organizing their excess reservists into maneuver units

The real French war plan bore no resemblance to Moltke's enemy estimate. Moltke thought that the French center of mass—10 corps—would be at Toul–Nancy when in fact it was 100 kilometers to the south-west, at Langres. Moltke thought that the French mobilization was twice as fast as it actually was—that it would be completed on the 13th day when in fact it would take until the 25th. The German army had at least nine reserve divisions on its 1881 order of battle. Moltke assumed that the French had at least six, while in fact they had none. Most important, it is clear that the French were not going to fight for Nancy. Moltke's enemy estimate was not only wildly inaccurate, it was even less perceptive than published evaluations such as Hoenig's. The reason for this is evident in Moltke's *Denkschrift* of December 1882 for an attack on Nancy–Lunéville. He began the *Denkschrift* by saying that it was curious that while the French and Russians were preparing for war, both had evidently adopted defensive strategies and would wait for the German attack. Moltke did not draw any conclusions from this conundrum. Moltke was allowing his anticipation of the inevitable *Titanenkampf* between the Latin west and the Slavic east on the one side and the Teutonic center on the other to determine his military evaluation of the situation. In fact, both his political and military estimates were seriously in error.

MOLTKE'S PLAN TO ATTACK NANCY

Moltke said in December 1882 that there were two gaps in the French fortress line: one to the north of Verdun, the other to the south of Nancy. The 1st Army should not try to move to the north of Verdun because it might be cut off by a French counterattack from Verdun to the north. Nor would Moltke advance through the 'Trouée de Charmes'. Instead, Moltke saw advantages in reaching the Meurthe before the French main body and now planned to launch an immediate offensive on Nancy–Lunéville. He expanded the offensive into a coordinated seven-corps attack.[51] In 1885 Moltke further refined the plan to

[51] Ibid. 114–17.

attack Nancy–Lunéville.[52] If the French didn't attack by the 18th day of mobilization, then the German army would launch a general advance. The 1st Army would demonstrate in front of Pont à Mousson to fix one and perhaps two French armies in place. The 2nd and 3rd Armies would attack Nancy and Lunéville. The French, said Moltke, could not let this challenge go unanswered and a general battle would ensue. Moltke's conviction that the French would fight a battle for Nancy had become an *idée fixe* which was immune to rational calculation.

1881: LEAGUE OF THE THREE EMPERORS

From 1880/1 on the German army therefore had a basic war plan for a two-front war, plus a variant for a one-front war against France. In a two-front war, the Germans would attack in the east and defend a position in the west somewhere in the vicinity of the Saar. Moltke retained this plan in spite of the fact that on 18 June 1881 Bismarck informed him of the provisions of the League of the Three Emperors.[53] This treaty expressly superseded the Austro-German alliance.[54] In case of a two-front war, Bismarck still wanted an offensive in the west.[55] Advocates of the *Ostaufmarsch* have always contended that Moltke's plans for a two-front war presciently foresaw and provided an infallible plan for the situation in 1914. It would seem to be warranted to doubt the practicality of planning in 1881 for a war that would only occur thirty-three years later. What is clear is that Moltke's planning after 1881 was completely out of step with Bismarck's policy. For the remainder of Moltke's tenure as Chief of Staff Russia was Germany's ally. Nevertheless, Moltke maintained a war plan that was based on an immediate offensive in order to catch the Russian army before it had completed its deployment. It is very difficult to envision a political situation where Moltke would have been allowed to execute such a plan. In the last years of his tenure as Chief of Staff, Moltke was planning to support his own political policy, and not Bismarck's.

WALDERSEE

In January 1882 Count Alfred von Waldersee was appointed as Moltke's assistant as *Generalquartiermeister.* In effect, Waldersee ran the operations

---

[52] Marchand, *Plans de concentration de 1871 à 1914,* 118–20.

[53] Kessel, *Moltke,* 680.

[54] *GP,* vol. 3, no. 532, Article VI, 178.

[55] W. von Schweinitz (ed.), *Denkwürdigkeiten des Botschafters General von Schweinitz* (Berlin 1927), ii. 173–4.

of the General Staff. Waldersee obtained the position solely because he was the senior available corps commander. Most important, Moltke insisted that his deputy be considered his presumptive successor.[56] Waldersee immediately set out to reestablish the high standards of work in the General Staff, which he obviously felt the aging Moltke had let slide.

Almost from the first, Waldersee fundamentally disagreed with Moltke's defense plan in the west: Moltke had always maintained that the French would fritter away their numerical superiority on secondary operations.[57] Waldersee contended that if the French really surrounded Metz and Diedenhofen with three corps and sent three corps on a fool's errand in Alsace, left a corps at Paris, and deployed two against Italy, the Germans would actually the outnumber the French ten corps to nine, his point being that the French would hardly be so accommodating. In 1883 he proposed to move strong forces right up to the border very early, in order to mask the German army's intention to stay on the defensive. He also argued that the French were strong enough to outflank Moltke's St Avold–Saaralben position. Waldersee proposed that the Germans occupy a position far to the south, from Saarunion to Saarebourg. Waldersee was hoisting Moltke on his own petard: he was proposing a *Flankenstellung* against a French attack in Lorraine. Moltke was unimpressed, and maintained that the French would merely bypass Waldersee's position to the north.

In January 1884 Waldersee wrote a *Denkschrift* which summarized his ideas on German strategy.[58] He expanded his attack on Moltke's strategy in the west. He said that the attack on Nancy was not as easy as it looked. The French would hold Nancy in strength early on and would at the very least dig field fortifications there. Waldersee argued that from his Saarunion–Saarebourg position the German attack could be better directed both against Lunéville as well as against the French fort at Manonviller than it could be from Moltke's position, which was further to the north.

In October 1884 Waldersee renewed his argument with Moltke over the conduct of the defensive in the west.[59] Waldersee said that Metz was not going to draw off nearly as many French forces as Moltke estimated: with 16 corps and 12 reserve divisions deployed in Lorraine, the French could use their numerical superiority to turn the left flank of Moltke's position and from Saarunion the French stood as close to the Rhine

[56] Kessel, *Moltke*, 685.

[57] H. Mohs (ed.), *General-Feldmarschall Alfred Graf Waldersee in seinem militärischen Wirken* (Berlin 1929), ii. 264–70.

[58] Ibid. 273–9.   [59] Ibid. 282–5.

crossings at Mainz as the Germans did. He said that the Germans could not risk the existence of the army in the west in a battle forward of the Rhine: the decisive battles had to be fought on the Rhine and the Vistula. It would be easiest to shift forces between these two fronts.

Since it became clear that Moltke was not going to alter his plans, Waldersee changed his tack and contended that the Germans could not afford to conduct Moltke's passive, positional defense. Of the total force in the west of nine corps and five reserve divisions, a corps and a reserve division would have to be left in the upper Alsace and a reserve division at Saarunion. With the remaining force of eight corps and three reserve divisions the Germans should try to conduct a mobile defense and attack the left flank of the advancing French army.

In November 1885 Moltke made a comprehensive reply to Waldersee's continual objections and he did not budge an inch from his 1880/1 plan. He continued to believe that the French would send one army into the upper Alsace, leaving only 12 corps for the main attack in Lorraine. If the French did attack, Moltke was now back to defending a position at Forbach–Saargemund. He still maintained that the French would have great difficulty turning the left flank of this position because of the woods at Dieuze and would have to attack frontally to the north of that town. If the French did not attack, the German right should demonstrate against Pont à Mousson while the main body advanced on Nancy–Lunéville. However, Moltke made the remarkable assertion that in a two-front war the most important characteristic that the German position in the west had to possess was that it offered a secure route of withdrawal to the Rhine. The position that best insured this withdrawal was his Forbach–Saargemund line. He maintained that the French could turn the right flank of Waldersee's Saarebourg–Saarunion position and reach the Rhine at Mainz before the Germans could retreat through the Vosges.

In three years of argument, Waldersee did not change Moltke's concept for the defense in the west. Moltke continued to assume that the French would conduct an unimaginative, not to say incompetent, offensive. The French would have to detach forces to watch the Italians and would invade the upper Alsace with very strong forces which would accomplish nothing. They would further weaken their main army by detaching strong regular forces to watch Metz. Last, they then had no choice but to attack the German Saar position frontally. In spite of all these favors the French would do for the Germans, Moltke said that the determining characteristic of the German position in Lorraine was that it had to provide the best possible route of retreat to Mainz and the Rhine.

Waldersee said that from 1879 to 1882 there had been no military coordination between the Austrians and the Germans. Waldersee obtained Bismarck's permission to talk with the Austrian chief-of-staff, Beck, but only on the condition that complete secrecy be observed and no binding promises be made. Waldersee and Beck met while they were both vacationing at the Mondsee near Bad Ischl in Lower Austria. Only at this time did Waldersee learn that the Austrians intended to deploy in Galicia, not on the Carpathians, and that this deployment would take three weeks. The Austrians then planned to take the offensive. Waldersee informed Beck that the Germans intended to deploy 20 divisions to the right bank of the Vistula and would 'cross the border' even before the concentration was complete. Waldersee promised to conduct offensive operations from Silesia into south Poland in order to protect the Austrian rail line. He would also put the Silesian rail system at the Austrians' disposition to facilitate the transfer of the Bohemian corps to the east. There was no mention of a grand double envelopment of the Russian armies in Poland or indeed of the objective of the simultaneous Austro-German offensive at all. Rather, the Germans and Austrians apparently intended to win conventional battles near to their own border and then exploit their victories in the direction of Warsaw. The question of a Russian withdrawal in the face of an Austro-German attack was apparently not considered.

Between 1882 and 1885 Waldersee refined Moltke's 1880 plan in the east.[60] In 1882 he ordered that reconnaissance of the Russian rail net be conducted and discovered that the Vilna rail line was one-third more effective than previously believed. At the same time, he moved some assembly areas to the east side of the Vistula. In 1883 he ordered units to plan for large-scale raids into Russian Poland and Lithuania as of the 1st day of mobilization. In September 1883 Waldersee said that a preventive war in the east was justified because the Russians were far from being ready ('noch keineswegs fertig').[61]

In 1884, he said the Russians had a total of 72 infantry divisions, at least 60 of which could be deployed for a war with the Austro-Germans. However, if the Germans attacked with nine corps during the first four weeks, they would still be numerically superior to the Russians. The Austrian army would be ready a week after the German. Together they would initially enjoy a significant numerical superiority over the Russians. Waldersee now made the startling admission that as late as 1883 the Germans had assumed that the Russians would evacuate Poland in the face of a German attack. Waldersee maintained that in

[60] Mohs (ed.), *General-Feldmarschall Alfred Graf Waldersee in seinem militärischen Wirken* ii, 247–50, 256–63.
[61] Ibid. 5.

1884 the Germans were certain that the Russians would mass around Warsaw. The Germans should send their main force against Warsaw and defend against the Russian army at Kowno. Likewise, the Austrians should send their main force against Lublin and defend on their right flank against Rowno. This should allow the Austro-Germans to defeat the Russian main army at Warsaw, but this was obviously not a great double envelopment of Russian forces in Poland.

Waldersee said that on the 21st day of mobilization the Russians would have 100,000–120,000 men at Kowno, 50,000 men at Grajewo (south-east of Lyck), and 50,000 men at Plock, and would then 'without a doubt begin their offensive' against Prussia. Waldersee maintained that it was impossible for the Germans to remain on the defensive in the east, but his reasoning was fundamentally different from Moltke's: given time, the Russians could assemble an army that was strong enough to conduct offensives simultaneously against Germany and Austria. The German border in the east was too long to defend and if the Germans stayed on the defensive, so would the Austrians, putting the Russians on an interior position between the two.

In 1885 Waldersee said that as a result of Russian reinforcements in Poland and the increasing capacity of the Russian rail system, the Germans would have to speed up their offensive.[62] This resulted in major changes to the German plan. The German forces were divided into two armies, the 4th Army with three corps and three reserve divisions in eastern East Prussia, and the 3rd Army with six corps and five reserve divisions around Thorn—26 divisions in total. The Bavarian army would no longer deploy to East Prussia. Waldersee continued to be concerned by the Russian rail net at Kowno. Instead of allowing the Russian Kowno army to march into East Prussia, Waldersee intended that the 4th Army would launch a spoiling attack on Kowno on the 10th day of mobilization with the forces then available—2½ corps, a reserve division, and a cavalry division. The 4th Army should arrive in strength at Kowno before the Russians did to break up the Russian concentration. The 3rd Army, advancing from Thorn, would lag far behind and even by attacking before the army was completely assembled, with only five corps and four reserve divisions, it would reach Pultusk on the 20th day of mobilization. The military balance was obviously changing in the east. Waldersee's concept of the operation was shifting from fighting a decisive battle on the Narew to conducting a spoiling attack to break up the Russian concentration.

---

[62] Mohs (ed.), *General-Feldmarschall Alfred Graf Waldersee in seinem militärischen Wirken* ii, 256–9.

WALDERSEE'S *GENERALSTABSREISEN*

As of 1882, Waldersee was entirely responsible for the *Generalstabsreisen.*[63] Under the septuagenarian Moltke the exercises had become slack. Since Moltke was applauded wherever he went, the joke circulated that the name *Operationstag* (exercise day) should be changed to *Ovationstag* (ovation day).[64] Waldersee immediately set about tightening up ship. More work was given out and the critiques became tougher. Officers had to ride hard to keep up with the 49-year-old Waldersee and his Guard Uhlan assistant, Schlieffen. Waldersee also instituted a major innovation. It was Waldersee's intent to use the staff rides to teach strategy and test the war plan. This was great improvement over Moltke's exercises, which focused on tactics, local security, and march organization in areas far from the likely seat of war.

In the 1883 exercise the (notional) main armies faced each other across the Sieg (on the east side of the Rhine, opposite Bonn) while a French army three corps strong advanced on Hof (north of Nuremberg).[65] The German army was led by Schlieffen. For the first time Bavarian officers participated in a *Generalstabsreise* and the exercise took part on Bavarian territory. The purpose of the exercise was ostensibly to show that the *Flankenstellung* on the Rhine would protect Bavaria and Württemberg from invasion, and that the south German forces should withdraw to the east, not to the south. That the south Germans would have been reassured by this exercise seems doubtful, for Waldersee found it necessary to delay the French advance by thoroughly destroying the south German railroads. Since track is easy to repair, thorough destruction presumably included large structures such as bridges and roundhouses. When the French entered south Germany, the population conducted a guerrilla war against the invaders. Schlieffen apparently was able to attack the left flank of the French army and annihilate it as it tried to retreat through the Thuringian forest.

The general situation for the *Generalstabsreise West* in 1884 was unusual: while the (notional) main armies of France and Germany were engaged in Lorraine, the Swiss allowed a French army of three corps to pass through their territory and into south Germany, advancing through the Black Forest. At the same time, a French army attacked north in the upper Alsace towards Strasbourg. The purpose of the exercise was to show that the left flank of the German main body in Lorraine would be protected by improved fortifications at Strasbourg

---

[63] Ibid. 109–29.   [64] Ibid. 22.
[65] The 1882 exercise concerned a Russian invasion of Silesia.

and a fortress at Mutzig, built after 1893 as Fortress Kaiser Wilhelm II. The Germans would also use their rail net to mass against the French in the Black Forest and defeat them. Waldersee said that the decisive battle at Oberndorf am Neckar would have been won by whichever side gained artillery fire superiority. Waldersee also rejected the use of garrison troops and *Ersatztruppen* as combat units. It was determined that an invasion of south Germany served only to weaken the French main effort in Lorraine.

The intention of the 1885 *Generalstabsreise Ost* was to show that the eastern front could be defended with four corps and three reserve divisions, which was a radical departure from Moltke's planning. This exercise is particularly interesting because the Kriegsarchiv in Munich has a copy of the General and Special Situations and a commentary by a Bavarian officer who participated in the exercise.[66] This is therefore the only surviving *Generalstabsreise Ost* conducted between 1862 and 1894. Schlieffen was Waldersee's assistant exercise director. In the General Situation Germany was allied with Britain. Germany declared war on France and Russia on 1 April. Austria was neutral, but had begun to mobilize. The mass of the German army was sent to the west because France could deploy more quickly than Russia. In the east the Germans exploited their faster deployment by launching a large-scale raid into Poland starting between the 5th and 12th day of mobilization. The Russian units in western Poland withdrew. The Russian force consisted of the 1st Army with seven infantry divisions at Kowno and the 2nd Army with 13 infantry divisions at Warsaw. The Bavarian officer, Captain Meyer, said that according to Bavarian sources the entire Russian army consisted on paper of 48 infantry divisions and 24 reserve divisions. Meyer noted dryly that the number of these divisions that were operational at any given time was an interesting question. Waldersee said that the Russian 2nd Army should be able to assemble at Warsaw, but if it could not, it would withdraw to Brest-Litovsk. This is an important point. Delbrück, Ritter, and the rest contended that the *Ostaufmarsch* would succeed because the Russians would defend in Poland and not withdraw to the interior of Russia. In 1885 Waldersee clearly did not believe that to be true. By the 28th day of mobilization the Russians had begun their offensive and the Germans withdrew along the north bank of the Vistula, thoroughly wrecking the railroads in Russian Poland as they went. Bad weather between 25 April and 15 May severely restricted operations.

The mission of the German forces was to prevent the Russians from entering the German core provinces. East Prussia could not be

---

[66] Bayerisches Kriegsarchiv, *Generalstabsreise 1885*, Generalstab 1233.

defended. Waldersee declared a *levée en masse* in eastern Germany: he gave the German commander the authority to use all the men in eastern Germany (East and West Prussia, Pomerania, Posen, and Silesia) who were of military age. The Commander-in-Chief East was also made Governor General of these provinces. The Landsturm had been called up and the population of East Prussia was conducting guerrilla warfare against the invaders. The German forces crossed to the west bank of the Vistula at Fortress Thorn and took up a position behind the lakes to the south of Thorn by 10 June—the 71st day of mobilization. If the Russians wanted to advance on Berlin, they would have to attack this strong position. If defeated, the Germans would fall back to a second position immediately to the rear. Captain Meyer made the exceptionally perceptive observation that the General Staff apparently intended to make large-scale use of rail mobility to surprise the enemy. The Russian advance on the German position took place from 10 to 12 June without a decisive result. At that point word arrived from Lorraine that the Germans had won a great victory. The exercise was then terminated. Moltke's peevish comment was that no matter how much they maneuvered, four German corps could never cover Berlin against 10 Russian corps. The *Generalstabsreise* also pointed out once again the inadequacy of the East Prussian rail net, which possessed only one double-tracked line. It was concluded that three double-tracked lines were necessary. The exercise also served to highlight the importance of Thorn in eastern defense.

Waldersee's 1885 *Generalstabsreise Ost* was the first exercise that we can identify as a free-play strategic war game. It marks a decisive improvement in strategic planning. To this time, planning had been Napoleonic: the Chief of Staff decided on a course of action and his staff executed it. There was never an independent test of the Chief of Staff's decision. Henceforth plans would be determined on the basis of intensive wargaming. In executing the plan during the opposing force wargame, unforeseen problems and possibilities became apparent. Stereotyped solutions were doomed—there were too many bright young staff officers participating who were uninterested in doing their opponents any favors and were eager to make a reputation for themselves by offering a better solution.

As a vehicle for training staff officers, Waldersee's 1885 *Generalstabsreise Ost* overflowed with innovations and was several orders of magnitude better than Moltke's. Moltke rarely played an important real-world situation, whereas in the 1885 exercise forces drawn from a prospective German war plan maneuvered against the enemy on the terrain they were expected to actually fight over. Instead of independent divisions or corps, as in Moltke's exercises, Waldersee maneuvered armies. In Moltke's exercises the size and location of all the friendly and opposing units was known. In the 1885 exercise the intelligence provided to the players was frustratingly realistic: the fog of war descended on the war game, and the players frequently had little idea of the enemy situation.

The 1885 *Generalstabsreise* went far to kill the *Ostaufmarsch*. It showed that, given East Prussia's poor railway net, the German forces now had little chance of overrunning the Russians in their assembly areas, and the Russians could simply disappear into the interior of their vast land mass. On the other hand, this exercise clearly demonstrated the truth of what Kirchhammer and Graham had written in 1879: the terrain and poor communications in eastern Germany could be used as an effective force multiplier for the defense. The period of bad weather between 25 April and 15 May was also a sobering reminder of the power of General Mud in eastern Europe. Last and not least, the recognition began to dawn that the rail system could be used not just for deployment, but in operations. The invader, moving at the rate of a marching man, could be confronted with defending forces moved by rail to appear in very unwelcome places. Schlieffen would expand this concept until it became the *Leitmotiv* of his operational doctrine.

In the 1886 *Generalstabsreise* Waldersee refined the 1885 exercise. The General Situation was the same: Britain and Germany versus Russia and France. Russia had been secretly mobilizing for a considerable period and had begun her deployment. It was therefore pointless for the Germans to attack. On the other hand, the German player was instructed not to surrender German territory without good cause. He was to prevent the Russians from marching on Berlin while at the same time preserving his force: a difficult mission indeed.

The Russian player was given a total of 10 corps and told that the Germans had apparently decided to commit their main force in the west. In the east it appeared that the Germans had deployed only five or six divisions. The Russian commander's mission was to take Berlin. He decided to be bold. The 1st Russian Army would occupy East Prussia while the 2nd moved on Berlin along the south bank of the Vistula.

The most important factor in this exercise was not forces, but time. The Russians began mobilizing on 10 July and commenced their forward movement on 30 July. The lead elements of the Russian offensive reached the Prussian border near Thorn on 9 August, the 29th day of mobilization. Waldersee said that the Russian reserve divisions would not be combat-ready and deployed until 20 August. The Germans won the battle in the west on 5 August and by 12 August moved three corps, two reserve divisions, and two cavalry divisions to Breslau. This was a nice touch, clearly illustrating the strategic power of rail mobility. From

Breslau the Germans had the Russian left flank and lines of communication with Warsaw at their mercy.[67]

Sometime after the Great War, *Archivrat* Greiner in the Reichsarchiv was given the mission to write a study on the following topic: 'What intelligence information did the German General Staff possess concerning the French mobilization and deployment in the period 1885–1914? What was the German enemy estimate? What were the actual French plans?' The result was a 157-page paper evaluating the German intelligence estimate in the west, perhaps the most remarkable intelligence document of the pre-war period.[68]

The fact that Greiner was directed to begin in 1885 is further proof that prior to that time the Germans did not consider the French to be a serious threat. Greiner begins his story with a bang: in 1885 the Germans had an agent in place, an official of the French eastern rail system in Paris who had access to the French mobilization and deployment plans. He delivered the French 1885/6 plans to the Germans in the spring of 1885. The Germans decided that the information he provided was completely reliable. The Germans had already obtained, in August 1884, the French covering force's order of battle and deployment plan, which they were able to update for the French 1885/6 plan.

On the basis of this treasure trove of information, the chief of the 3rd Department, Colonel Schlieffen, wrote his intelligence estimate. Schlieffen said that the French had available 18 corps and the Marine Division, 37 active army divisions in all, plus 17 reserve divisions, for a grand total of 54 divisions. The XIX Corps in Algeria and the division in Tunis were fixed in place. This came to a total of 714 infantry battalions, 303 squadrons of cavalry, and 419 batteries of artillery, including territorial units:[69] 1,033,086 men and 2,514 guns in all. The French would deploy 16 corps and 12 reserve divisions against Germany, two corps (XIV and XV) and two reserve divisions against Italy, and three reserve divisions against Spain. The deployment would be, from south to north: 1st Army (four corps) at Epinal–Charmes; 2nd Army (four corps) in reserve at Neufchâteau; 3rd Army (four corps) behind Toul; 4th Army (four corps) behind Verdun. These armies would complete

---

[67] After all this innovation, the 1887 *Generalstabsreise* is a disappointment: the exercise replayed the 1870 campaign. Schlieffen was the German commander.

[68] Greiner, 'Welche Nachrichten besaß der deutsche Generalstab über Mobilmachung und Aufmarsch des französischen Heeres in den Jahren 1885–1914? . . .', BA-MA W10/50267, 2–25.

[69] 168 territorial infantry battalions, 37 squadrons, 12 batteries.

their deployment by the 15th day of mobilization. Three groups of four reserve divisions each were deployed to the rear: 5th Army behind Belfort, 6th Army behind 2nd Army, 7th Army on the left rear at Vitry le François. They would complete their deployment by the 18th day. Greiner says that this information corresponds with that given by Marchand in his history of the French deployment, *Plans de concentration de 1871 à 1914*, except that Marchand said that the active army units would be ready by the 11th day of mobilization, that is, 3–4 days earlier than the Germans estimated, while the reserve divisions would not be ready until the 19th day, a day later than the Germans expected.

Schlieffen said that the strength of the French right was remarkable. In the 50-kilometer section of front between Epinal and Pont St Vincent the French had concentrated two armies (1st and 2nd), two groups of reserve divisions (5th and 6th Armies), and part of the 3rd Army, while in the 90 kilometers between Frouard and the Belgian border there was only the 4th Army. The rest of the 3rd Army and the 7th Army could be regarded as reserves for the wings. The French intent was clearly to defend the 'Trouée de Charmes'. The only offensive action that the French were expected to take was a raid by the 2nd Cavalry Division on the 1st day of mobilization. At the same time, wrote Schlieffen, the French had taken precautions against a German advance through Belgium. The left flank had been pulled far to the west to avoid the German attack and the French had concentrated most of their cavalry there.

1886: WALDERSEE RECOMMENDS THE *WESTAUFMARSCH*

Due to Schlieffen's new estimate, obliquely mentioned by Waldersee, the Germans could base their plan on hard data and not assumptions or opinions. Waldersee could now prove that the Germans would be faced in the west with nearly a 2 : 1 enemy numerical superiority.[70] In 1886, almost surely as a consequence of the new 1885 west-front intelligence estimate and the results of his 1885 *Generalstabsreise Ost*, Waldersee proposed that in case of a two-front war Germany should make her main effort in the west.[71] In doing so, Waldersee was only falling in line with what by then was the general opinion held in European military circles. In the current political situation, Waldersee maintained that simultaneous French and Russian mobilizations were unlikely. If the French decided for war, the Russians would probably hesitate before they did the same. Waldersee said that a victory in the west would be the

[70] Mohs, *Waldersee*, ii. 270.
[71] Schmerfeld, *Aufmarschpläne 1871–1890*, 120–2; Mohs, *Waldersee*, ii. 288–2.

best guarantor of security in the east and that being as strong as possible in the west was the best way to insure victory there. Operations in the west could begin on the 14th day of mobilization. The French would probably attack immediately and the decisive battle would be fought by the third week, before the threat in the east would have become acute.

Waldersee was stating the obvious: that France and Russia were not formally allies. It was up to the German political leadership, not the General Staff, to establish the degree of danger the Russians posed. In 1887 Herbert Bismarck would present a similar opinion. Referring to the Reinsurance Treaty, Herbert Bismarck said that 'It puts some pressure on the tsar and should, if matters become serious, keep the Russians off our necks six to eight weeks longer than would otherwise be the case. That is worth something.'[72] This is one of the first indications that the Foreign Office and the General Staff might be arriving at similar conclusions concerning the war plan.[73]

Waldersee said that the Germans should leave a minimum of forces in the east: four corps and three reserve divisions. These would not deploy but they would—so as not to antagonize the Russians—remain in their mobilization stations. If the Russians had not acted by the 14th day of mobilization, then these forces would be sent west, and would arrive in Lorraine by the 20th day of mobilization. Waldersee was proposing nothing more than the resumption of the war plan that Moltke himself had used in 1870.

If the Russians did mobilize, then the eastern army would deploy I Corps and 3rd Reserve Division to Insterburg. The remaining three corps and one reserve division would assemble at Thorn-Soldau, with a reserve division in Silesia.

Even if the Russians and French mobilized simultaneously, Waldersee did not want to split the German army in half, as Moltke planned. Waldersee would initially deploy 9 corps in the west and 7 in the east. He proposed to retain the Guard corps, its two reserve divisions, and the IX Corps in their mobilization stations. If the French launched an early attack, Waldersee wanted to send these forces to Lorraine. Their movement would take 10 days at the most, and an attack by an additional 100,000–120,000 men in Lorraine could be decisive. The likely final deployment was therefore 11 corps in the west, 7 in the east.

In 1886, Waldersee, Moltke's designated successor, using wargames

---

[72] Pflanze, *Bismarck*, iii. 251.

[73] Kessel acknowledges that while Moltke had virtually no contact with the foreign office, Waldersee was concerned with keeping the lines of communication with the Foreign Office open (*Moltke*, 705). Indeed, at their meeting in 1882, Moltke told Beck that 'his position was such that he was not dependent on the Foreign Office', (ibid. 707).

and intelligence information, had proven that Moltke's *Ostaufmarsch* was unworkable. He proposed to replace it with a *Westaufmarsch* that, given the political situation, had much to recommend it. In 1887 a radical deterioration in the German strategic position would force even Moltke himself to abandon the *Ostaufmarsch*.

Moltke had obviously not even convinced his most senior subordinates of the wisdom of the *Ostaufmarsch*. Waldersee was thirty-two years younger than Moltke and free of Moltke's romantic *Großdeutsch* sentiments. He was also only a year older than Schlieffen, and together they formed the spearhead of the new, intensely professional generation of General Staff officers. For the new men the war plan was a question of rational military calculation and not *Nibelungentreue*.

CHAPTER THREE

Fortresses, spies, and crisis, 1886–1890

FORTRESSES AND WAR PLANNING

Fortresses in general, and the Rhine fortresses Mainz, Coblenz, Cologne, and Wesel in particular, were vitally important to Moltke's war plans in the west. These fortresses would serve as bridgeheads on the left bank of the Rhine and formed essential supports for Moltke's Rhine *Flankenstellungen*. Moltke estimated that the French would also decisively weaken their field army to blockade or attack Metz and Strasbourg. After 1875 the French began constructing their own frontier fortresses, which then also assumed a very large role in German planning. All histories of strategy prior to the Great War assume that the fortresses on both sides were capable of fulfilling their assigned roles. In fact, that was not the case, and the rapid changes in European fortifications and artillery had profound effects on Moltke's war plans.

At the Treaty of Vienna in 1815 Prussia gained considerable territory on the Rhine. Since France was still felt to be a potentially revolutionary and aggressive power, fortifying key points in the new provinces was absolutely necessary. At Cologne a new series of fortifications, built according to the 'New Prussian system', were added to the medieval city wall by 1843. This consisted of 11 detached forts about 500 meters in front of the old enceinte.[1] At Coblenz a fortress system—Feste Kaiser Alexander—was built just outside the medieval wall on the south side of the Moselle, in the angle between the Moselle and the Rhine, while Feste Kaiser Franz was added north of the Moselle.[2] The intent of these detached forts was to keep the artillery battle away from the medieval wall. As long as this wall was not breached, the town was still capable of defending itself against infantry assault—in siege terminology it was still *Sturmfrei*.

Mainz was a *Bundesfestung*—a Federal Fortress. The core of the

---

[1] H. Bernhardt, *Geschichte der Stadt, Festung und Garnison Köln* (Cologne and Frankfurt am Main, 1959), 37.

[2] H. Neumann, *Die Klassische Großfestung Koblenz* (Koblenz, 1989).

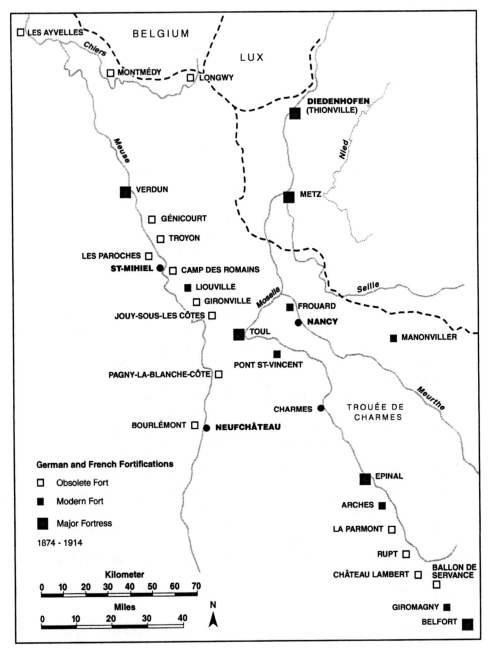

MAP 4. French and German Fortifications

fortress to 1862 still consisted of the 17th and 18th century bastions, counter-guards and ravelins, somewhat modernized against infantry attack after 1815. Between 1862 and 1866 two detached forts were built at Bingen and Gonsenheim. Despite the immense importance that Moltke assigned to Mainz as both his irreplaceable bridgehead on the west bank of the Rhine and the anchor for his Main river *Flankenstellung*, Mainz was weakly fortified. In Moltke's time Mainz possessed one permanent road bridge as well as a rail bridge that was probably unusable during hostilities. Mainz's suitability as a bridgehead was therefore questionable. Passing an army across one bridge, through a medieval city, and past the early modern fortifications would have been no easier at Mainz than it had been at Metz in 1870. Mainz also lies in a bowl in the Rhine valley: to the west the town was dominated by high ground. Enemy forces here could have made deploying Prussian forces from the town a dangerous undertaking.

REFORTIFICATION OF EUROPE AFTER 1871

Immediately on the conclusion of peace in 1871 the Germans began a complete re-evaluation of their fortress system.[3] According to the *Allgemeine Kabinetts-Ordre* of 24 June 1872 seven forts in the west were supposed to be able to withstand a formal siege against the new rifled artillery: Wesel, Cologne, Coblenz, Mainz, Metz, Strasbourg, and Rastatt. In 1872, none of these places could meet this criteria. The siege of Strasbourg in 1870 had demonstrated that only fully modern fortresses with forts far forward of the enceinte could withstand a modern siege. Even the detached works of the 'New Prussian system' were too close to the enceinte. Owing to the immense cost of the new fortress systems, only three forts in the west could actually be modernized. Metz was the first priority, and indeed the work on Metz stopped only in 1915.[4] Between 1872 and 1881 ten forts were built 3 kilometers apart and from 2 to 4 kilometers beyond the enceinte. These were generally polygonal in form, perhaps 300 meters long, and built of masonry. They consisted of underground shellproof rooms and a fighting platform that looked like the upper gun deck of a masted man-of-war. These guns had no overhead cover. The forts were intended to serve as the basis for the artillery duel with the attacking batteries. When the enemy attack sector was identified, the artillery in the forts

[3] Großer Generalstab, Ingenieur-Komitee Abteilung 4, 'Die Entwicklung des deutschen Festungssystems seit 1870', Geheim! n.d.[last update 1914?] Kriegsarchiv Munich, Kriegsministerium 4605/2, 5, 9–10, 82–3.
[4] R. Rolf, *Die deutsche Panzerfortifikation: Die Panzerfeste von Metz und ihre Vorgeschichte* (Osnabrück, 1991), 105–8.

would be reinforced by guns from the mobile fortress reserve and perhaps by infantry from the fortress main reserve (*Hauptreserve*).The forts therefore had a very high profile—up to 9 meters high—and were visible from a great distance. The traverses established on German fortresses to prevent enfilade fire were visible from even greater distances. Between 1872 and 1877 Strasbourg was similarly refortified with 9 forts on the west side of the Rhine (two more were added between 1877 and 1882). The Strasbourg forts were located up to 5,500 meters from the enceinte: the new belt of fortresses (*Festungsgürtel*) was 53 kilometers long. In 1873 the refortification of Cologne began with 12 major forts and 22 intermediate works, with a *Festungsgürtel* 40 kilometers long. The rest of the fortresses, including Mainz and Coblenz, remained essentially in their pre-1866 condition. In the east, Königsberg and Posen were refortified by 1883 and Thorn by 1885.

In 1874 the French Chambers approved the initial credits for the construction of Séré de Rivières famous system of fortifications.[5] It would consist of four great fortress complexes: Verdun, Toul, Epinal, and Belfort. The spaces between Verdun and Toul and between Epinal and Belfort were connected by isolated *forts d'arrêt et de rideaux* (*Sperrforts* to the Germans). The area to the north of Verdun was unfortified, as was the space between Toul and Epinal—the 'Trouée de Charmes'. The concept and construction of the French forts were similar to those of the Germans', and the French forts too had very high profiles. Séré de Rivières fortification system was fully integrated into the French defense plan, acting to cover the French deployment close to the border, then blunt and canalize the German attack and provide the basis for the French counterattack. The entire system was not compete until the mid-1880s.

In 1881 the French conducted a siege exercise against Verdun.[6] This was surely a mix of map exercise and staff ride—it is unlikely that troops were involved. The siege army was six divisions strong. The French employed two reinforced siege trains: 460 guns in 16 heavy artillery battalions, with three pioneer battalions and a large equipment park. The attack was directed against two of Verdun's detached forts, which held out for three months. It took another month to breach the city wall. Some 450,000 rounds of artillery were expended. These figures seem to agree with the sort of effort that Moltke believed would be required to take Metz.[7]

[5] S. Gaber, *La Lorraine fortifiée* (Metz, 1994).

[6] H. von Müller, *Geschichte des Festungskrieges von 1885–1905* (Berlin, 1907), 13.

[7] From 1880 real progress had been made in the use of mortar fire, which became much more effective than the demolition fire of 1870. Bolder spirits were also advocat-

HIGH EXPLOSIVES

The French and German refortification programs were complete by 1883. By 1886 all of the newly finished fortresses were obsolete. From 1884 to 1887 German artillerists conducted firing tests using shells filled with high-explosive against so-called 'target forts'.[8] The French conducted similar tests at Malmaison. The effects of high explosive rounds against permanent fortifications were terrific. Heavy mortar shells were capable of penetrating 4–5 meters of sand or 6–7 meters of loam or clay, then collapsing the shellproof rooms of the fortress, which included the barracks and ammunition magazines. They destroyed the exterior walls and filled in the ditches which insured the *Sturmfreiheit* (invulnerability to infantry assault) of the fortresses, demolished the breastworks and traverses, collapsed the entrances to the underground spaces, destroyed the guns and topside cover to such a degree that the upper works—which were the main fighting platform of the forts— were quickly rendered indefensible. In 1886 the German artillerist, Major Scheibert, declared that permanent fortifications were dead. Only field fortifications could be used in the age of the high-explosive shell.

The reaction among the German fortress authorities bordered on panic. As a result of further firing tests at Kummersdorf, the Inspector of Fortresses ordered an emergency building program late in 1886.[9] Owing to lack of money, only six fortresses could be protected against high explosive shells: Strasbourg, Metz, and Cologne in the west, Königsberg, Thorn, and Posen in the east. The initial re-inforcement consisted of removing the earth over the underground rooms and adding to the roof a layer of concrete about 1 meter thick. The work would commence with those detached forts on the most likely avenues of approach. In the end, the Germans decided to virtually abandon the masonry forts and build smaller infantry bunkers and artillery positions out of concrete in the intervals between the older works. It could safely be assumed that fortresses such as Mainz and Coblenz, which were already obsolete in 1870, were now death traps with a life expectancy under fire to be measured in hours.

---

ing the *Abgekürzte* or *Gewaltsame Angriff* which emphasized hurricane bombardments with field artillery to suppress the forts and the troops defending in the intervals. This would allow the assaulting infantry to penetrate between the forts and into the interior of the fortress.

[8] Ibid. 1–17.

[9] K.b. Mitglied der kaiserlichen Reichs Rayon Kommission, Berlin 11 März 1887 No 4985, Betreff: *Information in ingenieur-Dienstlichen Angelegenheiten: hier Umbau der Festungen; Beilage zum Kriegsministerialreskript vom 26 April 1887 No 5076*, Kriegsarchiv Munich 4581.

In fact, the German fortress system in the west was now reduced to two fortress complexes: Metz–Diedenhofen and Fortress Kaiser Wilhelm II at Mutzig west of Strasbourg. These fortresses were eventually provided with the sole means of defense against modern siege artillery: 'armored' works built out of reinforced concrete and steel. The decision to build these armored fortresses was not taken lightly, for they were very expensive. Fortress Kaiser Wilhelm II (KW II) was not begun until 1893, and five new armored works for Metz were begun only late in 1899. Therefore, from 1887 to the early 1900s none of the German fortresses in the west would have been of much assistance to the German defense. The rest of the fortresses in the west and east were largely left unmodernized. These included the forts essential for Moltke's plan to defend the Rhine: Mainz, Coblenz, and Cologne.

Mainz remained in the condition it had been in after the last building phase in 1862–6.[10] By 1890 the only improvements that had been made were that ammunition dumps and quarters for the garrison had been reinforced against high explosive shells. Repeated resolutions to make Mainz into a modern fortress were never carried out.

Coblenz remained essentially a pre-1860 'New Prussian system' fortress.[11] After the introduction of high explosives, the only improvement made was the reinforcement of the forward ammunition bunkers. Fortress Kaiser Franz on the north side of the Moselle was demilitarized in March 1890 and the remaining forts in January 1903.

In Cologne the existing installations were reinforced almost immediately and the work was completed by 1892.[12] At the same time, infantry and munitions bunkers were built in the intervals between the forts. The fact that Cologne was reinforced and Mainz was not is a strong indicator that the Germans actually rated the threat of a French attack through Belgium higher than the possibility that they would ever have to defend the middle Rhine.

High explosive had the same effect on the French fortifications. Séré de Rivières brand-new fortress line was immediately obsolete. Like the Germans, the French were not able to reinforce the entire line, but only the most important parts. This meant Verdun, Toul, Epinal, and Belfort. Only 6 of the 21 *Sperrforts* could be modernized.[13] Only one of these was located to the north of Toul. A German breakthrough

---

[10] 'Entstehung des deutschen Festungssystems', 344–53; G. Fischer, *Die Festung Mainz 1866–1921* (Düsseldorf, 1970).

[11] 'Entstehung des deutschen Festungssystems', 248.

[12] Ibid. 252.

[13] Gaber, *Lorraine fortifiée*, 14. These were Liouville halfway between Verdun and Toul, Frouard and Pont-St.-Vincent to the east of Toul, Manonviller, Arches to the south of Epinal, and Giromagny to the north of Belfort.

between Toul and Verdun was now practicable. The surviving intelligence documents show that the Germans were well informed about the state of the French fortresses. After 1887 the Germans did not rate the *Sperrforts* between Toul and Verdun very highly.[14] A German analysis noted that the forts provided fine targets and that they were not reinforced against high explosive shells. German intelligence estimates stated that the *Sperrforts* were hardly capable of resisting for more than a few days. Waldersee made a similar observation as early as 1889.[15]

BOULANGER AND BULGARIA

The collapse of the German fortress system could not have come at a less auspicious time. In October 1885 General Georges Boulanger entered the French government as Minister of War in the cabinet of Charles de Freycinet, himself the dynamic minister of war in the republican government of Gambetta in 1870/1. Boulanger proved to be a popular figure, a republican general who embodied the spirit of *revanche*. The cry was taken up by Paul Déroulède, anti-republican poet, publicist, and founder of the League of Patriots. In October 1886 a new journal, *La Revanche*, appeared, adorned with Boulanger's picture on the front page.

At the same time, Russian frustration over loss of influence in the Balkans in general and in Bulgaria in particular was leading to pan-Slavic agitation against Austria and Germany. Tension between Germany and Russia continued to be acute through the last half of 1887, in spite of the signing of the Reinsurance Treaty.

The crisis over Bulgaria and the Straits was at its peak in late 1887 and early 1888; the Boulanger crisis in the last half of 1888 and the first half of 1889. The foreign policy crises were aggravated by the death of Wilhelm I on 9 March 1888 and then the death of his son and heir Friedrich from throat cancer on 15 June 1888. The Emperor was now the 29-year-old Wilhelm II. Wilhelm's youth and inexperience were considered to be serious weaknesses in a military monarchy like Germany.

[14] Großer Generalstab 4. Abteilung April 1909, 'Mittlere Maas-Forts', Kriegsarchiv Munich, III bayerisches Armeekorps, Generalstab 180 Bund 9. Although this report is dated 1909, there is no indication that this was anything more than an update of a previous intelligence estimate and that the state of the *Sperrforts* had been known to German intelligence for a considerable period. Between 1880 and 1885 the German army had a manual titled *Angriffsverfahren gegen Sperrforts* which provided the doctrinal method for attacking French *Sperrforts*. It was last updated in 1885. After that, apparently, no further updating was necessary. Kriegsarchiv Munich, Kriegsministerium 4669.

[15] H. Mohs (ed.), *General-Feldmarschall Alfred Graf Waldersee in seinem militärischen Wirken* (Berlin, 1929), ii. 319.

Prior to 1886 the military threat to Germany was minimal. German success had forced massive military reforms in both France and Russia. Both countries had to introduce conscription and refashion their armies accordingly, construct rail systems to support the mobilization and deployment of the new conscript armies, and create General Staffs. This process did not seriously get under way in either country until 1874. By 1886 the conscript army, rail systems, and the General Staff were fully functional in France. This was not the case in Russia, and although real progress had been made, the construction of the rail system in particular had barely begun.

In 1886 the military situation changed radically to Germany's disadvantage. The French were, for the first time since 1871, ready and able to fight the German army. Given the tension in the east, it was reasonable to expect that Russia would be tempted to intervene in a Franco-German war. Worst of all, Moltke's last two-front war plans in 1880 and 1881 had been based on his estimate that the fortresses of Mainz, Coblenz, and Cologne would permit the Germans to hold the line of the Rhine while Metz and Strasbourg would tie down significant French forces. The development of high explosives reduced these plans to a shambles.

1887: MOLTKE'S *WESTAUFMARSCH*

Almost surely in reaction to the Boulanger crisis and the collapse of the German fortress system, in 1887 Moltke completely rewrote his plan for a one-front war against France.[16] The division of forces in the east and west was practically the same as that proposed by Waldersee in the preceding year: fourteen corps in the west and four in the east, with the eastern corps earmarked for transfer west if the situation allowed. On 5 February 1887 Waldersee wrote in his diary that he had convinced Moltke of the need for adopting his new plan, which could only be called a *Westaufmarsch*.[17] Moltke said that all indications pointed to the French initially standing strictly on the defensive. The French could, however, be expected to conduct raids at the start of mobilization in order to disturb the German deployment. Since the Germans had no reason to attack, at the start of the war the curious situation could occur where both armies stood on the defensive. This condition would not last long. On the one hand, the French had the positive objective—the recovery of Alsace-Lorraine. On the other hand the threat of Russian intervention could force the Germans to take the offensive. Moltke

---

[16] Schmerfeld, *Aufmarschpläne 1871–1890*, 122–8.
[17] Mohs, *Waldersee*, ii, 291.

apparently felt that the French would attempt to delay their offensive until the Russians attacked the Germans in the east. Moltke intended to stand on the defensive for as long as possible and attack only if the situation in the east required it.

Moltke now decided to initially occupy a position from Bolchen (Boulay) to Saarunion. Moltke said this position was 45 kilometers long. This·was a conservative estimate. It was far longer on the ground, by far the longest position Moltke had ever proposed to occupy. It should not be assumed that Moltke proposed to dig in along this line—quite the contrary. He expressly stated that the troops would occupy cantonments to the rear of the line, conduct refresher training, and occupy the position only if necessary. The position would be held by eight corps, with one corps and nine reserve divisions in reserve. Each forward division would therefore hold a position more than 3 kilometers long. The German deployment would be complete by the 17th day of mobilization. Moltke now said that the French deployment should be no faster than the German. The estimate of French strength and deployment was missing from the German files, along with the German order of battle and deployment.

Moltke thought that a French envelopment of his right flank was unlikely. A shallow envelopment would be hindered by Metz and stopped by the position on the Bolchen hill and the Nied. A German counterattack would then push the French into neutral Belgium. A deep envelopment through the Ardennes would bring Belgium and probably Britain into the war against France and would in any case come to a stop on the Rhine. It would be more likely that the French would try a shallow turning movement against the German left. This would be stopped by two corps in battle positions at Hemingen (Heming) south-west of Sarrebourg: Moltke's defensive line was therefore really at least 70 kilometers long. A deep French envelopment would have to cross the Vosges and would be brought to a halt by Fortress Strasbourg and forces in a defensive position on the Breusch to the west of Strasbourg. If the French attacked through the Belfort gap the upper Alsace was initially lost, but the French would gain nothing by crossing the Rhine into Baden. The French would therefore almost surely be forced to attack the German position frontally. The German defense, based on the firepower of the German artillery and magazine-fed rifles, should be able to defeat the French attack, at which point the Germans would counterattack: Moltke's old defensive–offensive strategy again, but with a difference. Moltke had committed so many troops to positional defense that his reserve consisted of a single active corps and nine reserve divisions. This is a far smaller and weaker reserve than in Moltke's previous plans, particularly since the reserve divisions were considered to have virtually no offensive combat power. It would appear likely that Moltke was hoping for the transfer of the eastern army to the western front. In case of defeat the Germans could withdraw through Mainz.

Circumstances in the east could force the Germans to take the offensive in the west. Moltke rejected a German envelopment to the north of Verdun. The German lines of communication would run parallel to the front and the enveloping force could be cut off from Germany. Rail communications were non-existent.

Moltke now also rejected the attack on Lunéville, saying that the terrain was too restrictive. Instead, the German advance would be directed on a narrow front against Nancy alone. Seven corps—half the army in the west—would advance on the city in Moltke's favorite phalanx formation. Four corps in the first line would initially occupy a front of 38 kilometers. This would probably narrow to a 15-kilometer front east of Nancy, where Moltke hoped to find the French. The first-echelon corps would march in a column of infantry divisions, that is, one division behind another. These would be followed by three corps in reserve, also presumably in a column of divisions. Moltke's concept was apparently to hammer the French with successive waves of divisions echelonned in great depth. This is the same concept as that of Moltke's plans between 1867 and 1870, indeed an even deeper deployment than the one he used at Gravelotte–St Privat. Sedan had been forgotten, as had 'marching separately and uniting on the battlefield'.

Waldersee transformed Moltke's plan into a complete *Westaufmarsch*.[18] He said that any troops left in the east would be missed at the decisive battle in the west. Troops left in the east might also excite Russian suspicions. When the Germans mobilized, every diplomatic effort must be taken to convince the Russians that there was no German threat against Russia. On the 11th day of mobilization, if the Russians had made no unfriendly moves, the redeployment of the four eastern corps to the west should begin. Between the 16th and the 20th days of mobilization these forces could arrive in the west and would participate in the decisive battle. If the Russians then assumed a threatening attitude, forces could be sent back east. In the meantime, security against Russian cavalry would be provided by four reserve divisions and the Landwehr.

1887: THE GERMANS EXPECT A FRENCH ATTACK

In the autumn of 1887 the 3rd Department received, handwritten, the march tables for all the units that used the Paris eastern railway. On the

---

[18] Mohs, *Waldersee*, ii, 292–4.

basis of this information Captain Rohr wrote an updated enemy estimate, which unfortunately Greiner could not find in the archives. The German estimate of the French rail deployment itself was in the archives and Greiner took great pains to evaluate it. Greiner said that this deployment agreed completely with the description given by Marchand for Plan VIII. Furthermore, he said that the French official history described the intent of Plan VIII as being purely offensive. In order to facilitate the offensive the French had moved their deployment closer to the border and the attack was scheduled to begin on the 11th day of mobilization. The French also produced a variant of Plan VIII which moved the deployment to the west in case the Germans launched an *attaque brusquée*.

Greiner did not overtax his sources: owing to the absence of Rohr's enemy estimate itself he could not state conclusively that the German army expected a French attack in 1887, but his inference was clear: Greiner believed that the Germans knew late in 1887 that the French had an offensive war plan.

1887: PREVENTIVE WAR AGAINST RUSSIA

In 1887 Moltke and Waldersee also became increasingly concerned at the increase in Russian strength. In November Waldersee predicted that the Russians were going attack in the spring of 1888.[19] Thereupon, Moltke sent an alarming intelligence estimate to Bismarck.[20] He wrote that for the last 14 years Russia had raised an army based on universal conscription and the result was that the Russian army was now a human steamroller. The active army of 824,000 men could be reinforced by 1,600,000 trained reservists—fully mobilized, the Russian army would number 2,424,800 men. The reservists would form 24 reserve divisions—the equivalent of 12 German corps. If one added territorial troops and Cossacks, the total force numbered 3,129,800 men. The infantry was being armed with magazine-fed rifles and the Russian artillery, though less mobile than the German, was more accurate and had a longer range. Training and mobilization were improving. In particular, the Russian rail net was growing. Kowno and Warsaw had received modern fortifications.

Given Moltke's previous east-front war plans, which assumed that the Russians would defend Poland, it is surprising that Waldersee and Moltke now both asserted that they had up to this time assumed that the Russians were incapable of defending Poland and if attacked would

---

[19] Ibid. 299–301.
[20] Schmerfeld, *Aufmarschpläne 1871–1890*, 137–50.

have withdrawn to the interior of the country as they had done in 1812. Owing to Russian reinforcement of the Polish garrison, this was no longer the case. These reinforcements included the XIV Corps and a Cossack division in Lublin in 1878, an infantry division in Vilna and one in Bialystok in 1883, and another cavalry division in Lublin in 1887.

To this point, Moltke's case was not very convincing. The probability that Russia could actually deploy 2½ million men in the field was nil. Moltke did not say how long it would take the Russian army to deploy the forces it actually had, or when the reserve divisions would appear. The Russians had added only four or five infantry divisions in Lithuania and Poland during the preceding ten years, the last having arrived four years previously, which does not appear to be a particularly energetic build-up. Moltke could only point to the recent arrival of a cavalry division in Poland. Moltke attempted to bolster his case by saying he had unconfirmed rumors that the Russians were planning serious troop concentrations near Warsaw. Waldersee and Moltke told Bismarck that the Russians were conducting a secret build-up 'as they had done in previous wars' (presumably Moltke meant 1877/8). Moltke concluded that there was 'no doubt' that the Russians were preparing for war. Moltke told Bismarck that when the Russians had completed their build-up they would attack and defeat Austria. Moltke had clearly been shaken by the Bulgarian crisis. He said that Russia was preparing for war because of pan-Slav agitation and the Russians' frustration over their lack of influence in Bulgaria. The Russians felt that the time was right because the Austrian infantry was poorly armed.

It seems likely that Moltke and Waldersee were also reacting as much or more to Rohr's estimate that the French had adopted an offensive war plan as they were to the threat of a Russian offensive. The possibility of a two-front war now seemed very real.

Behind this was the determining factor in Moltke's estimate, his conviction that it was inevitable that the Slavic east and the Latin west would attack the Teutonic center of Europe. Once again, Moltke was arguing that the only chance for the Austro-Germans was to launch a coordinated attack before the Russians were ready. That attack should begin in the winter of 1887/8. How it was to be conducted was not specified.

Bismarck had no authority to supervise Moltke's peacetime war planning. Until 1883 Moltke was, at least theoretically, subordinate to the War Minister. After 1883 he possessed the *Immediatrecht* and was responsible only to the Emperor. As Helmut Otto noted, Moltke determined the war plan entirely on his own.[21] Now that there was a serious danger

---

[21] H. Otto, 'Militärische Aspekte der Außenpolitik Bismarcks (1871–1890)', *ZMG*, Heft 2 (1967), 150–66.

of a two-front war, Bismarck laid down the law to Moltke. He told Moltke about the provisions of the Reinsurance Treaty, signed on 18 June 1887, and said that the *casus foederis* for the Austro-German alliance would occur only when Russia attacked Austria and not before. He said further that war with Russia meant war with France too and in that case he wanted to settle accounts with the French first before moving forces to the east. There would be no preventive war in the east and in case of a two-front war, the German army would conduct a *Westaufmarsch*. Bismarck also told the Austrians gently but in no uncertain manner that the German war plan was for a *Westaufmarsch*.[22] There was no question that the *Ostaufmarsch* was now both militarily and politically dead.

Gerhard Ritter believed that Moltke's fundamental political ideas were sound: after all, Moltke's war plans after 1871 were supposed to be based on Ritter's twin concepts of *Ermattungsstrategie* and negotiated peace. However, Ritter found the details of Moltke's planning were frequently disquieting, particularly Moltke's desire for an east-front offensive, which clearly ran counter to Bismarck's policies. Ritter squared this circle by maintaining that Moltke did not hold these views very strongly, that they were 'hypothetical, based on broad historical generalization, meant to envisage certain contingencies in an experimental way'.[23] Later historians were not so careful. In discussing Moltke's January 1880 war plan, Gordon Craig wrote that

What can be said with some assurance, however, is that Moltke's plans reveal not only the most careful consideration of the technical aspects of Germany's military position but also awareness of the political factors involved in war—the internal conditions of the countries opposed to Germany and the role of diplomacy in destroying the enemy coalition. Moltke possessed real political insight and in addition he had ... no hesitation in keeping the Chancellor informed concerning his operational plans.[24]

This is pure hagiography. As we have seen, Moltke formed his political ideas and war plans from geopolitics, Great German nationalism, and his own Darwinian conception of history.[25] Needless to say, all of these ideas were utterly foreign to Bismarck.

---

[22] E. Heller, 'Bismarck's Stellung zur Führung des Zweifronten-Krieges', *APG* 1926 Heft 12, 677–97.

[23] G. Ritter, *The Sword and the Scepter* (Miami, 1969), i. 229.

[24] G. Craig, *The Politics of the Prussian Army* (Oxford, 1964), 276.

[25] R. Peschke, 'Moltke als Politiker', *PJ* 158 (Oktober bis Dezember 1914), 16–35. Peschke's conclusion is similar.

GERMAN ENEMY ESTIMATE IN THE WEST, 1888–1890

In 1888 the German agent again supplied the 3rd Department with all the rail march tables for units that would use the Paris eastern rail line.[26] On the basis of these and the previous French plans, the 3rd Department produced its estimate of the French 1888/89 deployment. Greiner said that the German estimate corresponded to the new French Plan IX and that the German estimate of French intentions was identical to that given by Marchand. This was essentially the same as the variant to Plan VIII which would have been employed in case of the German *attaque brusquée*. The French also added four reserve divisions to the eastern army, including both of those from the Spanish front.

Greiner said that the French had found Plan VIII to be too daring. The left wing had been brought too far forward. The rail net was over-committed: two lines were required to transport three corps each at an unrealistically high rate of 54 to 58 trains a day. In addition, the French could not insure the security of the eastern parts of the rail net. The expected completion of the deployment was now pushed back a day and all the active corps but one or two were allotted their own rail line. The German army would therefore have been aware that the threat in the west had been reduced.

Although the French sources do not specifically mention it, the French also obviously were concerned about a German attack though Luxembourg and southern Belgium. The French deployed two cavalry divisions to the east of Verdun, extended the left wing of the 4th Army to Challerange, and deployed a group of reserve divisions by Reims. The French had also pulled their troops out of the Vosges and built a central reserve of reserve divisions, which they probably intended to deploy in the north. Greiner noted that in Plan IX the French moved the left wing back to the west to provide a buffer against the German right wing attack through the Ardennes.

In 1889 the German agent again supplied extensive information on the French deployment, including printed copies of the rail march tables for the covering force, detailed information on the deployment of all the corps using the Paris eastern rail line, and a warning that the active corps were to be followed by a corps *bis* (a second corps with the same number—e.g. III*bis*—composed of reserve formations). The agent received 6,000 francs for his pains. On the basis of this information, plus loquacious discussions in the French press ('sehr offen-

---

[26] Greiner, 'Welche Nachrichten besass der deutsche Generalstab über Mobilmachung und Aufmarsch französischen Heeres in den Jahren 1885–1914? . . .', BA–MA W10/50267, 2–25.

herziger Auslassungen') and the peacetime deployment of the French army, the 3rd Department arrived at their French enemy estimate in October 1889. Greiner was not able to confirm this plan from Marchand, who did not give any deployment times in his description of Plan X.

1888: *WESTAUFMARSCH*

In February 1888 Moltke wrote his last plan for a two-front war.[27] As far as the German army was concerned, this was a *Westaufmarsch*. Moltke was now forced to commit the mass of the German army—11 corps—in the west. Only 7 corps—351,000 men—could be deployed in the east. In spite of the fact that Bismarck had notified Moltke of the conditions of the Reinsurance Treaty, Moltke continued to plan for the principal offensive effort of the Austro-German alliance to be made in the east. The Austro-German offensive would now be spearheaded by 584,000 Austrians. This is rather surprising, considering that Moltke had acknowledged just two months before that the Austrian infantry weapon was inadequate. The plan was concerned almost solely with operations in the east: the west front was hardly mentioned. Moltke said that 935,000 Austro-Germans would be opposed by 757,000 Russians. One is left to wonder what happened to the Russian steamroller. Moltke said that the Russian deployment would take no less than five to six weeks. The Russians could then be expected to conduct a full-scale offensive either against Germany or Austria. The Austrians would complete their deployment only by the 28th day of mobilization: the Austrian deployment was only marginally faster than the Russian.[28] Even the German deployment to the east was not particularly impressive. Only one corps could be deployed to eastern East Prussia to join I Corps. The other five would have to detrain near the Vistula, on a 225-kilometer arc from Thorn to Ortelsburg.

Given time, the Russians could mass 418,000 troops in the western Ukraine. The Austrians would therefore have to attack first in this direction in order to secure their right flank. The Germans would advance east and arrive on the Orchys (Orzyc) river to the north of Warsaw by the 5th week. Since the Polish roads were miserable and the countryside impoverished or swampy, the Prussian corps would march 15–22 kilometers apart, keeping as close to the Prussian border as possible in

---

[27] Schmerfeld, *Aufmarschpläne 1871–1890*, 150–3.
[28] In Dec. 1887 the Austrians had told the Germans that they would be able to attack with 37 divisions (28 line, 9 Landwehr) from Cracow on the 12th day of mobilization—almost surely an over-optimistic estimate. Mohs, *Waldersee* ii. 302–5.

order to insure resupply. By the 5th week the Austrians should have reached Lublin. The Russian lines of communication would then be threatened from both sides and Moltke said that the Russians would be forced to advance from behind their Vistula–Bug river lines to attack the Germans or Austrians. Here Moltke's concept of the operation ends. By the 5th week the Russians would be near to completing their initial concentration. The Russians would have the initiative and would occupy a central position between the Austrian and German armies, which would have been about 200 kilometers apart. To advance any further, the Germans would have to cross the Narew.

In the February 1888 *Denkschrift* Moltke complained about the low capacity of the East Prussian rail lines. In a note written on 30 March 1890 Moltke said that the concentric Austro-German attack could be very successful—if the Germans could move their deployment assembly area about 200 kilometers to the east, so that the right flank was at Ortelsburg and not to the south of Thorn.[29] At a minimum, this required improving the Thorn–Allenstein rail line. Under these circumstances, it is hardly surprising that Moltke spent the last half of the February 1888 *Denkschrift* trying to figure out how to defend East Prussia.

In contrast to Moltke's previous assertions that Germany's eastern border was indefensible, Moltke now acknowledged that the problem was hardly as bad as he had once made it appear, even in the improbable event that the Russians made their main attack against East Prussia. The Russians were unlikely to advance between the Austro-German pincers to launch an attack on Posen or Silesia. The 6th Reserve Division would provide security for both provinces. The real danger point was East Prussia. Thanks to the rail lines from St. Petersburg and Moscow, the Russians could get to East Prussia as fast as the Germans: the first battle in the east could well be fought in East Prussia.[30]

Therefore, Moltke proposed to arm the Landsturm with locally stored weapons in order to stop Russian cavalry raids and reinforce the field army. This seems to be the first time such a drastic measure was proposed in a war plan. Apparently even Moltke was becoming concerned about German numerical inferiority. Nothing was done to implement this idea, but Schlieffen eagerly adopted it, making the same suggestion in 1893.[31] He then expanded on it to form a major element of his defense policy.

In East Prussia, the German forces occupied a central position between the Russian Niemen and Narew armies. If the Russian Narew

[29] Schmerfeld, *Aufmarschpläne 1871–1890*, 165–6.
[30] Ibid. 151–2.   [31] Ibid. 164–5.

army advanced, Moltke said, the Germans would attack it with all available forces. If, as was more likely, the Narew army stayed on the defensive while the Niemen army advanced, then the Germans would mass
against the Niemen army, 'whose position would become worse the
farther it advanced [into Prussia]'. In March 1888 Moltke stated that
even if both Russian armies advanced simultaneously, the Germans
could concentrate all seven corps on an interior position to mass
against one Russian army or the other.[32]

Therefore, in 1888 Moltke did not develop a war plan for a massive
invasion of Poland, but rather the concept for Tannenberg. The shift to
an east-front strategy based a defensive using interior lines was begun
not by Schlieffen, but by Moltke himself.

Delbrück, Ritter, and their followers maintained that Moltke's 1888
Ostaufmarsch was Germany's *Siegesrezept*, a formula for victory, the perfect
plan that would have assured German victory in 1914 had it only been
implemented. The 1888 plan, they said, provided for a powerful Austro-
German offensive to the east which would clear the Russians out of
Poland. They proved their case by mixing quotes from all of Moltke's
eastern war plans as though they were identical. Statements made in 1871
or 1879–80 are repeated as though they were still valid in 1888. They were
not. Politically, the *Ostaufmarsch* had been vetoed by Bismarck. Militarily,
the 1888 plan was a pale reflection of its predecessors. In 1888 Moltke
could only deploy 7 corps to the east and the German army never strayed
far from East Prussia. In 1888 Moltke made no mention of the Germans
crossing either the Narew or the Vistula, much less of taking Warsaw or
Brest, and the German and Austrian armies never linked up. Instead, the
purpose of any Austro-German offensive was to force the Russians to
come out from behind their river lines and attack. However, Moltke's real
concern was not to conduct an offensive to push the Russians out of
Poland. Rather, he spent most of the 1888 *Denkschriften* trying to decide
how to defend East Prussia against an early Russian double envelopment.

1888: MOLTKE'S LAST *WESTAUFMARSCH*

Moltke's last war plan was the west-front component of his 1888
Westaufmarsch.[33] Moltke's description of the French deployment was
general in the extreme. He said that the French would occupy a 150-
kilometer-long line behind their border fortifications between Epinal

---

[32] Ibid. 154–6. For a time in March 1888 the Germans apparently thought that the
Russians might launch an all-or-nothing offensive and, ignoring the Austrians, Silesia,
and East Prussia, advance directly on Berlin. Mohs, *Waldersee*, ii. 309.

[33] Schmerfeld, *Aufmarschpläne 1871–1890*, 156–62.

and Verdun, with the 1st and 2nd Armies on the right behind the upper Moselle and the 3rd and 4th on the left behind the Meuse. The French would enjoy a numerical superiority of almost 50,000 men—561,000 French infantry and 3,072 pieces of artillery against 514,000 German infantry, and 2,280 guns. Nevertheless, the French deployment showed that the French intended initially to conduct a strategic defensive operation. However, the French still had the positive political goal and would eventually switch to the strategic offensive.

Moltke intended initially to deploy eleven corps in the west. If Russia was not a belligerent, then forces would be shifted from the east, but the basic plan would continue to be in effect. Moltke's description of the German deployment was also fragmentary. By the 15th day the Germans would be able to defend in place with 376 battalions, by the 17th day the deployment would be complete (440 battalions, probably 11 corps and 14 reserve divisions, 36 divisions in total). The Germans could then assume the offensive. To the very end, Moltke continued to fiddle with his defensive position in Lorraine. The German army would now deploy into a line of cantonments 90 kilometers long in the vicinity of the Saar. On a line 50 kilometers long from Bolchen to Finstingen (Fénétrange) seven corps would occupy the front line and, for the first time, dig field fortifications. Seven reserve divisions would constitute the army reserve. The concept of the defense was little changed from the previous plan. He still considered an envelopment of the German right unlikely. The most probable French course of action was an attack on the German left, which Moltke intended to stop at Saarebourg. A French attack through Alsace would get no further than Strasbourg and the Breusch position. He said that if the six corps that the Italians had promised to send actually appeared, the Germans could think of attacking Belfort, the only point in France that had any value to the Germans. Such vain hopes demonstrate that the German army had run into a strategic dead end.

In May 1888 Moltke wrote his last operational *Denkschrift*, characteristically for his favorite west-front offensive operation, the attack on Nancy.[34] Moltke still said that this attack was the most suitable way to bring on a decisive battle. The main German attack would be made by six corps, covered by two corps on the right and the Guard Corps on the left. It was likely that the French would meet the German offensive halfway. The German main attack would then be delivered by four corps on a 15-kilometer front near Château Salins: Moltke's old phalanx battering-ram was making one last appearance. If the French defended Nancy, the position was a restricted one and could accommodate only

[34] Schmerfeld, *Aufmarschpläne 1871–1890*, 162–5.

three or four corps. The French would be fighting with their backs to the Meurthe and the Germans would attack it from three sides with six corps: the position would be blasted by 120 batteries of German field artillery. Moltke described the attack in detail, advancing from one small wood to another and prescribing the exact procedure for bombarding Ft. Frouard.

GENERALSTABSREISEN IN 1888 AND 1889

The 1888 *Generalstabsreise* was held in eastern East Prussia.[35] The General Situation said that Russia had begun secretly mobilizing on 30 July, whereupon Germany mobilized and declared war on 1 August (again, shades of 1914). The (notional) main armies would oppose each other near Thorn. The mission of the German 1st Army, with two corps, three reserve divisions, and two cavalry divisions, was to defend East Prussia and the left flank of the main army. The mission of the Russian 4th (Niemen) Army, with three corps, a reserve division, and three cavalry divisions, was to invade eastern East Prussia. On the first day of the exercise Waldersee was called back to Berlin to attend the funeral of Kaiser Friedrich. Schlieffen became the exercise director. Moltke requested permission to retire and on 10 August 1888 Waldersee became the Chief of the General Staff.

Waldersee's concept for the exercise was that the Germans would use their faster deployment to launch a spoiling attack towards Kowno. By the time they reached the Niemen the Russians would have assembled enough troops to prevent a German crossing. The Russians would counterattack and by 14 August they would enter German territory. To this point the exercise was probably conducted in Berlin as a map exercise. The *Generalstabsreise* proper could now begin. The Germans would have to withdraw and Fortress Königsberg would become a factor on the Russian right flank. Towards the end of the exercise the Germans would win a battle on the Narew and would be in a position to counterattack to the north with three corps. Whether this counterattack would come to the west of the Masurian Lakes or move to the east using Fortress Lotzen as a bridgehead, would be dictated by circumstances. The last part of the exercise therefore war-gamed a situation similar to that on 9 September 1914 at the First Battle of the Masurian Lakes. One of the participants on the German side in 1888 was a young Major von Benckendorff und von Hindenburg, who in 1914 would be the commander of the German army in East Prussia. (Another was Major Graf von Moltke, who in 1914 would be Chief of the General Staff.)

[35] Mohs, *Waldersee*, ii. 199–204.

Unfortunately, Schlieffen's exercise critique has been lost. Suffice it to say that at the Masurian Lakes in 1914 the Russians lost 125,000 men and the Russian 1st Army, though not destroyed, was rendered completely *hors de combat*. German losses have been estimated as low as 10,000 men.[36]

In the 1889 *Generalstabsreise West* the General Situation was somewhat improbable, but nevertheless had a serious purpose.[37] Germany and Italy were at war with Russia and France. Austria was neutral but mobilizing. The Germans deployed half their army in the east and half in the west. There were five French armies, each comprising four corps and four reserve divisions (except the 3rd Army, which had two corps and two reserve divisions)—18 corps and 18 reserve divisions in total. The 1st Army deployed against Italy. The 2nd Army assembled at Lyon with the mission of moving through Switzerland into south Germany. The 3rd Army would move from Belfort to attack the upper Alsace. The 4th army would concentrate at Lunéville and Nancy, the 5th at Toul and St. Mihiel. The 4th and 5th Armies would attempt to fix the German main body in Lorraine in place while the 2nd and 3rd Armies moved north on both sides of the Rhine.

The list of participants was a formidable one. The French were led by Schlieffen, the Germans by Graf von Haeseler, perhaps the most respected corps commander in the pre-war German army. The Chief of Staff of the Bavarian army also attended. Schlieffen and Haeseler were the commanders of the respective army groups and had control over operations both in Lorraine and on the Main river, as well as in south Germany. There was also an independent commander for the Austrian army. Such a situation could only have been played on a map as a strategic west-front war game—probably the first ever. The tactical part of the *Generalstabsreise* was apparently conducted in the Swabian mountains.

One of the principal purposes of the exercise was clearly to test rail mobility. The Germans withdrew two corps and two reserve divisions from the main body in Lorraine and moved them by rail to Stuttgart, where they formed the 4th Army. The Germans also carried out a massive program of rail demolitions in southern Germany, including the Rhine river bridges, tunnels, and the rail station in Freiburg im Breisgau. All the rolling stock and railroad personnel were evacuated to the north. The German main army in Lorraine, now only six corps and six reserve divisions strong, withdrew to the Palatinate and then crossed to the east bank of the Rhine. The Austrians were preparing to enter

---

[36] V.J. Esposito (ed.) *The West Point Atlas of American Wars 1900–1953* (2 vols., New York 1959), ii. Map 20–1.

[37] Mohs, *Waldersee* ii. 204–19.

the war and the 4th Army was told to be prepared to withdraw down the Danube to join them. The fortresses at Ulm and Ingolstadt were put on a war footing. Ulm and the defense of Munich were given particular attention. The Austrian army and German 4th Army then counterattacked, while at the end of the exercise the main German army was behind the Main river. Waldersee began the exercise critique by noting the paramount importance of the role of mass armies in modern warfare. However, he said that the use of reserve divisions on the front line would be the exception, not the rule. Operationally, the General Staff had to coordinate several large armies. These problems would be further complicated by the fact that the next war would likely be a coalition war.[38]

1888/1889: *WESTAUFMARSCH*

The only mention of a German war plan for the mobilization year 1888/9 was for a *Westaufmarsch*.[39] Since this plan went into effect before Moltke retired, it can be considered Moltke's last war plan, though it was probably actually written by Waldersee. The mass of the German army—fourteen corps—would be deployed in the west. Only the 4th Army (four corps) was to be left in the east. If the Russians had not acted by the 12th day of mobilization, these corps were to be sent to the west also. It was necessary to do everything possible to avoid alarming the Russians. In particular, large bodies of German troops would not be assembled on the eastern border. On the other hand, measures were to be taken to secure the border against Russian cavalry.

In case Russia became a belligerent, the 4th Army would have to defend the east. The best way to conceal the 4th Army's weakness from the Russians, and 'to give courage to the Austrian High Command' was for the 4th Army to use its faster deployment to launch a spoiling attack against the Russians. For this purpose, the 4th Army needed all the cavalry it could get, so a fourth cavalry division was assigned to the east.

1889/1900: *WESTAUFMARSCH*

In November 1889 Waldersee wrote the concept for his 1889/1900 *Westaufmarsch*.[40] He began by saying that the changed political situation required significant changes in the *Aufmarschplan*. Exactly what these political changes were, he did not specify. He may well have meant the impending expiry of the Reinsurance Treaty. (Bismarck resigned on 18

---

[38] The 1890 *Generalstabsreise* was practically a re-enactment of the 1866 campaign.
[39] Ibid. 294–7.   [40] Ibid. 314–17.

March 1890.) He said that now the Russians would intervene almost immediately in a Franco-German war. As a result, the army in the east had to be increased from four corps, four reserve divisions, and four cavalry divisions to five corps, five reserve divisions, and five cavalry divisions. That would leave 13 corps, 11 reserve divisions, and 5 cavalry divisions in the west. Two reserve divisions would protect the northern coasts. The deployment in the east was little changed: I Corps, 1st Reserve Division and 1st Cavalry Division in the east near Gumbinnen, the rest near Thorn, with a reserve division in Silesia.

Waldersee's estimate was that the Russians would conduct their main attack against the Austrians with two armies; one near Lublin–Kowel would consist of five corps, the second in the western Ukraine near Dubno with four corps—19 infantry divisions total. The Austrians would be able to assemble 28 divisions in Galicia. Against Germany, the Russians would be weak: they would deploy two small armies, one with two corps on the Niemen, a second with four corps on the Narew. The balance of forces would therefore be 15 German divisions against 12 Russian. Two Russian corps would be deployed against Romania. Initially, 43 German–Austrian divisions would be opposed by 31 Russian divisions. However, the mass of the Austro-German force would be Austrian and the principal theatre of war was in Galicia and the western Ukraine.

This was just the first wave of Russian troops: 8–12 Russian reserve divisions, three divisions from the Caucasus and the XV Corps would arrive later. It was therefore necessary for the Austro-Germans to attack as soon as possible. In the west, Waldersee said that he felt confident that the Germans were strong enough to defeat the initial French attack and then counterattack.

In April 1889 Waldersee wrote a *Denkschrift* in which he gave his plans for an offensive in the east.[41] Waldersee was already concerned that deteriorating relations between Austria and Serbia would force the Austrians to deploy two corps and several Landwehr divisions in the south. Nevertheless, for the first five to six weeks the Austro-Germans should be numerically superior to the Russians. However, he once again increased the German force in the east, to six corps.

Waldersee said that the I Corps group would cross the border on the 10th day of mobilization and reach the Niemen by the 16th day without meeting serious resistance. By crossing the Niemen and advancing on Grodno this group could attain local victories and break up the Russian concentration.

At the same time, the 4th Army would advance from Thorn and

---

[41] Mohs, *Waldersee* ii. 322–7.

should reach the Narew by the 20th day of mobilization, again without meeting serious resistance. The Germans should then seek to cross the Narew with three corps while two corps masked the Russian Narew fortifications. Having crossed the Narew, Waldersee had to admit that he had no idea what was going to happen next. He did acknowledge that high water might prevent a crossing of the Narew at all.

In February 1890 Waldersee wrote another plan for the east.[42] Waldersee said that the German intent had always been to fight a decisive battle in the east as early as possible, perhaps on the west side of the Narew, at the very latest on the east bank of the Narew–Niemen. The possibility of such a battle taking place had become very unlikely: it appeared that the Russians were now prepared to allow the Germans to cross the Narew and if necessary fall back into the interior of Russia, drawing the Germans after them. The Russians probably would first accept battle in the area of Lomja on the 30th day of mobilization at the earliest. There the Germans would find a carefully prepared Russian position. The Germans would be weakened by detachments to guard their right flank and their lines of communication would be poor.

Waldersee's solution was to move the German deployment to the east to a line Ortelsburg–Johannisburg–Lyck. Moltke said the same thing at roughly the same time. The problem was that the East Prussian rail net would not support such a deployment. The line Thorn–Allenstein needed to be double-tracked and there was no way to complete this work in time for the 1891/92 *Aufmarschplan*. In spite of that, Waldersee proposed to change the *Aufmarschplan* as though the rail lines could support his plan: Waldersee had obviously reached a strategic dead end in the east just as Moltke had in the west. Even under these favorable circumstances, the objective of the offensive was modest. Waldersee did not intend to destroy the Russian army. Rather, his aim was to conduct a spoiling attack while the Russians were still relatively weak. The purpose of this attack was primarily to gain time. The left-flank 5th Army would break up the Russian concentration in Lithuania. The 5th Army could also attack the Russians as they tried to cross the Niemen. Waldersee had less faith in the ability of the German army to carry the attack over the Narew. The success of such an attack was entirely dependent on the weather. It was possible during a hard frost or in the summer; during the wet months, in April, May, June, and November, a crossing was completely impossible. On the other hand, mild winters and wet summers could completely disrupt such calculations. If the Germans were unable to cross the Niemen and Narew, they would have no other choice than waiting until the Russians tried to

---

[42] Ibid. 327–30.

cross. If the war began during a wet-weather period, Waldersee said that the Germans would have to consider weakening the east in favor of the west.[43]

In February 1890 Waldersee also wrote a *Denkschrift* concerning a war in the west. He decided that Moltke's old offensive against Nancy was no longer very promising.[44] Even if the Germans took Nancy, casualties would be heavy and the French fort line would still be unbroken. It would be better to allow the French to attack, which they would have to do if they wanted Alsace-Lorraine back. The German position now reached its maximum extent, the complete Bolchen–Saarebourg line which incorporated both Moltke's and Waldersee's defensive positions. The French would reach this line by the 18th day of mobilization, giving the Germans time to complete their deployment as well as eight days to prepare it for defense. The Germans should contest every inch of Lorraine from the border to the Saar. The French would 'have' to attack the Bolchen–Saar position. The Germans might even be presented with opportunities for full-scale counterattacks. The Germans would then pursue the French for several days back to their fortresses. In case of a one-front war against France alone, Waldersee proposed to use the same plan.

Why the French 'had' to attack the German Bolchen–Saar line is not clear. They would have already overrun most of Alsace and half Lorraine. They could have easily sat down in front of the Saar, reduced Metz and Strasbourg, which were completely obsolete as fortresses, and waited either for the Germans to attempt the relief of the fortresses or for the Russian hordes to appear.

GERMAN ESTIMATES OF RUSSIAN INTENTIONS, 1871–1889

Between 1871 and 1887 the German army would appear to simultaneously have had three mutually exclusive Russian enemy estimates.

Moltke's estimate in his 1871, 1879, and 1880 *Denkschriften* was that the Russians would fight in Poland. Delbrück and Ritter maintained that Moltke was absolutely correct in the 1870s and that his estimate was still valid in 1914. This estimate is the basis of *Ostaufmarsch*: if the Russians withdrew to the east in the face of a German attack, the *Ostaufmarsch* faced serious difficulties.

---

[43] In Dec. 1890 Waldersee wrote a last enemy estimate in the east. It was somewhat changed from his Nov. 1889 estimate. Now he expected the Russians to deploy three corps on the Narew and four on the Niemen: a one-corps increase. Against the Austrians the Russians would employ six corps in Poland and five corps in the western Ukraine. Ibid. 341–3.

[44] Ibid. 331–5.

In his 1879 war plan as well as his 1871 and 1880 war plans for a joint Austro-German attack on Russia, Moltke said that the Russians would assist in their own destruction and immediately attack, in 1871 on Berlin, in 1880 on East Prussia. In January 1884 Waldersee also contended that the Russians themselves intended to take the immediate offensive. In November 1887 both Moltke and Waldersee maintained that the Russians were conducting a secret build-up in order to attack in the spring.

In January 1884 Waldersee flatly contradicted these estimates. He said that up to that time the General Staff expected that, if attacked, the Russians would retreat to the east. In letters to Bismarck written in November 1887, both Moltke and Waldersee said that up to that time they had expected that the Russians would withdraw to the east in the face of a German attack, as they had done in 1812.

The most likely method to unravel this tangle is as follows. The 1st (Eastern) Department of the General Staff probably believed that the Russians would withdraw in the face of a German attack and would not attack until the entire Russian army was assembled. Waldersee's statement in 1884 and those of both Moltke and Waldersee in 1887, in which they said that the General Staff had expected all along that the Russians would not fight in Poland, were referring to this real-world 1st Department estimate. By 1889 Waldersee had correctly concluded that the Russian *Schwerpunkt* would be directed against Austria, not Germany.

Moltke's *Denkschriften* of 1871 and 1879 were not war plans, but policy papers advocating an Austro-German alliance, so his contention that the Russians would defend in Poland was a means of winning debating points and not a serious enemy analysis.

In 1871, 1879 and in 1880, even after the conclusion of the Austro-German alliance, Moltke assumed that the Russians would launch an immediate attack. Moltke's objective from 1871 to 1887 was to argue for the necessity of an Austro-German preventive attack on Russia, not to present a serious analysis of Russian intentions.

WALDERSEE'S EVALUATION OF THE GERMAN WAR PLAN

Between 1891 and 1904 Waldersee wrote his 'Retrospectives', one of which included an evaluation of German war planning between 1870 and 1890.[45] Waldersee said that the Germans had overestimated French military capabilities in the 1870s. The Germans thought that the French were capable of conducting offensive operations long before that was the case. They also thought the French border fortifications were

---

[45] Ibid. 233–40.

capable of hindering a German attack long before they were actually ready. He recognized that into the 1880s the French were solely concerned with defending against a German attack and had no offensive intentions. Even at the time of writing these comments, Waldersee thought that the French would attack only if they could be certain of Russian assistance.

Waldersee said the same was true in the east, only more so. In the early 1880s the Russians had fewer troops deployed in western Poland and their rail net was less capable than it became later. Until the end of the 1890s the Russians had no thought whatsoever of conducting offensive operations against Germany. Indeed, if the Germans and Austrians had launched an early joint offensive, the Russians would have refused to accept battle and withdrawn in the north to Bialystok and in the south to Rovno. There was no possibility that the Russians could launch an early offensive; indeed, the Russians were incapable of attacking before decisive battles had been fought in the west. Even after 1891 Waldersee didn't think that the Russians could launch an early offensive. They might be able conduct large-scale raids with cavalry and light infantry, but it was too much to expect the Russians to launch a 'bolt from the blue'. The best defense against Russian raids was even earlier German raids.

The conclusion of the Austrian alliance in 1879 improved Germany's position in the east still further. Waldersee said that he therefore obtained permission to transfer two corps from the east to the west. Waldersee stood Moltke's strategy on its head. Moltke wanted an Austro-German alliance in order to conduct a preventive war in the east. Waldersee used the alliance to increase the size of the German army in the west.

Waldersee wrote that Moltke's concept (by which he probably meant the 1880 war plan) in the east was to march up the left (south) side of the Vistula, cross to the right (north) side at Wloclawek or Plock, attack the Russians from the south and throw them into the Masurian lakes. Waldersee said that Moltke was not familiar enough with the condition of the Vistula. He said that there were periods when the Vistula was uncrossable owing to flooding or floating ice, or when the ice layer was not strong enough to support the crossing. Furthermore, even when the Vistula could be crossed, an enormous quantity of bridging material was required and one bridge would almost surely not be adequate.

Waldersee said that when he joined the General Staff the rail net in East Prussia was inadequate to deploy the army on the right bank of the Vistula. He tried to propose improvements, but was opposed by the rail and finance bureaucracies and by the war ministry, which 'always had its own opinion'. Nevertheless, by 1891, when he left the General Staff, he had been able to improve the rail net to such a degree that the eastern forces could all deploy north of the Vistula and several days earlier than previously.

Waldersee said that he had neither agreed with Moltke's division of the army into two equal halves, nor had he agreed with Moltke's static defense in the west. Waldersee also criticized Moltke's defensive position in the west. He said that Moltke had never inspected it on the ground. Waldersee implied that he, Waldersee, had. He said that the flanks were not secure, especially to the south, where the French would have had no trouble marching through Saarebourg, into the Palatinate, and then on the Rhine. Nor was the position strong to the front. Immediately behind the position was the Saar, which could prove to be an 'uncomfortable obstacle' if the German army had to retreat. Moltke's position in the upper Alsace didn't even look good to Waldersee on the map, an impression that was confirmed when he inspected it on the ground.

WESTAUFMARSCH 1887–1914

There can no longer be any doubt that Schlieffen was not the originator of the *Westaufmarsch*. The *Westaufmarsch* was proposed by Waldersee in 1886 and adopted by Moltke in 1887. After 1886 the German army no longer planned to conduct an *Ostaufmarsch*—a serious offensive in the east. If there was to be an Austro-German offensive in the east, then the Austrians were the ones who would have to make the main attack. In 1887 there were signs that the Austrian army was not keeping pace with the other European powers thereafter the Austrian army stagnated while the rest of the European armies modernized and grew. The Austrian capability to attack in the east steadily declined.

The decision to employ the mass of the German army in the west was based on two factors. First and most important was Bismarck's refusal to tolerate planning for a preventive war against Russia as well as his insistence that, in case of war, Germany would conduct a *Westaufmarsch*. The second factor was the military crisis that Germany faced in the west. Owing to the 3rd Department's intelligence coup, after 1885 there could be no doubt that the French had recovered from the war of 1870/1 and had produced both an effective rail net and an army capable of conducting immediate offensive operations. Moreover, the German army could no longer rely on its fortress system. If the Germans withdrew to the Rhine, there was every prospect that they would never be able to take the left bank back again.

Moltke and Waldersee therefore adopted the *Westaufmarsch* in 1887. Waldersee added the caveat that everything possible was to be done to delay or avert Russian intervention in a Franco-German war. If the Russians showed no signs of hostility, the forces earmarked for the east should be sent to the west too. Even in the west, German long-term prospects were not good. The Germans might well have to withdraw to the Rhine. Neither Moltke nor Waldersee could develop a promising offensive strategy. Moltke's sole offensive option was a frontal attack on Nancy. Waldersee eventually gave up completely on conducting an offensive in the west. The Germans would have to conduct a defensive–offensive operation. The French army would enjoy all the advantages of having the initiative. The German counter-offensive, in turn, would probably go no further than the French fortress line.

The danger of Russian intervention in a Franco-German war was increasing. In a two-front war the Germans would be heavily outnumbered. The Russians would surely withdraw in the face of a full-scale Austro-German offensive, an *Ostaufmarsch*. The Russians could then mass 72 divisions. With some 48 French divisions, the two had a total of 120 divisions, whereas the Germans had 60 and the Austrians probably only 37, a total of 97 divisions. Even in 1887, the chances that the Austro-Germans could win a long war or a war of attrition were slim. The German army had run into a strategic dead end.

CHAPTER FOUR

Schlieffen's war plan, 1891–1905

GERMAN ENEMY ESTIMATE IN THE WEST, 1890–1895

From 1890 to 1895 the German General Staff continued for all intents and purposes to be perfectly informed about the French war plan.[1] On 19 May 1890 the German agent again supplied what amounted to all the rail march tables for the Paris eastern railway. He also told the Germans that this plan constituted a modification of Plan X, called X M (*modifié*), and was effective from 15 April 1890. Most of the changes were made because the Bricon–Chaumont rail line had been expanded to four tracks.

Greiner said that the agent supplied less information concerning the French mobilization plan for 1891/2.[2] This was still a very great deal, including the routes for all the active corps which used the eastern railway. Greiner said that a comparison of the German estimate with Marchand and the French official history was difficult, in particular because the French sources were so vague and the map attached to the German estimate had been destroyed. Nevertheless, it appeared that the Germans had an accurate picture of the French deployment in Plan XI. Greiner does not mention the intent of the French plan, which seems evident. The first priority was to defend the fortress line, probably in a defensive–offensive operation. The French would receive the German attack from behind their Moselle position, then maneuver and counterattack. The French deployment also provided for an easy transition from a defense behind the Moselle to an outright offensive into Lorraine.

The 3rd Department did not receive any new material from its agent

---

[1] Greiner, 'Welche Nachrichten besaß der deutsche Generalstab über Mobilmachung und Aufmarsch französischen Heerer in den Jahren 1885–1914? ...', BA–MA W10/50267, 2–25, 46–76.

[2] The German estimate (completed on 4 Oct. 1891) of the French Plan XI was now that the French would deploy: 1st Army (3½ corps) at Epinal; 2nd Army (four corps) west of the Moselle at Charmes–Pont St. Vincent; 3rd Army (four corps) west of Toul; and 4th Army (four corps) at St. Ménehould. The French would deploy a second echelon with two corps and three reserve corps forming the 5th Army—the reserve army— behind the center, with three reserve corps behind each flank. The third echelon would consist of four reserve divisions and eight territorial divisions.

concerning the French 1892/93 mobilization plan. It therefore assumed, correctly, that the previous year's plan was still in effect.

The French were debating the proper role of reserve forces in the main battle, and the 3rd Department had difficulty deciding whether the French intended to integrate the reserve forces with the active units, employ them as reserve corps, or use them separately as reserve divisions.

In February 1893 the French implemented Plan XII. On 9 April 1893 the German agent sent in handwritten information on all the French covering force and active army corps that utilized the Paris eastern rail system for Plan XII as well as for Variant I to the plan. Therefore, as in previous years, the General Staff had a detailed and accurate picture of the French deployment, which was similar to that of Plan XI.

In March 1894 the German agent reported that there were no changes to Plan XII, but that Plan XIII was in preparation. In the spring of 1895 he reported in for the last time, empty handed, explaining that access to the rail timetables had been restricted and that he was no longer able to obtain them. The 3rd Department essentially maintained the last firm estimate they had—Plan XII—until 1897/98. Nevertheless, the Germans were fortunate. Plans XI, XII, and XIII were very similar in concept, and Plan XIII was in force through the 1897/98 mobilization year.

DIECKMANN: 'DER SCHLIEFFENPLAN'

Owing to the recent discovery of the Reichsarchiv manuscript 'Der Schlieffenplan' as well as of a number Schlieffen's last exercises, a clear picture of Schlieffen's war planning emerges for the first time. This picture has nothing in common with the genesis of the 'Schlieffen plan' described by the Reichsarchiv or Gerhard Ritter.

The most important of these documents is Major Dr Wilhelm Dieckmann's 'Der Schlieffenplan'.[3] Dieckmann was a wartime officer and trained economic historian who was brought into the Reichsarchiv in 1920 to help write the *Kriegsrüstung und Kriegswirtschaft* (armaments and war economy) volume of the official history, which was published in 1930. He also worked on several other papers, including one on an aspect of the Schlieffen plan which is in Foerster's *Nachlaß*.[4] During the Second World War he was recalled to active duty as a replacement

---

[3] W. Dieckmann, 'Der Schlieffenplan', BA-MA, W10/50220.

[4] W. Dieckmann, 'Hat Graf Schlieffen während der ersten Marokkokrise 1905 den Präventivkrieg gegen Frankreich gefördert?' BA-MA N121/30 *Nachlaß* Foerster. Some of Dieckmann's other work is listed in M. Herrmann, *Das Reichsarchiv* (Berlin, 1993), 533–42, 601–2.

battalion commander. Major Dieckmann was arrested after 20 July 1944 as one of the Stauffenberg conspirators and executed by machine-gun fire in the courtyard of the Lehrterstrasse prison in Berlin on 15 September 1944.[5] Dieckmann left us a working manuscript some 270 typewritten pages long. The text includes numerous handwritten corrections. It is undated, but appears to have been written in the late 1930s, probably in conjunction with the other works on Schlieffen published in 1937 and 1938. Most of what Dieckmann presents becomes known to us for the first time. The manuscript gives summaries of Schlieffen's *Aufmarschpläne*. It also gives summaries of selected *Denkschriften* concerning force structure and operational planning as well as the texts for twenty other *Denkschriften*, which are included as annexes. Dieckmann also summarized selected *Generalstabsreisen*. He stated where information was not available and he made it clear when he was drawing inferences. It is unfortunate that the maps which Dieckmann prepared were separated from the manuscript and apparently lost (as were several annexes). Owing to the destruction of the Reichsarchiv, this manuscript is likely to remain the only source of information for most of Schlieffen's war planning. Dieckmann, too, was convinced that the Schlieffen plan was the culmination of Schlieffen's strategic thought, but the information that his manuscript provides leads to another conclusion.

It is interesting to speculate why, at this late date, Wolfgang Foerster directed that an analysis of Schlieffen's 1891–1905 war planning be written. The W10 file (Reichsarchiv working papers) in Freiburg shows that, as an internal procedure, the Reichsarchiv produced exhaustive studies which were never published as well as detailed first drafts that were drastically cut back before publication. Dieckmann's manuscript may therefore have been an internal working document. Had it been published, it would have been one of the most controversial military histories ever written. A strong possibility therefore exists that Dieckmann's manuscript was an experiment to determine what sort of problems such a book would raise.

Dieckmann's manuscript was apparently evaluated by Wolfgang Foerster.[6] Foerster wrote numerous question marks and critical

[5] Karl Demeter, *Das Reichsarchiv* (Frankfurt am Main, 1969), 48. Demeter discusses Dieckmann's work on the *Kriegsrüstung und Kriegswirtschaft* book on p. 30. Also S. Wegner-Korfes, 'Realpolitische Haltung bei Offizieren der Familien Mertz von Quirnheim, Korfes und Dieckmann', *MG* 25 (3) (1986) 226–33.

[6] 'Apparently' because the reviewer is identified only as 'F'. The tenor of the comments makes it clear that the writer is superior in rank to Dieckmann, an important factor in a Reichsarchiv made up of former officers and organized along military lines, and which would limit the possible reviewers to two or three individuals. This was also

comments in the margins of the first 43 pages (up to the *Aufmarschplan* of 1894/5). Foerster was obviously intimately familiar with Schlieffen's planning, had some very firm ideas concerning Schlieffen's strategy, and criticized Dieckmann when Dieckmann's interpretations did not agree with his own. Foerster's penultimate marginal comment was the most important: he took Dieckmann to task for suggesting that Schlieffen's war planning in the east in 1894 ran counter to German foreign policy. Foerster wrote, '?? Particularly nowadays one must avoid making such judgements.'[7] It was already clear to Foerster that Dieckmann had produced a view of Schlieffen's strategy which differed in many ways from his own ideas. Foerster did not have the work revised or the mission assigned to another historian, but apparently let the matter drop.[8] It is significant that Foerster did not criticize Dieckmann's summaries of Schlieffen's war plans and *Denkschriften*: we can therefore take them to be accurate.

SCHLIEFFEN AND FORCE STRUCTURE

Dieckmann's manuscript makes it clear that Schlieffen had two major concerns; one was war planning, the other force structure (that is, the size and composition of the army), and of these two, force structure was the more serious problem. Schlieffen maintained that the German army was numerically inferior to the French army alone; against a Franco-Russian alliance this numerical inferiority became alarming. One needn't consider a two-front war, Schlieffen wrote in 1899, a war with France by herself would be as much as the German army could handle.[9] Schlieffen understood that excellent German troop training and operational skill could go only so far to compensate for superior enemy numbers; in an era of *Millionenheere* (million-man armies), masses mattered. In a *Denkschrift* on 25 August 1889,[10] even before becoming Chief of Staff, Schlieffen wrote that the German army was numerically inferior to the French because, on average, Germany

Foerster's particular area of expertise in a highly compartmentalized archive where documents were made accessible purely on a 'need to know' basis. These factors together seem to point pretty clearly to Foerster.

   [7] 'Vor solchem generellen Urteil muß man sich zumal heute hüten. F'. Dieckmann, 'Schlieffenplan', 42.

   [8] Stig Förster says that the war caused the termination of this project. Stig Foerster, 'Der deutsche Generalstab und die Illusion des Kurzen Kriger, 1871–1914. Kritik eines Mythos', *MM* 54 (1995) 87. Nevertheless, the Forschungsanstalt finished the *Weltkriegswerk* during the war: Reymann, *Reichsarchiv*, Blatt 373. The war was therefore probably not the determining factor.

   [9] Dieckmann, 'Schlieffenplan', 172.

   [10] Ibid., Annex 2, 227–39.

conscripted about 55 percent of her available manpower, while France conscripted about 80 percent of hers. Such high levels of French conscription even compensated for France's smaller population and lower birth-rate.

Nevertheless, Schlieffen recognized that his chances of fundamentally altering German conscription policy were slim. Army peacetime force structure was under the authority of the War Ministry and subject to the budget powers of the Reichstag. In peacetime, Schlieffen could only recommend changes. Since political and financial considerations blocked increases in the peacetime army, Schlieffen fell upon the expedient of planning to create a massive number of new units immediately upon mobilization, when he would be the operational leader of the army and could insist that his demands be met. There was plenty of trained manpower available. When the German army mobilized, several hundred thousand trained reservists, who could not be absorbed by the field army, would be called back to the colors. Many reservists would be assigned during mobilization to replacement battalions (*Ersatzbataillone*) while waiting for a vacancy to occur in a regular line unit. In June 1891, Schlieffen wrote a *Denkschrift* which advocated that each army corps form the *Ersatzbataillone* into two infantry ersatz brigades for use as maneuver units in the field army.[11]

The drawback lay in the fact that such ersatz units would consist of men with rifles, and little else: few trained officers and NCOs, little artillery, no combat support or combat service support units—not even medical personnel. In addition, if the replacement units were transformed into field units they would then be unable to perform their real function—providing replacements to the field army. The War Ministry was unenthusiastic and no preparations were made to use *Ersatzbataillone* as maneuver units until after Schlieffen had retired. Ludendorff said that they first entered the German order of battle owing to his efforts in 1911.[12] The ersatz divisions that were committed to combat in 1914 were initially deployed only on or very near German territory, presumably to allow them to use local resources to make up for their lack of support units. Nevertheless, the use of *Ersatzbataillone* as maneuver units remained one of Schlieffen's favorite expedients, and formed the foundation for the December 1905 'Schlieffen plan' *Denkschrift*.

In July 1892 Schlieffen wrote a long *Denkschrift*[13] which proposed heroic measures to correct the problem of German numerical inferiority. He

[11] Dieckmann, 'Schlieffenplan', Annex 12, 281.
[12] E. Ludendorff, *Mein Militärischer Werdegang* (Munich, 1933), 137.
[13] Dieckmann, 'Schlieffenplan', Annex 13, 282–8.

aimed at nothing less than the full incorporation of all trained reservists into maneuver units of the field army. On mobilization, each infantry regiment would form an additional battalion from available reservists. Each army corps area would raise as many reserve and Landwehr battalions as there were personnel available to assign to them. In this manner, each corps area ought to be able to raise a reserve corps (instead of the current reserve division) and a Landwehr division in addition. In order to find cadres Schlieffen recommended that reserve division staffs should be broken up and the brigades subordinated directly to the corps headquarters. New reserve artillery units would have to be raised but finding combat support and combat service support units for the new formations was going to be difficult: the Landwehr probably wouldn't get any. Indeed, some active army support units would have to be reduced to provide horses for the new formations. Schlieffen concluded by saying that the creation of new units was essential and that such measures could not wait for the next army bill. Schlieffen's overriding priority was clear: he was willing to do whatever was necessary to create the maximum number of maneuver units possible. The War Ministry did not share this priority. At no time during Schlieffen's tenure as chief of staff was the war minister willing to create units with little equipment or cohesion, nor was he willing to fight with the Reichstag to get the money for Schlieffen's mass army. Schlieffen's proposal to create new units upon mobilization by using already trained excess reservists was never acted upon. Nevertheless, Schlieffen never forgot this idea, and it became the basis for his final *Denkschrift* in 1912.

A further development of Schlieffen's concept of the mass army is apparent in a *Denkschrift* that he wrote on 11 December 1893.[14] Schlieffen repeated Moltke's contention that the exposed position of East Prussia made it essential that, upon mobilization, the German government declare a *levée en masse* in East Prussia. The East Prussian Landsturm and Landwehr would be armed with locally stored weapons and ammunition and would defend their own villages against Russian cavalry as of the first day of mobilization. Behind this Landwehr/ Landsturm screen the active and reserve units would mobilize and then counterattack. On the one hand, this was a sensible precaution against the massive Russian cavalry raids that were expected immediately upon mobilization; on the other hand, this was, adapted to the local circumstances, the logical culmination of Schlieffen's idea of mass warfare, wherein the entire trained population would rise in arms.

Schlieffen continually argued for significant increases in the size of the German army by whatever means possible. In 1897 Schlieffen told

---

[14] Ludendorff, *Mein Militärischer Werdegang*, Annex 5, 246 ff.

the war minister that his goal was to increase the number of active corps from 20 to 27. In 1899 Schlieffen asked for the formation of seven new corps but only three were actually raised, and these (XVIII, XIX, III Bavarian Corps) were made up by reorganizing existing formations, not by raising new units.[15] In 1902 Schlieffen succeeded in getting the War Minister to agree that in wartime five additional corps would be created out of a mix of active and reserve units (XX–XXIII Corps and the Guard Reserve Corps) which were known as *Kriegskorps*. In 1903 War Minister von Einem reduced their number to three. No further active army corps were added to the German army before the war, except XX and XXI Corps, which were elevated from *Kriegskorps* to regular army formations in 1912.[16]

SCHLIEFFEN'S DEPLOYMENT PLANS

Dieckmann provides a summary of each of Schlieffen's *Aufmarschpläne*. These give us only the initial deployments on the border. Dieckmann did not have access to the *Aufmarschanweisungen*—the initial orders to the army commanders—or any other document stating the chief of staff's intent. Dieckmann had to try to interpret the chief of staff's concept of the operation from the deployment itself and from the results of the *Denkschriften* and General Staff rides.

We are able to both supplement Dieckmann and confirm his *Denkschrift* with a copy of the notes for a briefing concerning Schlieffen's east-front war planning held in May 1905.[17] The briefer was

---

[15] Dieckmann, Schlieffenplan, 77–80, 107.

[16] Reichsarchiv, *Kriegsrüstung und Kriegswirtschaft*, 66, 74–5; C. Jany, *Geschichte der preußischen Armee* (2nd edn., 4 vols., Osnabrück, 1967), iv. 296–7. In 1902 there were 19 reserve divisions, including 9 that had been organized into reserve 'corps' which consisted of little more than a reinforced reserve division staff. By 1910 the addition of large numbers of young reservists alone had caused the number of reserve divisions to increase to 27 and 13 reserve corps headquarters had been raised (I, III–IX, XII, XIV, XVIII, I Bavarian Reserve Corps and 3rd Reserve Division). Neither number increased further before 1914 (Reichsarchiv, *Kriegsrüstung und Kriegswirtschaft, Annexes*, Tabellen 11, 13, 18). In October 1914 six new reserve corps (XXII to XXVII Reserve Corps) and four Bavarian reserve divisions were activated.

[17] 'Operationen gegen Rußland, Mai 1905', BA-MA W10/50221, 3–4. Dommes said (1–2) that Moltke's deployment 'in the 1880s' in the east consisted of a center army between Johannisberg and Lyck with nine divisions, a left-flank army between Goldap and Stalluponen with eight divisions, and a right-flank detachment with four divisions at Soldau, 21 divisions in total. The concept was for the center army to cross the Narew at Lomja while the left-flank army moved on Ostrolenka and the detachment covered the right flank. The attack would start on the 16th day of mobilization. The Austrians would commit their main body in an attack to the east of Warsaw, leaving only weak forces to cover their right flank. The Austro-German objective was to force the Russians to fight before they had completely assembled. This was an accurate if very general and

almost surely von Dommes, a senior General Staff officer, and the officer being briefed was probably the younger Moltke, who was preparing to assume the duties of Chief of Staff.

Schlieffen's first operational *Denkschrift* was written in April 1891, shortly after he became chief of staff. Dommes said that in this *Denkschrift* Schlieffen asserted that the military situation that obtained when Field Marshal von Moltke wrote his war plans had changed. The Russians had significantly improved their combat readiness and had fortified the Narew line. The French could now deploy faster than the Germans and could also wait behind their fortress line and begin operations at a time of their own choosing. The Russians could defend on the Narew and Niemen and attack the Austrians. If Austria were defeated the Germans would have to fight alone against the Russians and the French. The Austro-Germans were outnumbered. The French had 20 corps and the Russians 21 for a total of 41 corps, while the Germans had 20 corps and the Austrians had 15 for a total of 35. The Italians had 12 corps, but they could not be brought into action.

In a *Denkschrift* written in December 1892 Schlieffen expressed his skepticism concerning an offensive from East Prussia.[18] He said that by dint of hard work the Russians had increased the speed of their deployment to the point that it was little slower than that of the Germans. The Russians would also be prudent enough to deploy behind the fortified lines of the Narew and Niemen. There was little possibility that the Germans would be able to surprise and overrun the Russians while they were still deploying. Moreover, Schlieffen said that he had reliable reports that the Russians had shifted their center of mass from the western Ukraine to Lithuania and Poland in order to be able to meet the expected German attack. Like Waldersee, Schlieffen said that the Russians would fight at Lomja. It was therefore difficult for the Germans to break the Narew line. Even if the Germans did so, the Russians would not fall back to the south, toward the Austrians, but toward the east, where their reinforcements and supplies originated. The Germans would not be able to destroy the Russian armies. Rather, they would fight a series of frontal battles. The Russians could withdraw into the limitless interior of the country, while the German lines of communication would become ever longer and less secure.

In a *Denkschrift* written in December 1892, Schlieffen recognized the

undifferentiated description, but it was intended only as background: by 1905 Moltke's planning was 25 years old and of historical interest only. It is worthwhile to note that there was no mention of an Austro-German double envelopment of the Russian armies in Poland.

[18] Dieckmann, 'Schlieffenplan', 10–11.

need for an Austrian offensive.[19] He wrote that if the Austrians did not
attack, but defended on the Carpathians, then the Russians would be
free to deploy troops on the south bank of the Vistula. They could then
attack directly toward Thorn, Posen, and Berlin. The Germans would
be forced to evacuate East Prussia. Schlieffen was obviously concerned
that, without direct German assistance, the Austrians would not attack
at all. If the Austro-Germans were to avoid defeat in detail, the two
armies had to be united. Since the Austrians had to stay in Galicia,
Schlieffen said that the Germans needed to deploy their eastern army
to Silesia and then move into southern Poland to link up with the
Austrians. In the 1893/4 plan in the east, Schlieffen decided to employ
this concept: three corps and four reserve divisions would deploy in
southern Posen and attack immediately towards Fortress Iwangorod.
They would reach the Vistula by the 22nd day of mobilization and cross
upstream from the fortress. Here the German eastern army would link
up with the left flank of the Austrian offensive.[20]

   This plan had two advantages: first, there was no possibility that the
Russians could defeat the German and Austrian armies separately;
second, the Germans did not have to make an opposed crossing of the
Narew. There were also two disadvantages: the first was that only four
divisions remained to defend East Prussia; the second was that there
was no chance of destroying the Russian army in Poland—the Austro-
German offensive would push the Russians directly to the rear and on
their base areas. The steady arrival of Russian reinforcements and the
lengthening of the Austro-German lines of supply would be certain to
bring the offensive to a halt somewhere near Warsaw.

   Schlieffen's *Aufmarschplan* for 1893/4 was a *Westaufmarsch*. He
deployed 16 corps and 15 reserve divisions (48 divisions in total) in the
west and four corps and six reserve divisions (15 divisions in total) in the
east.[21] Schlieffen was even less impressed than Waldersee with Moltke's
defensive position in Lorraine. He said that the French army had grown
so large that the French would surely move to turn both its flanks.[22] The
best alternative was for the Germans to forestall the French attack by
attacking first. Belfort-Epinal in the south was difficult to reach. He
said that there were few fortifications to the north of Verdun, but the
force moving to the north of Verdun would become isolated. Any

[19] Ibid. 15–16; Dommes, 'Operationen gegen Rußland', 5–6.
[20] This was the only one of Schlieffen's war plans that was known to the public. It first
appeared in H. Mohs (ed.), *General-feldmarschall Alfred Graf Waldersee in seinem
militärischen Wirken*, ii. (Berlin, 1929), 343–4, and then in more complete form in Konrad
Leppa, 'Schlieffen in Polen', *DW*, 3 (Dezember 1930), 1167–9.
[21] Dieckmann, 'Schlieffenplan', 17–18.
[22] Ibid. 12–27.

maneuver to the north of Verdun must be supported by a breakthrough between Toul and Verdun. This attack had to be covered on the left by an attack on Nancy. The German army was not strong enough to conduct three attacks simultaneously. Schlieffen therefore had to reject an envelopment of the north flank of the French fortress line. Schlieffen's conclusion was that the best places to attack the French fortress line were between Toul and Verdun or along the Moselle downstream from Epinal. Any attack on the fortress line must be preceded by an attack on Nancy.

The Reichsarchiv was intent on demonstrating that Schlieffen's strategic thought moved single-mindedly in the direction of the right-wing envelopment. Therefore it printed only garbled fragments of this *Denkschrift*, saying that it led Schlieffen to realize that he had to maneuver through neutral Luxembourg and south Belgium.[23] This conclusion collapses now that Dieckmann's summary of the entire *Denkschrift* is available. It is now evident that the intent of the *Denkschrift* was to argue for a reform of the heavy artillery in order to facilitate the breakthrough of the French fortress line. This led to the creation of the *Schwere Artillerie des Feldheeres*, the heavy field artillery. No outflanking maneuver to the north of Verdun was possible until this reform was accomplished. Therefore, Schlieffen did not even consider moving through Belgium for another three years.

In 1894 Major F. M. von Donat published an updated version of his 1870s pamphlet, *Die Befestigung und Vertheidigung der deutsch–französischen Grenze* (The Fortification and Defense of the Franco-German Border).[24] Donat said that after twenty-four years of sacrifice and work, the French felt that they were completely ready (*archi-prêt*). Recently individual French military writers had been saying that it was time to abandon the defensive strategy of the last two decades and adopt an offensive doctrine, which was more appropriate to the natural bent of both the French people and the army, clearly foreshadowing Grandmaison's *offensive à outrance*. Nevertheless, a majority of the French military writers still favored the strategic defensive. This was in large part because they feared that the German mobilization was more efficient than the French—perhaps as much as eight days faster.

The French felt that the Germans would attack between Luxembourg and the Vosges, which some French writers described as *la trouée enorme* (the enormous gap) or *la vide effroyable* (the terrifying

---

[23] Reichsarchiv, *Der Weltkrieg*, 52–4.
[24] F. M. von Donat, *Die Befestigung und Vertheidigung der deutsch–französischen Grenze* (1st edn., Berlin, 1879; 4th edn., Berlin, 1894).

void). The French had tried to block this avenue of approach with fortifications. The first line of defense, the French *Sperrforts*, would be able to put up serious resistance. The French forts opposite Belgium and Luxembourg, on the other hand, were not built to stop a German attack but to provide bridgeheads for a French offensive. Paris was fortified as no other place in the world, but required a large mobile reserve for its defense. The zone of operations would be delineated by the Aisne and Oise in the north, Paris in the west, and the middle Seine and the plateau of Langres in the south. This was the decisive area in 1814, 1815, and 1870. Northern France offered no terrain obstacles to a German invasion, but the approach march to the true zone of operations was so long that the French would have plenty of time to take counter-measures. The French would concentrate at Toul–Epinal. The Russian deployment would take about four weeks longer than the French. Since the 1870s French publications had openly acknowledged that if the French were forced to withdraw, they would do so toward the plateau of Langres, not Paris.

If the French attacked it would be through Lorraine toward Mainz and not north of Metz into the Eifel. The Germans would launch a concentric counterattack on Dieuze and Saarebourg. A French attack into south Germany was pointless. Donat rated the German fortifications highly. He said that an attack on Metz would require an assaulting force three times the size of the garrison. The German garrison of Metz would show to the world how a fortress was defended. Strasbourg would require a besieging army of 180,000 men. Mainz, Coblenz, Cologne and Wesel were still obstacles to a French attempt to cross the Rhine.

As far as fortresses were concerned, Donat was about ten years behind the times: his views would have been accurate until 1886. It may well be that he did not want to acknowledge that German fortresses, built at so much cost, were now worthless. Otherwise, his estimate of the military situation was perceptive and accurate.

GENERALSTABSREISEN OST

In 1938 the great military publishers Mittler and Son brought out Schlieffen's *Generalstabsreisen Ost*. It was a magnificent volume, including 15 large and 37 smaller maps: it was clearly a labor of love for both the General Staff and Mittler. Five *Generalstabsreisen* were described: 1894, 1897, 1899, 1901, and 1903. The *Generalstabsreisen* included the general and special situations, a detailed daily description of the conduct of the exercise, and Schlieffen's *Schlußbesprechung* (exercise critique). When one opens the maps and reads the 1894 *Generalstabsreise*

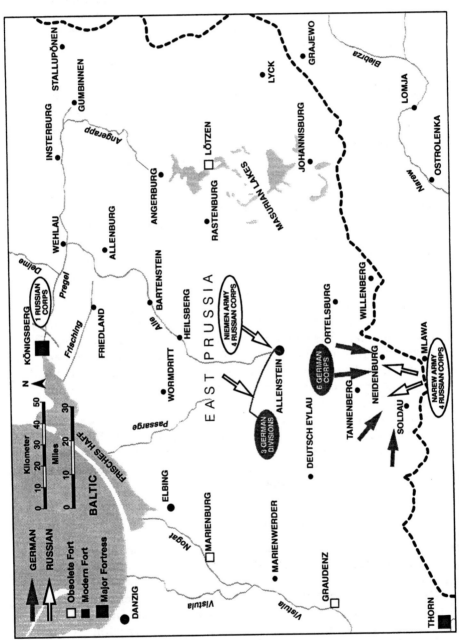

MAP 5. *Generalstabsreise Ost 1894*

it is clear why the General Staff was so proud of these exercises: in the 1894 *Generalstabsreise Ost* Schlieffen played the battle of Tannenberg.[25]

Moltke's war plans and *Denkschriften* usually called for an immediate Austro-German offensive against Russia, even though Russia was allied to Germany. Only with the Russo-French alliance concluded between 1892 and 1894 did Russia and Germany definitively become enemies. Therefore, the political situation in the 1894 *Generalstabsreise Ost*—a war between the Franco-Russian alliance on the one hand and the Austro-German on the other—is the first German staff ride in the east which corresponded to the actual political situation.

The Russians began the war with massive cavalry raids that were driven back only after they had effectively destroyed the East Prussian rail net. The German 1st Corps and 1st Reserve Division assembled at Angerburg–Insterburg, XVII Corps and the 35th Reserve Division at Soldau. By 15 June the Russian Niemen army, with six corps, had over-run half of East Prussia and was due south of Königsberg at Wormdritt. The Narew Army, with four corps, was north of Soldau: the German troops had fallen back in front of them. The total Russian force included 30 divisions, with 21 in the first echelon and 9, including the reserve divisions, arriving later in a second echelon. The Germans moved two more corps to East Prussia. II Corps had assembled at Thorn and four reserve divisions were along the Vistula. The Germans now had five corps and six reserve divisions available—16 divisions in total.

One of Schlieffen's wargaming techniques was for several officers to present their solutions. He then selected one of these from each side to continue the problem. Another technique was to appoint officers as corps and army commanders. These assignments would be rotated during the problem play. While Schlieffen certainly had a concept of the operation and set the parameters of the exercise, he interfered as little as possible with the solutions and play of the problem.

The German commander decided to exploit the momentary separation of the Russian armies and concentrate 13 divisions against the Narew Army, which was both closer and more dangerous. Only three divisions would try to delay the Niemen Army. The Russian commander, while recognizing the need for the Russian armies to unite, did not think that the Germans would offer serious resistance east of the Vistula.

On 18 and 19 June the Germans launched a concentric attack on the Narew army, with the main point of effort being directed against the Russian right flank. The Narew army suffered very heavy casualties

[25] Generalstab des Heeres (ed.), *Die Großen Generalstabsreisen—Ost—aus den Jahren 1891–1905* (Berlin, 1938), 1–50.

and was forced to withdraw back over the border and finally to the Narew river, where it was no longer a factor in the exercise. There was no serious pursuit of the Narew army: the Germans redeployed to the north-east against the Niemen army. On 22 June the Niemen Army and the German army collided. The left-flank German unit did not provide adequate security, so the Russians won the fight on this flank. The exercise was then terminated.

Schlieffen began the *Schlußbesprechung* by stating that an army's *Aufmarsch* is determined by the peacetime deployment, the rail net, and the configuration of the border. On the basis of uncomplicated calculations it was possible to say with practical certainty that the Russians would deploy two armies against Germany: one on the Niemen and one on the Narew. In the last fifteen years (that is, since 1880) the Russians had made remarkable strides in improving the speed of their deployment. Nevertheless, mobilizing and deploying the reserve divisions was still a slow process, as was bringing forward XII Corps. It was in the Russian's best interests to wait until the largest possible numbers of troops had been assembled. However, Schlieffen said that alliance considerations might force the Russians to attack before then, that is, the Russians might have to attack early to relieve German pressure on the French. That was what happened in this case (and what would happen in 1914). Of a total force of 30 divisions, the Russians had only 16 available when they began operations.

The Germans would surely be able to defend the Vistula, Schlieffen said, but there was no reason for them to delay a decisive battle: time was not on the Germans' side. Delaying a decision would merely allow the Russians to bring up additional forces. In addition, it was essential to exploit the division of the Russian armies and win a decisive victory before they could unite. Concentration against the Narew army was preferable. The attack must aim not just to defeat the Narew army, but to destroy it. This meant that the Germans must attack the Narew Army's right flank and push the army to the west, away from its lines of communication and the Niemen Army.

Schlieffen also made an important expansion of *Auftragstaktik*. Moltke had said that officers on detached missions must be permitted to use their own judgement, but that officers commanding units with the main body could ask their next higher commander for orders if necessary. Schlieffen said that the modern battlefield had grown to immense size and that many unforeseen circumstances could require a commander to make an independent decision. It was generally too time-consuming to wait for orders and communications, even telegraph lines, could fail. All commanders, but especially corps commanders, must be able to exercise their own judgement.

In addition, in modern battles holding a central reserve was rarely possible. Battlefields had become too large: the reserve would never arrive at the decisive spot in time. It was therefore necessary to deploy reserves at the decisive point from the very beginning of the battle, and that could only be on the flanks. The commanding general could not direct these forces: they must be employed by the senior commander on the scene.

Until 1888 Moltke had said that Germany's eastern border was too long to defend. The only possible German course of action was to over-run Russian Poland as early as possible. Waldersee was skeptical of this solution, but could think of nothing better than a spoiling attack on the Russian army while it deployed. The German army in the east would then stall for time until reinforcements arrived from the west. One of Moltke's last ideas was to use interior lines in the east to concentrate against one of the attacking Russian armies. Schlieffen transformed Moltke's static defensive–offensive into a dynamic operation. The Germans did not wait for the Russians in some 'impregnable' position, but seized the initiative by concentrating local superiority in a counter-offensive against a flank of the Russian offensive. Both armies would be in motion at the same time. Such a fluid situation would optimize German superiority in unit training, officer initiative, and the decentralized execution of orders. Mobile, offensive operations of this kind would become Schlieffen's *modus operandi*. For the rest of his career Schlieffen then tested this concept on both fronts in loosely structured, if not completely free-play, exercises: something neither Moltke nor Waldersee did either for the Saar position in the west or for the attack into Poland in the east. On the basis of the *Generalstabsreisen* Schlieffen then developed the concept of the operation for his war plans. These exercises also served to disseminate Schlieffen's mobile warfare doctrine throughout the General Staff.

AUFMARSCHPLÄNE, 1895–1897

Schlieffen provided two variants for the *Aufmarschplan* in 1895/6 in the east, for an army of 18 divisions. Variant A returned to Moltke's concentration in East Prussia. One corps and a reserve division would assemble on the Angerapp at Insterburg. The main group—four corps and two reserve divisions—would form up along the southern border of Prussia on a line Soldau–Neidenburg–Ortelsburg. Four reserve divisions would assemble at Thorn. There was also a reserve division in Silesia. Variant B repeated Schlieffen's concentration in Silesia from the previous year.[26]

---

[26] Dieckmann, 'Schlieffenplan', 44 ff. On p. 43 Foerster's marginal notes stop.

Dommes said that Schlieffen came to the conclusion in 1895 that the Russians might not concentrate against the Austrians after all, and that in fact they would attack Germany.[27] During a state visit to Austria on 15 June 1895, Schlieffen communicated his concern to the Austrians. According to Dieckmann, in the spring of 1895 Schlieffen abandoned the advance from Silesia to south Poland altogether.[28] Beck, the Austrian chief of staff, wrote to Schlieffen late in December 1899 or early in 1900 that he assumed that the Austro-German operation had now returned to the concept of the 1880s.[29]

The 1896/97 *Aufmarsch* in the east marked the complete return to the Moltke/Waldersee plan, with 15 infantry divisions conducting an advance from East Prussia on the Niemen and Narew. The main attack was directed on the middle Narew at Ostrolenka. The left flank was moved to the west at Neidenburg, which was presumably less exposed than Ortelsburg. There was no indication that this was anything more than a repetition of Waldersee's late 1880s spoiling attack to disrupt the Russian deployment and gain time. The *Aufmarschplan* for 1896/7 provided for 50 infantry divisions to deploy in the west. There was no apparent change in the mission from 1893/4.[30]

In 1896 the German military attaché in Vienna, Colonel Graf Hülsen, wrote to Schlieffen that Beck was complaining about a lack of information concerning the German deployment. Hülsen thought that the Austrians would use this as an excuse for inactivity if war broke out. Schlieffen provided Beck with the order of battle and the line of deployment for the German forces in the east. At the same time, he communicated to Hülsen his principal strategic problem: 'We cannot allow ourselves to be beaten by the French on the 15th–17th day of mobilization while the Austrians calmly deploy in Galicia. The outcome of the first battle will determine if a single Austrian crosses the San.'[31]

In 1894 Schlieffen wrote a *Denkschrift* giving his estimate of French military intentions. He thought that the French could mobilize and deploy as quickly as the Germans. Schlieffen, like Moltke, noted that for years the French had followed a defensive strategy, and he saw no evidence to indicate that this had changed. Schlieffen made one impor-

---

[27] Dommes, 'Operationen gegen Rußland', 6–7.

[28] Dieckmann, 'Schlieffenplan', 45.

[29] Dommes, 'Operationen gegen Rußland', 8–9.

[30] Dieckmann, 'Schlieffenplan', 45. Dommes said that the Silesian deployment was retained in the 1895/96 war plan. This doesn't square with a handwritten note on p. 7. Considering Schlieffen's views on this plan, if the Silesian plan was retained, then most likely it was worked out *pro forma*, with no intention on Schlieffen's part of actually implementing it (Dommes, 'Operationen gegen Rußland', 7–9).

[31] Dommes, 'Operationen gegen Rußland', 10–11.

tant observation in this regard, as had the elder Moltke before him, and as would the younger Moltke after him: when the French decided for war, they would shift to an offensive military plan.[32]

In 1895, General Köpke, an *Oberquartiermeister* on the Great General Staff, wrote a *Denkschrift* concerning an offensive in the west. In a two-front war, began Köpke, the Germans were going to be numerically considerably inferior to the French. Any German offensive would there-fore have to aim at strictly limited objectives. Both the attack between Verdun–Toul and one to the south of Toul involved numerous support-ing attacks which would overtax German strength. The risk involved in these attacks was high and the consequences of defeat were incalcula-ble. Probably only the offensive against Nancy planned by both the elder Moltke and Schlieffen was possible. In any case, possession of Nancy was of little military advantage and would serve mostly to increase morale. The attack on Nancy could be conducted only as a positional battle, or outright siege warfare, which would at best produce tactical success. Köpke was particularly concerned that in case of war the public would expect great victorious maneuver battles *à la* 1870/1, and would be unprepared for slow, costly, siege operations.[33]

Even Schlieffen noted in 1892 that military writers were openly spec-ulating that the Germans would march through Belgium in order to avoid the French border fortifications.[34] Nevertheless, according to Dieckmann, only in 1896 did Schlieffen begin to consider turning the French left by means of a march through the Ardennes.[35] His first *Denkschrift* on the subject was not written until 2 August 1897.[36] In it, Schlieffen began by explaining that the German army had to find an avenue of approach for its attack that was not blocked by French forti-fications. He then stated that there were only two such available: between Toul and Epinal—the 'Trouée de Charmes'—or to the north of Verdun. The 'Trouée de Charmes' was by far the less suitable. The line of the Moselle was itself a naturally strong position, and behind it the Germans would find assembled the entire French army. North of Verdun there was plenty of space to maneuver, but only if the German army could employ the entire breadth of the Ardennes in Luxembourg and Belgium. In that case, there was room for the German main force: two armies totaling eight corps (16 divisions). They would be protected on the right against the Belgian army by a flank guard of six reserve divisions, which would assemble at Aachen. The real threat, however, was from a counterattack from Verdun directed against the left flank of the German main body. To protect this flank, Schlieffen assembled a

[32] Dieckmann, 'Schlieffenplan', 49.   [33] Ibid. 54–5.   [34] Ibid. 57.
[35] Ibid. 62–3.   [36] Ibid. 63–71.

third army of eight reserve divisions between Diedenhofen and Metz, which would move to the north and north-west faces of Verdun. At this point Schlieffen discussed the real problem in outflanking the French line to the north, which was that when the two right flank armies came to the level of Verdun, they would be isolated from the rest of the German army, and the French could mass against them and destroy them. Ferron had made the same observation in 1879. Schlieffen's solution was to support the right flank armies with a fourth army, four corps strong and heavily reinforced with artillery, which would advance against the French fortress line between Verdun and Toul, seize one or two forts and force a crossing of the Moselle and link up with the right wing attack. To protect the left flank of this attack a fifth army, also of four corps, would attack Nancy. On its left, a sixth army of four corps would advance on the Meurthe between Nancy and Lunéville. Finally, a seventh army of five corps and three reserve divisions would guard the left flank until Nancy was taken, then it too would advance on the Moselle. One corps and three reserve divisions would hold upper Alsace; eventually, the corps would join the seventh army. This is not the first German plan for an offensive in the west: Moltke almost always planned to attack Nancy. This is, however, the first document in which Schlieffen planned for an offensive to the north of Verdun.

The *Denkschrift* also makes it clear why Schlieffen was so reluctant to outflank the French fortress line: no matter how simple and obvious such a maneuver might appear, it ran the serious risk that the French would overwhelm the isolated right wing. In fact, one of the principal conclusions that Schlieffen drew from the 2 August 1897 *Denkschrift* was that he didn't have the troops required to conduct the operation in this form. Even though the *Denkschrift* employed the entire German army in the west—an unlikely prospect in 1897—Schlieffen still found it necessary to plan for the use of three additional corps and a number of reserve divisions beyond what was available.[37] Therefore, the 2 August 1897 *Denkschrift* remained 'operational planning',[38] but had no effect on the *Aufmarschpläne* for 1897/8 or 1898/9.

Indeed, while the *Denkschrift* considered the problem of a mass offensive in the west, in these years the proportion of the army assigned to East Prussia was increased. The *Aufmarschplan* for 1897/8 deployed 48 infantry divisions in the west.[39] In the east there were 20 infantry divisions (up from 15 in 1896/7).[40]

[37] Dieckmann, 'Schlieffenplan', 66–7.   [38] Ibid. 73.

[39] Eighteen active corps, four reserve corps, and three reserve divisions

[40] Six active corps, two reserve corps, and four reserve divisions. Dommes notes for 1897/98 and 1898/99 are garbled. He appears to say that in the drafts of the *Aufmarschplan* for 1897/98 eight active corps and three reserve divisions were deployed

In 1898/9 an active army corps was taken from the west and added to the east, for a total of 46 divisions in the west and 22 divisions in the east.[41] In the west the right flank of the German army was deployed to the south border of Luxembourg, meaning there were no preparations to march into Belgium. The operational concept on both fronts was probably the same it had been under the last Moltke/Waldersee plans: active defense in Lorraine, spoiling attack from East Prussia.[42]

It has often been contended that Schlieffen switched to an attack through Belgium in 1897. The Reichsarchiv said that the concept for an attack through Luxembourg and south Belgium was first incorporated in the 1898/9 *Aufmarschplan*.[43] 'Der Schlieffenplan' shows that this was emphatically not the case. In fact, 'Der Schlieffenplan' shows a steady increase in the size of the East Prussian army to meet the growing Russian threat, from 15 divisions in 1894 to 22 in 1898/9.

1897: *GENERALSTABSREISE OST*[44]

The Russians attacked with a total of 12 corps divided into four armies. Counting second-echelon reserve divisions, the Russians had 36 infantry divisions available—about a million men. However, the campaign would not last long enough to allow the Russian reserve divisions time to deploy. Subtracting forces to watch Königsberg, the Russians had only 23 divisions in the first echelon for actual operations. This time the Russian 3rd and 4th (Narew) armies on the left waited until the 1st and 2nd (Niemen) Armies on the right advanced until they were all on line. By the 32nd day of mobilization the 1st and 2nd Armies had overrun half of East Prussia (to a line Allenstein–Neidenburg), with the 3rd and 4th Armies to the south of them. The Russian commander thought that the Germans would fight early. Instead, the I German Corps fell back to Fortress Königsberg, while the XVII Corps and the 35th Reserve Division delayed the Russian advance through East Prussia. The Germans also deployed all available Landwehr and Landsturm units in the field against the Russians.

---

in the east, 19 divisions in total. This is two more active corps and five fewer reserve divisions than Dieckmann, and one division fewer in total. The discrepancy is not fatal, and can be explained by a difference between the drafts and the final plan, or in the manner that the fortress mobile reserve (*Hauptreserven*) were counted (Dommes, 'Operationen gegen Rußland', 12).

[41] Dieckmann, 'Schlieffenplan', 107. Dommes' order of battle is again different. He says eight active corps and six reserve divisions, 22 divisions in total. This is one more active corps and two fewer reserve divisions than Dieckmann. Now, there is no discrepancy in the total number of divisions.

[42] Dieckmann, 'Schlieffenplan', 107.   [43] Reichsarchiv, *Der Weltkrieg*, 54.

[44] Generalstab, *Generalstabsreisen Ost*, 52–104.

On the 25th day of mobilization, the German army in the west defeated the French attack in Lorraine. The French army was not annihilated, but it was forced to withdraw behind the border fortifications. Thereupon the Russians received reports of German troop transport to the east. The Russians had to assume that as of the 30th day of mobilization the Germans could begin to receive reinforcements. By the 33rd or 34th day these could number four to six corps behind the Vistula or at Posen. In fact, the Germans transferred four corps and four reserve divisions to the east with an estimated time of arrival on the evening of the 36th day of mobilization. The Russian commander decided not to risk a crossing of the Vistula to the north of Thorn, but rather to cross the Vistula to the east of Thorn, at Wloclawek and Plock. The German commander decided on an offensive defense of the Vistula. As Schlieffen said in the *Schlußbesprechung,* the Germans were not in a position to keep an army of nine corps in the east indefinitely— these troops would soon be needed again in the west. Three corps formed an assault group on the lower Vistula behind the bridgehead over the Nogat at Marienburg with the intent of attacking the Russian right wing.

This is one of the first examples of Schlieffen's concept of mobile warfare. Schlieffen moved forces by rail to mass against an enemy flank. This movement was screened from the enemy by the Vistula and the XVII Corps. He then used his bridgehead at Fortress Marienburg to spring the trap on the advancing enemy armies.

The movement of the three German corps across the Nogat began on the 33rd day. By the 35th day the four-corps reinforcement had arrived from the west and had been deployed to the south of the assault group. On the 37th day superior German artillery broke the Russian resistance in front of the assault group. The Germans began to roll up the Russian right flank. The Germans continued to press to the south, until on the 42nd day of mobilization both armies were locked in a general engagement from Wloclawek on the Vistula to Soldau. Eight German corps and five reserve divisions defeated 10 Russian corps. The Germans broke the Russian center and right flank and sent the Russians in panic-driven flight to the south-east.

Aside from the further development of Schlieffen's operational doctrine of active defense based on rail mobility and surprise counteroffensives, the 1897 *Generalstabsreise* graphically illustrates the German strategy based on the concept of defense on interior lines. In this case, the Germans won a victory in the west on the 25th day, pushing the French back behind their border fortifications. They then transferred four corps to the east, where the Russians had overrun most of East Prussia. This still left 11 corps in the west. The German margin of

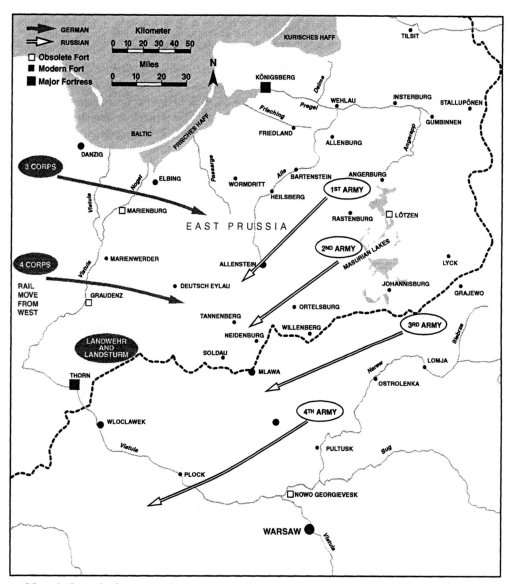

MAP 6. *Generalstabsreise Ost* 1897

victory—and margin for error—was razor-thin. By the 35th day these four corps were engaged. On the 42nd day the Germans won a largely frontal engagement with the Russians and pushed them back across the Vistula–Narew. At this point one supposes that at least four corps would be transferred back to the west. Such a procedure would avoid immediate defeat but, given Franco-Russian numerical superiority, could not be continued forever.

KRIEGSSPIEL, 1897

Between 1896 and 1905 Schlieffen held an annual winter war game.[45] Only the critique of the 1905 game has survived. Enough of the 1897 *Kriegsspiel* was described in Groener's *Nachlaß* to make it possible to understand the conduct of the exercise.[46] The situation was similar to that of Waldersee's 1889 *Generalstabsreise West*. The French estimated that the Germans would employ 20 divisions in the east. They intended to cross over the upper Rhine and turn the Germans out of their defensive position between Metz and Strasbourg. If the Germans did not fall back to the right bank of the Rhine then the French would re-cross to the left bank in their rear. A German offensive would be stopped by the French fortress line long enough for the French maneuver to be effective.

The French army consisted of 25 corps (66 infantry divisions). On 9 June the 6th Army (five corps) was deployed on the left between Verdun and Toul, the 5th Army (four corps) and the 4th Army (four corps) between Toul and the Vosges. The 3rd Army (four corps) had crossed over the crest of the Vosges and moved on the Rhine between Strasbourg and Colmar. The 2nd Army (four corps) crossed the Rhine near Freiburg and advanced into the Black Forest on Triberg. The 1st Army in the south (four corps) advanced on Villingen.

The Germans had deployed 18 corps in a position between Metz and Strasbourg, with a corps in the upper Alsace. The French therefore probably had a six-corps numerical superiority, that is, they were about 30 percent stronger than the German *Westheer*. On 9 June the German

45 Zoellner, 'Schlieffens Vermächtnis', *MWR Sonderheft 4* (Januar 1938), 48.

46 'Kriegsspiel 1897', *Nachlaß* Groener, BA-MA N 137/20. Also in The Papers of Wilhelm Groener, United States National Archives Microfilm Publication M 137, Roll 20. The 'Kriegsspiel' presents some interesting points, not least of which is how it got into Groener's possession in the first place. A letter dated 29 Apr. 1931 from an unidentified (the signature is illegible) historian at the Reichsarchiv said that the historian had been using the exercise for his research and thought that it might interest Groener. He was sending Groener a situation map and the initial special and general situations, and asked that Groener return them as soon as possible because they really belonged in the archives. Groener apparently never did give the documents back.

1st Army (four corps) was east of Metz. There was then a considerable gap between the 1st Army and the 2nd Army (three corps), which was north-east of Saarebourg. The 4th Army (four corps) manned the *Breuschstellung* to the west of Strasbourg and the 3rd Army (four corps) was moving east across the Rhine south of Mannheim. When the French crossed the Rhine, the German high command pulled one corps out of the 1st Army and two from the 2nd Army to form a 5th Army, which was moved by rail to Württemberg and off-loaded behind the line Stuttgart–Ulm. The Landwehr from Württemberg and Bavaria was committed to the front line.

From a Reichsarchiv historian's letter to Groener, we know that, while the German forces in Lorraine withdrew to the east, the German 4th Army was able to move three of its corps to the east bank of the Rhine. The Germans therefore gained local numerical superiority in Württemberg—10 or 11 German corps versus 7 French—and won a 'total' victory. The Reichsarchiv historian said that this was a masterpiece of Schlieffenesque conception and execution. It illustrates that even as early as 1897 Schlieffen was experimenting with the use of rail mobility in the west as a force multiplier to obtain surprise and numerical superiority for his otherwise outnumbered forces.[47]

STRATEGISCHE AUFGABEN

Schlieffen's General Staff *Schlußaufgaben* (General Staff test problems) were published by Mittler in 1937.[48] Initially they were *Taktische Aufgaben* (tactical problems) which dealt with corps-sized units. In 1897 they were expanded to involve army-sized units and in effect became *Strategische*

---

[47] It is clear from Groener's *Nachlaß* that he had practically unrestricted access to the material in the Reichsarchiv. Groener could have published Schlieffen's exercises and plans, but didn't. Instead, it was apparently Groener's intention to write a collection of Schlieffen's comments along the lines of the Military Maxims of Napoleon that were so popular in the 19th cent. Groener therefore collected *bon mots* from a wide range of Schlieffen's exercises. Groener's advocacy of the Schlieffen plan therefore cannot be attributed to ignorance of the facts. Rather, he distorted the truth with malice aforethought. (*Nachlaß* Groener, BA-MA N 137/20). The exercises cited included the 1896 *Generalstabsreise*, an *Operationsstudie* in January 1898, the *Generalstabsreisen* in 1898, 1900, both in 1903 and both in 1904, and the 1905 *Kriegsspiel*.

[48] Generalstab des Heeres (ed.), *Die taktisch-strategische Aufgaben aus den Jahren 1891–1905* (Berlin, 1937). The tactical problems from 1891 to 1896 were: 1891: I Corps against two Russian corps at Gumbinnen in East Prussia; 1892: XVI Corps as covering force at Metz; 1893: 5th Infantry Division in delay south-west of Saarbrücken; 1894: Two problems. The first seems to be based on the situation on 14 Aug. 1870 in front of Metz. The second was for XIV Corps in the defence in the upper Alsace; 1895: Cancelled due to Schlieffen's illness; 1896: Reserve and Landwehr units in the defence of Holstein against a corps attacking from Schleswig.

Aufgaben (strategic problems). At this point, if not earlier, the exercises were probably no longer conducted on the terrain but became map exercises.

Even in the second 'tactical' exercise in 1892, Schlieffen integrated strategic considerations.[49] He said that the Germans could conduct their deployment in the west on a line Diedenhofen–Metz–Saarebourg only if the French respected the neutrality of Luxembourg. If the French sent so much as one corps through Luxembourg, then the German deployment would be taken in the flank and rear. From the north bank of the Moselle the French could interdict the rail line that ran from Trier to Diedenhofen. The Germans would then have to pull their deployment back to the Saar. In the 1892 exercise the French VI Corps conducted a raid into Luxembourg on the 5th day of mobilization in order to disrupt the Trier–Diedenhofen rail line and push patrols into the Eifel.

In the 1898 *Strategische Aufgabe* the Russian Niemen Army, with eight corps, attacked into East Prussia. Two corps were at Tilsit, four at Gumbinnen–Angerburg, and two at Grajewo. A Narew Army of four corps was at Warsaw. The German army was still assembling: three corps and two reserve divisions were in a bow from the Kürisches Haff to Johannisburg covering the arrival of three corps and four reserve divisions.

Schlieffen said that the German solution was to concentrate against the nearest enemy army, defeat it, and then turn against the other enemy army. The German attack must be determined and decisive: if the Germans were held in place by one Russian army, the other would have time to attack the Germans in the flank and rear. The two Russian armies together would crush the Germans with sheer mass. If the German commander did not believe that he could win a decisive victory he would do well to withdraw over the Vistula.

Schlieffen said that it was difficult to predict the movements of the Niemen Army with any certainty. Indeed, it might not advance any further at all, but just sit tight. It was in the Germans' interest to attack the Niemen Army at once, before the two corps from Grajewo or the Narew Army could arrive. Schlieffen massed five corps against the center and right of the Niemen Army.

The German attack struck three Russian corps, destroying one outright and forcing the other two to retreat. Schlieffen said that this retreat would continue during the night, which would cause great confusion: the retreat itself was as damaging as a lost battle. Schlieffen

---

[49] Generalstab des Heeres (ed.), *Die taktisch-strategische Aufgaben aus den Jahren 1891–1905*, 13–14.

said that the entire German army, and not just one or two divisions, must pursue the defeated enemy without consideration for the fatigue of the German troops. The German pursuit could be effective in this case because the left-flank German units were closer to the Russian line of retreat than many of the Russian units were. The pursuit was continued to the Memel, where the Russians would have been able to set up a defensive position. In total, three Russian corps were destroyed, but three escaped intact.

GERMAN WEST-FRONT ENEMY ESTIMATE, 1898–1904[30]

In 1898 the French implemented a radically new war plan, Plan XIV. This plan was based on the theories of Bonnal, who in turn said that he was following the precepts of Napoleon. Bonnal modified Napoleon's *batallion carrée*, pushing forward an army as an advance guard. The Germans would attack the advance guard, whereupon the remainder of the French army would maneuver and attack. The French also decided that the active corps would consist of active units only. There would be no reserve corps—of a total of 17 reserve divisions, 12 would be assigned to the field army in the east, and the rest would be used on the Italian border and as fortress garrisons. The army in the east consisted of 40 infantry divisions and 12 reserve divisions, 52 divisions total.

As the advance guard, the 1st Army would be deployed at Nancy.[51] The rest of the French army was pulled into a tight group to the west of the 1st Army. This shifted the French army to the south. The left-flank 4th Army was moved south until it was west of Toul. The 3rd Army was moved south and west to Neufchâteau–Mirecourt, the 2nd Army south to Epinal. The 5th Army, in reserve, was now composed of 2½ active corps and remained at Chaumont. A group of reserve divisions was placed behind the left, center, and right of the deployment. This plan anticipated that the Germans would attack directly at the French center. It was clearly not intended to stop a German attack through Belgium, but could maneuver against the Germans once their right wing was north of Verdun. Plan XIV also facilitated a mass attack in Lorraine. Whether the French maneuver would be against the German right, or take the form of a breakthrough in the German center, was an open question. In 1903 the French implemented Plan XV, which maintained the essential features of the concept and deployment of Plan XIV, except that Plan XIV's five armies were reduced to four.[52]

[30] Greiner, 'Nachrichten', 42–95.
[31] A. Marchand, *Plans de concentration de 1871 à 1914* (Paris, 1926), Map Plan XIV after p. 139. [52] Ibid. 147–56.

It was retained as the French war plan until replaced by Plan XIV*bis* in 1907.

The only sources that the 3rd Department had for determining French intentions, Greiner said, were the French press and the reports of the German attaché in Paris. There was no evidence of agent reports or other sources. In the fall of 1897 the attaché reported that Plan XIV was a mobilization plan, not a deployment plan. The Germans were mostly concerned with the manner in which the French would utilize the reserve divisions—with the active corps or not? The 3rd Department continued to use the Plan XII estimate until 1904. In this estimate the 1st Army (four corps) was at Epinal–Belfort, the 2nd Army (five corps) was behind the 'Trouée de Charmes' (center of mass at Mirecourt) the 3rd Army (three corps) was strung out from Toul to the south-west, the 4th Army (four corps) extended the French left to the north of St. Menehould. The 3rd Department's estimate did not correspond to Plan XIV. It extended the French left 50 kilometers too far to the north, put four French armies on line when one was held in reserve, and failed to notice the change in the deployment of the reserve divisions. Most important, the Germans had no idea that the French would assemble the advance guard army at Nancy.

1899: SCHLIEFFEN'S *WESTAUFMARSCH*

In the *Aufmarschplan* for 1899/1900 Schlieffen provided two variants: *Aufmarsch* I was for a war on the west front alone; *Aufmarsch* II was for a two-front war. The only information Dieckmann provided for *Aufmarsch* I in this plan was that all 68 divisions were deployed in the west. There was, Dieckmann says, no actual *Aufmarschplan* in the archives.[53] Therefore, we know nothing of Schlieffen's concept for the operation. *Aufmarsch* II in 1899/1900 was similar to the deployment plans of the preceding years, with 45 divisions in the west and 23 divisions in the east.[54]

In October 1898 Schlieffen wrote a *Denkschrift* which changed the west front offensive into a counter-offensive.[55] This is clearly an experimental thinking paper. Schlieffen stated that the standard German deployment with one-third of her forces in the east and two-thirds in the west left Germany numerically inferior on both fronts. He therefore decided to test the idea of employing the mass of the German army in the west in a counter-offensive.

Schlieffen assumed that the French could complete their mobiliza-

---

[53] Dieckmann, 'Schlieffenplan', 118.   [54] Ibid. 126.
[55] Ibid. 119–23.

tion and deployment in two to three weeks, while the Germans would need four weeks. This contradicts other statements by Schlieffen that both sides would complete their deployments within days of each other. It may be that Schlieffen thought that deploying the mass of the German army in the west would take more time. It is more likely that by assuming a faster French deployment, Schlieffen could give the initiative to the French, and then analyze their offensive. Schlieffen frequently employed such a device in war games to require the German player to fight on the defensive. Schlieffen came to the conclusion that any French offensive would have to attack on both sides of Metz, with the right flank moving on the upper Saar and Strasbourg, while the left wing moved through Belgium and Luxembourg.

In this case, the most promising German counterattack was against the French left in the Ardennes. A frontal attack against the French fortress line was uninviting. It involved siege warfare which, even if successful, would bring little result, particularly as the defeated enemy could retire directly to the rear. Schlieffen said that the Germans should counterattack against the French left by sending two armies, the 1st and 2nd, through Belgium and Luxembourg. However, Schlieffen expressly stated that the envelopment could not be too wide. At the same time, while the three middle armies stayed on the defensive, the German left flank army, the 6th, would counterattack against the French right, which was presumably in Alsace. If the French did not attack at once, it would be a mistake for the Germans to wait for the French to advance: the situation in the east did not permit the Germans to be inactive in the west. If the Germans then launched a general offensive, the two right-wing armies, the 1st and 2nd, covered by a 7th Army of reserve divisions on the right and the 3rd Army on the left, would cross the Meuse between Sedan and Stenay.

If the right wing advanced across the Meuse, it was still essential to attack the French fortress line, first to tie down French forces, then eventually to break the fortress line to link up the German right and center. In the 2 August 1897 *Denkschrift*, Schlieffen had planned to attack the French fortresses on the Moselle between Toul and Verdun. He had to give up this project because the French were too strong, and substituted the old, much easier attack on Nancy. The 4th and 5th armies would move forward from their positions between Saarbrücken and Saarebourg against Nancy, to take the heights east of the city as well as Forts Frouard and Pont St Vincent. The center armies would then move to the south of Toul and through the 'Trouée de Charmes'. The 6th army would cover their left flank. This is exactly what Ferron had said in 1879/80 that the German plan would be.

Schlieffen also said that even in the case of a one-front war against

France alone, Germany still had to act in the east: the Russian army would not be idle, but would be preparing for eventual intervention, and the Germans would be forced to deploy more and more troops to meet this growing threat.

Henceforth the counter-offensive remained Schlieffen's preferred strategy: he would play it repeatedly in war games on both the west front and the east, culminating in his last great war game of November and December 1905.

On 1 October 1899, in the middle of the *Aufmarsch* year 1899/1900, Schlieffen changed the plan to implement his *Westaufmarsch*. Most important, Dieckmann said that the new deployment in the west was based on the October 1898 *Denkschrift*, that is, a plan for a counter-offensive in the Ardennes. An attack across the Meuse to the north of Verdun was clearly Schlieffen's second choice. Schlieffen changed the allocation of units from that of the October 1898 *Denkschrift*, weakening both flanks in favor of the attack on the center, which was therefore very strong, especially in active corps. Even so, the new plan only applied to *Aufmarsch* I, which was defined as being a situation in which Germany was at war with the Franco-Russian alliance, but Russia was not attacking in strength. It is also worth noting that in this war plan, even in this favorable one front strategic environment, Schlieffen could not afford to strip East Prussia bare of troops: under *Aufmarsch* I, Schlieffen still assigned a force of 10 divisions to East Prussia, with 58 divisions deployed in the west. In case of a two-front war, with the Russians attacking in strength, the previous plan, now *Aufmarsch* II, with 23 divisions in the east, would still be in force.[56] This presumably also involved a defensive–offensive operation in the west. The new *Aufmarsch* I marked an important addition to German war planning, but it did not break entirely with previous German planning. Conducting a strong counter-offensive in the west would be possible only in very favorable political circumstances; in case of a two-front war, Schlieffen's *Aufmarsch* II was little changed from the 1888 plans.

Under *Aufmarsch* II in the east the Germans would assemble on the line Thorn–Neidenburg–Masurian Lakes. A *Denkschrift* written by the Oberquartiermeister III (operations studies), Generalmajor von Lessel, said that the Russians were numerically superior and that the concept of the German plan in the east was to conduct a strategic defensive operation. The intent was to gain partial successes against the Russian

---

[56] Ibid. 127–34. Dommes says nine active corps and four reserve divisions, 22 divisions in total, one fewer than Dieckmann. Dommes does not mention *Aufmarsch* I, presumably because it was based on the assumption that the Russians were not attacking in earnest (Dommes, 'Operationen gegen Rußland', 12).

armies, which would be advancing in separate columns, divided by the Masurian Lakes.

Aufmarsch I for 1900/1 retained the same order of battle as the October 1899 plan: 58 divisions in the west and 10 in the east.[57] Although Dieckmann admitted that he lacked documentary proof, he said it appeared that the strength of the right flank was increased from two armies to three and the flank guard was reinforced so that the total strength of the right-wing armies increased from eight corps and five reserve divisions to 12 corps and six reserve divisions: more than half the strength of the Westheer. This would only be possible if the 3rd Army were relieved of its mission of providing protection against Verdun and integrated into the right wing with the two main-force armies (1st and 2nd). Dieckmann's interpretation must be treated with caution, since he was looking for opportunities to show that Schlieffen wanted to 'make the right wing strong'.

An *Operationsstudie* (operational study) written by General Hans Hartwig Beseler, then Oberquartiermeister III, on 18 January 1900, is the first document in which the concept of Schlieffen's *Westaufmarsch* is given fully.[58] Beseler wrote that the decisive operation would be conducted by the right wing, which therefore had to be made as strong as possible. The mission of the center armies, located to the south-east of Metz, was to support the right wing by fixing as many French forces in Lorraine as possible. The principal restriction on the strength of the right wing was the 90-kilometer stretch available between Liège–Namur on the right and Verdun on the left, which would accommodate 10–11 corps. When the right wing had defeated the French forces opposing it, it would swing to the south between Reims and Verdun. Once it had advanced until it was behind the French fortresses, it would attack the fortresses in the rear while the armies in Lorraine broke through their front. Where the Germans intended to break the French fortress line was left unspecified. The intent of the operation was to end the campaign with quick, decisive battles. Beseler saw the chief difficulty in the operation as the loss of surprise: it would hardly be possible to keep secret such a concentration of strength as that of the right-wing forces, and the French would surely take counter-measures. It is significant that this *Operationsstudie* was written not by Schlieffen, but by Beseler, one of the most respected and distinguished officers in the pre-war German army. This *Westaufmarsch* plan was clearly not Schlieffen's brainchild alone. This is not to say that the plan was complete; as Beseler said, there was still the problem of the enemy's reactions. Testing Schlieffen's *Westaufmarsch* against possible French plans, particularly

[57] Dieckmann, 'Schlieffenplan', 143–45.   [58] Ibid. 145–47.

against a French attack in Lorraine, would be a priority in subsequent staff rides and war games.

The Schlieffen *Denkschriften* of 1897 and 1898 and Beseler's *Operationsstudie* of 1900 were the basis of Schlieffen's strategy in the west, and not the 'Schlieffen plan' *Denkschrift* of December 1905. The goal was not to sweep around to the west of Paris but defeat the French army in battles near the frontier and then to break the French fortress line.

THE 1899 *GENERALSTABSREISE OST*

In the 1899 *Generalstabsreise Ost* Schlieffen assumed that Austria was initially neutral in a Russo-French war with Germany.[59] Without an Austrian offensive from Galicia, the Russians could ignore East Prussia and advance directly on Posen and Silesia. Such a situation would also occur if the Austrians were co-belligerents but stayed on the defensive in the Carpathians. The Austrian army was stagnating while the Russian army was growing and modernizing. Schlieffen clearly felt that the Austrians might soon be thrown on the defensive.

The Germans initially deployed four and a-half corps (nine divisions) in the east. The Russians left a portion of their army to watch the Austrians. Since the Russians had only two rail lines available, they did not assemble 12 corps in four armies in the area of Warsaw–Iwangorod until the 26th day. An army of 10 reserve divisions was at Kowno–Vilna. The Russians began operations with massive cavalry raids. They were met by Landwehr, Landsturm, and the divisional cavalry regiments, backed up by the cavalry divisions. On the 27/28th day of mobilization the Niemen Army's reserve divisions crossed the border into East Prussia and on the 35th day reached a line east and south-east of Königsberg. They were then dropped out of further exercise play. On the 30th day of mobilization two German corps were *en route* from the west. Schlieffen formed two corps out of units excess to standard corps authorizations. The Germans now had six corps and six reserve divisions on hand, with two corps and two reserve divisions arriving, plus the equivalent of seven Landwehr divisions. The Russian player was told that the Germans had four corps, plus two or three more en route; the location of the German troops was unknown. The Germans formed a Vistula Detachment with three reserve divisions to hold the Vistula fortresses. The Netze Army deployed between Posen and Thorn with three corps (seven divisions) by the 36th day of mobilization. The Silesian Army (center of mass Breslau) included five corps (14 divisions) and was ready by the 38th day. The German commander wanted

---

[59] *Generalstabsreisen Ost*, 106–74.

to draw the Russians onto the Netze Army and then attack the Russian left flank with the Silesian Army.

Schlieffen was not entirely happy with this solution. He said that the Landwehr and Landsturm should have been used as bait, and that the three corps of the Netze Army should have been used to attack the Russian left between Posen and Thorn. Schlieffen said that in 1870 and for part of 1871 the German army outnumbered the French, and could therefore fix the French with a frontal attack while turning one or both flanks. The best example of such a procedure was Sedan. Now the Germans were outnumbered. The Germans must therefore attack the enemy flank with maximum strength, while at the same time blocking his line of retreat. Only in this fashion could the German army win the sort of decisive victories which Germany needed if she were to win a war on two fronts.

The Russian commander decided to march on Berlin in the assumption that somewhere along the way he would force the Germans to stand and fight. He felt it likely that the Germans would mass at Thorn. The Russian army had a long approach march. The cavalry reached the German border on the 35th day of mobilization; the infantry did not reach the German border until the 38th day of mobilization. The Russians were deployed with the 1st and 2nd Armies in the north, generally facing the German Netze Army, while the 3rd and 4th were in the south, opposite the Silesian Army. The Russians had 408 battalions, 312 squadrons, and 1,560 guns; the Germans had 299 battalions, 148 squadrons, and 1,260 guns.

The two army groups maneuvered within the enormous arc from the Vistula at Wloclawek to Posen and finally to the border west of Lodz. The German Silesian Army moved to the north to strike against the center of the Russian position, at the junction of the 2nd and 3rd Armies, on the 45th day of mobilization. Schlieffen said that the attack was delivered frontally, and although the German artillery pushed in the right flank of the 3rd Army, the result was not decisive. The German commander in chief also did not order the Netze Army to attack boldly. The Germans won, but the situation would have quickly stabilized and Russian numerical superiority would have forced the Germans to withdraw somewhat. Neither side would have attained a tactical decision and the operation would have slowly ground to a halt. Schlieffen's lesson was plain. The Germans were not preordained to win. If the Germans attacked frontally, they would push the Russians back only to be stopped by superior Russian numbers. The result would be stalemate. This would be fatal: the Germans needed to be able to shift forces from one front to the other to obtain local superiority. The only operational method that the Germans could employ was to attack the enemy flanks and rear in order to destroy entire enemy corps.

Schlieffen's critique of this exercise contains warnings that were applicable on the Marne in September 1914. Schlieffen cautioned against over-reliance on command and control systems in modern warfare.[60] In peacetime exercises, he said, it is unavoidable that the senior commanders are extremely well-informed about the tactical situation and on that basis can issue daily operations orders that regulate the movement of subordinate units in detail. This peacetime procedure might lead to the impression that the command and control system would function perfectly in wartime. Given the distances involved on the modern battlefield, wartime reports would arrive late and orders would be overtaken by events. The execution of the operation would rest in the hands of subordinate leaders. They would be required to be thoroughly conversant ('voll und ganz durchdringen zu lassen') with both the intent of the higher headquarters and the general situation on the entire front and not merely the situation as it applied to their own unit. It was absolutely necessary that subordinate commanders insured that their decisions and orders conformed to the intent of higher headquarters. Subordinate leaders would truly do their duty only if they exercised the necessary initiative in order to bring the intent of the higher headquarters to fruition.

Major Hermann Kuhl was the commander of the Russian 4th Army during this exercise. Therefore, during the *Generalstabsreise Ost* in 1899, Schlieffen foresaw the problems that would arise in September 1914 and, in effect, told Kuhl exactly how he was to act. Kuhl apparently was not listening. He would later excuse his actions on the Marne by emphasizing the fact that communications with OHL in September 1914 were poor. In 1899 Schlieffen said that that was going to be the case. Kuhl would maintain that he didn't know what the overall situation was: Schlieffen said that it was Kuhl's job to find out. With a little initiative, Kuhl could have easily solved his communications problems with both OHL and the other army HQs. In fact, Kuhl was only too happy to lose contact with both OHL and the neighboring 2nd Army. This was because Kuhl was unsatisfied with the 1st Army's mission, which was flank guard. Rather than execute this mission, Kuhl tried to put the 1st Army in the position to win the campaign.

Schlieffen's warning concerning the proper and improper use of their initiative by senior officers was not an isolated occurrence. As early as the 1896 *Generalstabsreise* Schlieffen said that a great part of the reason for German success in 1870/71 was due to the initiative exercised by leaders such as the Prince of Prussia (Friedrich Karl) and Alvensleben. However, there were also cases of the abuse of initiative, of

---

[60] He would repeat this warning in detail in his 1901 *Strategische Aufgabe*.

which General Steinmetz was a prime example. With the first sort of leaders, Schlieffen said, the war is won; with the second, there is every prospect of being defeated.[61]

Aufmarsch II in 1900/1 was a true *Ostaufmarsch*, a massive deployment to the east the likes of which had not been seen since 1880: Schlieffen proposed to send 44 divisions to the east and only 24 to the west. Since Dieckmann once again did not have access to the planning documents, all that we know about the concept of the operation is what we can extrapolate from the deployment, which provided for five corps and 10 reserve divisions (20 divisions in total) to be assembled around Thorn, and nine corps and five reserve divisions (24 divisions in total) in eastern East Prussia.[62] Dommes said that the German military attaché in Vienna, Major von Bülow, told Beck that the Germans intended to attack in Poland with the advance against the Narew Army beginning on the 12th day of mobilization. Beck replied that the Austrians would complete their deployment on the 16th day and, if the Germans attacked, would begin their attack on the 18th day with eight corps in the direction of Lublin. Beck was concerned about his right flank, particularly because he could not be certain of the Romanians. The fact that we do not have Schlieffen's concept for this operation poses a serious problem in evaluating this plan. The plan was effective for only two years, and seemed designed for a special set of circumstances. There is the possibility that this was a plan for Austro-German intervention in a war between Britain and a Franco-Russian alliance. On the other hand, in his 1902 *Generalstabsreise Ost*, Schlieffen did conduct a genuine *Ostaufmarsch* which once again featured a German counter-offensive in East Prussia itself and not an attack into Russia.

Given the high proportion of active army corps it contained, Schlieffen intended that the second, East Prussian group, conduct the main effort. The limited capacity of the Prussian rail net east of the Vistula meant that assembling 24 divisions in eastern East Prussia would have been a very time-consuming process, which would have sacrificed any hope of achieving surprise. Nevertheless, with 44 German and some 30–40 Austrian divisions committed to an operation in the east, on the surface it would appear that the objective of the 1900/1 *Ostaufmarsch* was

[61] BA-MA *Nachlaß* Groener N 137/20.
[62] I Corps probably consisted of three divisions. Dommes says that 16 active corps and 13 reserve divisions were to be deployed between Thorn and Tilsit. This is probably 45 divisions, one more than Dieckmann gives. (Dommes, 'Operationen gegen Rußland', 12).

either a limited offensive to seize Russian Poland, or a strategic offensive against Russia proper. Nevertheless, Schlieffen never tested such an
operation.

Most likely, Schlieffen's intent was to force the French to attack
beyond their fortress line in order to rescue their Russian ally. In
November 1899 Schlieffen wrote a *Denkschrift* for just such a situation,
saying that the French 'could not avoid assuming the offensive'.[63] Given
that the French avenue of approach between Metz and Strasbourg was
severely restricted by German fortifications and the terrain, Schlieffen
felt sure that the French would extend their attack to the north to find
room to deploy their army. This would result in an attack to both the
north as well as to the south of Metz. Schlieffen wrote that when
the French left had passed beyond Metz it would lose the support of the
fortress line and be isolated from the rest of the army. The German
army would then mass against it and counterattack.

The essential factor for the German counter-attack was to conceal
the intentions of the German *Westheer*. The only forces that were to
march to the border were cavalry and border security. The *Westheer*
corps would remain for the most part in their mobilization stations.
When the French committed themselves, the German corps would
execute a prepared *Aufmarsch* to the area between Prüm and
Saarbrücken, on both sides of the Moselle, and attack the French left.
Schlieffen apparently used this situation as the basis of a General Staff
ride in 1900. In his exercise critique to this ride, Schlieffen expressed
his dislike of defensive positions and his preference for offensive
maneuver warfare.[64] No matter how excellent a defensive position the
German commander chose, Schlieffen said, given French numerical
superiority, the French could always outflank it. Even if the Germans
defeated a French frontal assault on the German position, the Germans
would not gain a decisive victory, for the French would merely withdraw
to their fortress line. A German frontal attack would also produce no
truly positive result. The best solution was to attack the French left with
forces massed directly by railroad from their garrisons. In case of
victory, the German pursuit might even bring the German army around
behind the French fortress line.

The decision that Schlieffen made at this time was not, as Ritter and
others have asserted, that Germany could only attack in the west.
Rather, Schlieffen determined that, because Germany was caught
between two very strong opponents, she had to use her interior position to win a decisive victory against one enemy before turning against

---

[63] Dieckmann, 'Schlieffenplan', 149–50.   [64] Ibid. 150–2.

the other. It was the decisive victory that was essential: which front it was fought on was left up to the circumstances at the time.

An anonymous article titled 'Die Befestigung und Verteidigung der deutsch-russischen Grenze' (The Fortification and Defense of the German-Russian Border) was first published in 1879 and updated three times, the last being in 1901.[65] The author begins by saying that even after the conclusion of the Russo-French alliance, there was no reason for hostility between Germany and Russia. The *Westaufmarsch* was the obvious German strategy. The French would be the driving force for war and Germany's most active enemy. If the French were beaten, there was every reason to expect that the Russians would make peace. An *Ostaufmarsch* would hit only air and would engage the Russians politically and militarily to no profit while the French would be advancing in the west. Even if the Russians were to fight in Poland, defeating them would have no lasting consequences, for victory over Russia would not affect French political will.

The German rail net in the east was suitable for the defense. There were four rail bridges over the Vistula into East Prussia. Two of these rail lines led to north-eastern East Prussia, while a major German rail line ran parallel with the border from Posen to Breslau. This would facilitate a defensive German deployment and troop movements.

On the other hand, rail communications from Poland into Germany were practically non-existent. One rail line ran parallel to the Vistula, but it was blocked by Fortress Posen. For a 400-kilometer stretch from Posen south to Silesia only one rail line crossed the border, and this was in the extreme south.

The Russian rail net was constructed primarily for civilian purposes. It was capable of conducting a tolerably efficient Russian deployment, but only against East Prussia. The Russian rail net was improving, but constructing the Trans-Siberian railway took priority over construction in Poland.

Most likely, the Russians would attack on two avenues of approach. One army would attack from Vilna to Königsberg while a second attacked from Warsaw down the Vistula. A landing on the Baltic coast was unlikely, as was a Russian invasion of Silesia. Even the route down the Vistula was not very suitable because it was exposed to attack from two sides and the Russians did not possess any rail bridges over the

---

[65] Anon., *Die Befestigung und Verteidigung der deutsch–russischen Grenze* (4th edn., Berlin, 1901).

Vistula downstream of Warsaw. The Russian army at Warsaw would therefore assemble on the right bank of the Vistula.

The terrain in East Prussia favored the defensive. The 180-kilometer length of the Masurian Lakes effectively closed the area to enemy movement. Thorn and the Vistula bridgeheads provided an excellent basis for defensive–offensive operations. This is probably where the Russians would encounter determined German resistance. The Russians could not bypass these fortresses, but had to take them before advancing to the west. Once over the Vistula, Danzig and Posen were also significant obstacles. The eastern border could therefore be considered secure against Russia.

The East Prussian fortresses would buy the Germans time. After the first mobilization had proven to be inadequate, the Germans would need this time to mobilize all their manpower and resources for the continuation of the war.

A German offensive against Russia was an unattractive proposition. Occupying vast stretches of Russian woods and swamp would accomplish nothing. The nearest important objective would be St Petersburg, 800 kilometers away. The prerequisite for an offensive against Russia would be the occupation of Poland. This was militarily possible, but politically pointless. Only the occupation of Russian national territory would put pressure on the Russian government to sue for peace. The mere occupation of Poland would lead only to a long, costly, and drawn-out defensive campaign against renewed Russian attacks.

Against a German attack, the Russians would conduct a defense in depth. The Russians were confident that, given time, they could assemble their vast resources and go over to the attack. The Narew–Niemen fortresses would secure the Russian deployment to the east of those rivers. The Russians would be able to conduct a defense on interior lines against an Austro-German pincer attack. The Austro-Germans would not be able to bypass Poland, rather they must first occupy it. The Russian rail net would be of little use to the Germans, first because of the different, larger, rail gauge the Russians used, and second because of an absence of lateral lines between the two main lines leading to St Petersburg and Moscow. The centre of long-term Russian resistance would be Brest-Litovsk. In the south, the fortresses of Rovno, Lutsk, and Dubno would form the base for a counterattack against the Austrians.

This should be considered an officially inspired pamphlet at the very least, perhaps it was even ghost-written by the General Staff. The pamphlet was dedicated 'to the German people' but the intended audience also included the Russians. The pamphlet insists that there are no issues that the Russians and Germans need to fight over, and that the

Germans had no intention of launching an offensive in the east. It would seem to reinforce the interpretation that the concept for the 1900/1 *Ostaufmarsch* was for a counter-offensive on either the east or west fronts.

1901: *GENERALSTABSREISEN*

In the first *Generalstabsreise* for 1901, the *Generalstabsreise West*, Schlieffen employed a *Westaufmarsch*: the Germans deployed 22 corps and 12 reserve divisions against France.[66] Six corps and four reserve divisions were deployed in the east. The Italians, although members of the Triple Alliance, were of little help and were able to fix few French forces on their common border. The French attacked through Luxembourg and Belgium on the 12th day of mobilization. In the west the decisive battle was fought close to the left bank of the Rhine, on the German–Belgian border. It resulted in a German victory on the 23rd day of mobilization, which allowed the Germans to transfer nine corps to the east.

By transferring nine corps to the east, Schlieffen left a force of 13 corps and 12 reserve divisions in the west: 38 of the 68 divisions available to the German army were still in the west, only 30 divisions were in the east. The French had been defeated, but not destroyed. In this case, a decisive victory in the west in Schlieffen's eyes meant the elimination of nine corps' worth of French combat power, about two armies. But the French army would not have been eliminated: it would still have demanded the attention of more than half the German army. Therefore, Schlieffen did not equate a decisive victory in the west with the total annihilation of the French army, as has often been contended.

In order to begin the transfer of forces to the east by the 24th day of mobilization, the decisive battle against the French had to be fought and won close to the German railheads. If the Germans had fought the decisive battle further west, say between Verdun and Reims, as Beseler had considered to be a possibility, then these German forces, no matter how victorious, would not have been available for immediate rail movement east.

This situation was then integrated into the second exercise of that year, the 1901 *Generalstabsreise Ost*.[67] The Russians waited in order to complete their mobilization before attacking. Therefore, the Niemen

[66] Dieckmann, 'Schlieffenplan', 153–4. The 1900 *Generalstabsreise* was conducted in the upper Alsace in order to determine if the area near Schlettstadt and Freiburg should receive permanent fortifications. The exercise was conducted in the greatest secrecy: all the participants wore civilian clothing. (Sächsischer Militärbevollmächtigter (4517), 18 Oct. 1900, Hauptstaatsarchiv Dresden).

[67] *Generalstabsreisen Ost*, 176–230.

Army, with six corps and eight reserve divisions, did not cross the border until the 24th day of mobilization. The Narew Army, with six corps, crossed the border on the 29th day. The Germans employed two armies in East Prussia. The 1st Army, with three corps and two reserve divisions, deployed on the Angerapp in the east. The 2nd Army, with three corps and two reserve divisions, deployed at Soldau. In the face of the Russian attack, the 1st Army fell back to Fortress Königsberg while the 2nd Army retired to the north. The Austrians crossed the border on the 20th day of mobilization. The Austrians pushed the Russian South-west Army north toward Brest-Litovsk. The transfer of the nine corps from the west took 10 days. Six of these corps arrived on the Vistula on the 34th day of mobilization.

After their defeat on the 23rd day of mobilization, the French immediately sent for help to the Russians, asking for a Russian offensive to take the German pressure off the French armies. The Russian Niemen Army continued its advance against the German 2nd Army, while the Narew Army advanced south-west on Graudenz and Thorn. The arrival of the German 3rd Army between Marienburg and Marienwerder on the 34th day caught the Narew Army by surprise. The German attack would have destroyed two Russian corps had not Schlieffen stopped the German advance in the interests of later problem play. At the same time, the German 1st Army attempted, unsuccessfully, to sortie from Fortress Königsberg. Three German armies, from north to south the 2nd, 3rd and 4th, now advanced from the Vistula to the east. However, on the 38th day the Russian Niemen Army defeated the German 2nd Army and was then able to send forces against the left flank of the German 3rd Army to the south. While the front between the German 4th Army and Russian Niemen Army stabilized, by the 41st day the Russian Narew Army had turned the open flank of the German 3rd Army, which would have resulted 'in a catastrophe of the worst kind for the Germans'.

In the exercise critique Schlieffen said that the most important factor in a war between the Triple Alliance and the Franco-Russians was Franco-Russian numerical superiority. In addition, Austria would have great difficulties overcoming the problems inherent in her deployment and would be slow to reach operational readiness. Germany's advantage lay in her central position. This advantage became a liability once Germany had to divide her army and was therefore outnumbered on both fronts. The Germans had to defeat one opponent while holding off the other. When there was no longer a threat on one front, the Germans had to use rail mobility to shift forces to the other front, gain numerical superiority there, and defeat that opponent. The initial battle must be truly decisive: a Solferino would not do. The Germans must win another Sedan, or at least a Königgrätz. Schlieffen said that an attack against the French fortress line would accomplish little in a two-front war. The Germans needed to wait until the French had advanced past their fortifications. Last, Schlieffen said that the Germans must always hold fast to one principle: attack the enemy's line of retreat. In a two-front war, Germany required complete victories.

The 1901 *Strategische Aufgabe* also concerned East Prussia.[68] The Russian Niemen Army deployed five corps by 3 June, with two reserve corps arriving on 6 June and two more reserve corps by 8 June. The Narew Army deployed with seven corps and one reserve corps by 7 June. The German army in East Prussia had deployed by 1 June with five active corps and three reserve corps (18 divisions), center of mass south of Königsberg at Bartenstein.

Schlieffen wrote an unusually long nine-page exercise critique. He began by saying that the German position was unenviable: the combined Russian forces were three times as strong in infantry as the Germans. If the Germans stayed put, their right flank was in great danger. If they advanced to the south, they would have the Frisches Haff to their rear and their left flank would be threatened by the Niemen Army. Schlieffen noted with obvious satisfaction that most of the officers had decided to attack the Niemen Army Group, which was the closest, and then turn on the Narew Army. After at least six major exercises in East Prussia, Schlieffen could feel that he was making some progress.

Schlieffen's solution stated his entire doctrine in a nutshell: the only way to surprise the enemy was by maneuver. The Germans could not effectively attack the Russian flank with one or two corps—they had to employ an entire army. To do this, the Germans needed to 'refuse' their left flank: bend it back so that the Russians could not immediately attack it. Schlieffen was obviously using Frederick the Great's Oblique Order as an example.

Schlieffen noted that there was a strong tendency in the German army to conduct frontal attacks. He said this observation was supported by reading the results of exercises such as this one, as well as corps general staff rides and published articles. By conducting frontal attacks officers sought to keep their forces massed together and insure the security of their lines of communication. These officers were only comfortable when their left flank was aligned with the enemy right,

[68] Anon., *Taktisch–strategischen Aufgaben*, 74–87. The 1900 *Taktische Aufgabe* was interesting because the students were required to analyze the situation first of a Russian army and then of a Russian corps to the south of Lyck, but the exercise had no strategic significance.

their right flank with the enemy left. The advocates of this procedure then argued about the best way to conduct frontal attacks in the face of modern firepower. The principal concern of such a procedure was to avoid losing a battle. If the enemy followed the same system the result would be indecisive battles and long-drawn-out wars. This condition was not tolerable in an age of million-man armies. The welfare of the nations and the expenditure of vast resources necessary to support million-man armies both required decisive battles and short wars.

A commander cannot be motivated by the desire to avoid defeat, Schlieffen said. His decisions must be driven by a burning desire to destroy the enemy. Thirty years ago (1870/71) we could engage the enemy frontally, Schlieffen observed. We enjoyed numerical superiority and had sufficient forces to engage the entire enemy front while turn-ing the flanks. Today we will never be numerically superior. At best, we can hope to have equal numbers; usually, we will be significantly outnumbered. It is the enemy who will be able to turn our tactics of 1870 against us.

We must find a means to fight, although outnumbered, and win, Schlieffen maintained. There is no universal solution to this problem, no formula for success. One thought, however, seems justified. If your forces are too weak to attack the entire enemy army, attack a part of it, preferably the flanks. The larger the enemy force, the more sensitive the flanks and the longer it will take the enemy to reinforce them when attacked. The flank of an enemy army should be attacked not with one or two corps, but with one or more armies, and the objective of these armies cannot be the end of the enemy line, but must be his lines of retreat. Ulm, the winter campaign in 1807, and Sedan were examples of such a *Vernichtungsschlacht*.

THE END OF THE *GROSSE OSTAUFMARSCH*, 1902/3

In the 1901/2 *Aufmarsch* II, Schlieffen reduced the forces in the east to 41 divisions, with 27 divisions in the west.[69] The 1901/2 *Aufmarsch* I deployed 10 infantry divisions in the east and 58 in the west.

In the 1902/3 *Aufmarsch* II, Schlieffen reduced the forces in the east to the levels of the previous plans: two-thirds (44 divisions) of the field army were deployed in the west, and only one third (24 divisions) in the east.[70] The experiment with the great *Ostaufmarsch* was now over.

---

[69] Dieckmann, 'Schlieffenplan', 154–5. Dommes says 16 corps and 11 reserve divisions, 42 divisions in total. Dommes, 'Operationen gegen Rußland', 12.

[70] Dieckmann, 'Schlieffenplan', 155–1. Dommes says nine corps and nine reserve divi-sions, 28 divisions in total. Dommes, 'Operationen gegen Rußland', 12.

Twenty-four divisions would give the German *Ostheer* near numerical equality with its probable Russian opponents. Dieckmann had no concrete information concerning the 1903/4 *Ostaufmarsch*. Dommes says that the *Ostaufmarsch* for 1903/4 was 'small' ('nur einen kleinen') and the *Ostaufmarsch* for 1906/7 was being planned for 3 corps and 7 reserve divisions: 13 divisions in total. He concluded his briefing by saying that Schlieffen had become increasingly skeptical of an eastern offensive because of the difficult terrain. Neither Austria nor Germany had any interest in a war with Russia and Austrian priority was for a war with Italy.[71]

From the mid-1880s to 1913 the German army maintained two *Aufmarsch* plans. After October 1899 these were called *Aufmarsch* I and II. Each plan generally had two components, a deployment to the east—*Ostaufmarsch*—and one to the west—*Westaufmarsch*. The use of the terms *Westaufmarsch* and *Ostaufmarsch* to refer to an offensive on those fronts seems to have originated after 1914, indeed after 1918. The improper use of the term *Ostaufmarsch* has led to the perception that since the German army during this period had an *Ostaufmarsch* it intended to conduct a massive attack to the east, *à la* Moltke's 1880 plan. As we have seen, this was incorrect. Except possibly for the brief interlude in 1900/1 and 1901/2 the intent of *Aufmarsch* II was not to make a serious attack to the east. Under *Aufmarsch* II, the German army in the east, with some 20 divisions, might launch a spoiling attack against the Niemen and Narew to disrupt the Russian deployment. Thereafter the Germans would use interior lines to defend East Prussia. No German Chief of Staff after 1888 (with the possible exception noted above) seriously contemplated an all-out attack in the east. There is no evidence that any *Generalstabsreise*, *Kriegsspiel*, or *Strategische Aufgabe* dealt with an operation even remotely resembling an eastern offensive. The very existence of an offensive *Ostaufmarsch* after 1888 is a myth.

Gerhard Ritter contended that the German army continued to prepare Schlieffen's 1900/1 and 1901/2 *Aufmarsch* II, which he, following Ludwig Beck, called the *Große Ostaufmarsch* (great eastern deployment) until 1913, when it was terminated by Moltke.[72] The existence of such a plan up to 1913 would demonstrate that a great eastern offensive was really still possible in August 1914. Moltke's supposed cancellation of the *Große Ostaufmarsch* in 1913 has even been interpreted by Fritz Fischer's supporters as an indicator that the Germans were going to conduct an aggressive war in the west. In fact, the so-called *Große Ostaufmarsch* was an aberration, an episode, which by 1914 had not

---

[71] Dommes, Operationen gegen Rußland, 12–14.
[72] G. Ritter, *The Sword and the Sceptre* (Miami, 1969), ii. 202.

existed for over ten years. The *Aufmarsch* II which was allowed to lapse in 1913 was almost certainly incapable of conducting an invasion of Russia.

In the 1902/3 *Aufmarsch* I, Schlieffen altered the deployment in the west significantly.[73] The 2nd–6th Armies (18 corps and 4 reserve divisions) were to deploy directly on the border with Luxembourg and France, from Echternach south, while the 1st Army (four corps, four reserve divisions) was echelonned behind the right flank, in a great bow between Eupen to the west of Bitburg. Dieckmann explained that Schlieffen had become convinced that the French were anticipating the right-wing attack north of Verdun, and would deploy strong forces on the Meuse to meet it. A frontal attack on this position was not at all to Schlieffen's liking. In the 1902/3 plan, therefore, Schlieffen decided to attack with his left and refuse his right. The 4th Army would attack between Verdun and Toul, the 5th and 6th against Nancy and the 'Trouée de Charmes'. Schlieffen hoped this would draw the French left out of its positions on the Meuse to attack into the Ardennes and across the Moselle to outflank the Germans east of Diedenhofen. Schlieffen then intended to conduct a counterattack against the left flank of this French force with the German 1st Army. This illustrates Schlieffen's preference for the 'backhand blow', that is, waiting for the enemy to attack and to commit himself, and then counterattack against the enemy's flank and rear.

In the spring of 1902 Schlieffen conducted a war game in which the Germans attacked the forts between Nancy and Toul while also attacking Nancy itself. In a note concerning this war game written on 16 May 1902, Schlieffen emphasized that in an attack in the west, both wings of the German army needed to support each other.[74] The attack on the Moselle fortifications would only succeed if supported by an outflanking maneuver to the north of Verdun. On the other hand, an outflanking maneuver to the north of Verdun would be exposed to defeat by overwhelming French forces if not supported by an attack against the Moselle fortresses. The German forces facing the French fortresses could not wait to conduct their attack until the right wing had unhinged the French line nor could they limit themselves to demonstrating or observing the enemy: they had to attack and fix French forces on the Moselle even as the right wing conducted its attack. The left-wing attack was vital to Schlieffen's *Westaufmarsch*.

Even though in the 1902/3 *Aufmarsch* II he had reduced the number of troops in the east to a level suitable only for a spoiling attack, on 5 December 1902 Schlieffen wrote a *Denkschrift* which analyzed the pos-

---

[73] Dieckmann, 'Schlieffenplan', 155–61.   [74] Ibid. 158–9.

sible conduct of a strategic attack by 13 corps and 10 reserve divisions—
36 divisions in total—in the east.[75] The main attack was conducted
frontally by nine corps and four reserve divisions from Thorn to the
Narew and then on to the Bug, where Dieckmann thought that the
Germans would link up with the Austrians. The main attack would be
covered on the left by an army (four corps, six reserve divisions) north
of the Masurian Lakes. The need for speed probably forced both a
reduction in the size of the force in eastern East Prussia and the assembly of the main force near Thorn. Schlieffen was apparently forced to
admit once again that any German attack in the east must be made
against the Narew, with all the disadvantages which were recognized as
far back as the 1880s. Because of this, the results of this *Denkschrift*
cannot have encouraged Schlieffen to launch the German main offensive in the east except as a means of drawing the French out of their
fortress line in the west.

Recently five of Schlieffen's *Generalstabsreisen* from 1902 to 1904 have
been discovered, four in their entirety and one summarized by
Dieckmann. They provide a fascinating view of the thoughts of one of
the great military thinkers of the twentieth century. Unfortunately for
proponents of the Schlieffen plan, none of these exercises resembles
the Schlieffen plan in the slightest.

1902: *GENERALSTABSREISE WEST*

In 1902 Schlieffen held two *Generalstabsreisen*, the first being conducted
in the west.[76] The French deployed the Vosges Army north-east of
Epinal with three corps, the 1st Army with two corps and the 2nd Army
with three corps near Lunéville, the 3rd with five corps near Nancy, and
the 4th with four corps near Verdun. The Germans employed 24 corps
in the west: the 1st Army near Metz with five corps, the Metz Army with
two corps, the 2nd Army at Saarlouis–Saarbrücken with three corps, the
3rd Army with four corps on the Saar south of the 2nd Army, the 4th at
Saarebourg with four corps, the 5th at Strasbourg with two corps, and
the 6th in Alsace with four corps. The Germans obviously did not
intend to attack through Belgium: indeed, the mass of both the French
and German armies were prepared to fight in Lorraine. Both armies
were deployed by the 14th day of mobilization.

The Germans had intended to wait in Lorraine for the French to

---

[75] Ibid. 165–6.

[76] '1. Große Generalstabsreise 1902, Geheim!' Kriegsarchiv Munich, Generalstab 1234.
Thirty pages long, handwritten in the German Standard style with nine maps. In this
form it was sent to all units with general staff officers so that they could stay current with
the latest strategic thought.

attack. The French intended to wait for the German attack. Both sides wanted to conduct a defensive–offensive battle. Schlieffen asked ironically if the Russians would allow the French to follow such a seemingly infallible plan, that is, would Russia agree to conquer Alsace-Lorraine on the Vistula and Oder while the French remained inactive?

Schlieffen said that it was far more likely that both the French and the Russians had reached a joint agreement to attack simultaneously.[77] Therefore the French would have to deploy between Epinal and Verdun with a detachment at Belfort. The French *Schwerpunkt* would attack between Metz and the Vosges. If the Germans defeated the French attack, the French would withdraw to their fortress line. The Germans would then have to break through the fortress line and after that they would still be faced with a long and difficult campaign, a *Volkskrieg*, in the interior of France. The Germans would hardly be able to conduct such a campaign in the face of Russian pressure in the east. The Germans therefore had to destroy the French, and this could only be accomplished by an attack on the French flanks and rear. The German army needed to attack both to the north of Metz against the French left as well as from Alsace against the French right.

The German army, faced with both a powerful French army and Russian pressure in the east, was not strong enough to conduct such an operation. Schlieffen therefore decided to increase the 19 available corps, each containing 24 infantry battalions, to 26 corps, each containing only 21 battalions. However, the new 26 corps would still contain the normal complement of artillery (how this was accomplished was not specified). Such an increase in the ratio of artillery to infantry was a prescient proposal. The most important point was that, once again, Schlieffen's principal concern was to create the maximum number of German maneuver units. Nevertheless, the French would still enjoy a slight numerical superiority.

The mass of the German army, 13 corps, was concentrated on the Saar, while the 1st Army, advancing through Luxembourg and followed by four reserve divisions, would turn the French left and the 6th Army, followed by three reserve divisions, would attempt to turn the French right in Alsace.

---

[77] Geyr von Schweppenberg said that the 1st (Russian) Department's records were destroyed during the Spartacist uprising in March 1919. He maintained that he was one of the few to have had access to these documents. He contended that the Germans had obtained a copy of the Russian 1902 war plan. (Leo Freiherr Geyr von Schweppenberg, 'Der Kriegsausbruch und der deutsche Generalstab', *WR* (1963), 151). There are also strong indications that the Germans were informed early on of the military clauses of the Franco-Russian treaty, especially the frequent German reference to the Russian 50–50 division of their army against Austria and Germany.

The French left-wing 4th Army and the German 1st and Metz Armies crashed together in a meeting engagement. The German 1st Army was massed in such depth and on so narrow a front that it was unable to outflank the numerically inferior French and the German frontal attack brought no results. Eventually, however, the Germans turned both French flanks and the French withdrawal became a rout, while the Germans pursued with long-range artillery fire.

In Alsace Schlieffen pointed out that Belfort provided the French with a sally-port which could threaten the flank of any German attack over the Vosges south of Strasbourg. The French, however, sent only one division east from Belfort and it was quickly defeated. The French Vosges Army had the mission of both protecting the right flank of the main body and attacking across the Vosges. The Germans attacked from Alsace, broke the French defense on the Vosges crest, and forced the entire French Vosges Army to withdraw.

In the centre the French assumed that the Germans would defend on the Saar. The French plan was to envelop the German left wing with the 1st Army, but in the face of strong German forces advancing out of the Vosges this army was forced to go over to the defensive. The French therefore decided to break the German line at Saargemund–Saarbrücken on the 19th day of mobilization.

Schlieffen said that the proper course of action for the German forces in Lorraine was to meet the French attack with a general advance. Officers who hoped to hold a defensive line, beat off a French attack, and then counterattack (Moltke's old defensive–offensive operation) were deceiving themselves. The attacker has the advantage of choosing the point of attack and would never do the defender the favor of attacking at the proper place. Nevertheless, the 4th German Army defended in place while the German 2nd and 3rd Armies attacked on the 18th day of mobilization. Two corps of the German 2nd Army hit a gap in the French line and broke through. The Germans also mounted a concentric attack by the 1st and Metz Armies on Pont à Mousson, the anchor for the French left flank. The entire French left flank had to withdraw toward Château Salins and Nancy. Schlieffen said again that German long-range artillery fire would have caught retreating French troops in the open. The French national headquarters would have had only an incomplete picture of the situation and that any orders they issued on the night of 18/19th days of mobilization would not have been able to establish a coordinated rearward movement.

However, the Germans were not able to close the trap and annihilate the French army. A large part of the French army would have reached the security of the French fortress line. The Germans would have been forced to attack this line and there was every prospect of the campaign into the interior of France consuming significant German forces.

Schlieffen said that the exercise did demonstrate that it would be difficult for the French to conduct an attack between Metz and the Vosges, even against numerically inferior German forces, so long as the Germans did not commit serious errors. There was no need for the Germans to block the avenue of approach in Lorraine with fortifications.

It seemed therefore likely that the French would seek to turn the German position in Lorraine by advancing to the north of Metz–Diedenhofen. The Germans must establish a strong right-flank army to block this French advance. The success or failure of this army would probably determine the outcome of the campaign.

However, if the French decided to defend on their left flank they could make a German outflanking maneuver to the north of Metz difficult if not impossible. An army based on Verdun could counterattack against the Germans as they moved between Verdun and Metz on Pont à Mousson. The French could also prevent the Germans from crossing the Vosges, not by adopting a passive defense as they had done in this exercise, but by attacking, especially down the Breusch valley.

Schlieffen pointed out that front lines were continually growing longer. It would do no good to try to fix the length of front according to doctrinal rules of thumb. Commanders would be forced to expand their front as far as necessary in order to accomplish their mission. A narrow defensive front held in depth (Moltke's old doctrine) was a one-way road to disaster the minute the enemy began to outflank the position. The increasing length of front meant that it was possible to break the enemy line, which had happened three times during this exercise. Long lines were particularly vulnerable if one unit stopped while the other continued to advance, creating gaps in one place while the units bunched up in others. Units must dress their lines ('mit Fühlung und Richtung marschiert werden') in order to prevent this. Nevertheless, the difficulty of conducting frontal attacks would force the attacker to fix the defender in place with a frontal attack while at the same time turning one or both flanks. This fixing attack must be a determined one, conducted by infantry: artillery fire alone would not do. Metz had once again proved its value, not as a fortress *per se* but as a secure base for the maneuver of the field army.

Schlieffen reiterated that subordinate commanders must use their initiative in order to realize the senior commander's concept of the operation. He said that the greatest weakness of modern armies was that this generally did not occur to an adequate degree.

It is not hard to see why the Reichsarchiv did not publish this exercise. The French army was not annihilated, the main battle was fought in the Vosges and Lorraine, and there was no trace of the 'Schlieffen plan'. In addition, Schlieffen's comments read like a critique of Kuhl's conduct on the Marne.

1902: GENERALSTABSREISE OST

This exercise was also not included in the General Staff's book *Generalstabsreisen Ost*.[78] The reason is not far to seek: Schlieffen played an outright *Ostaufmarsch* at a time when he was supposed to be perfecting the 'Schlieffen plan'. He also made extensive use of notional units. Since this was a glaring weak point in the 'Schlieffen plan' *Denkschrift* the General Staff surely wanted as little attention brought to this practice as possible.

Schlieffen began with a thorough discussion of the fact that, initially at least, the Russian forces were divided in two halves by the Masurian Lakes. This presented a window of opportunity in which the Russians could be defeated in detail. This opportunity was fleeting: the Russian advance would quickly result in the two armies linking up. The easiest and least risky German course of action was to counterattack from Thorn–Graudenz against the left flank of the Narew Army. However, the Russians would probably not be accommodating and would rest their flank on the Vistula. An attack against the right flank of the Russian Niemen army ran the risk of being thrown back into the Kurisches Haff. However, it was not possible to defeat a stronger enemy without taking risks.

The German army in East Prussia consisted of nearly half the entire German army: nine corps and eight reserve divisions. Schlieffen also deployed no less than eight Landwehr divisions in the east, which did not really exist at all. He also employed 17 Landsturm battalions in field operations and in the course of the exercise would form an ersatz corps out of the 24 *Ersatzbataillone* in East and West Prussia—Schlieffen's East Prussian *levée en masse* was making yet another appearance. In addition, the remaining German forces—11 corps, 11 reserve divisions—apparently did not deploy to the west but remained in their mobilization stations. This was initially a true *Ostaufmarsch*, a war on the east front only.

The Russians began the campaign with immediate cavalry raids. The center of mass of the German forces was concentrated in the middle of East Prussia. Schlieffen acknowledged that such a concentration could

[78] '2. Große Generalstabsreise 1902, Geheim!' Kriegsarchiv Munich, Generalstab 1235; also Hauptstaatsarchiv Dresden Generalstab XII Armeekorps, KA (P) 9195. Twenty-six pages long, handwritten in the Standard style with eleven maps.

not be conducted by the damaged East Prussian rail net, but would have to be made by foot-march. This was possible because the Russians did not attack until they had finished deploying on the 26th day.

The Russian forces consisted of 11 corps and 8 reserve divisions. When the Russians had completed their mobilization one army of five corps and three reserve divisions advanced to the north of the Masurian Lakes and two armies of three corps each, followed by a total of four reserve divisions, advanced to the south. The Russians had little intelligence on the location of the German main body owing to the screen provided by German Landwehr and Landsturm units on the border. The Russian intent was to crush the German forces with a concentric attack.

The German commander wanted to allow the Russians to attack his position on the Angerapp and then counterattack against his flank— Moltke's old defensive–offensive strategy. Unfortunately, the Russian commander refused to cooperate. The Russians stopped their own forward movement when they detected that the German left wing was advancing. On the 28th day, while the German Landwehr and Landsturm held the line of the Masurian Lakes, the German commander concentrated the remainder of his forces against the Russian northern army and launched a general advance, with five corps attacking the Russian front while three more corps enveloped the Russian right flank. Three Russian corps were annihilated and the rest attempted to withdraw. Schlieffen said that it was essential for the Germans to begin the pursuit immediately the next day and not rest on the battlefield, as often happens. The pursuit was continued until the 31st day, the German forces moving parallel to the withdrawing Russians as well as attacking the rearguards, when the Russians were forced to cross the Niemen using only one bridge, at which point the Russian northern army disintegrated.

On the 29th day the Germans had turned three corps around to confront the Russian forces advancing from the south; on the 31st day they were followed by four more. The commander of the Russian southern armies decided to advance directly north behind the Masurian Lakes in order to relieve the pressure on the Russian northern army and cut off the German forces. Schlieffen said that this also exposed the Russian armies to complete destruction: it would have been better if the Russians had moved to the south of the lakes to link up with the northern army.

In order to march north the Russians had to cover their left flank against Thorn. They assigned this task to the 3rd Army, which now consisted of only one corps and four reserve divisions. This force was too weak and the 3rd Army was continually forced to withdraw to the east by a German army made up of reserve divisions. Meanwhile the Russian 2nd Army continued its advance to the north, carefully shadowed by four German Landwehr divisions. Two other German Landwehr divisions were not so cautious and were dealt a severe defeat by a Russian corps.

The main armies were engaged on the 34th day, each trying to turn the other's western flank. The IX German corps was successful and the Russians were forced to retreat. Six Landwehr divisions had, however, blocked all but one road in the Russian rear. Schlieffen said that even if the Russians had been able to defeat the Landwehr divisions, the delay this occasioned would have been fatal for the Russian army.

This exercise clearly illustrates Schlieffen's developing doctrine: a true mass German army conducted mobile counter-offensive operations on German territory in order to fight battles of annihilation against the attacking enemy army.

1902: *STRATEGISCHE AUFGABE*

The 1902 *Strategische Aufgabe*, continuing the line of thought Schlieffen had developed in the 1902 *Generalstabsreise West*, concerned a French attack to the north of Metz. On the left flank the French 1st Army, with five corps and six reserve divisions, was deployed behind the Meuse with center of mass at Verdun on the 13th day of mobilization. On the right flank there were three divisions at Belfort. The remainder of the French army, 28 infantry and 10 reserve divisions, was deployed between Epinal and Nancy. These 38 divisions would advance between Metz and Saarebourg, securing their left against Metz and their right against Strasbourg. The mission of the 1st Army was to attack the German right flank. The success of the entire French offensive rested on the 1st Army attack. This was therefore designated the main attack and given priority of support. It was not necessary for the 1st Army to respect Luxembourg's neutrality. The French estimated that the German army was half to two-thirds the size of the French and would defend near the border. For exercise purposes it was assumed that all of the works at Diedenhofen and Metz that were either in construction or planned were complete.

The German army in the west consisted of 14 corps and 10 reserve divisions, probably 38 divisions in total (the total French force was 20 corps and at least 14 reserve divisions—54 divisions at a minimum). This meant that there were 30 divisions in the east: for all intents the Germans were conducting an *Ostaufmarsch*. The German *Westheer* assembled between Metz and Saarbrücken.

Schlieffen again wrote a long (10-page) evaluation of the exercise.

Some officers had decided to conduct a frontal attack toward Nancy. Schlieffen said that such an attack was directed at the strongest sectors of the French defensive front and was utterly pointless. Schlieffen said that the French left wing would appear north of the Moselle at or below Sierck, where it was isolated from the main army and was faced with crossing the Moselle while their left flank was exposed to an attack from Trier. An attack directly on the French left would, however, merely push it back to Verdun. In order to destroy the French 1st Army it was necessary to attack simultaneously from Trier as well as from Diedenhofen against the French 1st Army's lines of communication.

Schlieffen's solution was to hold the line of the Moselle between Metz and Diedenhofen with four Landwehr divisions and from Diedenhofen to Sierck with a Landwehr division and four reserve divisions. He moved seven corps from Lorraine to the north to attack the French 1st Army while it was isolated north of Metz. Four corps would cross the Moselle north-east of Sierck and attack the French left. Three cavalry divisions would sweep wide to attack the French rear. Three more corps would attack from the west of Diedenhofen to the north. The French would be caught in a double envelopment and destroyed or, more likely, would try to withdraw quickly to Verdun. The victorious German army would then stand to the north of Diedenhofen and would be able to operate against the left flank of the French main body.

Schlieffen said that few officers had chosen to conduct his concentric attack against the French left. Most attacked north-west from Metz-Diedenhofen or between Metz–Sierck. This would merely lead to a frontal battle. The best that one could hope for would be a gradual German advance, while the main French army closed in on the German rear. This would not do: what was necessary was to conduct a double envelopment to obtain the quick destruction of the French 1st Army.

1903: *GENERALSTABSREISEN*

In 1903 Schlieffen played a *Generalstabsreise West* and then a *Generalstabsreise Ost*. In the *Generalstabsreise West*, Schlieffen again conducted an *Ostaufmarsch*.[79] Therefore, the French had a 2 : 1 numerical superiority. Schlieffen's solution was to use the rail system to mass against the French left while it advanced through the Ardennes. Two armies (eight corps and four reserve divisions) assembled in the Rhineland and attacked up the left bank of the Moselle. They were supported by two corps advancing from the Saar and another force of three corps and six reserve divisions attacking from Metz–

---

[79] Dieckmann, 'Schlieffenplan', 164–5.

Diedenhofen. Seven reserve divisions would hold the line from Saarlouis to Saarbrücken, with two corps behind their left flank. Once again Schlieffen appears interested in the *Ostaufmarsch* solely because it would put pressure on the Russians, who in turn would demand help from their French ally. This would force the French to come out of their fortifications and attack in order to divert German forces from the east. The French would then advance close enough to the German rail net for Schlieffen to deliver a crushing counteroffensive.

The 1903 *Generalstabsreise Ost* was a staff ride in name only. In fact, it was really a huge east-front war game, with 21 officer-players, most as army commanders. Schlieffen said that the French and Russians had agreed to launch simultaneous offensives against Germany by the 18th day of mobilization.[80] (During the 1911 staff discussions the French and Russians would agree on simultaneous attacks by the 16th day of mobilization.) It became clear to the Russians that the Germans were conducing a *Westaufmarsch*, leaving only five corps plus their reserve divisions in the east. Furthermore, it appeared that the Germans were planning to delay back to the fortified Vistula line. By the 29th day of mobilization the Russian Niemen Army (six corps, with a reserve corps and two reserve divisions en route) was approaching Allenstein, halfway through East Prussia. The Narew Army (six active corps, two reserve corps) had crossed to the right bank of the Vistula and was south of Wloclawek. The French had launched their main attack in Alsace-Lorraine. On the 29th the Russian high command received word that the French had taken heavy casualties in Lorraine and had been forced on the 27th day to retreat behind the Moselle and Meuse in order to prepare to resume the offensive. German losses had also been very heavy and the German pursuit was tentative. It was now important for the Russians to conduct a determined offensive in order to relieve the pressure on the French. The Austrians had attacked into the western Ukraine but were stopped by the Russian defense, based on the fortresses of Lutsk, Kowel, and Dubno. The Austrians had not attacked to the north against Lublin–Kholm.

By the 32nd day the Niemen Army was a day's march from the Vistula north of Thorn, while the Narew Army was crossing the border to the south of Thorn. The Germans knew that the French would renew the attack in the near future, but until then they had a window of opportunity in which they could obtain local superiority in the east. It was decided to transfer 11 corps to the east—the maximum force that could be moved by rail in a reasonably short period of time. Once again, Schlieffen had also created two corps from excess units and deployed

---

[80] *Generalstabsreisen Ost*, 232–310.

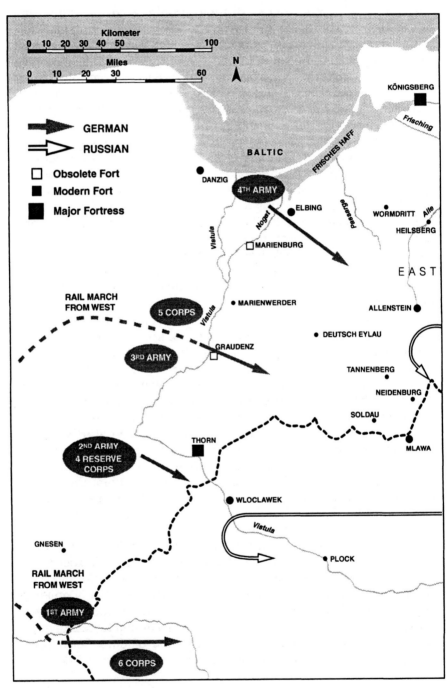

MAP 7. *Generalstabsreise Ost* 1903

them to the east: the German force in the east amounted to 18 corps. This would probably leave 7 corps in the west, plus 10 reserve divisions and Schlieffen's usual mob of Landwehr and Landsturm. Schlieffen had clearly decided to heed his own advice and mass against one opponent at a time. The Germans, with 18 corps and some 9 reserve divisions, would significantly outnumber the Russian's 12 corps and 8 reserve divisions.

Schlieffen was going to play his favorite trick on the Russians—allowing them to advance to the German border while the Germans massed a large force by rail for a surprise counteroffensive. The 5th Army (two reserve corps) held Königsberg while three corps conducted a low-risk delay through East Prussia to the Vistula bridgeheads north of Thorn. The 4th Army (four corps) concentrated by rail behind the lower Vistula. The 3rd Army (five corps) was transported from the west and off-loaded behind Graudenz. The 2nd Army (four reserve corps) assembled at Thorn. The 1st Army (six corps) from the west off-loaded to the east of a line Posen–Breslau. The lead elements of the rail move from the west arrived on the evening of the 30th day, the last combat troops late on the 34th or early on the 35th day.

The Russians were aware that the Germans were moving troops from the west, but had no idea how many or where they were being sent. On the 32nd and 33rd days both Russian armies were marching concentrically on Thorn.

On the 32nd day the German commander in the east gave his concept of the operation: double envelopment of the enemy flanks; annihilation of the enemy army by cutting it off from its route of retreat over the Narew and Vistula.

The German left wing started the attack on the 32nd day, with 5th Army successfully breaking out of Königsberg while 4th Army crossed the Nogat. On the 33rd day the Austrians attacked with two armies of three corps each against Lublin–Kholm.

By the 34th day the Russian situation was becoming critical. The German 4th and 5th Armies were enveloping the Russian right at an operational depth. The German 3rd Army was assembling on the Russian right and the German 1st Army was unopposed on the Russian left. Both the Niemen and Narew Armies began to withdraw to the south while the Russians moved troops west from Warsaw to try to shore up the open left flank.

The Niemen army was unable to get away. It was fixed in place by frontal attacks while the German 3rd and 4th Armies crushed its flanks and German cavalry closed it off to the rear. On the 37th day it was completely encircled north-west of Soldau and by the 38th day it was annihilated.

The Narew Army lived only slightly longer. At the end of the exercise on the 40th day it was being encircled to the west of Warsaw, with the 1st and 2nd German armies to the front while the 3rd Army turned its right flank. The Narew army's rear area was also infested with German cavalry. At the same time, the Austrians had taken Brest-Litovsk.

In the exercise critique, Schlieffen stated the fundamental problem of German strategy. In the west, the Germans had only been able to drive the French back behind the Meuse and Moselle. If they did the same in the east and drove the Russians behind the Narew and the Vistula they would soon be forced to transfer corps back to the west to meet the renewed French attack. In the meantime, the Russians would recover and the Germans would be forced to shift forces back to the east. The long-term effect of this procedure would be to completely wear down the German army.

In a two-front war, Schlieffen said, the Germans could only win by destroying the largest number of enemy units possible, first on one front and then on the other. The means to accomplish this were well known. Frederick the Great used the technique repeatedly, as did Napoleon in 1800, 1805, 1806, and 1807. Moltke did the same in August and September 1870. The method was to attack an enemy flank and rear with all or at least with the largest part of one's forces and make the enemy army fight with a reversed front. If the enemy was attacked on both flanks, as at Leipzig, Gravelotte, and Sedan, he could be encircled. Schlieffen did not mention Cannae.

1904: END OF DIECKMANN'S MANUSCRIPT

In the 1903/4 *Aufmarsch* I, Schlieffen assigned 65 divisions to the west and 10 to the east.[81] Dieckmann wrote that the now-missing map 9 showed that Schlieffen had returned to the deployment of 1901/2, which called for a three-army attack through the Ardennes. Dommes says that Schlieffen reduced *Aufmarsch* II to a small force, without being more specific.

At this point, Dieckmann's manuscript ends—just when it was getting interesting. That it does so is practically incomprehensible. A few more pages of text would have sufficed to provide, for the first time, detailed information concerning the Holy Grail of German war planning, the Schlieffen plan *Denkschrift*, as well as the *Aufmarschpläne*, *Kriegsspiele*, and *Generalstabsreisen* for 1904 and 1905. An indication of the direction Dieckmann was taking can be seen in his table of contents. Dieckmann divided 'Der Schlieffenplan' into three parts. The first

---

[81] Dieckmann, 'Schlieffenplan', 162–5; Dommes, 'Operationen gegen Rußland', 12.

section, pages 1–45, was titled 'The operations plans of the Great General Staff in the first half of the 1890s'. The second was titled 'The envelopment plan' (pages 46–175). The last chapter in this section, 'The fortress problem and the operations plans of the chief of staff', was apparently never written, nor did it have any page numbers. The same is true for the entire third and last section, titled 'The encirclement plan'. It included three chapters: 'The Franco-English Entente and the Russo-Japanese War'; 'The great chance'; 'Bülow's victory over Schlieffen'. It would appear, however, that Dieckmann had written a draft of the last chapters. It would seem reasonable to suspect that Dieckmann had come to the commonly held conclusion that Schlieffen had written the 1905 *Denkschrift* as a plan to conduct a one-front preventive war against the Franco-English Entente while the Russians were occupied in Manchuria and that Bülow had blocked its execution. The problem with this conclusion is that it would contradict the paper Dieckmann had written in which he argued that Schlieffen did not advocate preventive war at this time. If so, Foerster did not agree with Dieckmann's preventive war thesis. Dieckmann had already drawn sharp criticism from Foerster for his political opinions. Foerster's criticism seems justified. Dieckmann did not support his political views with serious research, and his paper would have been much better off without them. Nevertheless, we do not know whether Dieckmann stopped work just short of completion (for whatever reason) or whether Dieckmann did complete the manuscript, and the offending parts were later excised.[82]

By providing detailed information for the first time concerning Schlieffen's planning from 1889 to 1904 Dieckmann's 'Der Schlieffenplan' dramatically expands our perspective on Schlieffen's war planning. The contention that Schlieffen's strategic thought consisted of a switch from an east- to a west-front offensive leading to the culminating Schlieffen plan must now be rejected. Taken in

---

[82] It may be that Foerster himself tried to write an essay on Schlieffen's war planning. The file containing Dieckmann's manuscript includes three other documents. One is a review of Foerster's *Graf Schlieffen und der Weltkrieg* by Max von Szczepanski, with Foerster's shorthand notes in the margin. The other is an unsigned thirteen-page handwritten draft, in Standard script, titled 'Einige Bemerkungen über die Entstehungsgeschichte des Schlieffenplanes' (Some Notes on the Development of the Schlieffen Plan) in what appears to be Foerster's handwriting. The draft does not go beyond 1897. The third is a 26-page fragment of a typewritten draft which primarily concerns the 1905 *Denkschrift*. The authorship is uncertain, the page numbers are different from Dieckmann's manuscript, and it provides little that is new. It is also obviously a rough draft: entire pages are lined out. It is probable that Dieckmann's manuscript survived because it was in Foerster's office when the Reichsarchiv was bombed.

[83] Greiner, 'Nachrichten', 95–7.

conjunction with Schlieffen's exercises, 'Der Schlieffenplan' shows that Schlieffen's thought was moving in an entirely different direction—toward the use of strategic rail mobility, mobile warfare, and counteroffensives in operational depth. On both fronts he clearly preferred to conduct a counteroffensive against French and Russian attacks. Any advance into France was ideally a continuation of this counteroffensive. Only in the unlikely event that the French stayed on the defensive did Schlieffen reluctantly envisage an offensive into France. At no time did Schlieffen commit himself to one perfect plan. In case of war, he clearly intended to adapt his plan to the changing political, strategic, and operational situation. Dieckmann's manuscript also demonstrates Schlieffen's early and continual concern over the inadequate strength of the German army. Most important, there is practically nothing in this manuscript to support the contention that the Schlieffen plan *Denkschrift* was the culmination of Schlieffen's strategic thought. In fact, it demonstrates that this *Denkschrift* was an isolated aberration.

1904: GERMAN ENEMY ESTIMATE IN THE WEST[83]

Until 1904 the 3rd Department had always reckoned with the possibility of a French offensive. With the start of the Russo-Japanese War, it was practically certain that in case of war the French would initially conduct a defensive–offensive operation behind their border fortifications. For this purpose, the 3rd Department felt that the French would have to extend their left to the north. The new enemy estimate therefore shifted the 2nd Army farther north in the direction of Toul, the left of the 3rd Army moved north to Bar le Duc, and the left of the 4th Army was moved about 60 kilometres to the north-west, at Rethel. The 3rd Department now estimated that the French left was about 100 kilometers farther to the north than was actually the case. The 3rd Department expected the French to be strung out in a line between Epinal and Rethel, when in fact they were massed in a *battalion carrée* behind Nancy.

1904: TWO *GENERALSTABSREISEN WEST*

The French deployment for the 1st *Generalstabsreise West* in 1904 was similar to the Plan XII estimate, assuming a flank army near St Menehould and large concentrations in depth behind Nancy and Epinal, with groups of reserve divisions evenly distributed behind the flanks and center of the active army forces.[84]

---

[84] 'Geheim. Übersicht über die Operationen der 1. großen Generalstabsreise 1904' (Secret. Summary of the Conduct of the 1st Great General Staff ride in the West for 1904)

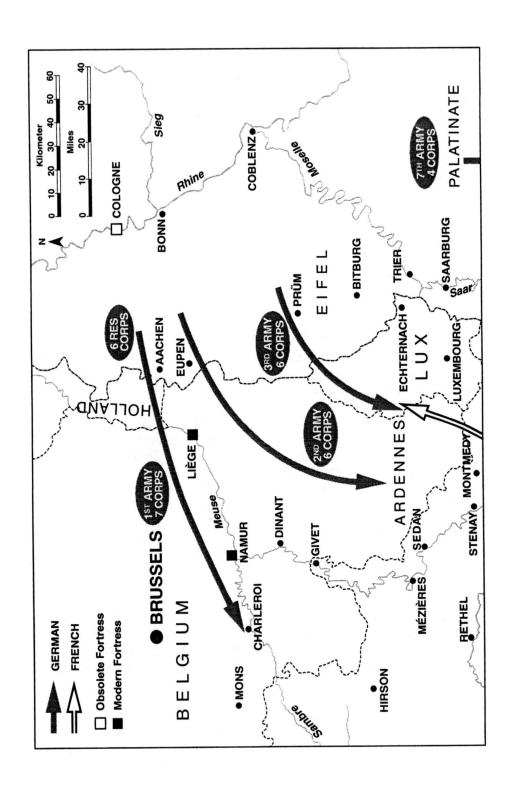

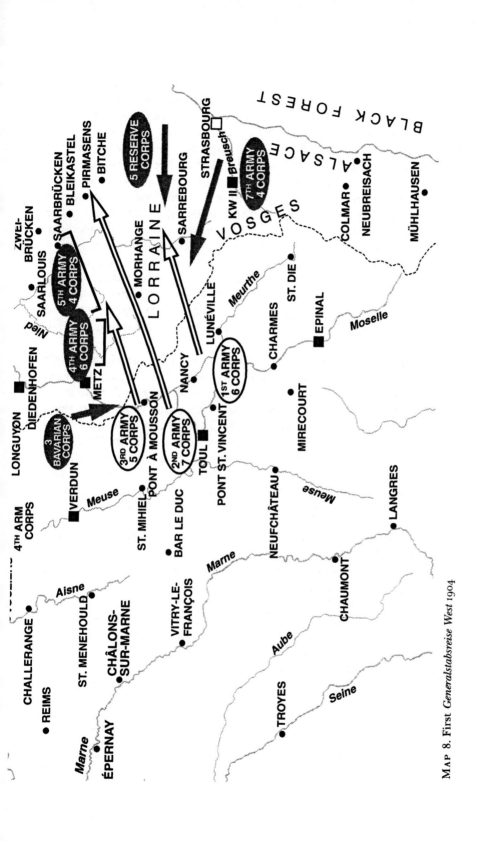

MAP 8. First *Generalstabsreise West* 1904

Schlieffen's German army in this exercise was considerably different from the actual German army. Instead of the total of 19 reserve divisions actually available, he had 16 reserve corps. In addition there were 14 Landwehr divisions, which did not really exist at all, to be used for rear-area protection. Schlieffen said that one may well ask where all the reserve corps came from. His answer was that, because the German army had chosen (in this exercise) to march through Belgium, there were a great many missions that required reserve forces: occupying Belgium; covering Belgian, Dutch, and French fortresses; securing the flanks. When the war really starts, Schlieffen was saying, if we need the units, we'll raise them. Clearly, Schlieffen had not given up his goal of completely using available manpower, and expected to use the pressure generated by total war to overcome the obstacles to his program of raising as many units as possible. On the other hand, Schlieffen was also saying that the attack through Belgium and northern France only had a chance of succeeding if the German army had many more units than were actually available.

The German deployment consisted of a mass of 17 corps in a triangle Aachen–Wesel–Cologne, connected by a screen of six corps in the Eifel to a group of German forces with six corps near Metz, with nine more corps echelonned to the rear toward the Palatinate. Most of Lorraine was held by reconnaissance forces only. There was a army of reserve divisions to the north-east of Strasbourg and three corps in Alsace.

Schlieffen then discussed the invasion of Belgium at length. He began by saying that Britons and Americans who had studied the problem had, as practical people with few scruples, come to the conclusion that the Germans were going to march through Belgium in the next war. The Belgians had come to the same conclusion, and had built Liège and Namur largely for the purpose of blocking that attack. Only the French didn't completely agree. They were so convinced of German aggressiveness that they expected the Germans to attack directly against their fortress line, at which point they would maneuver and counterattack. This counterattack could only come through Belgium and Luxembourg, so any way one looks at it, all the possible participants thought the war would spill over into Belgium.

Schlieffen said that there were two ways for the German army to conduct its right-flank envelopment of the French fortress line. The first was to extend the German right wing as far north as Mézières. This

BA-MA, PH 3/659. Schlieffen's exercise critique was 24 pages long, handwritten in Standard style and included eight maps. On the cover was written 'Foerster' in large block letters with a blue pencil, as well as the number 1474 in the lower right-hand corner. The Militärarchiv also has a second copy, PH 3/660, which has no maps.

meant that when the right wing crossed the Meuse the German army would be divided into two halves with the united French army occupying a central position between them. The result of such an operation would not be favorable. The second possibility was to march all, or a significant part, of the German army around the French left. Instead of attacking the French on a line Verdun–Belfort, one would attack them on a line Verdun–Lille, where there were no fortifications to get in the way. The problem with this course of action was that the approach march through Belgium was so long that all chance of surprise was sacrificed. Furthermore, this attack necessitated crossing Dutch territory. Last, the German army was so large that the deployment assembly area must extend as far south as Strasbourg. This presented the French with a flank to attack.

We are so used to the Schlieffen plan myth that we commonly assume that the right-wing attack was a brilliant, innovative idea. From Schlieffen's introduction to this *Generalstabsreise* alone, it is obvious that it was no great secret that the Germans could attack through Belgium into northern France. Schlieffen's discussion of this operation can hardly be considered a ringing endorsement for such an attack. Rather, from the list he cited of problems it posed, Schlieffen quite clearly thought that the attack had very little to recommend it. Schlieffen was not endorsing such an attack: he was warning against it. It should therefore come as no surprise that Schlieffen preferred to conduct counterattacks near his own railheads.

Given a situation in which the French learned that the Germans were deploying on the lower Rhine, Schlieffen asked several officers to work out the French reaction. Many decided that the French should conduct a second deployment by rail to northern France, there either to occupy a defensive position on a line Reims–Verdun or Paris–Verdun, or to conduct a counterattack. Schlieffen felt that this would take too long. He agreed with those officers who decided to attack the German left flank in Lorraine. Schlieffen said that this would produce a battle of Leuthen on a larger scale. The Germans would be forced to respond by sending their centre and right to the south, just as the Austrians had done at Leuthen. The only thing that would prevent this was if the Germans created around Metz and Strasbourg fortified zones from which armies could sally to conduct counterattacks. The fortified zone of Metz would force the French to divide their forces in order to advance to the north and south of it. Such fortified zones would also force the French to detach prohibitively large forces to guard them.

On the 16th day both the French and German armies began their advance. The French attacked with 18 corps and four reserve divisions (40 divisions in all) in Lorraine between Metz and Strasbourg while a smaller army of five corps and seven reserve divisions (18 divisions in total) advanced along the left bank of the Moselle towards Trier. The Dutch and Belgians had allied themselves with France. The British were not mentioned.

The German mission was to assemble as many corps as possible in the area Metz–Strasbourg to oppose the French advance in Lorraine. The German 1st Army entered Holland, the 2nd moved south-west into the Ardennes, the 3rd south south-west into the Eifel, the 4th was stationary near Metz, the 5th and 6th moved side-by-side to the south in the Saarland and Palatinate, the Reserve Army remained north-east of Strasbourg, and the 7th Army stayed west of Strasbourg. To the 19th day the French maintained their advance on both sides of Metz, while the German right wing armies—1st, 2nd, 3rd—continued moving south-west through Belgium, the Ardennes, and the Eifel. The German 4th, 5th, and 6th Armies began to assemble on a line Metz–Zweibrücken, facing south. There was a great deal of inconclusive fighting near Strasbourg. On the 19th the French occupied a defensive position with 10 corps to the south of the German Metz–Zweibrücken line.

Schlieffen took this opportunity to talk about positional warfare. A defensive position of this length (and by this he meant a hasty defense, not a defense that had been prepared for a considerable period) must have weak areas, even gaps. It is the job of the attacker to conduct careful reconnaissance and use the terrain and periods of darkness to bring his artillery and infantry forward and attack to discover where these weak points are, then exploit these to create a penetration. In this exercise, 10 German corps attacked 10 French, with one German corps breaking through the French line. It exploited this penetration and defeated a French reserve corps, which was inferior in artillery to the German corps. A French corps then conducted a mass counterattack. Having discussed the proper way to conduct an attack in modern warfare, Schlieffen now pointed out the wrong way. The French corps in question attacked on a front of 3 kilometers—practically a solid mass of infantry—apparently expecting that the moral effect of such a horde would sweep all before it. Schlieffen would have none of it, judging that it would have been destroyed by artillery without having achieved anything at all.

In part because of undue emphasis on the Schlieffen plan, Schlieffen has always been accused of harboring a monomaniacal fascination with outflanking the enemy. Here, as in many other places, he showed how properly conducted frontal attacks could defeat a hasty positional defense, allowing the attacker to mass against weak points in the defense.

The decisive battle took place on the French left flank. Here the

French commanders placed their trust in what they thought was a strong anchor for their left flank on the small but prominent Wallersberg hill. Schlieffen said that concentrated artillery fire would have quickly rendered the hill untenable, regardless of the heroism of the defenders. The French left was turned by three Bavarian corps and several cavalry divisions attacking out of Metz, while the French right was likewise turned by several German corps attacking from Strasbourg. (Given Schlieffen's continual use of fortresses as offensive spring-boards, it is astounding that the chief of staff of the German 1st Army in September 1914, none other than Kuhl, failed to guard against an attack from Paris.) At this point Schlieffen noted that if one is in a bad position, it is better to retreat early than to be destroyed. The French force in Lorraine was enveloped on both flanks and annihilated. Meanwhile, the battle to the north of Metz had degenerated into a side-show: the right-wing German 1st Army hardly made contact with the enemy. The exercise was over on the 21st day of mobilization.

In his final comments, Schlieffen said that a French offensive in Lorraine was a difficult undertaking, but that it would have been more effective if the French had not split their forces by sending them to the north and south of Metz. The French should have sent the entire force between Metz and Strasbourg, thereby having more forces available to guard the flanks. He repeated his previous statements concerning the importance of Metz and Strasbourg as fortified areas that should primarily be used to support offensive operations, and restated his mistrust of defensive positions. In conclusion, he said that what was important in the attack was artillery, not massed infantry.

This *Generalstabsreise* took place less than two years before Schlieffen's retirement. Superficially, it has three points in common with the December 1905 *Denkschrift*. First, Schlieffen used notional units both in the 1904 exercise and then on a massive scale in the 1905 Schlieffen plan *Denkschrift*. Non-existent units can hardly be used in a war plan. For this reason alone, the Schlieffen plan could have been an exercise or a policy paper, but not a war plan.

Second, in the 1904 exercise the German army was initially deployed in a formation which seems similar to that of the 1905 *Denkschrift*. The three armies of the right wing contained no less than 17 corps and extended far to the north along the Belgian border. This was a function of available deployment space and efficient use of rail capacity and was not a unique characteristic of the Schlieffen plan. By 1904/5 the German army in the west included 50 or 60 divisions; in 1914, 70 divisions. Counting non-existent divisions, the Schlieffen plan had to move and deploy 96 divisions! There was neither the rail capacity nor the physical space available to send the entire German army to Lorraine in

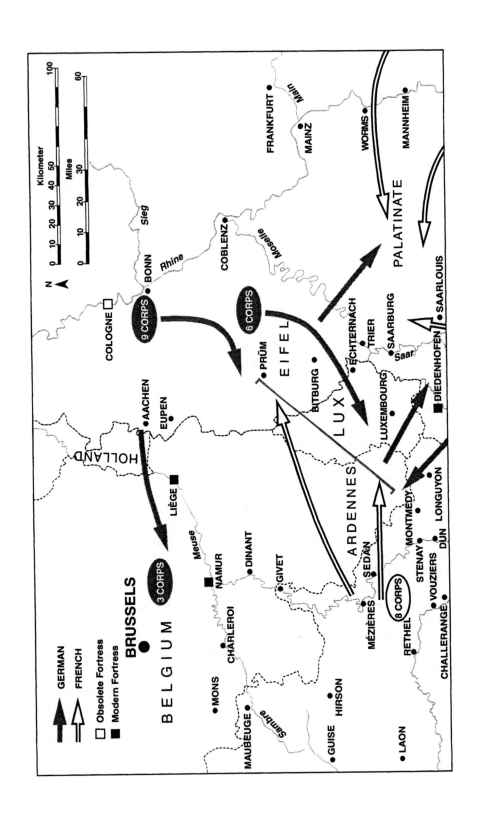

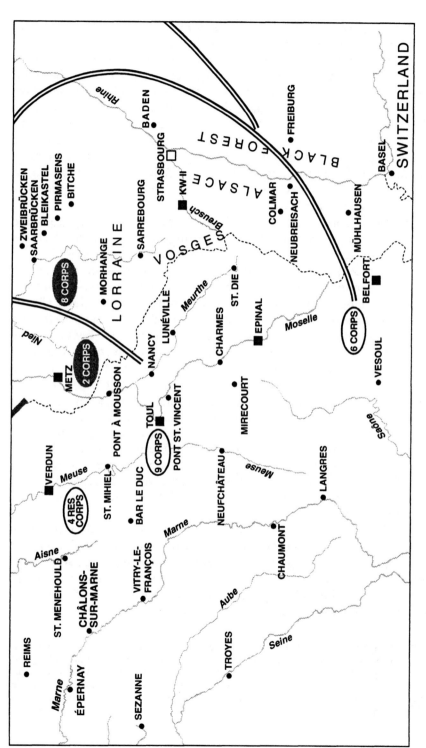

MAP 9. Second *Generalstabsreise West* 1904

1904 or 1914, not to speak of the fantasy army of the Schlieffen plan. The German army had to deploy along the lower Rhine.

Third, the most important factor in this exercise is that the plan for the right wing attack never survived contact with the enemy. By taking the offensive in strength in Lorraine, the French seized the initiative and forced the Germans to fight the decisive battle in a place of their choosing. The climactic battle took place between Metz and Strasbourg. The mission of the three right-wing armies became one of protecting the rear of the main battle, and they spent most of the exercise foot-marching south, not west, through Belgium. All in all, if the 1st 1904 *Generalstabsreise West* was a test of the 'Schlieffen plan', then the 'Schlieffen plan' failed badly.

Schlieffen conducted a second *Generalstabsreise West* in 1904.[85] He began his critique by saying that the starting situation for the Germans was the same as in the preceding exercise, with two exceptions. Because of doubts that Germany could raise so large a force of reserve corps, the Germans would have no reserve corps but rather 23 reserve divisions, which was close to the actual German strength of the time. Clearly there was serious resistance among the General Staff officers to the use of notional units on such a large scale. The Landwehr divisions were also eliminated. The Germans deployed in three groups: nine corps around Aachen and the Ruhr, six corps at and north of Trier, ten corps in Lorraine and one in Alsace. As in the first 1904 staff ride, Schlieffen stated that it was the German intention to attack on the line Lille–Verdun. For exercise purposes the German fortifications on the upper Rhine—which were not very formidable anyway—did not exist. The Belgians still allied themselves to France; the Dutch were mentioned in passing later on; the British weren't mentioned at all. The French were also allocated several reserve corps and additional infantry divisions—proof that Schlieffen did not play favorites when handing out notional units.

The French initial deployment was modified so as to allow a French attack into upper Alsace on the 13th day of mobilization. The French also deployed in three groups: the right wing with eight corps, with the mission of crossing the upper Rhine; a centre group of six corps between Lunéville and the Vosges; and a northern group of nine corps at Verdun which would advance along the Moselle.

---

[85] 'Übersicht über die Operationen der 2. großen Generalstabsreise 1904', BA-MA PH 3/661. This exercise critique, also handwritten in Standard style, is 22 pages long and includes eight maps. On the top part of the cover, the bottom half of the name 'Foerster' in block letters and blue pencil is visible. Foerster also annotated several passages in the critique with blue pencil. In the lower right-hand corner of the cover is the number 1475. There is a second copy, 662, which has no maps.

The French received reports that the Germans were deploying on the lower Rhine, but stuck to their plan to cross the upper Rhine. The Germans learned of the French deployment and abandoned their plan to march on Lille–Verdun. Instead, the Germans repeated their actions of the previous exercise and marched their center and most of the right-flank forces directly to the south, this time to engage the French left on the Moselle. The German 1st Army moved into north Belgium as originally planned, but it could accomplish nothing alone. Schlieffen said that he could agree with neither decision. Schlieffen's view was that if the Germans had continued to march on Lille–Verdun, the French would have had to turn back to protect Paris. Schlieffen also said that by crossing the Rhine, the French were doing the Germans a favor, because troops on the right bank of the Rhine would be out of the battle. However, Schlieffen did not feel strongly enough about the attack through northern France to test it in this exercise. Indeed, given that he had done everything to insure that the French could cross the upper Rhine early and easily, such radical changes would have been inconsistent with the initial concept of the exercise. Instead, he allowed his officers to implement their own decisions, to see how they would conduct battles on interior and exterior lines.

The opposing plans resulted in such extensive troop movements that the first exercise map was entitled simply 'Marches' and the exercise proper did not get under way again until the 22nd day of mobilization. In south Germany, the French crossed the Rhine unopposed and turned north, extending their right as far east as Tübingen in order to get room for all eight corps to deploy. The French left entered the Ardennes and had begun to wheel towards the Moselle when the Germans conducted a counterattack out of Metz with three corps and crushed their right flank. The mass of the German army was now on a line between Metz and Trier, facing north and attacking both flanks of the French left wing, driving it to the north. The French center was attacking north-east in Lorraine and the French right was moving north on the right bank of the Rhine. The German army on the Moselle was operating on interior lines between two groups of French forces: the French left, north of the Moselle; the French right and center in Lorraine and Baden. The two French groups in turn were on exterior lines separated by the German army and the Moselle.

Schlieffen said that the only hope for the French left was to escape the double envelopment by retreating. They did not do so because the commanders in the centre were not paying enough attention to what was happening on the flanks. He said they would have been better off if they had remembered the close-order drill regulations and marched forward by dressing on the man to their left, just as the Japanese had done in Manchuria, and not exposing their flanks.[86] This section was marked on the margins with Foerster's blue pencil. This phrase 'Augen links, Fühlung rechts' has been used frequently, and out of context, by Schlieffen's detractors to give the impression that Schlieffen wanted to conduct his battles in a rigid, linear, mindless manner: exactly the way that the arch-militarist would want to fight. Schlieffen was, in fact, warning his officers against a lack of mutual cooperation that would lead to gaps which the enemy could exploit. If these exercises prove anything, it is that Schlieffen expected that the next war at all levels would be a 'swirling maelstrom' and he conducted exercises that would prepare his officers for such conditions.

The Germans did not destroy the French left-wing group because the German commander began to feel the pressure from the French center and right closing in on his rear. On the 26th day he redeployed three corps from his left flank attack to cover his rear, and on the 27th day he sent two more. The German envelopment was fatally weakened and the French left was able to withdraw. These five corps were unable to accomplish anything against the French center and right, as the main German army was now outnumbered in both directions. When the exercise ended on day 31, the Germans were in danger of being encircled and destroyed.[87] Schlieffen's exercise critique was not concerned with the German right wing but rather with driving home the one vital principle concerning operations on interior lines: mass against one enemy and decisively defeat him before turning against the other. An 'ordinary victory' against one force or the other will only result in the eventual destruction of the army fighting on interior lines. Schlieffen used Napoleon's failure to destroy Blücher at Ligny to illustrate his point: the result of this omission was Waterloo.

The second *Generalstabsreise West* in 1904 had even less in common with the Schlieffen plan than did the first. Schlieffen's stated opinion notwithstanding, the French invasion of south Germany succeeded and the German army was annihilated. There is no evidence that marching the German right wing through northern Belgium would have rescued the situation. Instead, the Germans needed to fight a better battle on the Moselle. If the two 1904 exercises have any connection with the 'Schlieffen plan', they show that the necessity to deploy part of the German army along the lower Rhine was a liability, not an asset.

[86] 'Es wäre hier entschieden etwas mehr Exerzier. Reglement zu wünschen gewesen, etwas Augenlinksnehmen und Fühlung rechts, um etwas von den methodischen Verfahren der Japaner, die in dieser Weise ganz gewiß nicht vorgegangen waren, sondern immer gewartet haben, bis der Nachbar heran war.', 15.

[87] As Schlieffen said, 'Es kann sich nun jeder die Sache ausmalen, wie er will, jedenfalls steht sie nicht gut für die Deutschen.' (You can look at this situation anyway that you like, but its still not good for the Germans), 20.

THE 1904: *FESTUNGS-GENERALSTABSREISE*

The 1904 *Festungs*-(Fortress) *Generalstabsreise* was held along the German fortifications on the Vistula.[88] The Germans initially deployed six corps in the east while the Russians attacked with 16 corps. They quickly overran East Prussia with the exception of Königsberg and the Germans were forced to withdraw to the Vistula. This would be very curious if, as proponents of the 'Schlieffen plan' have maintained, the Russian army was no threat to Germany because of the war with Japan. Even at the height of the Russo-Japanese War (the Japanese had attacked Port Arthur on 8 February) the German army was fully conscious that it would have to fight outnumbered and that it was very likely that few reinforcements could be sent from the west.

On the 28th and 29th days of mobilization the Germans won a 'decisive victory' in the west which permitted them to transfer a grand total of three corps to the east. The German army in the west had few forces to spare, 'decisive victory' notwithstanding. It would be safe to assume that 'decisive victory' could not be equated with the total annihilation of the French army. The exercise director noted that the Russian commander feared that the Germans would shift massive forces to the east. Even if this were possible, he said, the troops would first have to be marched to the railheads and the rail movement itself would take a week. The Russians would have plenty of time to conduct their offensive.

1905: *GENERALSTABSREISE WEST*

Generalleutnant von Zoellner's 1938 article gives the only relatively complete description of Schlieffen's 1905 *Generalstabsreise West*. It is not made clear whether Zoellner was writing from personal experience or whether he got his information from the Reichsarchiv. The *Militärwissenschaftliche Rundschau*, in which the article appeared, was the official publication of the General Staff. The article, 'Schlieffens Vermächtnis' (Schlieffen's Legacy), is frequently cited because, according to Zoellner, during the 1905 *Generalstabsreise West*, Schlieffen's last, Schlieffen 'laid his cards on the table' and revealed his concept for the Schlieffen plan.[89] Zoellner strongly hints that this plan was synonymous

---

[88] 'Festungs-Generalstabsreise 1904', Kriegsarchiv Munich, Generalstab 1240. Most of the exercise was concerned with an attack on Marienburg using field artillery and an attack on Graudenz with heavy siege artillery.

[89] '... deckt er den Reiseteilnehmern gegenüber seine Karten vollständig auf und spielt mit ihnen seinen Umfassungsplan in großen Zügen durch.' (Zoellner, 'Schlieffens Vermächtnis', *MWR Sonderheft 4* (Januar 1938) 48). True. But the encirclements took place in the Ardennes and Lorraine, not south of Paris.

with the December 1905 *Denkschrift*,[90] without ever directly saying so. Subsequent historians have cited Zoellner as proof that at this time Schlieffen tested the concept of the Schlieffen plan and then transformed this concept into a working war plan.

The exercise was once again not a staff ride in the conventional sense, but a strategic war game. Zoellner said that Schlieffen played the German side himself,[91] and used a German deployment that was similar to that of the 1905/6 *Aufmarsch* I, in which all 72 divisions were deployed in the west. The right wing included 61 divisions (23 corps and 15 reserve divisions) in six armies deployed from Metz to Wesel. The left flank was relatively weak, including only 11 divisions (three corps and five reserve divisions). In fact, Schlieffen played three exercises, with the French side played independently by three General Staff officers, Lieutenant Colonel Freiherr von Freytag-Loringhoven, Colonel von Steuben, and Major Kuhl.

Schlieffen discussed the right-wing attack in detail, saying that it would have to bypass Liège, Namur, and Antwerp and that it could expect significant opposition on French defensive lines at Lille–Maubeuge and again at La Fère–Laon–Paris, which has been taken as proof of the assertion that Schlieffen was now trying out the Schlieffen plan. This is hammering the evidence into shape to fit a preconceived idea. On the contrary, once again Schlieffen, like Ferron, Beseler, and many others, was obviously showing the difficulties involved in an advance through northern France. It is therefore not surprising that in none of these three war games did the German right wing even enter northern France. Rather, in this exercise, as in all of Schlieffen's west-front exercises, the decisive battles were fought in Lorraine or Belgium.

Freytag-Loringhoven decided to meet the German right flank head-on with a French offensive on a line Luxembourg–Namur–Brussels. Schlieffen approved of the concept but faulted the execution. The French offensive was defeated by an attack out of Metz to the north against the French right as well as by an attack against the reserve divisions holding the French left. The use of Metz as an offensive springboard places this exercise firmly in the context of Schlieffen's previous exercises, whereas in the December 1905 *Denkschrift*, Metz is merely an

[90] 'Schlieffens Operationsplan für den Zweifrontenkrieg ist durch den Weltkrieg allgemein bekanntgeworden.' (Schlieffen's operations plan for a two-front war has become well-known through the world war): Zoellner, 'Schlieffens Vermächtnis', 7. Disingenuous, since the Schlieffen plan was for a one-front war. The article continually uses terms that support the Schlieffen plan theory: for example, Zoellner contends that there is no question that Moltke 'watered down' the Schlieffen plan, 52.
[91] Ibid. 48–52.

anchor for the right wing. How the German right wing would conduct its advance into Picardy, the Champagne, and beyond, was never tested for the decisive battle was fought in Belgium.

Steuben decided to launch the French main effort between Metz and Strasbourg. According to the Schlieffen plan concept, the French were performing a *Liebesdienst* and the German right wing should have continued its movement into northern France. Under identical circumstances, during the second 1904 *Generalstabsreise West*, just a few months before, Schlieffen said that the 'school solution' to this problem was to continue the attack with the right wing on Lille–Verdun. In this exercise Schlieffen did nothing of the kind. Schlieffen said that in view of the fact that the French main body had advanced east of the Moselle (and out of their border fortifications), he could shift forces from the right wing to the left. He marched two armies directly south to engage the French to the east of Metz. Half of the 3rd Army was sent by rail to Alsace to attack the French right flank. The right wing was reduced to two armies, which were engaged with second and third-rate reserve and territorial divisions. This exercise was a replay of the first 1904 *Generalstabsreise West* and had nothing in common with the Schlieffen plan *Denkschrift*.

Kuhl decided to attack on both sides of Metz. Kuhl had expected to find the Germans weak between Metz and Strasbourg, which Zoellner says 'was not the case' ('sich als unzutreffend erwies'). Zoellner said that the French attack soon found itself in serious difficulty. Schlieffen then sent 'significant reinforcements' to Lorraine and as usual conducted a strong counterattack from the Rhine against the French right wing, which was decisive.

Zoellner said that this exercise demonstrated the flexibility of Schlieffen's war plan. That is surely true, but the plan in question was the Schlieffen *Westaufmarsch*, not the Schlieffen plan. Nothing in this exercise bore any resemblance whatsoever to the Schlieffen plan. By 1938, however, the Schlieffen plan was dogma and the details of Zoellner's description have been ignored. Far from being a confirmation of the Schlieffen plan concept of a decisive enveloping attack by the right wing, in this exercise Schlieffen demonstrated that he was always quite willing to fight the battle with his left wing in Lorraine, if that was where the French came out of their fortifications.

It is also interesting to note that two of the most prominent advocates of the importance of the Schlieffen plan *Denkschrift* were Freytag-Loringhoven and Kuhl. Both were prolific writers on the subject, especially Kuhl, who nevertheless never mentioned participating in this exercise. Freytag-Loringhoven did give it passing notice.[92] Had they

---

[92] H. von Freytag-Loringhoven, *Menschen und Dinge* (Berlin, 1923), 103–4.

described this exercise in detail in the early 1920s, they would have destroyed the contention that the Schlieffen plan was the concept for the German war plan.

1905: THE GREAT *KRIEGSSPIEL*

The *Generalstabsreise West* in 1905 was not, however, Schlieffen's last exercise. In November and December 1905 he conducted his last *Kriegsspiel.*[93] This was by far the most ambitious exercise of Schlieffen's career, perhaps the greatest war game in modern military history. In it, Schlieffen played both fronts simultaneously to the 42nd day of mobilization. For advocates of the 'Schlieffen plan' as well as for those such as Ritter who saw in Schlieffen only aggressive militarism, this war game is a bitter disappointment for in this, Schlieffen's last, greatest exercise, he conducted a strategic defensive on both the east and west fronts.

In the exercise critique, Schlieffen said that it was advantageous for Germany to wait until one of her enemies crossed the border and then attack him. Usually the counteroffensive should be made to the east, because there the Germans had the greater prospects of not just throwing back their opponent, but of decisively defeating him. He said the disadvantage of this plan was that Germany might be attacked on both fronts simultaneously. His concept for the operation was to conduct a strong initial *Aufmarsch* in East Prussia with 16 divisions (five corps and six reserve divisions). When the Russians had committed themselves to attacking, he would reinforce the eastern force with an additional 22 divisions (eight corps and six reserve divisions). This total of 38 divisions was all that the East Prussian rail net could support. This was not sufficiently superior to the expected Russian force of 33 divisions (11½ corps and 10 reserve divisions) to ensure German victory. The German army must exploit the two advantages it possessed in East Prussia, Königsberg and the Masurian Lakes. As with Metz, Schlieffen advocated building Königsberg into a fortified zone in time of war. He said that in four weeks adequate field fortifications could be built along the Deime, Pregel, and Frischung. The Russians crossed the border on the 27th day of mobilization. By the 30th day they had reached a line Königsberg–Soldau. With the arrival of their massive reinforcements, the Germans launched surprise counteroffensives on three avenues of approach: out of fortress Königsberg against the right flank of the Niemen Army; out

93 'Chef des Generalstabes der Armee I Nr 13083 Z. Berlin, den 23. Dezember, 1905. Kriegsspiel November/Dezember 1905 Schlußbesprechung. Geheim!' BA-MA PH 3/646. Maps *Nachlaß* Schlieffen BA-MA N 43/133. The Bayerisches Kriegsarchiv also has a complete copy, with maps, Generalstab 1237.

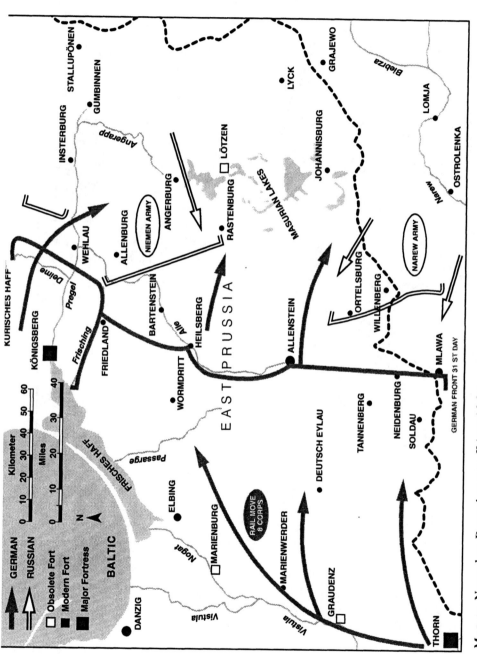

MAP 10. November–December 1905 *Kriegsspiel Ost*

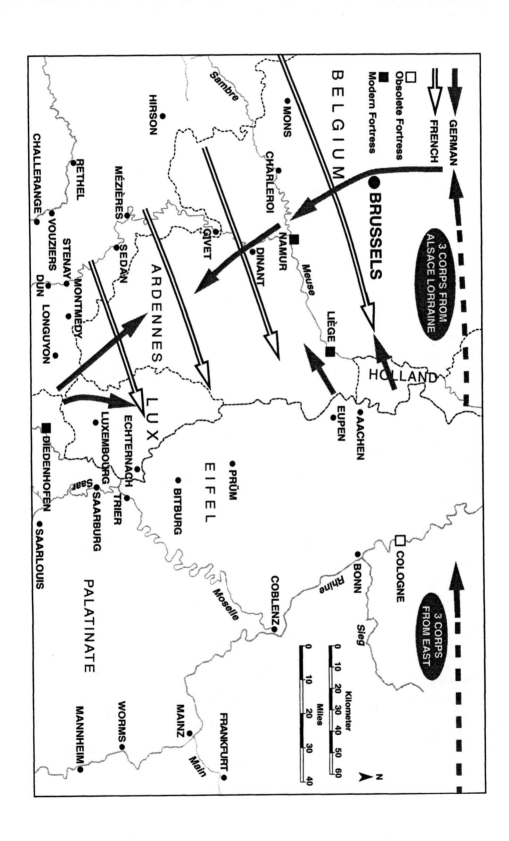

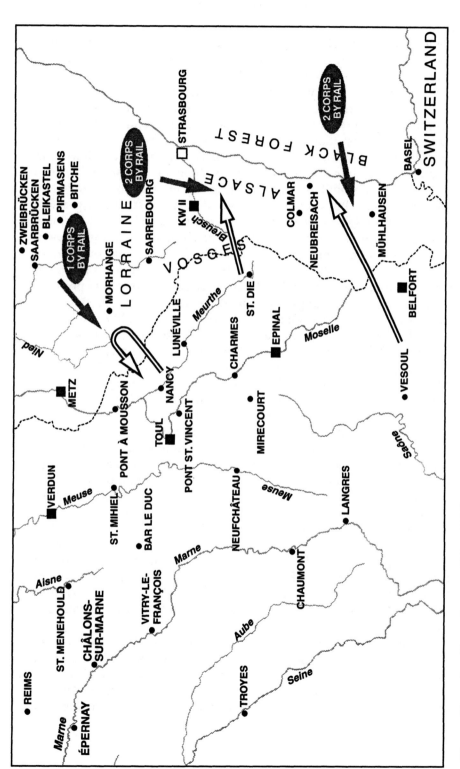

MAP 11. November–December 1905 *Kriegsspiel West*

of the lake district against their inside flanks of both armies; and against the left flank of the Narew Army. Both Russian armies were annihilated and by the 35th day of mobilization the transfer of troops to the west could begin. There was no pursuit into Russia.

Schlieffen then gave his officers some last thoughts on the character of the next war. He said that in the future it would be very easy to allow operations to degenerate into positional warfare: the war in Manchuria had demonstrated that. Nevertheless, the German army must always seek to win decisive victories in maneuver battles, and never allow a war of attrition to drag on indecisively for 'one or two years'. Such a protracted war would produce nothing but mutual exhaustion and economic chaos. But even if positional warfare did set in, long defensive positions might offer weak spots where the attacker could achieve a breakthrough. In mobile operations, the German army would generally try to envelop the enemy flank. Schlieffen said that one should never conduct a shallow turning movement but envelop the enemy flank with a strong force while attacking his front to fix him in position.

Returning to the *Kriegsspiel*, Schlieffen said that the French were twice as strong as the Germans and therefore clearly held the initiative. Schlieffen gave the French 58 active and reserve divisions (in Plan XV the French had 51 divisions). In addition, the French had 12 Territorial divisions, for a grand total of 70 divisions. The Germans had 37 infantry divisions (11½ corps and 14 reserve divisions). With the 38 divisions in the east, Schlieffen was employing 75 German divisions in total, 3 more than were actually on the German order of battle.

The deployment plan and force structure which Schlieffen gave to the French for this war game is strongly reminiscent of the French general Michel's 1911 war plan. Both the war game and Michel's plan were based on the exhaustive use of trained French manpower. Michel wanted to add more reservists to the active units. Schlieffen utilized French reserve and territorial divisions in the front line. In both Schlieffen's exercise deployment and in Michel's plan, the French mass of maneuver was on the left wing and this left wing extended all the way to the English Channel. On the far left wing of the French forces, Schlieffen deployed the British Expeditionary Force, the first time British units appear in a German exercise. South of Verdun, Schlieffen's French deployment consisted largely of reserve and territorial divisions.

Schlieffen's German deployment consisted of six corps between Cologne and Aachen, a screen of cavalry and Landwehr from there to Metz, three corps in Lorraine, one at Strasbourg and one at Mühlhausen. The two south German corps and the three Bavarian corps remained in their mobilization stations. Schlieffen scraped the bottom of the German manpower barrel, employing Landwehr, Landsturm, and ersatz units on the front lines, especially in Alsace.

The French crossed the Franco-Belgian border on the 23rd day of mobilization, at which point Belgium and Holland allied themselves with Germany. At the same time, the French attacked into Alsace and Lorraine. Schlieffen said that it was essential for the Germans to hold Lorraine and the right bank of the Moselle as a base for a counterattack against the French left wing and sent all the Bavarian and south German corps there by rail to counterattack; by the 26th day these forces had driven back the French attack in both provinces with heavy losses. In Schlieffen's opinion a pursuit through the 'Trouée de Charmes' led nowhere and involved considerable risk; therefore, from the 27th day he began to transfer three corps north. By the 31st day the French had reached a line Antwerp–Liège and had crossed the Belgian–German border south of Liège. By the 33rd day the three German corps being transferred from the south had arrived in Antwerp with the prospect of three more arriving from the east by the 37th day. Schlieffen said that the proper course of action was to attack south from Antwerp with these first three corps against the French flank; such an attack carried with it a considerable element of risk, but no great deeds could be accomplished without risk (a direct quote from Moltke). Such an attack would be unexpected and should achieve surprise. In order to make this outflanking attack from Antwerp effective, however, the French armies had to be fixed by a frontal attack, even if the attacking forces were inferior to the defenders. The French reaction to all these unexpected moves would be hasty and uncoordinated and this would to some degree counterbalance the risk the Germans were taking.

The German envelopment was directed on Namur, which was still in Belgian hands. This gave the envelopment operational depth, but nothing like the strategic depth envisaged by the envelopment around Paris in the December 1905 *Denkschrift*. By the 37th day the left-flank French army had been surrounded inside the triangle Namur–Liège–Antwerp and the German enveloping force had crossed the Meuse at Namur. On the 39th day the Germans launched an attack from Metz–Diedenhofen to the north-west against the right flank of the French main body. By the 42nd day three French armies were surrounded in the Ardennes and a fourth was surrounded west of Luxembourg. The exercise was then terminated. Concerning the British army, Schlieffen quoted Lord Roberts, who had said publicly that it would be the 'height of insanity' to involve the British army in a continental war, for which it was poorly prepared; Schlieffen said that Roberts should know what he was talking about.

In his last and most ambitious war game, Schlieffen tested concepts which had nothing to do with the Schlieffen plan. Given a simultaneous Franco-Russian offensive, Schlieffen replied with a strategic defensive on both fronts. When the Franco-Russian armies approached the German border, Schlieffen used the German rail net to mass uncommitted forces against the two Russian armies in East Prussia and destroy them. At the same time, he conducted an active defense in the west, retaining five corps in their mobilization stations and then committing them by rail to obtain local superiority against the French forces invading Alsace and Lorraine and crushing them. Finally, he used rail mobility to redeploy forces from the east and from Alsace to attack the flanks of the French main body in the Ardennes and destroy it.

We have reviewed almost all of Schlieffen's many exercises since 1902, the sole exceptions being the *Kriegsspiele* for 1902, 1903, and 1904, which were not to be found. None of these bears the slightest resemblance to the concept of the operation in the Schlieffen plan. It would appear that Schlieffen never tested this concept in a war game or staff ride at all. This would be very curious were the Schlieffen plan *Denkschrift* truly Schlieffen's *magnum opus*.

There is even an indication in Groener's *Nachlaß* that Schlieffen's actual war planning was moving in the direction set out by Schlieffen's last exercises. In a letter to the Reichsarchiv in 1923 Groener said that in one of Schlieffen's last *Ostaufmarsch* plans the defensive in the west was based on rail mobility. At this time, Groener was working in the *Eisenbahnabteilung*. Groener said that he saw this plan, which he then called an *Aufmarschstudie*. The Germans would initially deploy only a few corps in the west to insure border security. The rest of the *Westheer* remained in its mobilization stations. The rail movement for these units was worked out, with neither the movement day nor the unloading points being specified. At the appropriate time they would move and attack. This is the same concept as the one Schlieffen used in the 1905 *Kriegsspiel*.[94]

THE 'SCHLIEFFEN PLAN'

Historians have assumed that in the Schlieffen plan *Denkschrift*, which was written in early 1906, Schlieffen could afford to leave East Prussia undefended because the Russian army had been made combat-ineffective by the effects of the Russo-Japanese War and the Russian Revolution of 1905. This assumption is disproved by the German intel-

---

[94] BA-MA *Nachlaß* Groener, N 46/41, Blätter 58–9.

ligence analysis for 1905[95] and 1906[96]. The 1905 report gives no indication whatsoever that the Russian army had collapsed. The 1906 report covers Russian troop strength and capabilities in the 1905–6 time frame in great detail. The report said that in 1906 the Russians could still deploy about 25 infantry divisions against Germany and 22 infantry divisions against Austria (as opposed to a pre-1904 deployment of 30 divisions against Germany and 30 against Austria). Even Ludendorff[97] and Groener[98] acknowledged that Schlieffen's last real war plan for 1905–6 deployed 10 divisions in the east. This is consistent with *Aufmarsch I* in which Russian intervention was expected eventually, but not immediately. Published military analyses, such as *Streffleurs österreichische militärische Zeitschrift*[99] and *Lobell's Jahresberichte*,[100] while acknowledging that the Russian army had weathered a short but severe crisis, give no indication that the Russian army was combat-ineffective. In any case, the Schlieffen plan was written in January and February 1906, two years too late. It should have been written in February 1904, when the Japanese attacked Port Arthur. Peace talks between Russia and Japan began on 9 August 1905, the Treaty of Portsmouth was signed on 5 September 1905 and the Russians immediately began to redeploy their army to European Russia. By February 1906 the Russo-Japanese war had been over for six months and Russia's internal situation was rapidly stabilizing.

There are two massive inconsistencies in the Schlieffen plan: the wholesale use of non-existent units and leaving East Prussia undefended against an invasion by 25 Russian divisions. A modern military historian has apparently gone so far as to say that the Schlieffen plan is proof that Schlieffen was a 'senile idiot'.[101] Schlieffen was neither senile nor an idiot. There is a rational explanation. The only possible answer is that the Schlieffen plan *Denkschrift* was not a war plan at all.

Ritter, and those who followed him, did not understand the *Denkschrift* because they stood it on its head. The point was not to

[95] 'Großer Generalstab, 1. Abteilung, Nr 23, Zusammenstellung der wichtigsten Veränderungen im Heerwesen Russlands im Jahre 1905', Kriegsarchiv Munich, Generalstab, 207.

[96] 'Großer Generalstab, 1. Abteilung, 1 Nr. 44, Jahresbericht 1906 Rußland, Abgeschlossen 5. Dezember, 1906'. Kriegsarchiv Munich, Generalstab 207.

[97] E. Ludendorff, 'Der Aufmarsch 1914', *LV Folge* 31 (24. Dezember 1929); also *DW* (4. Januar 1930), 3–4.

[98] *Testament des Grafen Schlieffens*, 202–3.

[99] *Streffleur's XLVII Jahrgang (der ganzen Folge 83.) Jahrgang 1906*, 130–9, 144, 285ff, 481–6, 655–7, 666 ff., 812–23.

[100] *Lobell's Jahresberichte über das Heer- und Kriegswesen*, XXXIII. *Jahrgang 1906*, Generalleutnant, ed. Pelet-Narbonne (Berlin, 1907), 206–42, esp. 240–1.

[101] Förster, 'Der deutsche Generalstab' MM 54 (1995), 78.

develop a radically new scheme of maneuver, but to readdress the issue which Schlieffen had felt throughout his career to be the most serious problem facing the German army: Germany's failure to utilize exhaustively either her trained manpower or her total available manpower. In the *Denkschrift*, Schlieffen employed the total German force and added to it all the units he thought could be raised using Germany's trained manpower: given equipment and prior planning, reserve corps could be created from reserve divisions and ersatz divisions created outright by using trained reservists. Schlieffen had been recommending such a course of action since 1889. Using this expanded force, he then discussed the campaign that could be conducted. His principal interest was focused on the possibility of a battle in Belgium or on the Franco-Belgian border, which was in keeping with his previous war games and staff rides. The *Denkschrift* to this point consisted of arguments already well known to its recipient, Moltke. Schlieffen then presented the worst-case scenario: the French might successfully hold a line Verdun–Paris, at which point the Germans would have to go around to the west of Paris. Only at this point do six of the ersatz corps enter the picture in order to invest the north and west sides of Paris. This is the first and almost certainly the only time Schlieffen presented such a strategy (if there were ever another such occasion, Wolfgang Foerster would have surely made use of it). In any case, Schlieffen said the German army was probably too weak for such an operation. The obvious implication was that if Germany wanted to be able to meet any eventuality, she needed even more maneuver units and must raise an army based on universal conscription as the French had done.

Moltke's marginal notes to the *Denkschrift* were entered on a copy dated 1911. If the *Denkschrift*, dated December 1905, but actually written in January 1906, was really the template for all subsequent German war planning for the next nine years, Moltke's comments on the plan surely had to have been made before 1911. The explanation for the 1911 date for Moltke's notes is related to the 'Schlieffen plan' maps, which Ritter assumed to be part of the *Denkschrift*. Schlieffen's drafts make mention of only one map (scale 1:300,000);[102] nevertheless, in the final hand-written copy of both the January and February 1906 documents as well as the two typed copies, reference to nine maps was entered in the margin. The original file in Freiburg contains 11 maps[103] (six of which were reproduced with some alterations by Ritter). Map 6 (scale 1:800,000) in the Freiburg file shows the entire Schlieffen plan concept of a great wheel around Paris. This map is really a summary of two other

[102] *Nachlaß* Schlieffen BA-MA N 43/137, 125, 144, 197.
[103] *Nachlaß* Schlieffen BA-MA N 43/141K.

maps: map 2, titled German advance to the 22nd mobilization day, and map 3, titled German advance from 22nd to 31st mobilization day. Both these maps are 1:300,000 scale and show the daily straight-ahead routes of march of each corps, but nothing else. There are no enemy forces, no combat, no operational or tactical maneuver. In fact, in the entire map file there are only four very general (not to say crude) sketches showing French positions or movements. One would be hard put to argue that these represent a serious consideration of the French reaction to a German attack through Belgium. One map, number 10, gives the presumed French deployment but it is dated 1911. On the reverse side of the last map, number 11, is a handwritten note saying that it was Schlieffen's map from 1906–1912. However, the 3rd Department's estimate changed in 1907 and again in 1911/12.

The 'Schlieffen plan' maps, maps 2, 3, 6, and 7, are absolutely unique: there is nothing remotely like them in any surviving German plan or war game. These maps show one thing: how long it would take to march to the Somme. The answer is: to the 31st day of mobilization. Map 3 also shows the march around Paris but does not even bother to measure how long it would take to march from the Somme to the area south of Paris: an educated guess would be at least another 20 days or to the 51st day of mobilization. Even if the campaign ended at this point (and there is one arrow pointing generally from Fontainbleau towards Langres, 200 kilometers away), in a two-front war it would take nearly as long again to march the troops back to German railheads for transfer east. Schlieffen proposed, after all, that fortresses such as Liège and Lille, which block the rail lines, be bypassed. Bucholz and Herwig contended that Schlieffen maintained that the campaign would be over in 40 days after mobilization.[104] This was unlikely. By the 40th day the right wing had not even circumnavigated Paris. In any case, Schlieffen never made any such statement in the *Denkschrift*. They are confusing the 'Schlieffen plan' with Moltke's conversations with the Austrian Chief of Staff, Conrad, shortly before the First World War.

Map 3 is also interesting because on it the German *Schwerpunkt* is clearly south of Lille. Only four corps pass north of Lille, two in the first echelon and two in the second. Because the right wing bypasses Lille, at this point these four corps are separated by a 35-kilometer gap from the next corps on the left, and are very vulnerable to defeat in detail in exactly the area where Schlieffen said that he expected a battle. Not only does the right flank man not 'brush the Channel with his sleeve', but at its closest point the right flank is over 40 kilometers—two days'

---

[104] H. Herwig, *The First World War. Germany and Austria–Hungary 1914–1918* (London, 1997), 46; A. Bucholz, *Moltke, Schlieffen and Prussian War Planning* (New York, 1991), 209.

march—from the coast. The mapmaker attempted to compensate for these problems, for in map 7 he restarted the exercise at the 19th day of mobilization, this time sending six corps north of Lille. Even so, at the closest point—Ypres—the right flank is still 35 kilometers from the Channel. In any case, this variant was not adopted and not reflected in map 6, the final 'Schlieffen plan' map.

Maps 5 and 5a (scale 1:800,000) show the German reaction to a major French attack into Lorraine (the French forces are not shown). Schlieffen's instructions for such an event are contradictory. On the one hand, he wrote that the French were performing a *Liebesdienst* and that the Germans should continue the right-wing attack. This is the interpretation given by the Schlieffen School. Schlieffen also said in another passage that in this case the Germans should alter their operation as little as possible: the Moselle must be secured and the German right extended only as far as La Fère. This is far short of Paris, and passing to the west of Paris was obviously out of the question. In maps 5 and 5a a good part of the right wing—eight corps—actually moves to the south-east to take up a position on the north side of the Moselle to the east of Metz: this is 'securing' the Moselle with a vengeance. In map 5a, the German army is almost evenly divided with half to the west of Metz between Diedenhofen and St. Quentin, and half to the east and south of Metz in the Palatinate and Lorraine. Maps 5 and 5a are direct descendants of the *Generalstabsreisen* of 1904 and 1905 (and as we shall see, of Moltke's *Generalstabsreisen* of 1906 and 1908) and are unrelated to the Schlieffen plan. The mapmaker clearly could not conceive of allowing the mass of the French army to march practically unopposed through Lorraine. On the other hand, there is nothing in the *Denkschrift* that would lead one to believe that Schlieffen intended to cover the line of the Moselle and Lorraine with half the German army. Indeed, the essential element in the 'Schlieffen plan' is exactly the opposite: everything was to be sacrificed to make the right wing strong. Nevertheless, these alien maps are annotated on Schlieffen's handwritten *Denkschrift*. These maps were surely not Schlieffen's, but were added later.

All these inconsistencies can only be resolved by concluding that the maps and the typed copies of the *Denkschrift* are not contemporary with Schlieffen's January and February 1906 handwritten documents. Rather, the typed copies, Moltke's marginal notes and the maps were produced in 1911. At this time, the question of radically increasing the size of the German army was becoming acute. Since Schlieffen's *Denkschrift* addressed just such a problem, Moltke directed that it be re-evaluated. The only part of the operational problem in the *Denkschrift* with which Moltke was not intimately familiar was the march around Paris and the critical question here was the length of time it would take:

hence maps 2, 3, 6, and 7 which were generated to brief Moltke on this question. Moltke's evaluation of the *Denkschrift* was not favorable; in particular he disagreed with the fact that the Schlieffen plan provided only for a one-front war as well as with Schlieffen's opinion of the French *Liebesdienst* in Lorraine. The necessary number of ersatz corps were not created and it was never planned to send the ersatz formations that actually were formed to the right wing. Aside from the Schlieffen plan *Denkschrift*, there is no evidence of any kind that the German army at any time planned to move to the west of Paris, ever intended to abandon Lorraine or ever conducted an exercise to test either idea.

Critics of the Schlieffen plan have always cited these maps as proof of Schlieffen's mechanical, militaristic mindset. They contend that these maps prove that Schlieffen tried to determine the entire course of the campaign in advance, without taking any consideration of French actions. Such an intent has also been said to have contributed significantly to German guilt in starting the first World War: Schlieffen had allegedly bequeathed to Moltke an aggressive war plan which had a rigid timetable. In order to maintain this timetable in August 1914, the Germans had to attack immediately. Therefore, for Germany alone mobilization meant war. The preceding analysis demonstrates that these assertions are completely unfounded. These maps and the Schlieffen plan *Denkschrift* had nothing to do with the real German war plan. There was no German timetable and in fact it was the Franco-Russian attack plan that provided for a joint offensive by the 15th day of mobilization.

After February 1906 Schlieffen wrote nothing more concerning the Schlieffen plan. This is not to say that he was inactive—far from it. Freed of the demands of active duty, he wrote extensively. In *Der Krieg in der Gegenwart* (War in Modern Times), Schlieffen described how armies would have to adapt to accommodate true mass warfare and modern firepower and communications. In *Cannae*, he established the double envelopment as the ultimate form of battle of annihilation. To support the *Cannae* thesis, he rewrote military history. For example, his history of the 1866 campaign was really a modified exercise critique, a demonstration of the way Schlieffen would have conducted a strategic double envelopment of the Austrian army. *Cannae* was also probably the inspiration Groener, Foerster, and Kuhl used to develop the Schlieffen plan: just as Schlieffen invented a battle of annihilation in 1866, Groener, Foerster, and Kuhl used the Schlieffen plan to show how the Germans should have annihilated the Anglo-French in 1914.

If we are to arrive at a correct appreciation of Schlieffen's 1905 *Denkschrift*, it will only be by considering it as the first of the series of books and articles he wrote after his retirement and not as the last of his war plans. The war plans were firmly rooted in the present—there is no room in a real war plan for imaginary units and other flights of the imagination. Schlieffen's writing after January 1906, however, uniformly describes how things must change to meet the challenges of the future, and this challenge was the *Millionenheer.*

Schlieffen wrote one last operational *Denkschrift* on 28 December 1912, just before he died. Ritter again focused on the scheme of maneuver, which involved an attack along the entire western front. Many historians claim to see in this *Denkschrift* the culmination of the *Cannae* strategy. In fact, Schlieffen's last concern was the same as his first in 1889: the need to completely utilize Germany's manpower. Schlieffen had reached the same conclusions as had General Michel in 1911: at mobilization, the active army must be expanded by incorporating practically all trained reservists followed by Landwehr, Landsturm, and *Ersatztruppen*: for one last time, Schlieffen was advocating the *levée en masse.* To provide cadres, unnecessary echelons of command, which to Schlieffen meant corps headquarters, would be eliminated: the current 36 corps were to be replaced by 51 oversized divisions containing active army and reserve formations. The dilution of artillery support and the difficulties in the command and control of this mass army had to be accepted. This huge force would enable the German army to support the right wing with an attack all along the front to fix the French in place. Both Schlieffen and Michel decided that these armies had to fight the decisive battle in Belgium because that was the only place such masses could be controlled and maneuvered. Neither man found a hearing prior to the outbreak of the war but once the initial maneuver battles in the summer and autumn of 1914 were over, both the French and German armies were transformed into the mass armies advocated by Schlieffen and Michel.

Gerhard Ritter's interpretation of Schlieffen's strategy was that, first, Schlieffen abandoned the elder Moltke's east-front offensive for a west-front attack and that, second, he developed this west-front offensive into the perfect plan, the right-wing attack around Paris. This interpretation has been accepted by all subsequent historians. It is entirely wrong.

The *Ostaufmarsch* had already died in the crisis of 1886–8. Moltke's last plan was for a *Westaufmarsch,* as were all of Waldersee's plans. By 1890 both Moltke and Waldersee recognized that the Russian army in Poland had grown too powerful and the Russian deployment too effective for a German offensive in the east to succeed.

Dieckmann's *Schlieffenplan* manuscript shows us that Schlieffen maintained Moltke's *Westaufmarsch* plan virtually unchanged, first as the sole war plan, then after 1899 as *Aufmarsch* II. In 1900/1 he even revived for a time Moltke's full-scale *Ostaufmarsch* of 1880.

From the 1898 *Denkschrift* to the 1905 *Generalstabsreise* and the 1905 *Kriegsspiel* Schlieffen's operational thought was moving in the direction of the use of rail mobility to launch surprise counteroffensives to encircle and destroy the enemy on or near friendly territory, and not toward deep penetration into enemy territory.

There never was a 'Schlieffen plan'.

CHAPTER FIVE

Moltke's war plan, 1906–1914

GERMAN ENEMY ESTIMATE, 1906/1907

In 1906 the French adopted Plan XV*bis*, which was refined in 1906 and again in 1907. The 1907 version was in force until the spring of 1909. In spite of the designation as a modification of Plan XV, Plan XV*bis* was in fact based on an entirely different concept.[1] The French left was extended significantly to the north. The 2nd Army (four corps) was deployed between Epinal and Belfort. The 1st Army (four corps) was far forward, echelonned behind Nancy. The 3rd Army (five corps) was north and west of Toul, the 4th Army (five corps) west of Verdun, and the 5th Army (two corps), on the left flank, had its center of mass at Vouzieres. Marchand was coy concerning the reasons for the adoption of a radically new plan.[2] It seems likely that this plan served the same defensive–offensive purposes as its predecessors. It also allowed the French to immediately parry a German attack through the Ardennes. In addition, as Schlieffen had foreseen, the time would come when the French would decide to attack both to the north and to the south of Metz. Plan XV*bis* was the first French plan that could easily conduct such an operation. In this regard, Plan XV*bis* is the predecessor of Plan XVII. The 1907 version also bore a striking resemblance to the German estimate of 1904.

In the summer of 1906 the 3rd Department received an intelligence windfall.[3] Agent 35 supplied it with the deployment of all the active

---

[1] A. Marchand, *Plans de concentration de 1871 á 1914* (Paris, 1926), 156–64.

[2] 'Il utilise les résultats de diverses études faites depuis 1903 et consacre d'une façon très nette une certain nombre de principes parfois énoncés antérieurement mais toujours abandonnés'. (It made use of the results of several studies conducted since 103 and was clearly based on a number of principles which had been espoused previously and then rejected). Greiner, without stating any evidence, said that the French adopted this formation in March 1906 because they had information that the Germans were going to invade Belgium. Greiner, 'Welche Nachrichten Geraß der deutsche Generalstab über Mobilmachung, und Aufmarsch französischen Heerer in den Jahren 1885–1914? . . .', BA-MA W10/50267, 2–25, 98. This is unlikely. Rumors that the Germans would move through Belgium had been circulating for more than two decades.

[3] Greiner, 'Nachrichten', 100–12. Agent 35 said that the march tables were prepared by officers, but over the years the inevitable changes had been made by civilian employ-

French corps in the form of their rail routes of march. His information was in fact most similar to Plan XV*bis* issued in 1907. The Germans were now aware of the presence of strong French forces to the north of Verdun.

On the basis of this information, the 3rd Department issued a new enemy estimate. Greiner said that the 3rd Department January 1907 estimate corresponded to the 'operational idea' of Plan XV*bis*, but many of the details were wrong. The 3rd Department thought that the French had 14 rail deployment lines when they only had 9; therefore it made the French even stronger than they really were on their left, and weaker in the centre. The French concept was still seen as strategically defensive, tactically offensive.

Of exceptional importance was an agent report in January 1907, which said that the French and British had concluded a military convention.[4] The joint operations plan provided for the English to deploy their army on the Meuse, on the French left flank.

1904–1906: THE BAVARIANS PREPARE A BREAKTHROUGH BETWEEN TOUL AND VERDUN

At the same time that Schlieffen was supposedly perfecting the right-wing attack around Paris the Bavarian General Staff was preparing to conduct a diametrically opposite operation, a breakthrough between Toul and Verdun. The Bavarian Army enjoyed an enviable position within the German Army. While Army commanders were appointed in peacetime, they were called Army Inspectors and enjoyed little authority. The Bavarian Army had its own permanent command structure and General Staff. In wartime this would become an army headquarters. Probably only the Bavarian Army headquarters (and perhaps the Saxons) could practice their wartime mission in peacetime.

In the winter of 1904/5 the Bavarian General Staff played a war game testing an attack on the 'Position de Nancy'.[5] The French had made their main attack between Metz and the Vosges with a supporting attack north of Metz. Between the 15th and 19th day of mobilization the French attack was defeated and thrown back on the fortress line. On the 21st day the 2nd German Army would attack the *Sperrforts* between Metz and Verdun while the 3rd (Bavarian) Army attacked the 'Position

ees under officer supervision. Agent 35 became friends with three of these civilians. He convinced them that he was a good French patriot, and in conversations they gave him the information he needed. Needless to say, a textbook piece of espionage.

[4] Ibid. 105.

[5] 'Festungskriegsspiel über die Position de Nancy 1905', Kriegsarchiv Munich, Generalstab 1289.

de Nancy'. The defensive position at Nancy was analyzed in detail. Unfortunately, the actual conduct of the exercise was not in the file.

In November and December 1906 the Bavarian Army conducted an *Operationsstudie* (operational study) for an attack to break the French line of *Sperrforts* between Toul and Verdun.[6] This was serious preparation for a wartime mission. Both the *Operationsstudie* and the assumed French deployment were classified *Streng Geheim* (Top Secret). The French deployment was similar to the 1907 3rd Department enemy estimate. The exercise director was the Chief of Staff of the Bavarian Army.

The French army was deployed from Rethel in the north to Belfort in the south. The army designations were not provided, but it appears that there was one army (four corps) north of Verdun, a reserve army (four corps) south-west of Verdun, an army (five corps) around Toul, an army (three corps) near Epinal, and a small army (two corps) near Belfort. The intent of this deployment was to enable the French either to attack to the north or south of the Verdun–Toul position, or defend against a German attack. The line between Verdun–Toul was to be held with the minimum of forces. The first requirement was for the French players to develop a defense against a breakthrough of the Verdun–Toul line by a German army of four to five corps reinforced with a siege train—heavy artillery and engineers. The French were also required to plan field fortifications for their position, assuming that they had seven days available and almost unlimited civilian manpower.

The German army deployed from Trier to Strasbourg. With its right wing at Trier, the German army would at the most enter Luxembourg and the southernmost tip of Belgium. By the 13th day of mobilization the German combat troops and their combat trains had deployed. The field trains would arrive by the 15th day, the Landwehr brigades by the 17th day. The Germans estimated that the French deployment would have been completed by the 14th day at the latest. The German 1st and 2nd Armies on the right would begin their advance through northern Lorraine and Luxembourg on the 12th and 13th days. They would close up on the French border and be prepared to attack over the Meuse to the north of Verdun. The detailed deployment was shown only for the 3rd (Bavarian) Army, which occupied an assembly area behind Metz. With eight corps, this was a powerful force. On the 13th day the German headquarters in Mainz ordered the general advance of the German armies to begin on the 14th day, and said that the headquarters itself would then move forward to Saarbrücken.

The concept of the German operation was for the right flank (1st

[6] K. b. Generalstab, 'Studie eines Durchbruchs durch die Maas Linie Toul-Verdun, November/Dezember 1906 Streng Geheim!' Kriegsarchiv Munich, Generalstab 1293.

and 2nd Armies) to attack toward Sedan while the left flank attacked toward Epinal. The 3rd Army mission was to attack the Meuse line between Verdun and St. Mihiel. The 3rd Army would break through the fort line in order to prevent the movement of enemy forces against the 1st and 2nd Armies. The 3rd Army would secure its right flank against the southern half of Verdun while the 2nd Army closed off the northern half. It was expected that the French would defend in place on the *Côtes Lorraines*. The French *Sperrforts* had been built on this ridge, which was located on the east bank of the Meuse. To the south of the 3rd Army, the 4th and 5th Armies were to break through the 'Trouée de Charmes' between Toul and Epinal and advance in the direction of Chaumont. The 4th Army would presumably be able to advance only slowly against Nancy.

From the 14th to the 17th day the 3rd Army drove back the French covering forces, on one occasion encountering such heavy French artillery fire that the German troops could not take their objective. The tactical situation in the 3rd Army sector was very realistic—strong enemy forces on dominating ground with heavy enemy artillery fire from 75mm, 120mm, and 155mm guns which prevented the Bavarian infantry from advancing and forced the Bavarian artillery to displace its guns. The French also made extensive use of barbed wire obstacles.

On the 17th day the Germans launched a general attack. The 1st and 2nd Armies were ordered to cross the Meuse to the north of Dun to envelop the French left flank. Strong enemy forces were reported at and to the north of Reims.

The Bavarian advance was conducted according to the principles of formal siege warfare. On the night of the 17th–18th days of mobilization the Bavarian infantry occupied a *Schutzstellung* to protect the artillery, which also moved forward at that time. On the night of the 18th–19th day three Bavarian corps launched an attack on the French main position, which was a complete failure in two corps sectors and only partially successful in the other. A general attack on the 19th made little progress owing to the weight of French artillery fire. The French also launched local counterattacks. On the 18th and 19th days the French and Germans conducted a furious artillery duel, in which the Germany artillery was at a severe disadvantage because it could not observe the fall of shot because of the terrain and range. On the evening of the 19th day the 2nd Army reported that it had opened the attack on the north side of Verdun and had put effective fire on Fort Douaumont. The 4th Army reported that it had silenced Fort Frouard and expected to be able to take the place on the 20th day.

On the 21st day III Bavarian Corps attacked Fort Troyon, but was turned back by wire obstacles and heavy defensive fire. Progress elsewhere in the

Bavarian army sector was slow or non-existent and the troops were tiring. In the 2nd Army sector it appeared that the French would defend at Reims. The 4th Army reported that it was making progress against the south side of Nancy and Fort Pont St. Vincent. On the 22nd day the French forces opposing the Bavarians fell back to the west bank of the Meuse, except at Fort Camp de Romains, which they continued to hold. The exercise was then ended.

In his 'critical comments' to Moltke, the Chief of the Bavarian General Staff concluded that the two French corps defending in the sector would have been attritted and fought out and would have had no alternative but to withdraw to the west bank of the Meuse. Forts Troyon, Camp de Romains, and les Paroches would then have fallen in a couple of days. Moreover, they would have been unable to hinder further German operations.

If the Schlieffen plan was the German war plan in late 1906, it is difficult to understand why the Bavarians would conduct such major exercises to test a breakthrough of the French fortress line. On the other hand, these exercises were perfectly consistent with the concept of the operation enunciated in Beseler's 1900 *Denkschrift*, which envisioned an attack on the French fortress line to fix the French forces in place, followed by an attack from the front and rear to break through the French fortress line.

MOLTKE'S 1906 AND 1908 *GENERALSTABSREISEN*

If Moltke had adopted or even just inherited the Schlieffen plan as his war plan, it would be natural to assume that he would conduct an exercise to test it, particularly since such an exercise had not yet taken place. Since the Reichsarchiv never published any of Moltke's operational work or allowed access to it, it was not possible to verify this theory. Now, thanks to recent acquisitions at the Militärarchiv in Freiburg, we know the content of two of Moltke's earliest *Generalstabsreisen*, the staff rides in the west in 1906 and 1908

For the *Generalstabsreise West* of 1906,[7] Moltke provided East Prussia with a strong army: six corps and nine reserve divisions, 21 infantry divisions in all. This exercise was therefore testing the western component of *Aufmarsch* II: simultaneous French and Russian offensives. This would be incomprehensible if the Germans really considered that the Russian army was not combat-effective at the beginning of 1906, as the Schlieffen plan assumed. In the west, the right wing with 15 corps (30

---

[7] 'Geheim! Große Generalstabsreise 1906', BA-MA PH 3/663. Twenty-three pages, typewritten, with maps.

divisions) deployed between Diedenhofen and Eupen, with a corps at Metz, 7 corps (14 divisions) in Lorraine, two corps at Strasbourg, and two corps in Alsace. This is clearly not the Schlieffen plan deployment.

Moltke stated that it was not in the French interest to violate Belgian neutrality and therefore the French would attack in Lorraine. This attack was conducted *en masse* with 14 corps. Moltke had to acknowledge that such a horde would be practically impossible to supply and would have virtually no ability to maneuver. The French left-flank army, to the north of Verdun, contained nine divisions and four divisions attacked in Alsace.

In the face of this mass French attack in Lorraine, the German commander decided immediately to launch his main attack through Belgium with the three right- wing armies. This was the solution which Schlieffen advocated, but never carried out, in the second 1904 *Generalstabsreise.* Moltke disagreed with this solution; he preferred the same maneuver as the one Schlieffen actually used himself in the 1905 *Generalstabsreise*: counterattack by the right wing through Metz. Moltke said that one needed to be clear about the purpose of the right wing: it was to force the French to leave their fortress line and fight in the open. If the French launched their main attack in Lorraine, then the decisive battle would be fought in Lorraine and that was where the German right wing needed to march. This statement was practically the only part of Moltke's planning which was made public by the Reichsarchiv. It has been repeatedly cited to demonstrate that Moltke did not understand the concept of the Schlieffen plan.

In fact, Moltke allowed the German right-wing advance through Belgium to proceed! On the 15th day the Germans also counterattacked against the French invasion of upper Alsace, but this maneuver failed to trap the French forces. The Germans then abandoned Alsace altogether. On the 18th day the Germans were forced to send two corps from the right wing to reinforce the left. By the 20th day the decisive battle was being fought by 10 French and 10 German corps on a 70-kilometer long west–east line from Metz to Bleikastel. A mass German frontal attack to the east of Metz failed in the face of the 'murderous fire of modern weapons' while the French slowly turned the open German left flank. On the 21st day the last three corps of the German 3rd Army had to be sent from the right wing to Metz. The German right wing (1st and 2nd Armies) encountered no significant French forces and spent the exercise foot-marching through the Ardennes. Moltke ended the exercise without allowing it to come to a climactic battle of annihilation. According to the results of this exercise, the German army would be forced to meet a French attack in Lorraine with at least equal force. The decisive battle was fought in Lorraine long before the

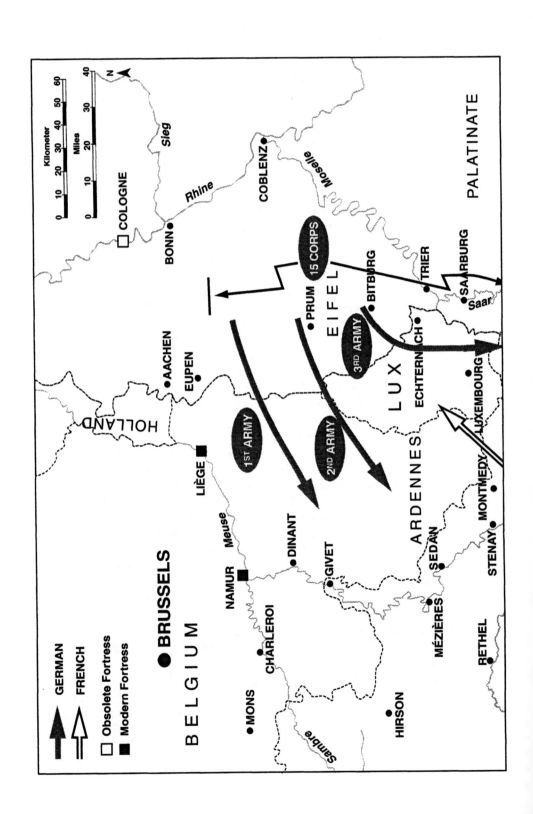

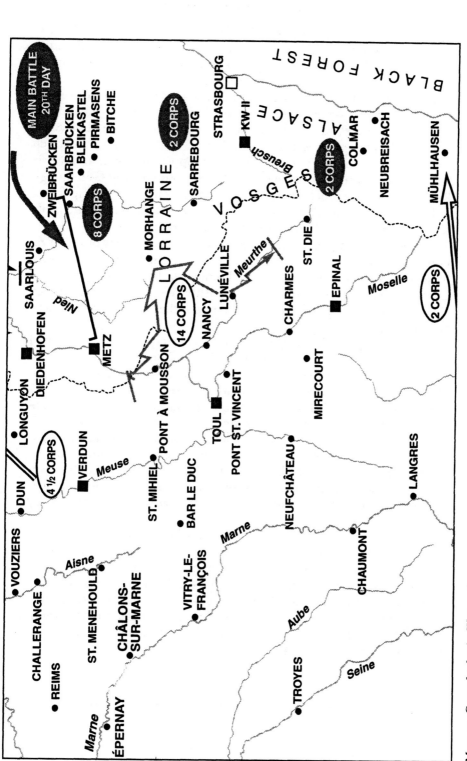

MAP 12. *Generalstabsreise West 1906*

right wing, marching through the Ardennes and northern France, could make itself felt. The course of action advocated in this situation by the Schlieffen plan *Denkschrift*—to continue the right flank attack through France—was emphatically rejected.

Moltke's *Generalstabsreise West* of 1908 also survived.[8] This exercise, of all the German exercises, most closely approximates the situation in 1914 and is the best indicator of Moltke's intent at that time. It plays the pure *Westaufmarsch*: a war between France and Germany in which Britain has promised to provide effective support for France and Russia has not yet declared her belligerency. Moltke also said that even though Russia was not yet a belligerent, the Germans must keep strong forces in East Prussia to guard against her later intervention. Italy would probably exercise a benevolent neutrality toward France.

The French completed their deployment by the 9th day of mobilization. Moltke stated again that it was not in the French interest to violate Belgian neutrality and therefore the French would most likely attack in Lorraine. The British would land in Antwerp if the Germans had already violated Belgian neutrality; otherwise they would land in Calais and Boulogne.

The French and Germans were numerically equal. The French had 21 corps and 19 reserve divisions (61 divisions in total), the Germans 31 corps, including both active and reserve corps (62 divisions in total). Moltke's French exercise deployment was a reasonably good approximation of the French Plan XVII in 1914. Two armies were in Lorraine with a third army to the north of Metz and a fourth army on the left flank of the third. The French were able to launch their attack on the 11th day of mobilization. Belgium said that she felt threatened by the German deployment and allied herself to France. Moltke said that even if France violated Belgian neutrality, Germany must assume that Belgium would ally herself to France. On the 13th day the British army landed in Antwerp.

Moltke said that if France were certain of British and Belgian cooperation her best course of action would be to launch her main attack immediately with 15 corps and 9 reserve divisions from a line Verdun–Maubeuge to a line Diedenhofen–Liège in the Ardennes while remaining on the defensive between Belfort and Verdun with 6 corps and 10 reserve divisions. After the 8th day of mobilization, however, it was too late for the French to change their deployment from an attack in Lorraine to one in the Ardennes.

[8] 'Große Generalstabsreise 1908', BA-MA PH 3/664. Thirty-six pages, typewritten, with eight maps.

The Germans deployed four armies between Metz and Aachen, an army echelonned behind Metz, one in Lorraine and one in southern Lorraine and in Alsace: practically the deployment used in 1914. The Entente had a numerical superiority of 311 infantry battalions, but Moltke seemed to feel that this would be offset to a large part by German qualitative superiority. The German intent was to launch the main attack with the right wing into Belgium and Luxembourg, but the German army would fight a decisive battle wherever the French main force was to be found.

Moltke said that if the French launched their main attack between Metz and Strasbourg, the 3rd, 4th, 5th, and 6th Armies would swing south to occupy a line Metz–Coblenz and attack with a strong right wing to the south-west. The 1st and 2nd Armies would guard the right flank of the main body to the north of Metz and the 7th Army on the left would fall back to the north along the left bank of the Rhine.

The most likely French course of action was a main attack with the left wing between the Meuse and Verdun. This would be met by the German right wing, whose *Schwerpunkt* would be in an enveloping movement by the 1st and 2nd Armies on the right or a breakthrough by the 4th and 5th Armies on the left; the 6th Army would cover the left flank of the main body in Lorraine. The French might also attack on both sides of Metz. In this case, the 1st and 2nd Armies would march south.

Moltke said that the great difficulty would lie in determining what strategy the French were using. He then repeated a common concern of all soldiers before the Great War, saying that no one had any experience in conducting a war with a mass army. In the face of these questions, deciding on his own strategy was no higher than Moltke's third priority problem.

The French attacked on both sides of Metz. The German 1st, 2nd, 3rd, and 4th Armies on the right marched directly south. The 5th held the Moselle to the north-east of Metz, the 6th the Nied to the south-east, the 7th held the line Han (south-east of Metz)–Saarebourg. On the 13th and 14th days 9 French corps attacked 8½ German corps defending a position on the German Nied.

On the 15th day the German 2nd and French 4th Armies were maneuvering against each other in the Ardennes with the German 1st Army echelonned to the right rear of the 2nd and the 3rd Army arriving to the left rear of the 2nd. The French 3rd Army was defending Luxembourg and the German 4th had crossed the Moselle to attack it. The German 6th, 7th, and 5th Armies (west to east) were defending a position on a line Metz–Saargemund–Pirmasens against frontal attacks by the French 2nd and 1st Armies. The French frontal attacks failed, as,

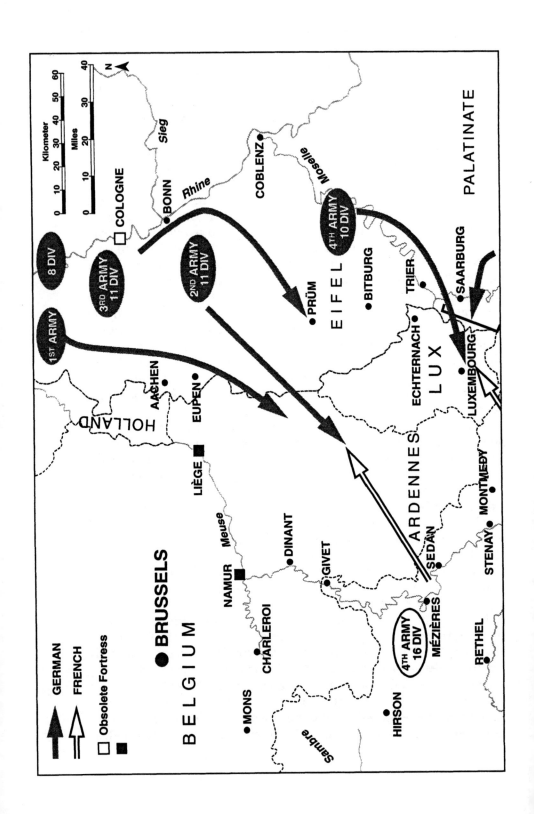

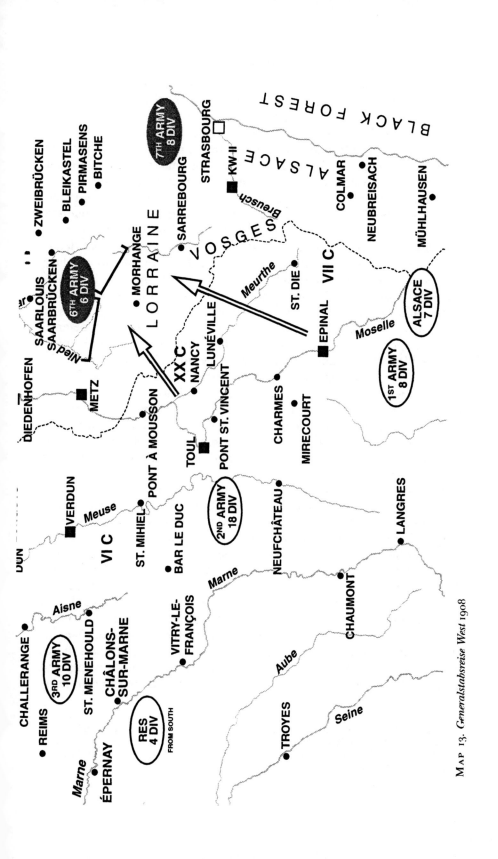

MAP 13. *Generalstabsreise West* 1908

BLACK FOREST

ALSACE

LORRAINE

VOSGES

7TH ARMY
8 DIV

6TH ARMY
6 DIV

STRASBOURG

KW II

Breusch

SARREBOURG

MORHANGE

SAARBRÜCKEN

SAARLOUIS

ZWEIBRÜCKEN

BLEIKASTEL

PIRMASENS

BITCHE

COLMAR

NEUBREISACH

MÜHLHAUSEN

ST. DIE

Meurthe

LUNÉVILLE

NANCY

EPINAL

VII C

Moselle

ALSACE
7 DIV

1ST ARMY
8 DIV

CHARMES

MIRECOURT

XX C

PONT ST. VINCENT

TOUL

PONT À MOUSSON

METZ

DIEDENHOFEN

Nied S.

VERDUN

Meuse

ST. MIHIEL

VI C

BAR LE DUC

2ND ARMY
18 DIV

NEUFCHÂTEAU

LANGRES

CHAUMONT

Marne

DUN

Aisne

CHALLERANGE

REIMS

ST. MENEHOULD

CHÂLONS-
SUR-MARNE

ÉPERNAY

Marne

3RD ARMY
10 DIV

VITRY-LE-
FRANÇOIS

RES
4 DIV
FROM SOUTH

Aube

Seine

TROYES

Moltke said, frontal attacks would fail no matter how overwhelming the attacker's superiority in infantry. Nevertheless, the Germans were unable to prevent the defeated French forces from successfully with-drawing to their fortress line. The Germans, said Moltke, were now faced with a difficult second campaign. In his opinion, the first battle would come quickly and might well decide the final outcome of the war but it would be followed by a long war in the enemy heartland.

Moltke's analysis of the situation in the west in 1908 was founded directly on the German intelligence analyses and the results obtained by Schlieffen's last staff rides. This concept has nothing in common with the Schlieffen plan *Denkschrift.* Rather, the Germans had deter-mined that because of the Anglo-French Entente British military support for the French was practically certain and therefore a French offensive into the Ardennes and north Belgium was likely. In such circumstances, the Belgians would side with the Entente regardless of German actions. There was also no provision for a pure French defense because every chief of staff from Moltke the elder to the younger Moltke himself maintained that it was very unlikely that there would even be a war at all unless the French wanted one, and if the French wanted a war, then the French would attack. Moltke was not planning to invade France but rather to meet the French offensive head-on.

Six of Moltke's eight *Schlußaufgaben* have also survived, those from 1907 to 1911 and 1913. With one exception, these are all strategic exer-cises—*Strategische Aufgaben.* They give additional insight into Moltke's strategic thought.

In 1907 Moltke played a *Westaufmarsch*.[9] Only seven divisions were initially deployed in East Prussia. The Russians had attacked with a Niemen Army of three to four corps and a Narew Army of six to seven corps. These had crossed the border on 30 August. On the afternoon of 1 September three German corps began to arrive in west–central Prussia 'from other areas' with one en route. In the *Schlußbesprechung* Moltke said that this problem could be solved by digging in and allow-ing the Russians to attack. Fortunately none of the officers had chosen this solution. If we defeat the enemy attack, Moltke said, the enemy would retain his freedom of maneuver and would move to outflank us the next day. Eventually we would be forced out of our position. It was necessary not just to throw back the enemy attack, but destroy him and this could only be accomplished by attacking. Since the German army

---

9 Sächsisches Hauptstaatsarchiv Dresden KA(P) 9195 (XII Corps) contains both *Aufgaben* and the *Schlußbesprechung,* with pp. 2 and 3 of the latter missing. Groener's *Nachlaß* contains the *Schlußbesprechung* BA-MA N/46 111. The Hauptsttatsarchiv Stuttgart has a copy of the two *Aufgaben* M33/1 (XIII Corps) Bündel 35.

was not strong enough to attack both Russian armies, it had to concentrate against one. The Niemen Army would probably withdraw in the face of a German attack. Even if it stood and fought, the Germans would probably not be able to deal with it before the Narew Army appeared in the German rear. A German attack on the Niemen Army would be largely frontal and in modern combat frontal attacks are long, drawnout, and bloody affairs. Recent experience had shown that a decision could be won only by enveloping an enemy flank. Moltke's solution was to attack the left flank of the Narew Army and drive it into the Masurian Lakes. I Reserve Corps would delay the Niemen Army on a position along the Alle. Three corps would block the Narew Army's attack at Allenstein in the middle of East Prussia while two corps attacked the Narew Army's left flank. Moltke said that this was safer than attacking the right flank of the Narew Army. Even if the Niemen Army did break the German defensive line on the Alle it could not threaten the decisive right-wing attack of the German main body, whereas if the German *Schwerpunkt* were on the left, the Niemen Army might pose a danger. In 1894 Schlieffen's solution was that the Germans had to risk an attack on the Russian right in order to destroy the Narew Army.[10]

The German deployment in the 1909 *Schlußaufgabe* was an *Ostaufmarsch*: the German army in the west contained only 23 divisions.[11] The 1st Army was in Lorraine with three corps. The 2nd Army was on the east bank of the Rhine defending southern Germany with three corps. The 3rd Army with five and a-half corps was in reserve on the Saar. The French attacked with the mass of their forces (8–11 corps) in Lorraine supported by an attack with an army to the north of Diedenhofen and another with about six corps in Alsace. Groener took part in this exercise.

Moltke said that in the next war the Germans were going to be severely outnumbered and they were not going to be given any easy problems to solve. The French also had their difficulties, as their armies were divided into three parts by Metz–Diedenhofen and the Vosges–Strasbourg. The Germans must therefore attack before the French had a chance to unite their forces. This attack must strike at the heart of the French army: partial success would not be adequate.

A German counterattack into Alsace was out of the question. The Germans would not be able to mass a significant force there. In addition, it was completely immaterial to the Germans whether the French could

---

[10] The situation for the 1908 *Schlußaufgabe* was for a defense against a landing of three corps (100,000 men)—pretty obviously the British army—in Denmark: Hauptstaatsarchiv Stuttgart M33/1 (XIII Corps), Bündel 35.
[11] Ibid.

cross the Rhine into Baden. Except for a few Landwehr brigades the Germans should pull all their troops out of Alsace.

A counterattack against the French army in Luxembourg had attractive advantages. However, in the current situation the Germans could not turn the French left in time. A German frontal attack in Luxembourg would accomplish nothing, because at the same time the French main body would drive the Germans out of Lorraine.

Only victory over the French main army in Lorraine would be decisive. VIII Corps would defend the Moselle to the east of Diedenhofen. It would probably take too long for the XIV Corps and XIV Reserve Corps to move by rail from Alsace to Lorraine, but the movement must begin anyway. Therefore, the Germans had eight corps for the decisive battle in Lorraine, and would certainly not be numerically superior to the 8–11 French corps there. There would be four ways to attack the French: frontally, on their eastern (right) flank, the western (left) flank, or both flanks.

Advocates of the frontal attack noted that the French would have to make their flanks so strong to guard against Metz and Strasbourg that they would advance in a wedge formation and the tip of the wedge could be snipped off by a pincer attack. Moltke said that such an attack would, in fact, merely drive the French directly to the rear. The Japanese had pushed the Russians back in Manchuria with frontal attacks to little result. At the same time the French army in Luxembourg would cross the Moselle in the German rear and the campaign would end in a disaster for the Germans.

The German deployment did not permit a strong attack on the French right. Nor with only eight corps could the Germans conduct a double envelopment. The only possible solution was an attack against the French left. The Germans had to be conscious of the fact that the French would recognize the threat to their left and would be very strong there. Tactically this would be a frontal attack. The Germans would be faced with successive French defensive positions and fresh French forces. The operation might drag on, a situation the Germans could not tolerate. The German army needed quick, decisive victories. Nevertheless, this attack had the advantage, that it would be directed against the strategic flank of the enemy army and that was the most important thing. The area to the south-east of Metz was the most sensitive point in the entire French operation. A victory here must have decisive results. Moltke said that the majority of the officers had come to this conclusion, but that most had not been ruthless enough in its application. Many expected that if the Germans withdrew to the east the French main body would follow and so present a flank to attack. Moltke said that there was no reason that the French would make such an obvious mistake. It was better to stick with the principle that the enemy will act in the most effective manner possible.[12]

A surprise attack could only be launched through Fortress Metz. This attack should be conducted using the entire 3rd Army, supported by all of Metz's available guns and troops. The French could not fall back, but had to stand and fight to defend their flank, and it would be likely that the Germans would push in the French flank. At the same time, the German 1st Army would occupy a defensive position behind the Nied with the left flank on the Saar south of Saargemund. Moltke noted that this operation was risky, but that it was impossible to defeat an enemy that was twice the German army's strength without taking risks.

It should be clear that Moltke was presenting his solution to the situation that the 6th Army faced in Lorraine in August 1914: the Germans should not have attacked frontally but rather out of Metz against the French left. Moltke also said that if the Germans were able to begin the war with an attack into France they must anticipate a similar French counterattack from one of their great fortresses, by which he meant Verdun, though the warning could equally well have been applied to Paris in the first week of September 1914.

In his scenario for the second requirement Moltke said that tactically the Germans had been forced to conduct a frontal attack and that the situation had quickly became critical. Nevertheless, the entire French army in Lorraine was forced to retreat and for mass armies this was a difficult operation. Crowds of disorganized French troops blocked the roads and it was impossible to deploy them again.

However, the I Bavarian Corps was being hard pressed by the enemy. The German XVIII Corps was coming up on its right flank. The XVIII Corps commander had to decide either to march his corps immediately to the assistance of the I Bavarian Corps or press on against the strategic objective, the French rear. Of 170 officers taking the test, 117 went straight to the assistance of the I Bavarian Corps. Moltke said that the situation did not justify such a step. The best that would be accomplished would be a lengthening of the front. Many officers thought they could do both. Moltke said that this half-measure would accomplish neither purpose. Moltke's solution was for XVIII Corps to continue the attack directly against the enemy rear. This would give the best prospects of destroying the enemy and be the surest method of bringing relief to the I Bavarian Corps.

---

[12] Moltke noted that captive balloons had the ability to detect troop movements far into the enemy rear. Future campaigns would begin with attempts to destroy enemy balloons. That was why in this exercise the assumption had been made that the French balloons had all been destroyed. For the moment, Moltke said, the Zeppelin provided the Germans with the superior air reconnaissance platform.

Moltke's solution to the second requirement is of particular importance for any evaluation of the German 3rd Army's performance in the 1914 Marne campaign. Three times the 3rd Army went straight to the assistance of hard-pressed neighbors and missed chances to conduct an operational penetration of the French center. Both in 1909 and in 1914 Moltke favored the bold solution: he was practically alone. Either the timid solution or some half-measure was the choice of most of the General Staff officers both in the exercise and during the campaign.[13]

The initial situation for the 1911 *Schlußaufgabe* was similar to that of 1907.[14] The Germans conducted a *Westaufmarsch*. Only six divisions were initially deployed in East Prussia. The Russians attacked from the Niemen with seven to eight corps. The German army withdrew in front of the Russian advance. The Russians formed another army of six corps at Warsaw which was moving north-west on 14 May. Three more German corps 'became available' with the lead elements arriving beginning 16 May.

Moltke said that the Russians knew that their Niemen Army was nearly three times stronger than the German army in East Prussia and thought that the Germans would withdraw and defend the Vistula. Here the Germans would be able to hold up the Russian advance for a considerable time. The Russians had therefore sent a second army from Warsaw down the right bank of the Vistula to turn this defensive line. The Russians would know that the Germans had sent reinforcements to the east, but would not know where they would be employed. Once they had detrained, however, the Russians would become aware of their presence.

The German mission was to defeat the two Russian armies in detail. Most of the officers chose to attack the Warsaw Army. Moltke agreed. He did not believe that the Germans could gain numerical superiority over the Russians in East Prussia, while the Warsaw Army would be forced to advance between Thorn and Posen. In the second requirement the Germans decided to attack the Warsaw Army as it advanced up the south bank of the Vistula. The three arriving corps were directed to Posen. The three German corps in East Prussia crossed to the west bank of the Vistula at Thorn. The German force opposite the Russian Warsaw Army therefore included all available active and reserve units, plus the equivalent of more than three Landwehr divisions. The troops were assembled by 19 May and the German attack began on 20th May.

Most of the officers decided to attack the Warsaw Army's left flank. Moltke said that then the Germans would be pushing the Warsaw Army

---

[13] The 1910 *Schlußaufgabe* played a French attack from Alsace into Baden. Hauptstaatsarchiv Stuttgart M33/1 (XIII Corps), Bündel 1.
[14] Ibid.

toward the Niemen Army. Moltke's solution was a double envelopment with three corps attacking from Posen and three from Thorn. He said that this concept more clearly realized the intent of annihilating the enemy (*Vernichtungsgedanke*). The Germans could afford to hold their centre with four Landwehr brigades which would withdraw in the face of an enemy attack. This was pure *Cannae*.

Moltke said that in his initial order the Army commander would deploy the corps and coordinate the attack, but he would not try to predict the course of the battle. The conduct of the battle was the province of the corps commanders. During the battle the Army commander would make his intent known to the corps commanders through liaison officers. The corps commanders were given objectives: the method of attaining them was left up to the corps commander's discretion. This was exactly the procedure that Moltke would use in relation to the Army commanders in 1914.

Moltke said that the reports from the front on 23 May did not present a complete picture but the outline of the course of the battle could be recognized. There had been heavy fighting and only on the 2nd day of the offensive had it been possible to force back the enemy flanks. The enemy had been defeated but not yet destroyed. All the officers recognized that destruction of the enemy was the objective but the methods of accomplishing this differed.

A correct estimate of the enemy's most likely course of action was therefore the primary task. A major problem was the probability that the Niemen Army would intervene. The Niemen Army's location and movements were known with a high degree of accuracy owing to air reconnaissance from dirigibles and aircraft. These reconnaissance assets, Moltke said, would become even more effective in the future. Some officers thought that the Niemen Army was an immediate threat, others that it was not. There was also the question of the Warsaw Army's intent. Some officers thought it was already withdrawing, others that it would defend in place and wait for the Niemen Army to arrive.

Moltke said that the evaluation of the Russian situation was relatively easy. Only one corps from the Niemen Army was across the Vistula and it was a day's march to the east. Six Landwehr brigades could defend the Vistula against attempts by the rest of the Niemen Army to force a crossing. The Warsaw Army was tangled up in the lake district south of Thorn. Withdrawal was difficult and it was possible that the Russians would dig in and attempt to defend in place. All available German forces must be concentrated against the Warsaw army to achieve its destruction. It was essential to close the sack behind the Warsaw Army with the Guard and XVII Corps. The troops would be tired but it was necessary to push them on.

In the 1913 *Schlußaufgabe* Moltke employed an entirely new *Ostaufmarsch*.[15] In a one-front war against Russia the mass of the German army (1st–4th Armies) deployed in Posen and Silesia. The 5th and 6th Armies deployed in East Prussia on the east side of the Vistula. The concept was for the 1st–5th Armies to launch a concentric attack into Poland while the 6th Army covered the left flank. The exercise was concerned with 6th Army operations. Moltke's comments on the students' solutions were pure Schlieffen, emphasizing the need to take the initiative even when the situation was unclear—as would always be the case.

None of these six problems had any connection with the Schlieffen plan. They were all conducted in East Prussia, Lorraine, and Alsace, not in Belgium or northern France. They all dealt with Schlieffen's principal concern—how to fight outnumbered and win—and they generally featured Schlieffen's solution to that problem: rail mobility, surprise counterattacks, and the use of fortresses to aid maneuver, with the emphasis being on the destruction of the enemy. Moltke also made extensive use of Landwehr units, especially in the east. Moltke's contribution was to point out the increasing effectiveness of firepower on the battlefield. His exercises are obviously not as sophisticated and daring as Schlieffen's, but there is no indication that Moltke was trying to do anything else than develop the doctrine presented in Schlieffen's last exercises.

According to the Reichsarchiv, Moltke changed the Schlieffen plan in two stages.[16] Moltke's sin was that he supposedly diluted the strength of the decisive right wing in favor of the left. In the 1908/9 plan he assigned the XIV Corps to cover the upper Alsace. From 1909 on, the 7th Army was deployed to the area around Strasbourg, its strength eventually reaching three corps. The Reichsarchiv said that it had no documents which could explain the change in the deployment. The only indications the Reichsarchiv could find were the marginal notes that Moltke made in 1911 on the Schlieffen plan *Denkschrift* itself and some comments (of dubious value) that he made in 1915. There was no evidence that the Reichsarchiv, which otherwise prided itself on expanding archival materials by interrogating key personnel, ever obtained an explanation of Moltke's changes to the deployment plan from any of the operations officers. It was all a mystery.

Comparing Moltke's exercises with Schlieffen's of 1904 and 1905 it is clear that whatever changes Moltke made in the deployment, he adhered to Schlieffen's real operational concept of the counteroffensive.

---

[15] 'Schlußaufgabe 1913', Hauptstaatsarchiv Dresden, KA (P) 9195.
[16] Reichsarchiv *Der Weltkrieg, Band I, Die Grenzschlachten in Westen* (Berlin, 1925) 61–4.

PLAN XVI

The adoption of the two-year law in France in 1905 led to significant growth in the French order of battle, including an increase to 22 corps and the assignment of a reserve infantry brigade to most of the corps. There were also 12 reserve divisions available for the field army. These troop increases, plus the prospect of British participation in a war with Germany, led to the adoption of a much more confident Plan XVI in 1909. The plan provided for five armies to deploy on line from the east of Reims in the north to Belfort in the south, backed up by a reserve army of four corps behind Verdun.[17] As Greiner noted, this concentrated 10 corps in the front line opposite Lorraine with an army of two corps on each flank. The French now also had ten deployment rail lines available instead of nine.

In September 1911 the new chief of staff of the French army, Joffre, introduced the first variant to Plan XVI.[18] The left wing was significantly strengthened. The reserve army, 6th Army, was moved north to Reims–Ste Menehould, where it was directly behind 5th Army. This concentrated a mass of six corps on the left flank. The right-flank 4th Army was also increased to four corps. The combat troops and their trains would finish movement by the 11th day of mobilization. The entire deployment would be complete by the 17th day.

GERMAN INTELLIGENCE ESTIMATES, 1911–1914

Owing to a lack of new information, the 3rd Department retained the 1907 enemy estimate (Plan XV*bis*) until 1911.[19] In 1909 it was acknowledged that the estimate was based on a wide range of indicators of uncertain value, and could be partially or totally wrong. Greiner said that up to 1909 the Germans thought that the French expected the Germans to launch a frontal attack from Lorraine and the Vosges, with a German attack through Luxembourg and south Belgium being considered a strong possibility, but not a certainty. The French military literature seemed to indicate that after 1909 the French expected the German main attack through Belgium and Luxembourg. The French no longer felt that the Germans would launch a serious attack in Lorraine. The Germans would only deploy weak forces in Lorraine, which would demonstrate against the French fortress line or stand on the defensive. Indeed, they suspected that the Germans might even transit Holland and advance to the north of the Meuse.

[17]   Marchand, *Plans de concentration*, 169–89; Greiner, 'Nachrichten', 112–18.
[18]   Marchand, *Plans de concentration*, 181–9.   [19] Greiner, 'Nachrichten', 121.

In November 1911 the 3rd Department wrote a political-military appreciation of the German situation, which the Militärarchiv in Freiburg obtained from the East German military archive.[20] The *Denkschrift* began by saying that any consideration of Germany's military-political situation must be based on the possibility of war with France. It did not appear in November 1911 that France was seeking war with Germany. The factors in France which served to maintain the peace were universal conscription, colonialism, and the government's own interest in self-preservation. The elements which could lead to war were the propaganda of the French nationalists, the support which France would receive from her allies, the recent reawakening of French self-confidence, and the excitability of the French national character. A successful war promised France revenge, national power, glory, and the return of Alsace-Lorraine. In any war, France would therefore be the political aggressor. Germany, which had no other continental goal than the preservation of the status quo, was therefore politically on the defensive. However, in terms of *Weltpolitik* Germany had offensive political goals—colonial and naval expansion—which must come up against British interests.

The *Denkschrift* said that French confidence had increased significantly in the recent past, particularly in the army. This was in good part because of the assurance that the Triple Entente would stand together in a war against Germany. The Russians had recovered from the effects of the Japanese war and the 1905 revolution. Above all, the French were encouraged by the certainty that the British would support them in a war against Germany. At the same time, pro-war propaganda was stirring up the easily excited French population. German military prowess was being called into question, particularly by the British military expert, Colonel Repington, who said that the latest *Kaisermanöver* showed that the French army was in many areas superior to the German, while the German army had in many areas sunk to the status of a second-rank power. Numerous books, including those written by senior French officers, proclaimed French military superiority. Success in aviation (the cutting-edge technology of the early twentieth century) further built French self-confidence. As a consequence France, borne on a wave of popular enthusiasm, could go to war at any time.

Given the current political constellation, an isolated Franco-German war was impossible. The corollary to this was that the outcome of the war would largely depend on the degree of support given to Germany and France by their allies. Italian adherence to the Triple Alliance was purely formal: there was no possibility that Italy would fight if opposed

[20] BA-MA PH 3/529 'Die militär-politische Lage Deutschlands Ende November 1911'.

by British sea-power. The best that could be expected of Italy was that she did not attack Austria. If Italy declared war on Austria, Austria would be crippled in the east. For their part, the Austrians would rather attack Italy and defend in the east. On the other hand, if Russia were neutral, Austria would remain neutral also, and Germany had nothing to fear from a war with France and Great Britain.

In any possible war, the General Staff maintained that the German *Schwerpunkt* must be directed against France. If Russia was a belligerent in a Franco-German war, Germany could deploy to the east only the minimum forces necessary to defend the eastern provinces. The war would be decided in the west. France was the most dangerous opponent and the Germans had the prospect of reaching a quick decision in the west. If France were defeated in great battles, the French lacked the manpower reserves necessary to conduct a long war. If the Russians lost the initial battles, they could always withdraw into their vast interior and drag the war out for an unforeseeably long period. Germany's entire effort must be directed at winning the war on one front before turning to the other.

The Italian–Turkish War had complicated Italy's relationship to the Triple Alliance. Germany now ran the risk of losing a friend (Turkey) or an ally (Italy). The General Staff decided that the Turkish alliance was more useful in a European war. Military reforms had increased the offensive capability of the Turkish army. Turkey alone could threaten Britain on land. A Turkish campaign against the Suez canal and Aden would divert significant British forces from the continent. The Turks could also assist against the Russians. In conjunction with the Bulgarians, the Turks could keep the Romanians in check.

The numerical balance was shifting in favor of the Entente. In the last five years, owing to rail construction and a more effective distribution of peacetime garrisons, the Russian army had halved the time needed to complete its deployment. The Russians had raised six new corps by reorganizing fortress and reserve troops. The Russians had spent vast sums on new field guns and heavy artillery. The most important improvements in the Russian army had already been completed. The General Staff concluded that it was no longer correct to say that Russia was not capable of conducting a European war.

The British had also done all they could to increase their military strength. By drawing in their colonial garrisons, the British would be able to put an army of 150,000 men onto the continent. Britain would not be unhappy to see a war between Germany and France. The British recognized that a German defeat would present an opportunity to eliminate the German fleet. To achieve this objective, the British were willing to commit their entire strength to the war.

In an isolated Anglo-German war, the British would rely on a naval blockade to destroy German trade and industry. The British would also seize the German colonies. There was no military solution for an Anglo-German war. The British would never land troops on the mainland and a German invasion of Britain was impossible, even if the Germans won a naval battle. A German naval victory could never bring the war to a favorable conclusion. Even if the British lost a naval battle and suffered severe losses, given Britain's vast fleet Britain would still retain naval superiority. Germany could injure Britain only by seizing the Low Countries. That, however, meant war with France. The French could never tolerate a combat-ready German army in Belgium. If Britain declared war on Germany, the only possible German response could be the mobilization of the entire army for a war with France, before France mobilized and attacked an unprepared Germany. Germany's strength, now as in the past, rested on her military power.

The General Staff traced the cause of the current tension in European politics back to the Morocco crisis of 1905. Prior to that time a reduction in the military spirit and interest in defense was discernable in France. The Moroccan crisis caused a complete reversal in French defense policy and also revived and strengthened French chauvinism. The second Moroccan crisis of 1911 only reinforced these tendencies. Franco-German tensions then led to a European arms race. All the powers in Europe were anticipating a great war.

Only Germany and her Austrian ally had not taken part in the European military build-up. Austria had done nothing for years to strengthen her army. Significant expansion of the German army had been blocked by financial considerations. In particular, there was a glaring failure to completely utilize Germany's manpower. The General Staff did not say so outright, but the implication was clear—Germany had devoted all of her resources to the fleet and that was dangerous.

The course of European politics in the near future would be decided by war, the General staff maintained. This war would judge whether the individual states had demonstrated the inner strength that alone justified their future existence. The General Staff concluded that German defense policy needed to move in two directions: toward a further build-up of the fleet as well as the reinforcement of the army through genuine universal conscription.

There is no evidence in this intelligence estimate that the General Staff contemplated an aggressive war. The General Staff was pessimistic: since 1905 tensions had been increasing and would probably lead to war. The General Staff saw the attack coming most likely from France, but perhaps from England, with the Entente acting in concert in any case. The Entente was ready: the Austro-Germans were not. Neither the

Austrian nor the German armies had kept pace with the Entente build-up and they were losing the arms race. Fritz Fischer said that on 8 December 1912 the Kaiser, supported by Moltke, held a 'war council' to prepare for a war of aggression. In fact, there would have been little point to a preventive war, for which the Entente alone was prepared. Many modern historians maintain that in July 1914 Moltke advocated a preventive war before the Russians had completed their Great Program army expansion. Rather, the General Staff had said that in 1911 the Russians had recently increased the speed of their mobilization, added six corps to their order of battle, and were now ready for war. Moltke's concern in July 1914 was that Entente superiority, which was already considerable, would become overwhelming in 1917 when the Russian Great Program was to be completed.

This estimate was probably decisive in motivating the General Staff to simplify the German war plan. The strategic situation was plain and it was serious. There was no need for two *Aufmarsch* plans. Any war would begin with coordinated and nearly simultaneous Franco-Russian offensives. By 1913 they were amalgamated into one plan, with nine divisions in the east and the rest of the German army in the west. This involved taking terrific risks in East Prussia.

On the basis of the 1911 intelligence estimate the 3rd Department wrote a *Denkschrift* in May 1912 titled 'Aufmarsch und operative Absichten der Franzosen in einem zukünftigen deutsch–französischen Krieg' (French Deployment and Operational Intentions in a Future Franco-German War).[21] This represented a fundamental reassessment and revision of the German intelligence estimate. It was updated on 9 November 1912, updated again for the 1913/14 plan, and finally reviewed a last time in April 1914. This is therefore the final German west-front intelligence estimate. It is an unusually thorough document, some 70 pages in total, and is worth a detailed summary.

The 3rd Department acknowledged that it had no hard intelligence data concerning the French deployment or intentions. Apparently the only important agent material it possessed concerned the transfer of the North African units to France. It believed, however, that it could develop an accurate estimate using published works by French military authors.

---

[21] Ibid. 123–9; Großer Generalstab 3. Abteilung, Mai 1912, 'Aufmarsch und operative Absichten der Franzosen in einem zukünftigen deutsch-französischen Kriege', BA-MA PH 3/628. This copy was obtained from the Militärarchiv der DDR. The BA-MA has a typed transcript of the *Denkschrift* which had been made by the Americans who had captured it after the First World War. The original had belonged to the IV Corps. The Americans apparently had returned the transcript to the BA-MA. The maps were missing, which probably goes a long way to account for the fact that this *Denkschrift* has never received the attention it deserved.

As long as the French thought that the German main effort would be made in Lorraine, the *Denkschrift* began, the French massed their forces at Toul–Epinal. Now that the French thought that the Germans would make a major effort in the Ardennes, they had moved their deployment to the north. In particular in the October 1911 issue of the *Revue militaire générale* General Langlois said that a German *Westaufmarsch* was a practical certainty and that it was virtually impossible that the Germans could stay on the defensive in the west. The Germans would leave a minimum of forces in the east and seek an early decision against France. General Bonnal said that the Germans would not leave more than two to three corps in the east. The Russians could not tie down more than a maximum of four German corps. In 1911 Bonnal said that the Germans would send 20–22 corps against France. The German intelligence estimate noted that everyone in France, Belgium, and Britain expected the Germans to attack through Belgium ('anderslautende Meinungen kommen überhaupt nicht mehr auf'). The *Petit Parisien* and *Est Republican* said as much in 1909. The *Armée et democratie* wrote in April 1911 that the Germans had no other choice. Senator de Lamarzelle said in the Senate on 6 April 1911 that the need to find room to deploy the army by itself forced the Germans to march through Belgium.

Captain Sorb wrote that there were two schools of thought in the French army concerning the German offensive. The 'old school' thought that on the 12th day of mobilization a 'strong German army' (eight corps plus reserve troops) would cross the Belgian–Luxembourg border and would reach the French border on a line Mézières–Montmédy on the 16th day, when the strong German left wing would attack on a line Nancy–Raon l'Etape. Langlois had presented such a scenario in 1906.

The 'new school' thought that the mass of the German army would deploy on the right wing, which would march through Belgium, while only weak forces would be deployed in Lorraine. The German right wing would extend to the north of the Meuse. In 1910 'Junius' wrote in the *Echo de Paris* that the German mass of maneuver would attack through south Belgium and Luxembourg on Maubeuge–Montmédy while a 'strong detachment' with much cavalry would advance through Holland and north Belgium on Lille. In 1906 a member of the Chamber of Deputies named Rousset warned of a German advance as far north as Lille. Foch wrote that the Germans would advance north of the Meuse at Namur. Many French field-grade officers (Colonel Cordonnier, commander of the 119th Infantry Regiment; Colonel (retired) Biottot, formerly commander of the 162nd Infantry Regiment at Verdun, and Commandant Imhaus) thought that the Germans would conduct a deep outflanking maneuver through Belgium. Many French officers thought that the German objective was Lille or St Quentin.

Cordonnier and Biottot expected the Germans to make diversionary attacks in Lorraine. Foch said that the Germans would stand on the defensive in Lorraine. Commandant Imhaus said in *Armée et démocratie* in December 1911 that Metz would serve as the pivot for the German right-wing attack. He was seconded by General Cherfils in *Echo de Paris* on 21 April 1912, who expected a bold German offensive ('mouvement offensif audacieux'). As of 1910 the 'new school' was gaining adherents in France, Britain, and Belgium. The German intelligence estimate even concluded that the French expected a German *coup de main* on Liège.

The German intelligence estimate concluded that the French expected the Germans to make the main attack through Belgium and Luxembourg. The Germans felt that the French were not uncertain what the German right would do in Belgium, but rather what the German *left* would do in Lorraine. The real question for the French was between the 'old school', which expected a German attack on the front Verdun–Toul, and the 'new school' which expected the Germans to stay on the defensive in Lorraine. French apologists, in particular Joffre, would attempt to justify French defeats in the battle of the Frontiers and the retreat to the Marne by claiming that the German right wing had been much stronger than anticipated. This was an *ex post facto* explanation. The real cause for French confusion was the German intentions in Lorraine.

The French expected the German mobilization and deployment to be completed in 10–12 days. The German approach march through south Belgium and Luxembourg would take 5–7 days, that is, to the 16th–18th day of mobilization. The German forces moving to the north of the Meuse would take 21–22 days to reach the French border. This was essentially accurate. The French also expected the Belgians to withdraw to Antwerp and the Italians to join the winning side.

Until 1911 the German intelligence estimate concluded that the French intended to conduct a strategic defensive operation. This was clear from Bonnal's 1906 book *La prochaine guerre* (The Next War). However, after 1911 there were signs of increasing military confidence in France and therefore a turn to the doctrine of the strategic offensive. The 3rd Department said that French confidence had grown because of the prospect of British support and Italian neutrality in a war with Germany. The French thought that the German army was less capable than their own ('systematisch wurde das deutsche Heer herabgesetzt'). They believed that their troops were better trained than the Germans. In the 1911 Balkan war the German-trained Turkish army was badly beaten: this was taken to be an indicator of the poor training of the German army itself. The French thought that they had achieved numerical parity with the German army, while enjoying technical superiority, especially in the most modern equipment, such as aviation.

The 3rd Department said that the offensive spirit was strong in the French press, military literature, and in Parliament. The war minister and other representatives of the government were using the word 'offensive'. An important indicator of the new French offensive doctrine were the writings of Colonel Boucher, *La France victorieuse* (France Victorious) and *L'Offensive contre l'Allemagne* (The Offensive against Germany), in which Boucher, with all the authority of a one-time chief of the operations section of the French General Staff, strove to show that the French army was superior to the German, regardless of whether the Germans were attacking or defending.

Nevertheless, the French were not yet really serious about launching a strategic offensive. The French would initially still be on the strategic defensive, but they were increasingly emphasizing the counterattack. This estimate was repeated in 1913, when the 3rd Department noted that there were even more calls for a strategic offensive, but it felt that the French still had not adopted an outright offensive war plan. (This was perfectly accurate: Plan XVII was not implemented until April 1914.) As proof of this estimate, Major Mordacq's views on the German offensive were cited. Mordacq wrote that the Germans would launch an offensive on a very broad front ('sur un front énorme') with the *Schwerpunkt* directed on Dun–Stenay (that is, south of the Meuse in the Ardennes) against the French left flank. The Germans would try to divert French attention with supporting attacks between Belfort and Verdun. Mordacq said that the German plan left them no means to maneuver: it was merely a 'brutal push straight ahead which took not the least notice of the movement of the enemy'. The French would win by using their railroads to maneuver. Therefore, the French would deploy in depth.

The German intelligence estimate said that the French High Command had replaced General Michel with Joffre in the spring of 1911 in order to institute a more aggressive war plan. Joffre had moved the French leftmost army nearer to Hirson-Maubeuge. This army would march 'under all circumstances' into Belgium. It could be supported by a second army of three corps located between Stenay and Montmédy. French military literature mentioned sending forces towards Namur to secure the French left flank and assist the Belgians and British, who would operate against the German right. The French were still uncertain as to whether the German attack would come to the north or south of the Meuse. The 3rd Department thought that Joffre estimated that

the German right wing would need two days to reach Liège and a
further five days to reach the French border. In this time he could
concentrate forces on Hirson–Maubeuge and deploy them either to
cover the Sambre–Meuse, or to move north to meet the Germans on
French soil.

However, the French mass of maneuver would still assemble on a line
Epinal–Toul–Verdun, and the main French counterattack would come
either from Verdun to the north of Metz or into Lorraine. The French
were conscious of the fact that an attack into Lorraine was a difficult
undertaking. Bonnal had said that it was impossible. General Maitrot
agreed, adding that the French should also not attack into the upper
Alsace. Captain Sorb said that the terrain was difficult and the Germans
would probably reinforce their defense with field fortifications. Metz
and Strasbourg threatened the flanks of the French attack, while the
entire French army was in danger of encirclement by a German attack
through Sedan. Sorb felt that the French should extend their deployment more to the north.

The French would not deploy all the way to the Channel (as Michel
had proposed) for in that case they would expose the right flank of
their main body to an attack from Lorraine (Metz) and they ran the
danger of being thrown into the sea (shades of 1940). Therefore, if the
Germans did launch their main attack through Belgium, the French
would not be able to outflank the German right but would only be able
to meet the German attack in a frontal battle.

The 3rd Department estimated that the French army included 22
active corps with 45 infantry divisions (plus 20 attached reserve infantry
brigades), perhaps 18 reserve divisions and 12 Territorial divisions. The
active army would deploy by the 10th day of mobilization, the reserve
divisions by the 13th, the Territorial divisions by the 18th. Greiner said
that the 3rd Department still thought that the French had 14 rail
deployment lines available. The 3rd Department's map of the French
deployment carried the caveat that the estimate was based on 'uncertain sources'. In the front line there was, from north to south: I Corps
at Maubeuge; a left-flank army of four corps at Vouziers–
Rethel–Mézières; a center army of four corps at Toul; a southern army
of five corps at Epinal and an enormous mass of maneuver, two armies
with seven corps concentrated west of Verdun–Nancy. Six reserve divisions were deployed behind the left flank at Laon–La Fère, four behind
the right flank at Lure–Vesoul and no less than eight reserve divisions
would be added to the mass of maneuver.

Greiner said that the General Staff estimate of the French deployment was once more far from the mark. In 1912/13 the 3rd Department
estimated that the French left consisted of an army at Maubeuge. This

extended the French left too far to the north and made it too strong. In fact, the French left was much weaker and went only as far north as Mézières. On the other hand, the 3rd Department still thought that the French would deploy in depth when in fact they intended to deploy almost on line and much closer to the border. The order of battle was completely inaccurate. The senior General Staff intelligence officer at this time, who was responsible for this estimate, was Hermann von Kuhl.

The only offensive action that the French would take at the outset would be an immediate attack by the VII Corps from Belfort into the upper Alsace. This was seen as a means for the French to get a cheap propaganda victory and occupy time until the main battle took place on the 15th–17th day of mobilization in Lorraine or on the 20th–22nd day in Belgium or northern France. Once the French had begun their rail deployment, changes in the deployment were no longer possible.

The 3rd Department thought that the French could not count on the British army. Captain Sorb wrote in the *Revue militaire générale* (1910–11) that the value of the Entente should not be overestimated. The British would use the opportunity provided by the war to destroy the German fleet and would provide full diplomatic support to France, but would not send the British army to France out of fear of a German invasion. The 3rd Department was aware of the 1911 British–French military staff discussions. It said that the French wanted the British Expeditionary Force (BEF) to land at Dunkirk, Calais, and Boulogne. The British would probably base their army on Lille. The French I Corps was deployed at Maubeuge to link up with the BEF. The British would probably advance from Lille on Namur–Liège.

The primary concern of French intelligence would be to determine if the Germans would enter Belgium and Luxembourg and in what strength. Attacks by agents against German bridges and rail installations were also considered possible. The French would employ masses of cavalry in Belgium and send them deep into the country. It was also possible that the French would use airships to attack the Rhine bridges as well as German Zeppelins and Zeppelin bases.

There were only two possible French courses of action. In the first, the Germans attacked both in Belgium and in Lorraine. The French, according to Bonnal, Foch, and Sorb, would then maneuver to concentrate superior forces against one half of the German army while conducting an economy of force operation against the other. It would be unlikely that the French would make their main effort between Metz and Strasbourg. The French would probably choose to meet the German right wing. They could either move forward to the Meuse between Givet and Namur, while the British and Belgians advanced between Namur and Liège, or they could hold a line in northern France. According to an article in the *Journal des Sciences Militaires* of April 1912 the mission of the French left-wing army was to defend in place and not yield a step in order to give the maneuver army time to conduct the counterattack. The 3rd Department felt that the most likely French counterattack would be from Verdun to the north-east. Colonel Biottot suggested an attack from Verdun toward Luxembourg to unhinge the German right wing and said that the French had played a war game concerning such an operation in March 1912. In this case the French left would either join in the attack or defend on the Meuse, Argonne, and Aisne.

In the second course of action the Germans attacked with the mass of their army through Holland–Belgium–Luxembourg. Only weak German forces deployed in Lorraine. These would defend or conduct diversionary attacks. In 1912 the 3rd Department did not think that the French would respond with a major attack in Lorraine. By 1914 a major attack in Lorraine seemed more likely. The 3rd Department said that in 1913 many articles in the French military journals had been advocating a French counteroffensive in Lorraine: Captain Felix in the 15 May 1913 issue of the *Journal des Sciences Militaires*, General X (presumably still Ferron, now a general) in the 8 September issue of *France Militaire*, General Lacroix, and so on. The German right wing would be delayed by the fortifications of Maubeuge and the northern army while the French mass of maneuver attacked the weak German forces in Lorraine with overwhelming numerical superiority.

If the Germans attempted a very wide envelopment the French would defend on the lines Maubeuge–Lille or Sambre–Oise. The German forces in Lorraine would be fixed in place by the French army attacking from Epinal. The French could also withdraw deep into the Champagne, to the line Reims–Laon–La Fère. The army at Toul could counterattack to the north from the line Verdun–La Fère against the German right wing's lines of communication. Mordaq had discussed this possibility in his book *Politique et Stratégie*.

This second course of action employed the same concept as the Schlieffen plan—a strong right-wing attack with only weak forces left in Lorraine—with one important exception: the Schlieffen plan employed 96 divisions, whereas in the 1911–1913 time frame the Germans really had less than 70 divisions available in the west. Lacking at least 26 notional divisions a Schlieffen plan style attack was no brilliant, original concept but a garden-variety outflanking maneuver. The possibility of a strong right-wing attack had been recognized by French military writers and its strengths and weaknesses analyzed. The principal disadvantages were the long approach march and the multiple lines of defense the French could occupy, particularly on the Meuse and between Paris and Verdun. German weakness in Lorraine was seen to give the French an opportunity for a decisive victory. Far from being an infallible prescription for victory, like any other course of action the strong right wing attack had advantages and disadvantages and these were well understood by both sides long before the war.

The direction of the withdrawal of the French left wing had been widely discussed in the French press. The 3rd Department said that it was certain that the French would not fall back on Paris. If necessary, the mass of the French army would pull back to the middle Loire. The *Monde Illustré* had said in February 1906 that the main body of the French army could withdraw if necessary to Orleans on the Loire, with the right flank on Lyon and the left on Paris. The *Petit Journal* had presented a similar opinion in May 1906. The 3rd Department agreed. It also said that the Morvan—the plateau of Langres—was still important in case of a French withdrawal.

In case of a serious defeat, the 3rd Department was of the opinion that the French did not have the manpower to raise new armies on the scale of 1870/1. On the other hand, the initial German victories would not be on the scale of Metz and Sedan in 1870. Even if the Germans won significant victories at the beginning of the next war, strong elements of the 2 million-man French field army would be able to withdraw to the middle Loire, and the subsequent German operations would not be easy. Significant forces would have to be detailed to watch the French border fortifications. The German advance on the middle Loire would be flanked by Paris and Lyon. Fortress Paris was enormous and would be difficult to deal with. It is clear from these last statements that the German army from 1912 to 1914 did not plan to attack to the north and west of Paris, as provided in the 'Schlieffen plan', but rather to the east and south of Paris on the middle Loire. Nor did the General Staff think that they could end the war in the west in a month with one immense Cannae-battle. Even if the French lost the initial battles, strong French forces were sure to find refuge along the Loire or at Langres.

An initial French offensive was considered extremely difficult— much more so than the German offensive—and therefore was very unlikely, unless the Germans committed significant forces in the east. The 3rd Department was implicitly saying that an *Ostaufmarsch* would assist and encourage a French offensive. If the French did attack, the most likely French course of action would be to attack on both sides of Metz. The attack by the French right between Metz and Strasbourg was extremely difficult and the left-wing French armies would be separated from those on the right by Metz. The further advance by the French left would be in eccentric directions toward the Moselle and the Rhine and would be blocked by these rivers. A French advance across the upper Rhine into south Germany would be cut off.

In December 1912 the 3rd Department issued an intelligence esti-mate titled *Vermutete Erste Maßnahmen der Franzosen 1913/14*. (Anticipated Initial French Actions 1913/14).[22] The 3rd Department thought it likely that the French would take immediate action on the flanks at the start of the war. On the left, I Corps, and perhaps also II Corps, would prob-ably assemble at Maubeuge and then enter Belgium to secure the line of the Meuse from Namur to Givet. At the same time a large cavalry corps of up to four divisions was expected to move into the Belgian Ardennes and Luxembourg. On the French right flank an early attack by the French VII Corps and 8th Cavalry Division against Mühlhausen was anticipated. The French were also likely to send light infantry detachments to seize the Vosges passes. It is clear from these documents that the General Staff expected the French to begin hostilities immedi-ately at the start of the war. There was no reason for Moltke to believe that the attack on Liège might have any particular significance.

These analyses show conclusively that both the French and the Germans had weighed all the possible permutations of their own and their opponents' courses of action. There were no brilliant secret war plans. The trick, as Moltke had said in 1906, was in discerning which plan the enemy had actually adopted. In any case, war is not about plan-ning but fighting. War plans notwithstanding, the army that fought best was likely to win the initial battles.

Historians would later accuse the General Staff of criminal negli-gence for having violated Belgian neutrality. They contend that the propaganda advantage the Entente gained by the German attack into Belgium was immense and far more important than any military advan-tage the Germans obtained. The German General Staff was too mili-taristic and out of touch to recognize this. In fact, in the period before the war the French military press openly discussed that, purely as a matter of military necessity, the decisive battle would probably be fought in the Ardennes. Probably in order to keep their own options open, the French military writers did not assign any particular military, diplomatic, or moral importance to the violation of Belgian neutrality by either side.

Most important, before the war neither the French military writers nor the German 3rd Department made British intervention on the continent contingent on German violation of Belgian neutrality. The British had concrete political and strategic goals to pursue in a European war, the foremost among them being the elimination of the

[22] Greiner, 'Nachrichten', 129–33.

German fleet. In large part on the strength of the agent report in January 1907 of a joint Franco-British war plan, the General Staff could expect with a high degree of certainty that the British would intervene on the side of the Entente. In the 1908 *Generalstabsreise West* Moltke said that the British and Belgians would ally themselves with France and that the most likely French course of action was to attack with their main effort in the Ardennes. This appreciation was surely given concrete confirmation by Haldane's statement to Lichnowsky on 3 December 1912 that Britain would not stand idly by and watch Germany crush France.

In addition, by late 1912 the General Staff intelligence estimates also make it clear that there was little prospect that Germany could quickly defeat the Entente. The war would involve several campaigns and would not be concluded by driving the French army into Switzerland in forty days.

In February 1914 the 1st (Russian) Department issued a special intelligence estimate, 'Die Kriegsbereitschaft Russlands' (Russian Military Readiness). This was a warning to the German army that the Russians were not to be taken lightly. The estimate listed seven pages of improvements in the Russian army since the Russo-Japanese war, including an increase in the size of the army, stronger cadres, better equipment and training, expansion and improvement of reserve forces, and faster mobilization and deployment. In summary, the estimate said that Russian readiness had made 'immense progress' and had reached hitherto unattained levels. This was due in particular to the extraordinary acceleration in mobilization speed provided by the introduction of a 'period preparatory to war' (*Kriegsvorbereitungsperiode*).[23] This was in fact a secret mobilization. These alert measures included the disguised call-up of reservists, horse purchases, and the uploading of ammunition, rations, and animal fodder.[24] German intelligence was especially sensitive to the Russian use of secret mobilization because it had detected unmistakable signs that the Russians had conducted one such secret mobilization during the Balkan crisis in the winter of 1912/13. At that time the Russians had retained conscripts in the army who ought to have been discharged while simultaneously calling up the next conscript class, which increased the peacetime strength of the Russian army by 400,000 men. The Russians had also conducted an unusual number of practice mobilizations and reserve exercises, prepared the

[23] Hauptstaatsarchiv Stuttgart M33/1 (XIII Corps), Bündel 1. Kriegsarchiv Munich, AOK 6 Bund 925. In the copy issued to the Bavarian 6th Army the sections referring to the Russian *Kriegsvorbereitungsperiode* are highlighted in red.

[24] G. Frantz, *Rußlands Eintritt in den Weltkrieg* (Berlin, 1924), 193–200. Frantz provides German translations of captured Russian mobilisation regulations.

rail system for troop movements and massed troops on the Austrian border.[25] Both in 1912/13 and in 1914 the German General Staff would exercise great restraint in the face of the secret Russian mobilization. Nevertheless, the Russian army was obviously trying to steal a march on the Germans—an enormously destabilizing factor in times of international tension.

The Russians would implement the *Kriegsvorbereitungsperiode* at 0326 hours on 26 July 1914. German intelligence got wind of this almost immediately. The General Staff intelligence summary issued on 28 July 1914 said that the Russians were apparently conducting at least a partial mobilization and that the *Kriegsvorbereitungsperiode* had 'probably' been declared in all of Russia.[26] It said it was certain that Russia was taking military measures in areas bordering Germany which could only be considered as preparations for war. The 29 July 1914 German intelligence summary reported troop concentrations near the border of all arms in up to multi-regimental strength, the recall of reservists, and the preparation of rail rolling stock.[27] The Russians had obviously begun a secret mobilization and in addition were preparing to begin deployment. The fact that the German army thought that the Russian army had been mobilizing since 27 July, if not earlier, must be considered in any evaluation of German actions during the July crisis.

The Reichsarchiv said that at the outbreak of war the Russians had 114 divisions in European Russia, with 18 more available later from the east. The Serbs had 11 divisions, for a total of 125 Entente divisions immediately available in the east. In the west the Reichsarchiv said that the French had a field force of 62 divisions (22 active corps and 18 reserve divisions). The Belgians and English had six divisions each. This makes an Entente field force of 74 divisions in the west. The Entente therefore could employ a grand total of around 200 divisions.

The Reichsarchiv said that the Germans had 87 division equivalents (including the 6 ersatz divisions), the Austrians 49, altogether 136 divisions. On the decisive western front, against 74 Entente divisions the Germans deployed 68 divisions in the field (23 active corps and 11 reserve corps).

In the east, nine German divisions (three corps, three reserve divisions) were opposed by 18 Russian divisions (9 active corps). This potentially left about 100 Russian and Serbian divisions against 49 Austrian. In

[25] 'Nachrichten über die militärische Lage in Rußland: Politische Spannung 1912/1913', Kriegsarchiv Munich, Generalstab 925.

[26] *Nachrichten* #2, Generallandesarchiv Karlsruhe GLA 456/553 (XV Corps). Also Haeften, Generalmajor, 'Der deutsche Generalstabschef in der Zeit der Spannung Juli 114', *DOB*, 28(24)(24. Juli 1924) 185–8.

[27] *Nachrichten* #3 Generallandesarchiv Karlsruhe GLA 456/553 (XV Corps).

the east both the Germans and Austrians were outnumbered 2 : 1.[28] Over time, the Austro-German situation would probably become worse as the French and British drew forces from their empires and the Russians mobilized their steamroller. If war were purely a mathematical exercise, the Entente should have won in a matter of weeks.

THE FRENCH AND RUSSIAN WAR PLANS

Since the conclusion of the Franco-Russian military alliance in 1894 the two General Staffs had held frequent, if not always annual, conversations. In 1902 these ceased altogether and resumed only in 1910. This was not accidental: 1910 was the first year that the Russian General Staff's operations officer, Danilov, said that he could observe real improvement in the Russian army after the debacle of 1904/5.[29] At the 1910 conference the French promised that, in case of war, they would launch an immediate offensive against Germany, and asked the Russians to do the same between the 15th and 30th day of mobilization.[30]

The Franco-Russian military conference of 1911 was of decisive importance on the road to war. While there was no German 'war council' on 8 December 1912, as Fritz Fischer maintained, the Allies were coordinating a detailed offensive war plan in 1911. As Joffre reports, the French delegate, General Dubail, obtained the Russian commitment to attack Germany on the 16th day of mobilization, when the Russian initial deployment was completed, without waiting until the reserve divisions or units from the east arrived. It was agreed that only a determined joint offensive against Germany would insure success.[31] Such an agreement had always been the French objective. It was a commitment that the Russians had always avoided making in anything other than the vaguest terms, because of their slow mobilization and deployment, their preference for fighting the Austrians, and their lack of interest in fighting the Germans. In one of their last meetings before the Russo-Japanese War, in 1901, the Russian Chief of Staff, Kuropatkin, promised the French that he would mobilize and deploy by the 40th day. He did not allow himself to be pinned down to a promise to attack the Germans at a specific time.[32] Presumably he was giving himself plenty

---

[28] Reichsarchiv, *Der Weltkrieg*, i. 39, 67, 69.

[29] W. C. Fuller, Jr., 'The Russian Empire', in E. R. May (ed.), *Knowing One's Enemies: Intelligence Assessment Before the Two World Wars*, (Princeton, 1984), 111.

[30] B. W. Menning, *Bayonets before Bullets: The Imperial Russian Army, 1861–1914* (Bloomington, IL, and Indianapolis, IN, 1992), 242.

[31] J. J.-C. Joffre, *Mémoires 1910–1917* (2 vols., Paris, 1932), i. 129.

[32] D. Collins, 'The Franco-Russian Alliance and the Russian Railways', *HJ* 16 (1973), 782.

of time to bring up his reserve divisions and forces from the east. Kuropatkin's timetable had an additional advantage for the Russians: by the 40th day of mobilization the decisive battle would probably have been fought in the west.

Joffre visited the Russians in 1913 to insure that the joint attack plan was properly coordinated. Joffre explained to the Russians on several occasions that the most probable German course of action was to commit their main body against the French, and that it was therefore urgently necessary that the Russians attack as soon as possible, even if it meant doing so with only a portion of their forces. Joffre said that the Grand Duke Nicholas, the Russian commander-in-chief designate, expressed to him several times that he understood the need for an early Russian offensive. Tsar Nicholas said that he would attack on the 15th day with 11 corps in the Niemen army and 9 corps in the Narew army. Joffre recommended that the Narew army be directed down the Vistula on Thorn.[33] According to L. C. F. Turner, the Franco-Russian Military Convention of September 1913 'confirmed the opinion expressed at the conferences of 1910, 1911, and 1912 that Germany will direct the greatest part of her forces against France and leave only a minimum of troops against Russia.' The Convention went on to say that the allied plan must be to attack Germany simultaneously from both sides with the maximum forces.[34] Time was particularly crucial for the Russians. The Russians, alone of all the Powers, were attacking at less than full strength. The Russians therefore had every incentive to begin their mobilization before the other Powers. The need to mobilize early and strike quickly was an integral part of the Franco-Russian offensive war plan and was not, as Ritter and others would have it, the unique characteristic of the German war plan.

The 1911 agreement was the foundation of all further French and Russian war planning, which thereafter would undergo a fundamental change in both countries. On the basis of this agreement the French would replace the defensive–offensive doctrine of Bonnal with Plan XVII, which was the expression of the *offensive à outrance*. The Russians would change their normal defensive war plan against Germany with Schedule 19, which provided for simultaneous offensives against Germany and Austria-Hungary.

In 1911, therefore, the military stage was set for the outbreak of the war. The Russian general mobilization on 30 July 1914 set the clock ticking on the Franco-Russian offensive, which would start on the 15th day

---

[33] Joffre, *Mémoires*, 131–3; Fuller, 'Russian Empire', 104.
[34] L. C. F. Fuller, 'The Russian Mobilisation in 1914' in P. Kennedy (ed.), *The War Plans of the Great Powers*, (London, 1979), 257.

of mobilization—14 August at the very latest. Schlieffen had predicted that this would be the case at least since 1902: indeed, he had built his entire counterattack doctrine around it.

PLAN XVII

It has generally been assumed that the Plan XVII deployment is fairly well known. The 1st Army (five corps) was deployed near Epinal, 2nd (five corps) at Mirecourt–Toul, 3rd (three corps) behind Verdun, 4th (three corps) initially in reserve between St Menehould and Bar-le-Duc, 5th (five corps) on the left at St. Menehould–Stenay–Hirson.[35] The Cavalry Corps (three divisions) was on the far left at Mézières and Sedan. Joffre claimed that he did not have a preconceived scheme of maneuver.[36] Nevertheless, the concept of the operation was purely offensive: 'in all cases, the intent of the commanding general is, once the armies are deployed, to attack the German army.'[37]

Plan XVII is normally described as having a variant which would be implemented if the Germans invaded Belgium. In this variant, the 4th Army would move from its reserve position to the north of the 3rd Army, and the 5th Army would move north toward the Belgian border. All five French armies would be on the forward line. In fact, Joffre implemented the 'variant' on 2 August 1914,[38] which was the 1st day of mobilization for both the French and German armies. The German army entered Luxembourg on the 2nd, but had not yet even sent their ultimatum to Belgium, much less attacked Liège. The Germans had just begun to mobilize, and aside from security forces no troops would move toward the border until around 6 August. The French could therefore have had no indicators whatsoever of the German deployment. Nor would the French begin their deployment for several days. Therefore, the 'Plan XVII' deployment as generally depicted is irrelevant. The real French deployment provided for five armies on line, with three of those armies, the French mass of maneuver, to the north of Verdun.

Given a deployment that placed three of the five French armies on the Belgian border, a war plan which called for an *immediate* French attack and an alliance that specified an offensive against Germany by the 15th day of mobilization, the French were going to enter Belgium, irrespective of whether the Germans did or not. It will surely be argued

---

[35] Ministère de la Guerre, État-Major de l´Armée, Service Historique, *Les Armées Françaises dans la Grande Guerre, Tome Premier, Premier Volume,* 19 ff.; *Annexe,* 21 ff.; *Cartes,* Carte No. 7, 8.

[36] Joffre, *Mémoires,* 129.   [37] *Les Armées Françaises* 1.1.1. 54.

[38] Joffre, *Mémoires,* 234.

that the French political leadership would never have allowed Joffre to invade Belgium. In fact, the French government approved of the war plan and was fully aware of its significance.

The question of Plan XVII seems to have been painful for Greiner. He tiptoes around it, without ever getting to the important point: that German intelligence had practically no idea of the scope of the changes in the Russo-French war plans since 1911.[39]

In comparison with Plan XVII, the German 1912 estimate of the French deployment was wrong on four counts. It extended the French left flank only to Maubeuge, where it was now weaker than the actual French left and much too far to the west and south. In addition, the German estimate still gave the French a huge mass of maneuver in depth behind Toul–Verdun and the French were initially expected to stand on the defensive. As Greiner noted, the 3rd Department had failed to understand that the French intended to deploy their entire army on line along the border and then launch an immediate offensive. Last, the German estimate of the French order of battle at all levels was erroneous.

Nevertheless, there is at least one strong indication that the French adoption of Grandmaison's *offensive à outrance* had not gone unnoticed by the General Staff.[40] A long article in the last issue before the war of the General Staff's professional publication, *Vierteljahresheft für Truppenführung und Heereskunde* (Quarterly Journal for Military Studies and Leadership) accurately and perceptively traced the rise of the *offensive à outrance* in some detail. It would have been difficult to have ignored such a development, because Grandmaison had published a book explaining his doctrine. The new French doctrinal manuals were also made public: the 28 October 1913 *Instruction sur la conduite des grands unités* (the French doctrinal operations manual at army group, army, and corps levels) as well as the 2 December 1913 *Service en campagne* (division level and smaller units) and the 20 April 1914 manual for the individual soldier. All these documents emphasized the offensive, including Grandmaison's famous statement that 'the French army, returning to its traditions, recognizes no other law in the conduct of operations but that of the offensive.' The objective was to destroy the enemy in a battle of annihilation. The new regulations stated Joffre's concept of the operation in his wartime General Instruction Number 1 almost verbatim: 'The offensive will begin as soon as the army has

[39] Greiner, *Nachrichten*, 136–57.
[40] Captain Baare, 'Neue taktische Anschauungen im französischen Heere', *VTfHK*, 9(3) (1914), 396–418. Also, Captain Baare, 'Taktische Fragen aus den französischen Armeemänover 1913', *VTfHK 9(1)* (1914), 390–5.

assembled.' German intelligence estimates were skeptical that a complete change in French doctrine could have permeated the entire French army in so short a period of time, but the French had clearly stated their intent.

The Reichsarchiv published an enormous history of the war, including an entire volume on preparations for the rail deployment alone, but did not reveal anything more than fragments of the 1914 *Aufmarschanweisungen* to the army commanders. It is almost certain that Moltke wrote a *Lagebeurteilung*—his analysis of the situation and concept of the operation. This was not published either. Nevertheless, in addition to the few pieces of the *Aufmarschanweisungen* published in the official history, the *Aufmarschanweisungen* for three armies survived the destruction of the Reichsarchiv. The American army captured the German 5th Army's records at the end of the Great War. Some time after the Second World War the Americans returned a typewritten English translation of the 5th Army's *Aufmarschanweisung* to the Militärarchiv in Freiburg.[41] The US Army War College also retained a copy. Even more important was the survival of the Bavarian 6th Army's *Aufmarschanweisung* at the Kriegsarchiv in Munich.[42] Since the 6th Army had operational control over the 7th Army in Alsace, the 7th Army *Aufmarschanweisung* also survived.[43] Just as important, the Bavarian Chief of Staff, Krafft von Dellmensingen, did write a *Lagebeurteilung* for the left wing of the German army, which is to be found in his *Nachlaß*.[44] These orders, together with Moltke's subsequent operations orders during the campaign, allow us to reconstruct Moltke's concept of the operation in France in 1914. This concept had nothing whatsoever to do with the 'Schlieffen plan'.

The concept of the operation was contained in the fourth section of the *Aufmarschanweisung*, 'Besondere Weisungen' (special instructions). These began with a general appreciation of the political situation. Holland was not expected to declare war on Germany. Belgium's position was uncertain. The intervention of the British army was considered 'not unlikely'. The British could move through Holland, occupy

---

[41] 'Aufmarschanweisung 5. Armee', BA-MA PH 3/284.

[42] 'Aufmarschanweisung für Oberkommando 6. Armee', Kriegsarchiv Munich, AOK 6, Bund 369 Nr. 45. This was handwritten in the German Standard style. There is also a typed transcript in the Kriegsarchiv Munich, *Nachlaß* 145 Krafft von Dellmensingen.

[43] 'Aufmarschanweisungen für Oberkommando der 7. Armee'; Kriegsarchiv Munich, *Nachlaß* 145 Krafft von Dellmensingen.

[44] *Nachlaß* 145 Krafft von Dellmensingen, Kriegsarchiv Munich.

Antwerp, or land at Calais–Dunkirk and move to link up with the French left wing.

The concept of the German operation was for the main body to advance through Belgium and Luxembourg into France. The 5th Army would act as pivot for the German movement by maintaining contact with Metz–Diedenhofen. The speed of the movement of the main body would be determined by the movement of the right flank. This was the entire concept as stated in the *Aufmarschanweisungen*. In addition, each army received its own mission statement.

As we have seen, the Reichsarchiv was selective in its choice of the documents it made public: it released only fragments of documents and followed the 'Schlieffen plan' party line in its interpretation of the facts, but it apparently never falsified documents outright. The Reichsarchiv was therefore forced to admit that the mission of the 1st Army on the right flank was to march on Brussels 'to protect the right flank of the army' ('die rechte Flanke des Heeres zu decken').[45] Later, the Reichsarchiv, as well as Kuhl (the Chief of Staff of the 1st Army) and Groener, would contend that the concept of the 'Schlieffen plan' was for the 1st Army to deliver the decisive blow, continually turning the left flank of the French army. Such an interpretation finds no support either in the *Aufmarschanweisungen* or in Moltke's subsequent operations orders. The 1st Army's mission throughout the campaign, from the initial *Aufmarschanweisung* to the end of the battle of the Marne, was always principally to act as flank guard.

Moltke clearly intended that the 2nd Army conduct the main attack. The army was led by Germany's senior active general officer, Wilhelm von Bülow. Moltke would give Bülow operational control over the 1st Army on his right and the 3rd Army on his left. The 3rd and 4th Armies were instructed to march on the Meuse.

Both the 6th Army and the 5th Army were told that the 5th Army had been deployed on a narrow front and in depth for a specific purpose: this formation would allow the 5th Army to swing south-east through Metz if the French attacked early and in strength into Lorraine. This would have changed the entire character of the campaign. The 4th Army would have had to cover the 5th Army's rear and the operation would have looked exactly like one of the *Generalstabsreisen West*. Metz was to be expanded into a fortified zone: seven Landwehr brigades reinforced with artillery would dig in along the Nied river (*Niedstellung*). Moltke clearly felt that the French could launch their main attack into Lorraine.

The commander of the 6th Army, Crown Prince Rupprecht of

[45] Reichsarchiv, *Der Weltkrieg, Band* I, 73.

Bavaria, was given operational control of all the forces in Alsace-Lorraine, which in addition to his own army meant principally the 7th Army. His mission was to guard the left flank of the main body as well as to prevent the French from transferring forces against the German right wing. Initially, he was to plan to accomplish this by advancing on a very wide front against the Moselle below Fort Frouard (that is, to the north of Nancy–Toul and in the direction of the *Sperrforts* between Toul and Verdun) as well as on the Meurthe (that is, on Nancy and the 'Trouée de Charmes'), while at the same time taking Fort Manonviller. His mission would also be accomplished if the French attacked into Lorraine with superior forces. If the German forces in Lorraine were forced to withdraw, they were to retreat to the east of Metz in order to insure that the left flank of the main body was still protected. A French attack into the upper Alsace would be favorable for the German operation so long as the French did not advance north of the line Feste Kaiser Wilhelm II-Breusch–Strasbourg (the *Breuschstellung*). If the 6th and 7th Armies were not opposed by superior enemy forces, elements of the 6th Army might be instructed to attack over Metz or to the south of Metz to the left bank of the Moselle (i.e., between Toul and Verdun).

Initially, the mission of the 7th Army was to drive back weak enemy forces attacking into the upper Alsace. If the French attacked with superior forces into the upper Alsace, the 7th Army was to withdraw to Strasbourg and the right bank of the Rhine. The principal mission of the 7th Army was to send the strongest possible forces to cooperate with the 6th Army.

The Bavarian chief of staff, Krafft von Dellmensingen, wrote his analysis of the mission in Alsace-Lorraine (*Lagebeurteilung*) between 2 and 5 August 1914.[46] Krafft began by saying that the four active army corps would be combat-ready by the evening of the 11th day of mobilization, the Bavarian I Reserve corps by the 13th day. The 6th Army could therefore advance no earlier than the 12th day.

If the French launched their main attack into Lorraine it was the mission of the German forces in Alsace-Lorraine to give the right wing time to turn to the south-east to support the left wing.

Krafft said that the 6th Army needed to fix the French by attacking, yet preserve the flexibility to withdraw if the French appeared to attack in strength. At the same time, the Army must be ready to cross the Moselle further north at and to the south of Metz. He said that this was a complicated mission, but one that had to be solved.

[46] 'Eine Beurteilung der Lage verfaßt in München 2–5. 8. 1914', *Nachlaß* 145 Krafft von Dellmensingen, Kriegsarchiv Munich. This is a handwritten paper (in Standard script) 18 pages long.

An offensive against the Moselle and Meurthe could not be conducted as an all-out attack that sought to destroy the enemy. Nevertheless, the enemy had to gain the impression that a full-scale attack was being conducted against the line Toul–Epinal. Making the attacking force appear stronger than it actually was would be difficult: the French were not to be easily fooled. In order to deceive the enemy, the attack would be made on a 70-kilometer front from Nancy to the north-east of Epinal. This was a much wider sector than was doctrinally appropriate for five corps and might convince the French that the Germans were committing a stronger force. The Germans would there-fore advance in multiple parallel columns, instead of deploying in depth. Such a broad formation would also facilitate a change to a defensive posture. Krafft said that the French had been digging in on the 'Position de Nancy' for weeks. To make a German attack on the Moselle–Meurthe appear plausible as the German main effort, the 'Position de Nancy' nevertheless had to be engaged, but this would best be done by using mobile heavy artillery from Metz's artillery reserve.

If the French attacked at once in strength the main body of the 6th Army would withdraw without offering serious resistance. The enemy would be delayed by rearguards and cavalry. At any time during the withdrawal the Army must be ready to turn and attack, in case the enemy stopped or even withdrew. The 6th and 7th Armies would then take up a position from the *Niedstellung*, along the Saar to the south-east of Metz and presumably on the *Breuschstellung*. The Saar position was 80 kilometers long, straight-line distance, and holding it with the five corps of the 6th Army would not be easy: the 6th Army would have to be augmented by XV Corps from the 7th Army. Krafft said that the posi-tion had been reconnoitered during a *Große Generalstabsreise*. The 6th and 7th Armies would hold this position until they were able, in conjunction with forces from the right wing, to counterattack. The further the French attacked into Lorraine, the more vulnerable their flanks became to counterattacks from Metz and Strasbourg (Schlieffen's favorite maneuver). If the French pressed their attack to a line Metz–Nied–Saar–*Breuschstellung*–Strasbourg the German counter-attack would hit them from three sides and the Germans had good prospects of destroying the French forces.

Krafft then discussed the measures necessary to conduct the third mission, the attack to the west of Metz. Most of the 6th Army would have to redeploy to the east of Metz. Although Krafft did not say so, from here the 6th Army might also attack the flank of a French offen-sive out of Verdun. However, it would seem that the objective of such a maneuver would most likely have been to break through the French fortress line between Toul and Verdun.

This assumption is supported by a brand-new plan written by the Great General Staff for exactly this operation, and updated on 31 July 1914 with an intelligence analysis of the French forts.[47] The plan provided for an army of seven corps to break the fort line supported by an attack on the 'Position de Nancy' in the south while another army enveloped Verdun to the north. Four corps would be employed as the *Schwerpunkt*, supported by 13 battalions of heavy artillery, 14 heavy mortars, and one battery of each of the super-heavy 305mm and 420mm guns later used at Liège. The plan noted that except for Louville the *Sperrforts* had been built by Séré de Rivières and were unmodernized and should fall easily. The attack should take four to six days: two days' ammunition was allocated for the field works and two days' ammunition for the *Sperrforts*.

On 10 September 1914 Moltke wrote a letter to Rupprecht stating that an attack on the 'Position de Nancy' should only be made in conjunction with the breakthrough attack which he had planned for the 6th Army to conduct between Verdun and Toul. It now appeared that this operation it was no longer feasible.[48] There was no mention anywhere in the *Aufmarschanweisungen* of the 6th Army conducting a rail movement to Belgium to join the right wing, as some commentators—including Krafft—suggested after the war.

The nature of the French attack in the upper Alsace was seen as an indicator of French intentions. If the French attacked in the upper Alsace in strength, then it was very likely that the main French effort would be made in Alsace-Lorraine. If the French did not attack in the upper Alsace, or if the attack there was weak, then the French were probably not going to make their main effort in Alsace-Lorraine.

If the French did not attack in strength in the upper Alsace, it was important that the 7th Army not allow itself to be distracted in the south but to close up on the left wing of the 6th Army. If the French did make their main effort in Alsace-Lorraine, then the 7th Army would defend the left flank of the German position on the *Breuschstellung*. In both cases, the mass of the 7th Army should move from their assembly areas by rail march, not by foot-march. The 7th Army had to be prepared in all cases to attack south of the Donon toward St Die to take the French in Lorraine in the right flank.

From these considerations, Krafft determined his initial deployment and his special orders to the subordinate units. Each army chief of staff probably wrote a similar document. Krafft's *Lagebeurteilung* shows what

[47] 'Angriffsentwurf gegen die Sperrforts der mittleren Maas', BA-MA W10/50589.
[48] 'Generaloberst von Moltke 10.9.14 Brief an S.K.H. Kronprinz Rupprecht von Bayern', BA-MA W10/51063.

elements made up his decision-making process. These were very similar to the problems that the General Staff had addressed in intelligence estimates and strategic exercises over the preceding twenty-five years. Krafft's *Lagebeurteilung* had not the slightest thing to do with the 'Schlieffen plan'. Krafft still considered it possible that the French would make their main effort in Alsace-Lorraine. If they did, then the main battle would be fought in Lorraine. He thought it almost certain that the French would commit strong forces in his sector and that it was likely that the French would outnumber his army group. He clearly did not feel that by deploying strong forces in Lorraine the French were dooming themselves to certain destruction. Krafft did not commit himself to a course of action in advance, but he seemed to believe that the 6th Army would probably conduct a diversionary attack on the French fortress line followed by a defensive battle in Lorraine. Although the German right wing was designated the main German force, there was no mention of the right wing passing around to the west of Paris. Had it intended to do so, Krafft would have had to be prepared to fight almost alone for two months—a factor that surely would have entered into his calculations. On the other hand, he specifically mentioned in two places that if the French launched their main attack early in Lorraine then the right wing would march to the southeast and that the two German wings would make a coordinated and hopefully decisive counterattack. Indeed, one of the first possible scenarios considered by the *Aufmarschanweisungen* to the 5th and 6th Armies was that the French would attack very early into Lorraine. The 5th Army would then attack through Metz against the French flank. The 4th Army would then have to cover the rear of the 5th Army. This was a scenario straight out of the *Generalstabsreisen West* and the very antithesis of the Schlieffen plan.

LIÈGE

An aspect of the German war plan which has received universal condemnation was the German attack on Liège. Moltke intended to conduct a *coup de main* before the fortress had been 'armed'. Therefore, the German forces entered Belgium on 4 August (3rd day of mobilization) and conducted an attack on the night of 5–6 August.

After the war this was decried as an especially rank case of militarism. The attack on Liège is one of the key elements in the argument that for the German army alone mobilization meant war. It was allegedly planned without the knowledge of the German chancellor. Most important, it supposedly cut off all further chances of negotiations and made full-scale warfare inevitable. In 1931 Churchill wrote:

Nearly three weeks before the main shock of the armies could begin [on 25 August?] . . . six German brigades must storm Liège. It was this factor which destroyed all chance that the armies might mobilize and remain guarding their frontiers while under their shield conferences sought a path to peace. The German plan was of such a character that the most irrevocable steps of actual war, including the violation of neutral territory, must be taken at the first moment of mobilization. Mobilization therefore spelt war.[49]

There are no contemporary sources which support this theory: this is another case of *ex post facto* reasoning. By 1915 the major figures in the German government and military were already preparing to defend their actions in the histories they all knew would be written after the war. Nevertheless, in a discussion with Freytag-Loringhoven on 2 May 1915, Bethmann contended that he had maintained in July 1914 that mobilization would not mean war. Bethmann said he was opposed to the General Staff's insistence that German troops immediately enter *Luxembourg*. Belgium wasn't even mentioned.[50] Freytag argued that the German army could not have stood inactive in the west while the Russians entered Berlin, to which comment, he said, Bethmann did not reply. Karl Helfferich, at that time State Secretary in the Chancellor's office, nodded his head in approval of Freytag's comments.

Nor are there contemporary indications from the Entente that the attack on Liège interrupted any budding diplomatic initiatives. The Russians declared general mobilization at 1800 hours 30 July, 1st day of mobilization 31 July. This started the 15-day clock moving on the Russo-French offensive against Germany. The French therefore declared general mobilization at 1630 hours 1 August, 1st mobilization day 2 August. The Germans did not mobilize until half an hour later. The French therefore did not respond to German 'aggression' but rather solely to meet their treaty obligations to the Russians to attack by the 15th day of Russian mobilization.

Gerhard Ritter contended that the Russian army was capable of mobilizing and deploying while at the same time continuing to negoti-ate: the Schlieffen plan however required that Germany mobilize and attack France immediately. The German war plan has been universally condemned for being too 'rigid'. According to this charge Schlieffen had developed the perfect war plan which did not admit of change or deviation. For Germany alone, mobilization meant war. Essentially, this argument rests not on proofs but on caricature: the Germans were mili-tarists, militarists are rigid, therefore the German war plan must have been rigid: QED.

49 W. Churchill, *The World Crisis: The Eastern Front* (London, 1931), 93.
50 H. von Freytag-Loringhoven, *Menschen und Dinge* (Berlin, 1923), 278.

This theory has three fundamental problems. First, this book has shown that no German Chief of Staff from the elder Moltke on would have allowed the Russians to deploy their enormous steamroller without taking decisive counter-measures: in 1914 the fully deployed Russian army was as large as the entire Austrian and German armies combined. Second, the Schlieffen plan was not the German war plan. The Russo-French alliance had the offensive war plan, not the Germans. Schlieffen's real intent, which was adopted by Moltke, was to counter-attack against the Russo-French invasion of Germany. Third, all the European General Staffs expected hostilities, especially raids to disrupt deployment, to begin immediately with the declaration of general mobilization.

Moltke's motivation in attacking Liège is clear. The Anglo-French General Staffs had succeeded keeping their talks and the British 'Continental Commitment' secret from the British Cabinet and Parliament. No one has ever asked what the *German* reaction would be if they learned of the plan to immediately send the BEF to the Continent. However, the Germans had the best intelligence system in Europe. By January 1907 the General Staff had a credible agent report concerning the secret Anglo-French agreement. German intelligence was also informed of the 1911 Anglo-French staff conversations. As of 1911, German intelligence estimates began to warn of the increasing Entente readiness, aggressiveness, and the growing possibility of an Entente attack. British intervention became a topic of discussion in the French military press. In 1912 Haldane told the Germans that British intervention was a practical certainty. The Germans had to assume that Belgium would then side with the Entente regardless. This led to a series of German measures, among which, in 1911 or 1912, were preparations for a *coup de main* on Liège. If Liège remained in Belgian hands, then the lines of communication of any German advance to the north side of the Meuse would be in danger. Liège might also serve as the anchor for the Entente's defense of the Meuse line or indeed as the bridgehead for an Entente counterattack into the Ardennes or even north Germany. The decision to attack Liège therefore arose out of the German appreciation of the political–military situation in 1911–12 and had nothing to do with the Schlieffen plan.

After mobilization, military actions followed their normal sequence. At 1410 hours on 2 August, the first day of mobilization and two days before the attack on Liège, Joffre received permission for complete freedom of movement from the French government.[51] By 5 August the Reichsarchiv says that reconnaissance and counter-reconnaissance

---

[51] *Armées Françaises* I.I.I. 69–70.

patrols were in contact all along the border in Alsace and Lorraine, even earlier in East Prussia.[52] There is no evidence that these actions had anything to do with the attack on Liège. When Joffre does mention the attack on Liège in his memoirs it is only to remark that on 6 August he received word that the Germans had been driven back with loss.[53] He does not say that the attack had any particular military significance, let alone political or diplomatic importance. Joffre would attack in strength into German territory on 7 August. Nothing that Joffre says would lend any support to the idea that the attack on Liège cut short an Entente plan to hold back the French attack in favor of negotiations.

In August 1914 Churchill's mind, as First Lord of the Admiralty, was focused not on possible negotiations but on destroying the German battlecruiser *Goeben* in the Mediterranean. On the early morning of 4 August the *Goeben* bombarded the cites of Bône and Philippeville in an attempt to disrupt the movement of troops from Africa to France. This was an act of war of a bit more concern to the French than the attack on Liège. At 1030 hours on 4 August, about the same time that German troops entered Belgium, the British battlecruisers *Indomitable* and *Inflexible* sighted the *Goeben* and began shadowing her, though Britain was not at war with Germany. At 1400 on 4 August the British flotilla commander learned of the British ultimatum to Germany, which expired at midnight. (There is no indication that the British ultimatum was connected with any specific German military operations against Belgium.) At about the same time, the *Goeben* made full speed. The British gave chase, but the *Goeben* was faster, and she succeeded in losing the British at 1939 hours, only shortly before her power plant broke down. The British began a full-scale search the next morning, 5 August, and had they found her, there certainly would have been a battle. The fact that no fight took place was a great disappointment to Churchill.

The main British fleet had mobilized and deployed to its war stations in the North Sea on Churchill's sole authority on the morning of 29 July. The British had promised to protect the coast of France against German attacks. It is clear from Churchill's book *The World Crisis* that, had the German High Seas Fleet at any time thereafter presented itself, the British would have accepted battle with light hearts.

In his capacity as a British propagandist in 1931, Churchill maintained that, but for the attack on Liège, the diplomats could have had three weeks to work out some kind of peaceful arrangement. In his capacity as head of the British navy in August 1914, Churchill was trying

[52] Reichsarchiv, *Der Weltkrieg, Band I*, 108, 125.
[53] Joffre, *Mémoires*, 244.

to arrange a big naval battle in the Mediterranean or, better yet, in the North Sea, as soon as possible.

THE FRENCH ATTACK IN LORRAINE

The French opened the campaign with an attack from Belfort into the upper Alsace by the reinforced VII Corps on 7 August, the 6th day of mobilization. General von Heeringen, the commander of the German 7th Army, took advantage of the fact that Crown Prince Rupprecht had not arrived to take command to move his army south to counterattack. Heeringen was motivated not by strategic considerations but by the desire to make a reputation for himself as the first German army commander to win a battle in this war. His conduct of the campaign did his reputation and career no good at all. Heeringen did not coordinate his attack and the French were merely pushed back. Heeringen's army was now tired, disorganized, and far from the expected main battle area in Lorraine. He then failed to effectively use his rail assets to move the army north, and one of his corps commanders, afraid that the French were attacking across the Vosges, foot-marched his corps instead of moving it by rail.

On 14 August, the 15th day of Russian mobilization, the French 1st and 2nd Armies began their attack into Lorraine and the German 6th Army's situation began to deteriorate. Krafft abandoned his initial plan for a fixing attack and began a slow withdrawal. The Germans suffered a serious reverse in the Vosges when the French overran a German brigade which was at the west end of the *Breuschstellung* covering the 'arming' of Feste Kaiser Wilhelm II. It was feared that the French would take the unprepared fortress. In the evening an intelligence estimate arrived at 6th Army headquarters from the *Oberste Heeresleitung* (OHL), the German high command, which said that the French were going to make their main effort in Lorraine: the 6th Army, with 10 divisions, was opposed by up to 16 French corps and 6 to 8 reserve divisions, a total of 38 to 40 French divisions. This was some 60 percent of the French field army: a scenario straight out of the *Generalstabsreisen West*. Such a massive French attack in Lorraine, Krafft later wrote, would have meant that the decisive battle would have been fought there, Schlieffen plan or no Schlieffen plan.[54] It appeared that the French advance was aimed right at the west flank of the *Breuschstellung* and Strasbourg. The 7th Army was still trying to untangle itself from its counterattack into the upper Alsace and would not arrive in Lorraine for several days. OHL

[54] K. Krafft von Dellmensingen, *Die Führung des Kronprinzen Rupprecht von Bayern auf dem linken deutschen Heeresflügell bis zur Schlacht in Lothringen in August 1914* (Berlin, 1925), 9.

alerted both the 4th and the 5th armies on 14 August to be prepared to attack through Metz.[55] Krafft began coordination with the 5th Army for just such an eventuality. The fear of a French attack in Lorraine was also the reason that Moltke sent the six ersatz divisions to reinforce the 6th and 7th Armies and not to East Prussia as he had initially intended.

The French advance into Lorraine was slow and cautious. This, combined with intelligence gathered from actual contact with the enemy, led both the 6th Army and then the OHL by 16 August to suspect that the French were not so strong in Lorraine as was initially believed. The 6th Army began to consider going over to the offensive, but had to wait until the 7th Army arrived before it could do so. On 18 August the German right wing began its advance. The 7th Army, which had finally assembled to the west of Strasbourg, began a slow slog through the Vosges in an attempt to turn the French right flank. On 20 August, the 19th day of mobilization, the 6th Army attacked.[56] The Reichsarchiv said that the Bavarians were outnumbered, with 328 battalions and 1,766 guns in all of Alsace and Lorraine against 420 French battalions and 1,648 guns.[57] In spite of that and of the fact that the attack was purely frontal, the French were thrown back everywhere in disorder. Aggressively led Bavarian units attempted to pursue the French through the night and into the next morning without being able to reestablish contact; no large French units were destroyed and the French lost few guns. On 22 August the French artillery began to show its teeth. Many Bavarian units were caught in the open and took heavy casualties. Bavarian counter-battery fire proved ineffective against French guns in defilade positions and directed by forward observers.

The second volume of the Bavarian official history, published in 1929, says that on 22 August Rupprecht and Krafft had determined that they had done their job in Lorraine and wanted a change of mission.[58] The French 1st and 2nd Armies were in no condition to interfere with the German offensive in the near future. The German left flank was secure and the right-wing attack on the Sambre and Meuse had begun. Krafft asked OHL at that time if he should execute the '3rd contingency' in the *Aufmarschanweisung*, that is, to redeploy the 6th Army to the east of Metz. The Bavarian official history would have one believe that Krafft and Rupprecht wanted to move the Bavarian army to the right wing, preferably by rail to Belgium or perhaps by foot-march through Metz.

[55] Reichsarchiv, *Der Weltkrieg, Band I*, 132, 184–5.
[56] K. Deuringer, *Die Schlacht in Lothringen, Band I und II* (Munich, 1929).
[57] Reichsarchiv, *Der Weltkrieg, Band I*, 593.   [58] Deuringer, *Lothringen*, ii. 372.

This was an attempt to put the Bavarians on the right side of the 'Schlieffen plan' legend. By this time the right wing had been advancing for five days and was almost on the Franco-Belgian border. It would have taken two to three days to move the Bavarians to the railheads and another four or five to move them by rail to Aachen, where, owing to rail demolitions in Belgium, they would have had to detrain to foot-march forward. By this time it would have been the beginning of September, the right wing would have been approaching Paris, and the Bavarians would have been hundreds of kilometers from any battle-field. There is no evidence to support the contention that a rail move was ever considered before early September, when the situation was entirely different. Foot-marching the Bavarians through Metz to the right wing would have been exhausting, time-consuming, and would have caused chaos in the rear areas: it was also never seriously considered until September. Rupprecht and Krafft probably did expect a new set of orders, but most likely these would have been for a formal attack on the French fortress line between Toul and Verdun. This would require OHL to pick a point of attack and allocate heavy artillery and ammunition from Army reserves.

OHL was not ready to make such a step. The Bavarian heavy artillery was still attacking the *Sperrfort* at Manonviller. Operations against fortresses in Belgium occupied the attention of a good part of the German heavy artillery and were reducing the ammunition stocks. Attacks on the fortresses in northern France were also going to get priority.

On 24 August Moltke felt the need to transfer forces to the east. The 6th Army was close to the German railheads and could have been in East Prussia far more quickly than the units he did send, which had to foot-march back through most of Belgium. The entire point of the German defense on interior lines was to use the speed of rail movement as a force multiplier. Alternatively, preparations needed to be made to break through the French border fortifications. Moltke did neither.

On 22 August OHL had ordered the 6th Army to attack south to try to encircle the French 1st Army in the Vosges. The Bavarian official history said that OHL believed that on 23 August the French would continue to withdraw in Lorraine. Instead the French 1st and 2nd Armies stopped their retreat and on 24 August the French began to counterattack against the Bavarian right. On 25 August the Bavarians encountered murderous French artillery fire and counterattacks which stopped their advance cold.[59] The 4th Ersatz Division and some Bavarian units broke under the rain of French shells.

[59] Ibid. 411–13.

On 25 August OHL told the 6th Army that the ultimate objective for the German left wing was to break through the 'Trouée de Charmes'.[60] This was a clear demonstration that Moltke was still thinking in the same terms as Beseler's 1900 *Denkschrift*: that one of the principal missions of the campaign in the west was to break the French fortress line by attacking it in the front and rear. However, Moltke did not back up this concept by allocating to the 6th Army large quantities of heavy artillery or artillery ammunition. By 26 August French attacks had forced the 6th Army to go over to the defensive. For their part the French continued to commit considerable resources in Lorraine, especially artillery and shells. On 27 August the French stopped attacking and the front stabilized.

The OHL operations order for 28 August gave the 6th and 7th Armies the mission of breaking through the 'Trouée de Charmes', but only if the French began a general withdrawal. Nevertheless, Moltke was unhappy with the lack of Bavarian progress in Lorraine. Eventually the Bavarians convinced OHL that the German forces in Lorraine were fought out and needed infantry replacements, rest, and heavy artillery in order to continue the attack. Krafft was told that he did not need to attack, but was also instructed to fix as many French forces in Lorraine as possible. Schlieffen had warned expressly against making such an error.

In early September it became clear that the German 4th and 5th Armies were not going to break the French fortress line from the rear and that the 6th Army could not penetrate it from the front. At the same time there was growing concern that the French would move forces to northern France by rail and be joined there by British forces landing from the sea: these would then threaten the German lines of communication along the Meuse in Belgium. It was therefore decided on 5 September to move the 7th Army to Belgium, beginning on 8 September. By this time the Germans had completed repairs on a considerable part of the Belgian rail net and troops could be moved by rail into Belgium itself. On 8 September the 6th Army was ordered to move too. Both armies were heartily glad to see the last of Lorraine. These troop movements from Lorraine to Belgium had nothing to do with the Schlieffen plan.

THE CAMPAIGN IN FRANCE

On 14 August the right-wing German 1st Army crossed the Meuse to the north of Liège. On 17 August Moltke issued his operations order for the

---

[60] Reichsarchiv, *Der Weltkrieg, Band I*, 593.

right-wing attack that was to begin on 18 August. The order was short. There was no mention of the 'Schlieffen plan' or anything resembling it. The most important instruction was that the 1st Army was placed under the operational control of the commander of the 2nd Army, Bülow. Their mission was to clear Belgium. The 3rd Army was to cooperate with the armies on its flanks. By 20 August the 1st and 2nd German Armies were halfway through Belgium and Bülow had reports that the French were concentrating on the Sambre–Meuse between Charleroi and Dinant. Bülow turned the 1st and 2nd Armies south to fight them. Kuhl, adhering to the pre-war intelligence estimate that he had written himself, was convinced that the BEF was somewhere to the north at Lille. He therefore oriented its formation to the north-west and was completely off balance when he did make contact with the BEF some 70 kilometers to the south-east of Lille, at Mons.

The French were conducting their main attack on their left, in the Ardennes. By 21 August the French 5th Army was approaching the angle of the Sambre–Meuse, the 4th Army was crossing the Belgian border to the south, and the 3rd Army was on the right flank of the 4th Army. According to Joffre's plan of 18 August the 5th Army, with the British on their left flank, was to turn the German right flank while the 4th and 3rd Armies broke the German center.

In the Ardennes, the German 4th and 5th Armies met the French 3rd and 4th Armies in a pure meeting engagement on 22 August. The Reichsarchiv history contended that the French enjoyed a considerable advantage in infantry (377 French battalions versus 236 German) and a lesser advantage in artillery (1,540 French guns to 1,320 German).[61] Nevertheless, the two German armies were completely victorious. Attempts have been made to explain the French defeat by asserting that it was the Germans who actually outnumbered the French, or that the French 4th Army was hit in the left flank, both factors being the result of the Schlieffen plan. In fact, it seems the French did have the stronger forces but that little generalship was involved on either side. What was decisive in the Ardennes was the superiority of the German infantry at company, battalion, and regimental levels. In practically every case, the French infantry was thrown back in disorder.

On the right flank the Germans did have a considerable numerical superiority: 358 battalions and 2,164 guns to Entente forces totaling 257 battalions and 1,120 guns. The German army commanders were unable to translate this near 2–1 advantage into a decisive victory. On 23 August the Saxon 3rd Army attempted to blast its way across the Meuse by attacking with massive artillery support on a narrow front between

[61] Ibid. 646.

Namur and Givet. The Meuse valley here is very steep and weak French forces were able to prevent the 3rd Army from gaining a useful foothold on the west bank (101 German battalions versus 17 French!). Only when the futility of the frontal attack was completely evident did the 3rd Army make a half-hearted attempt to cross the Meuse to the south of Givet, where there were practically no French troops. Since the 3rd Army did not provide this force with a bridge train, the French were able to keep it on the east bank by simply blowing up the existing bridges.

In the center, Bülow attacked on 23 August straight across the Sambre between Namur and Mons. The French 5th Army and the Belgians were numerically stronger than the 2nd Army, but the German infantry once again demonstrated its superiority and the 2nd Army pushed the Entente forces off the river line. The French 5th Army was able to withdraw directly to the rear during the night of 23–4 August. It appeared that by moving south-west the 3rd Army still might have a chance on 24 August to cut off the French 5th Army. It did not do so because of insistent cries for help during the night of the 23–4 August from Bülow. The 3rd Army therefore moved directly to the west toward the 2nd Army and any possible chance of cutting the French off was lost.

On the far-right German flank the 1st Army faced the BEF—potentially 120 German battalions against 52 British and French, with the British left flank hanging in the air. A decisive German victory would have profoundly affected the war. If the 1st Army could have mauled or better yet destroyed the BEF, it would both have sent a shock through the British Empire and exposed the left flank of the entire French army. Instead, the 1st Army was slow to react. Even the Reichsarchiv was critical of Kuhl, noting that although the reports from three of his corps made the situation absolutely clear, Kuhl still failed to take energetic measures to concentrate his army against the British.[62] Kuhl thought he was faced with only two British divisions and was absolutely convinced that strong British forces were at Lille. Only two of the 1st Army's five corps were engaged at Mons. Instead of acting boldly and directing the right-flank III Corps to envelop the British left flank, Kuhl launched III and IX Corps in frontal attacks on the British position, with the German left lined up against the British right and the German right against the British left.

The BEF withdrew on the night of 23–4 August and the 1st Army completely lost contact with it. The 1st Army then decided that the BEF had withdrawn east to Maubeuge and moved to trap it there. In fact, the BEF had retreated to the south. As a consequence, the 1st Army was

[62] Reichsarchiv, *Der Weltkrieg, Band I*, 420–1.

unable to exploit the golden opportunity it was given to destroy the isolated British II Corps at Le Cateau on 26 August. Although the II Corps was fixed in place with open flanks for most of the day, the 1st Army was so badly deployed that Kuhl was unable to outflank and destroy it.

Nevertheless, the German army had won all of its initial battles with the French. Nowadays this is hardly cause for comment. In fact, the completeness of the German victories came as a profound shock to the French and something of a surprise even to the Germans. This success has been incorrectly attributed to the brilliant Schlieffen plan. It was the result of superior German training at the tactical level. Ironically, as Hermann Stegemann pointed out in 1917, the Germans were too successful. The very extent of the German victories made it appear that the Germans had launched a planned war of aggression against an unprepared France.[63]

Victory in the Battle of the Frontiers had bought the Germany army two or three weeks in which the French army was incapable of attacking. The opportunity now presented itself to exploit Germany's interior position and rail mobility to inflict a severe defeat on the Russians. Such a course of action also would require the Germans to go on the defensive in the west, staying in close proximity to the German rail net. Having defeated the Russians the Germans could have then transferred forces from the east to the west to meet the second French attack. Alternatively, Moltke could have continued the attack with the entire army in the west until the right and left wings could break the French fortress line, as in Beseler's 1900 *Operationsstudie.*

On 24 August—the 23rd day of mobilization—OHL decided to transfer six corps to the east. This was consistent with the concept of many of Schlieffen's exercises, for example, the 1897, 1899, 1901, and 1903 *Generalstabsreisen Ost.* In fact, Schlieffen never played an exercise in which the French army was first completely annihilated in the west and then the mass of the German army was transferred east. Even in the 1903 *Generalstabsreise,* the one occasion when he transferred a really large force—11 corps—from the west to the east, the French army had withdrawn behind its fortress line and was preparing to renew the attack. Had Moltke sent six corps immediately by rail to the east while standing on the defensive in the west he would have been well within the parameters established by Schlieffen.

Having arrived at Schlieffen's bold 'school solution', Moltke replaced it with disjointed *ad hoc* measures. He tried to go one better than Schlieffen and secure victory on both fronts at the same time. On

---

[63] H. Stegemann, *Die Geschichte des Krieges, Band I,* (Stuttgart and Berlin, 1917) 100–1.

25 August he reduced the force that would be sent from the west from six corps to two corps, which had just taken Namur (Guard Reserve Corps from the 2nd Army, XI from the 3rd). Because of the Belgian rail demolitions both corps had to foot-march to Aachen in order to board the trains. This consumed several days. The advantage provided by rail mobility and interior lines was that it gained time. The forces to be transferred from the west needed to be as close as possible to the German railheads. This meant that the mass of the forces should have come from the German left—the 6th and 7th Armies in Alsace and the 5th Army near Metz. The 7th Army in particular was disposable, since it was becoming painfully clear by 25 August that the 7th Army would never accomplish anything in the Vosges. On 26 August Moltke decided to transfer V Corps from the 5th Army to the east. On 30 August he rescinded the order and returned V Corps, which by that time had marched to the German railheads near Metz, back to 5th Army control. At the same time, Moltke allowed the German pursuit in the west to continue. On 26 August the 8th Army in East Prussia reported it had begun the counterattack at Tannenberg and predicted that the attack would be successful.

In the Reichsarchiv discussion of Moltke's decision on 24 August to transfer forces to the east, the official history for the first time maintains that the concept of the Schlieffen plan was for the decisive effort to be made by the 1st Army.[64] The proof was the fact that Moltke did not transfer any 1st Army forces to the east. The real reason was surely that the 1st Army was so far from the German railheads that it was impractical to move any of its corps by rail. Kuhl and Groener made much of the fact that Moltke did not move OHL to a point in eastern France where he could exercise close and continual supervision directly over the decisive right wing. This is presented as evidence that Moltke did not understand the Schlieffen plan. In fact, Luxembourg city was a well-chosen position for the headquarters. From here Moltke had land-line communication with Berlin, Austria, and East Prussia as well as with Alsace and Lorraine. It was practically in the centre of the German west-front deployment. Communications with the centre armies (3rd, 4th, 5th) were very good and with the left wing (6th and 7th Armies) were excellent. Bülow (2nd Army) ought to have been able to take care of himself and the 1st Army should not have needed detailed instructions to perform a simple flank-guard mission. Luxembourg city was also large enough to accommodate the imperial entourage. Moltke's choice of Luxembourg for the headquarters does not prove his incompetence. Rather, it further shows that the plan at this point was to break the

[64] Reichsarchiv, *Der Weltkrieg, Band I*, 434.

French fortress line between 'Trouvée de Charmes' and Toul and that the 1st Army was not the *Schwerpunkt* of the German effort. The German headquarters at Luxembourg was in the immediate vicinity of the principal German operation.

On 27 August Moltke issued his first complete operations order since the start of the campaign.[65] This order had absolutely nothing at all to do with the 'Schlieffen plan'. Moltke believed that the Battle of the Frontiers had inflicted very heavy casualties on the French army and that the mission of the German army now was to pursue the battered French units in order to prevent them from being reinforced. As much French territory as possible must be captured to withdraw resources from the French defense effort. The main German effort was to be made by the 2nd Army advancing on Paris. What the 2nd Army would do when it got there was not stated. Moltke's concept was clearly to exploit the German victory. According to Generaloberst Moritz Freiherr von Lyncker's diary (Lyckner was the chief of the Kaiser's military cabinet) on 31 August Moltke said he intended to attack between Reims and Verdun and thought that the decisive battle would be fought there.[66] The 1st Army's mission was to 'advance on the lower Seine'. Attempts have been made to portray this as the prelude to the 1st Army advancing to the north and west of Paris as provided for in the Schlieffen plan. Advocates of this theory never even address, much less explain, how, unsupported, the five corps of the 1st Army were to circumnavigate Paris: in the Schlieffen plan the 1st Army should have been seven corps strong and, more important, followed by six ersatz corps to screen Paris. In fact, Moltke's instructions were for the 1st Army to guard the right flank of the main body against forces that Moltke felt the French might well concentrate on the lower Seine.

The German 3rd Army's instructions were to attack to the south-west. It was opposed only by French rear guards and it appeared that it had a glorious opportunity to drive deep into the rear of either the French 5th Army on its right or the French 4th Army defending on the Meuse to its left. However, on the morning of 27 August the German 4th Army said that it was unable to cross the Meuse in the face of the French 4th Army's resistance and needed immediate assistance. Hausen, the 3rd Army commander, therefore shifted his advance from a southwesterly direction to the south-east, aiming not for the French 4th Army's rear

[65] 'Allgemeine Anweisungen an die 1. bis 7. Armee für den Fortgang der Operationen' (General Instructions to the 1st through 7th Armies for the Continuation of Operations) 27 Aug. 1914 *Streng Geheim!* Generallandesarchiv Karlsruhe GLA 456/659 Blätter 160–3. Five pages, handwritten in the Standard style.

[66] Generaloberst Moritz Freiherr von Lyncker, diary extract sent to Reichsarchiv on 20 Feb. 1925, BA-MA W10/51062.

but for its left flank. The French 4th Army then withdrew unhindered to the south. Hausen's decision was in direct contravention of both Moltke's instructions as well as Schlieffen's doctrine: Schlieffen maintained that the intent must be to destroy the enemy, not merely to push him back, and to accomplish that the objective must be the enemy's line of retreat, not his flank. Hausen was apparently unwilling to take the risk that the French would fight a successful battle on interior lines, first throwing the German 4th Army back across the Meuse and then turning on the isolated German 3rd Army.

The German right wing was still numerically far superior to the Anglo-French forces opposing it. The BEF was essentially *hors de combat* after Le Cateau. In order to cover the BEF's withdrawal the French 5th Army had to fight a delaying action on 29 August on the Guise. This was another parallel battle between the German 2nd Army and the French 5th Army. The 2nd Army asked for assistance from the 1st Army on its right, but the 1st Army was too far to the west to intervene. Not only was there no effective German pursuit after the battle, but Bülow decided that the 2nd Army was so tired that he ordered a rest day on 31 August while the French withdrew.

On 31 August the 1st Army, which had been moving generally to the south-west, swung to the south-east in an attempt to outstrip the French 5th Army on its left. This has been described as 'Von Kluck's turn' and has been called the end of the Schlieffen plan. In fact, the 1st Army had little alternative: it was still responsible for securing the flank of the 2nd Army. After the battle on the Guise the 2nd Army would have to pursue the French 5th Army to the south. The 1st Army could hardly remain on the lower Seine doing nothing, but had to move to protect the 2nd Army's flank against Paris.

By dint of remarkable forced marches, on 2 September IX Corps of 1st Army reached the Marne at Château Thierry far in front of the 2nd Army. At this point Moltke reminded 1st Army that its mission was flank guard and ordered it to echelon itself behind 2nd Army. The overall mission for the right wing, Moltke said, was to turn the left flank of the French armies. Moltke's intent was to push the French army onto the Swiss border. This was the first time such an operation was mentioned. Apparently Moltke felt that the French had been completely beaten.

Kuhl had convinced himself that the British and French were going to make a stand north of the Seine and ordered the 1st Army to continue its advance past Paris to the south. Kuhl would later contend that he had moved south of Paris because the 1st Army was best placed to attack the French left: by continuing the attack to the south, instead of guarding the flank against Paris, he said he was really acting in the spirit of Moltke's 2 September orders. IV Reserve Corps was left to watch Paris. Reserve corps had no reconnaissance aircraft or corps artillery and in addition IV Reserve Corps had detached one of its four infantry brigades for garrison duty in the rear area.

Kuhl had badly miscalculated. The British and French had withdrawn out of range: the 1st Army's attack was a classic *Luftstoß* which hit only air. By 5 September the 1st Army, except for the IV Reserve Corps, was all alone well to the south of the Marne. At this point, Moltke issued his third operations order, which was delivered by officer courier.[67] Moltke's intelligence summary said that the French had avoided the outflanking attack of the 1st and 2nd Armies. There were indications that the French were withdrawing forces from their right and center. Elements of the French army had reached Paris. It was therefore not possible to force the French army to the south-west and against the Swiss border. Moltke had harbored the hope of such an outcome for no more than three days. Now it was likely, Moltke wrote, that the French would shift forces to their left wing to protect Paris and threaten the German right. He reverted to the concept of Beseler's 1900 *Operationsstudie*. The 1st and 2nd Armies were to take up a front opposite Paris and operate offensively against any French attack from that direction, the 1st Army between the Oise and Marne, the 2nd between the Marne and Seine. These armies should deploy far enough away from Paris to allow them freedom to maneuver. The 4th and 5th Armies were faced with strong enemy resistance. Nevertheless, they should attack to the south-east to open the 'Trouée de Charmes' for the 6th Army. The 5th Army would also take Forts Troyon, Les Paroches, and Camp de Romains. It was not yet possible to foresee if the 4th, 5th, 6th, and 7th Armies would be able to drive significant elements of the French army into Switzerland. The 3rd Army would attack towards Troyes. It would be prepared to attack to the west across the Seine to assist the 1st and 2nd Armies or to the south or south-east to assist the left wing. In the meantime the 6th and 7th armies would fix the greatest number of enemy units as they could and attack through the 'Trouée de Charmes' as soon as possible.

On 5 September the French 6th Army began to move east from Paris to attack the German right. It was met by a reconnaissance in force conducted by the German IV Reserve Corps. Once the French threat was clear Kluck and Kuhl sent II and IV Corps north to reinforce IV Reserve Corps in place. This left a large gap in the middle of the 1st Army's deployment. It would have been far better to have withdrawn IV Reserve Corps and fought further to the north and east, where the 1st

---

[67] 'Anweisungen für die 1. bis 7. Armee' (Instructions for the 1st through 7th Armies) 5 Sept. 1914, GLA Karlsruhe GLA 456/659.

Army could have kept its corps together, covered the 2nd Army's flank, and drawn the French away from the protection of the guns of Fortress Paris. Kuhl later maintained that it would have been impossible for IV Reserve Corps to break contact and withdraw. Given the fact that even the BEF had repeatedly been able to conduct just such a maneuver, this is a dubious assertion. The 1st Army probably refused to pull back to the north-east for two reasons. First, the 1st Army was not going to be the first German army to conduct a withdrawal in this war. To withdraw would have also involved an admission that their advance for the last three days had been a mistake and—horror of horrors—that the 1st Army had been outmaneuvered by the French. Second, if the 1st Army came in close proximity to the 2nd Army, then OHL might well place the 1st Army under the operational control of the 2nd Army again. The 1st Army's leadership wanted to avoid this at practically all costs. Schlieffen had continually warned that gaps could appear in the modern battle front, especially when one army moved while its neighbor remained stationary. He had repeatedly encouraged his pupils to exploit such enemy mistakes in order to rupture their front. Kuhl had now presented the British and French with just such a gap.

At the same time, the French counterattack fixed the 1st Army's left-flank corps, III and IX, in place on the right flank of the 2nd Army. Initially, Kuhl placed these corps under the operational control of the 2nd Army, but as French pressure on the 1st Army in front of Paris increased, Kuhl recalled both corps on 8 September. They had no difficulty in breaking contact and conducting a prodigious forced march to the north. There was now a 50-kilometer gap—or more—between the 1st and 2nd Armies. The BEF was slowly entering this gap and the French 5th Army was turning the right flank of the German 2nd Army.

Meanwhile, on 6 September the German 3rd Army was advancing into an open gap between Foch's 9th Army in the west and the French 4th Army in the east. To later German critics, this seemed like another opportunity for the 3rd Army to boldly push through the gap and break the French centre. Instead, Hausen let the right-flank corps commander attach his corps to the end of the 2nd Army line on the right while the left-flank corps did the same with the 4th Army on the left. The open gap in the French line was never exploited. Even the BEF showed more enterprise.

At this point Moltke paid the price for shifting two corps to the east. If Bülow still had the Guard Reserve Corps his position would have been much stronger. More important, if Hausen still had XI Corps and the Saxon Cavalry Division, which had also been sent east, then the 3rd Army would have automatically ruptured the French center whether Hausen intended to do so or not. Nevertheless, the French 9th Army was in a precarious position, particularly after Hausen's pre-dawn attack on the morning of 8 September crushed the French 9th Army's right flank.

The gap between the German 1st and 2nd Armies became a source of concern to OHL on 8 September. Moltke sent the OHL Intelligence Officer, Lieutenant-Colonel Hentsch, to clarify the situation. Moltke was apparently concerned that if he went to the front himself he would leave the field clear for a palace intrigue conducted by the war minister, Falkenhayn, and the chief of the military cabinet, Lyncker: a justifiable fear, as it turned out. Moltke's instructions to Hentsch were that if the right wing was withdrawing he should direct the 1st Army to the Aisne at Soissons, that is, to the north-east where it could protect the 2nd Army's right flank. When he arrived at 2nd Army headquarters Hentsch was told that the French were turning the Army's right flank, which Bülow said he would have to pull back. Bülow complained that by withdrawing III and IX Corps the 1st Army had exposed his right flank. The 1st Army's instructions, Bülow said repeatedly, were to cover the flank of the 2nd Army. He could see no point in the 1st Army's attack on the French 6th Army, because the French could easily withdraw to Paris. The 1st Army, on the other hand, ran the risk of becoming isolated.

At 1st Army Headquarters on the early afternoon of 9 September Hentsch discussed the situation with Kuhl; the Army commander, Kluck, did not participate in the conference. It appears that Kuhl wanted at all costs to avoid being brought back into the orbit of the 2nd Army. His initial solution to the operational problem was that the 2nd Army should stand fast while the 1st Army finished off the French opposite them. Hentsch maintained that that was not possible because the 2nd Army's right flank was in the air. Kuhl then argued that for the 1st Army to withdraw to Soissons it would have to conduct a dangerous flank march in the face of the enemy. Kuhl contended that the 1st Army had to withdraw almost directly to the north. This was an eccentric withdrawal, a favorite late-nineteenth century maneuver. The younger Moltke himself had often advocated using this maneuver. In theory, the 1st Army would have then occupied a form of *Flankenstellung* on the left of any French attempt to outflank the 2nd Army. Kuhl clearly hoped that from this position he could disguise the fact that the 1st Army had conducted a withdrawal, while staying independent of the 2nd Army. He also hoped to be able to later resume the offensive. In the end, Kuhl agreed to move to Soissons, but when Hentsch had gone he conducted his eccentric withdrawal straight north anyway.

The attack of the French mass army was not to be stopped by such artificial maneuvers as eccentric withdrawals. The 1st Army was forced on the defensive and was never able to counterattack. Nevertheless, in the next week OHL would send repeated instructions for Kuhl to move the 1st Army to the east to cover the 2nd Army's flank. The 1st Army was even put under the operational control of the 2nd Army again. Kuhl would not budge, even at the risk that the French would exploit the gap between the 1st and 2nd Armies a second time. This time the gap was only closed at the last minute by the arrival of forces from the left wing. The withdrawal of the 2nd Army forced the entire German right wing to pull back. The Germans had lost the battle of the Marne.

CHAPTER SIX

Excuses and accusations

Before the war, French military writers had said that the Germans were mentally too slow to win a maneuver battle against the intellectually alert French. The battle of the Marne seemed to have proved them right. Within six weeks after the Germans began their withdrawal from the Marne it was clear to the senior German commanders and General Staff officers that at some point there would be a search for the guilty parties. These officers were sure to see their names added to the list of history's conspicuous military failures.

Lyncker's diary entries show that the race to assign the blame was already on by 10 September 1914. Lyncker wrote that it had been a mistake on Moltke's part to transfer the XI and Guard Reserve Corps to the east and that Moltke had allowed control of the army to slip out of his grasp ('die Zügel schliefen am Boden'—the reins were trailing on the ground—a phrase that would later be used continually by German officers to describe Moltke's leadership). Lyncker was scathing concerning the performance of the General Staff as an institution: there was no question that everyone recognized that the General Staff had failed.[1] On 13 September Lyncker wrote that the General Staff as a whole had been unable to conduct a coordinated operation. The 1st and 2nd Armies had acted as they saw fit, completely out of control. Moltke's nerves were not equal to the strain. The General Staff had put the army into a very bad position. In addition, Lyncker said that it was hard to understand how Kluck could have got himself into the situation he was in.

It should come as no surprise that the first organization to write its version of the battle was 1st Army HQ, which had a report ready on 19 October 1914, a truly remarkable achievement under the circumstances.[2] The text of this and the other wartime reports has been lost,

---

[1] '... wenn der Feldzug gewonnen werden sollte, so würde dies das Verdienst der Truppe, nicht aber des Generalstabes sein. Dieser hat seine Sache nicht gut gemacht, daß kann man jetzt wohl ohne Widerspruch behaupten' (If we win this campaign, it will be because of the troops, not the General Staff. It can stated without fear of contradiction that the General Staff has performed poorly). Lyncker diary, BA-MA W10/51062. Needless to say, this passage did not find its way into the official history.

[2] Notes for the preparation of the *Weltkriegswerk*, BA-MA W10/51063.

but later accounts make it clear that the tenor of Kuhl's report was to place the blame for the Marne on the 2nd Army and OHL in general and Hentsch in particular. The working papers for volume IV of the official history note that Hentsch then prepared a report that was expressly identified as a reply to the 1st Army's report. The 2nd Army's report was ready on 31 October.

In 1915 Freytag-Loringhoven began writing the official history of the campaign. The results were never published and were probably destroyed in the bombing of Potsdam. By this time Moltke had been sent back to Berlin as the Chief of the General Staff Rear Headquarters and by accident happened to see the draft of Freytag's book. Moltke wrote a letter to Freytag to complain about the tack Freytag had chosen. Most of this letter was printed in Moltke's posthumous memoirs, but the first page was not. The letter was, however, preserved in the official history working papers, covered with Reichsarchiv marginal markings. What the first page shows is the beginning of the Schlieffen plan myth.[3]

Moltke noted that when Freytag's book would eventually appear it would be the first book to be based on official archival sources and would therefore exercise a great influence concerning judgements on the planning and conduct of the initial campaign. Moltke said that Freytag had concentrated on Schlieffen's planning, with the emphasis on the attack through Belgium. Moltke's nine years of work were characterized as modifying Schlieffen's plan in order to accommodate the changing political situation, nothing more. Moltke was obviously outraged that he had been demoted to a cipher. Prophetically, Moltke said that such an approach would make it appear that the Germans had planned aggression in Europe and the violation of Belgian neutrality years in advance with malice aforethought.

OFFICIAL INVESTIGATIONS

The subject of the Marne remained a hot topic of conversation among German officers. Hentsch explained his version of events to a subordinate, Captain Schubert, on 25 August 1915.[4] He told Schubert that Bülow was concerned for the security of his right flank after the 1st Army had withdrawn III and IX Corps. Bülow wanted to withdraw his right, but feared that even then the 2nd Army was threatened if the 1st Army did not protect his flank. Hentsch said that the 1st Army was in no immediate danger, but that its attack on the French 6th Army was going to bring no more than local success, which would be of no assistance to

---

3 Letter Moltke to Freytag Berlin, 26 July 1915, BA-MA W10/51063, Blatt 66–70.
4 Letter, Schubert, 27 May 1927, BA-MA W10/51062.

the 2nd Army. In any case, the French would use the Paris rail net to reinforce their 6th Army and in 48 hours the 1st Army would be forced to withdraw anyway. It was Hentsch's opinion that Kuhl's mistake had been made on 5 September when, instead of watching Paris, he sent the 1st Army crashing (*vorgeprellt*) to the south, only to have to rush back north again. Now, Hentsch said, Kuhl was claiming that he had been on the verge of a great victory on 9 September when he was ordered to withdraw. Hentsch reported back to Moltke that the centre armies, 5th, 4th, and 3rd, did not need to withdraw: Moltke did that on his own later, apparently concerned that the French were massing against the 3rd Army. Hentsch had heard that Freytag had finished his history of the campaign and he was anxiously awaiting Freytag's conclusions.

Accusations continued to be made in the German army that Hentsch was responsible for losing the battle of the Marne. Hentsch requested an official investigation into his conduct, which Ludendorff granted. Hentsch's statement for the investigating officer was made public by Müller-Loebnitz after the war.[5] Hentsch contended that he was given the authority to order not just the withdrawal of the 1st Army, but of the entire right wing. On the morning of 9 September the chief of staff of the 2nd Army told Hentsch that the 2nd Army's problems began when the 1st Army withdrew III and IX Corps. The 2nd Army could hold the Marne if the 1st Army protected their right flank. Hentsch said that the 2nd Army was fully justified in making this demand. Early that afternoon Hentsch arrived at 1st Army HQ. He was not initially disposed to order the 1st Army to withdraw. Rather, he wanted the 1st Army to protect the 2nd Army's right flank. On arrival at 1st Army HQ he found that the 1st Army was withdrawing its own left and Kuhl told him that even if the 1st Army won on 9 September, it could not support the 2nd Army on the 10th. Hentsch then ordered the 1st Army to withdraw because (1) the 2nd Army was already withdrawing, (2) he had seen for himself how dangerous the gap was between the 1st and 2nd Armies, and (3) even the 1st Army did not believe that it would decisively defeat the French forces it was facing. Hentsch thought that the only way he could get the 1st Army to protect the 2nd Army's flank was by making the 1st Army pull back. On his return to OHL no one objected to the actions he had taken. He maintained that everyone was pleased that by keeping the left wing (3rd, 4th, 5th Armies) in position it was possible to take the Meuse forts and encircle Verdun. He maintained that he had 'created a new basis for the continuation of the operation'. The

---

[5] W. Müller-Loebnitz, *Die Sendung des Oberstleutnants Hentsch* (Berlin, 1922), 57–9. The originals are in BA-MA W10/51062. I have been unable to find any discrepancies in Müller-Loebnitz's transcription, but my summary is drawn from the original at Freiburg.

entire sense of Hentsch's statements was that the mission of the 1st Army was flank guard and that OHL's offensive intent was to break the French fortress line. The objective of the operation was to execute Beseler's 1900 *Operationsstudie.*

The investigation's results were published in a General Order dated 24 May 1917 that was distributed down to divisional level.[6] The official determination was that Moltke had told Hentsch that if the right wing had begun to withdraw, Hentsch had authority to direct the movement so as to close the gap between the 1st and 2nd Armies, with the 1st Army to fall back to Soissons. Lieutenant-Colonel Hentsch was under these circumstances authorized to give binding instructions in the name of OHL. On the morning of 9 September the 2nd Army had already independently made the decision to withdraw behind the Marne. Hentsch agreed with this decision. Once at the 1st Army HQ he invoked his authority from OHL and instructed the 1st Army to withdraw. He was completely justified in doing so, as the 2nd Army had initiated the withdrawal of the right wing. Whether the 2nd Army was justified in pulling back was a question which could only be answered by later research. No reproach could be made concerning Hentsch's conduct.

Hentsch died in March 1918 after an unsuccessful operation to remove large gall stones. Hentsch's surgeon said that many in the army still held him responsible for the loss of the battle of the Marne.[7] Rumors circulated after the war that Hentsch had committed suicide out of shame and remorse.

The official investigation may have found that Hentsch had acted properly, but the Reichsarchiv did not. In October 1921 Wilhelm Müller-Loebnitz, a former General Staff lieutenant-colonel and then *Oberarchivrat* in the Reichsarchiv completed *Die Sendung des Oberstleutnants Hentsch* (The Mission of Lieutenant Colonel Hentsch), which was published in 1922. Müller-Loebnitz made Hentsch responsible for the loss of the battle of the Marne. He charged that Hentsch had not acted in the spirit of his instructions. In a statement on 3 March 1920 Tappen, the OHL operations officer, said that his intent, and that of Moltke, was that both armies should hold their positions and that 'rearward movements had to be prevented absolutely.' Tappen and Dommes (both in 1917 and 1920) said that nobody in OHL was thinking of a withdrawal and that Hentsch never had any authority to order one. In his book *Bis zur Marne* (To the Marne) Tappen became even more certain of this. However, on 10 September 1914 Tappen had written in his diary

[6] BA-MA PH 3/60. The original investigation report was apparently destroyed in the bombing of the Reichsarchiv.

[7] Letter Dr. Ramstedt, 1 Nov. 1929, BA-MA W10/50162.

that the 1st Army had caused the withdrawal on the Marne by recalling the IX Corps and creating a gap between the 1st and 2nd Armies.[8]

Müller-Loebnitz said that the fatal error was Hentsch's agreement with Lauenstein, the 2nd Army's Chief of Staff, on the morning of 9 September to the effect that the 1st Army had to cover the right flank of the 2nd Army, even if both had to fall back to get this done. Müller-Loebnitz said that according to his instructions Hentsch should have encouraged the 2nd Army to stand fast. There was no immediate pressure on the right-flank division of the 2nd Army. This, said Müller-Loebnitz, was the tragic guilt that Hentsch carried for the rest of his life, guilt he vainly attempted to expiate by the brilliant performance of his subsequent duties.

Müller-Loebnitz also attacked Hentsch's professional ability. He said that Hentsch's reports were full of factual errors and his operational decision-making was not logical. It was pointless for the 1st Army to have covered the 2nd Army's flank, Müller-Loebnitz maintained: the French and British could always have outflanked the 1st Army too. Hentsch could not have known on the afternoon of 9 September that the 2nd Army was actually withdrawing. Therefore, he ordered the 1st Army to pull back, acting entirely on his own initiative because of pessimistic preconceptions which had no relation to the actual situation on the ground. Nevertheless, Kuhl, like a good soldier, obeyed orders. Müller-Loebnitz does confirm that in its report of 19 October 1914 the 1st Army was already blaming Hentsch for the defeat on the Marne. The 1st Army maintained that it was 'advancing victoriously on Nanteuil and was in the process of rolling up the French envelopment when Lieutenant-Colonel Hentsch [ordered] . . . a withdrawal to the Aisne'.

According to Müller-Loebnitz, Bülow was at least as guilty as Hentsch. As Bülow's own statement of 31 October 1914 showed, his decision to withdraw was, like Hentsch's, not based on an accurate picture of the situation, but on preconceived and unfounded assumptions. Bülow underestimated the success of his own army on 8 September and was unduly pessimistic concerning the condition of his own troops, his right flank and the 1st Army's situation. The decision to withdraw the 2nd Army was not justified. Müller-Loebnitz said that in the deposition for Hentsch's 1917 investigation, the 1st Army's position was that it could have defeated the French 6th Army and then turned on the BEF. The 2nd Army's withdrawal made it impossible to execute this plan, because the 1st Army had to withdraw to protect his own left: the 1st Army turned the 2nd Army's own arguments around and used them against the 2nd Army.

[8] BA-MA, *Nachlaß* Tappen, Diary.

Müller-Loebnitz then discussed the results of the 1917 investigation. In addition to Ludendorff's general order of 24 May 1917, Müller-Loebnitz acknowledged that a report on the case written by a Major Kaupisch concluded that had Hentsch not 'ordered' the 1st Army to withdraw, it would have had to do so anyway, because there was a 60-kilometer gap between the two armies, and four long columns of enemy troops had entered this gap. Müller-Loebnitz then contended that the 1917 investigators had got it all wrong. The testimony of Moltke, Tappen, and Dommes showed that Hentsch's primary mission was to encourage the armies to stand fast. He was not to initiate a withdrawal but only to coordinate one if it had already begun. Müller-Loebnitz said that Hentsch's pessimism led him to an incorrect interpretation of his instructions. It was Hentsch on 8 September who encouraged Bülow to withdraw and then he did the same with Lauenstein on the morning of 9 September. Hentsch did not inform OHL on 8 September of the 2nd Army's intention to withdraw; therefore, on 10 September, when Hentsch made his report, OHL was faced with a *fait accompli*. In fact, maintained Müller-Loebnitz, there was no necessity for the 2nd Army to withdraw on 9 September. The 2nd Army should have waited for the results of the 1st Army's attacks. The 1st Army's decision to attack the left flank of the French 6th Army was a bold one which could have turned the tide for the German armies. Indeed, Müller-Loebnitz says that the 1st Army should have been bolder yet, and attacked the British as they crossed the Marne.

Müller-Loebnitz's final conclusion was that once the 2nd Army had begun to pull back, formally Hentsch was justified in requiring the 1st Army to withdraw also. Nevertheless, the German army was not forced by the enemy to withdraw. Tactically, the Germans were winning. Rather, the decision to withdraw was made, unforced, by certain senior officers. The German army was not beaten on the Marne, it was ordered to retreat by its own leaders. The real miracle of the Marne was that experienced German officers (Hentsch and Bülow) could commit such a series of mistakes, misunderstandings, and omissions.

In 1926 volume IV of the official history expanded the circle of guilty parties to include Moltke.[9] The official history maintained that Hentsch probably had a second, private interview with Moltke just before he left OHL in Luxembourg and during this interview Moltke may have given Hentsch the authority to order a withdrawal. Moltke and Hentsch were now equally at fault.

Müller-Loebnitz said that in 1917 Colonel Matthes, the operations officer (Ia) of the 2nd Army, could not remember clearly what was said

---

[9] Reichsarchiv, *Der Weltkrieg*, iv: *Der Marne-Feldzug. Die Schlacht* (Berlin, 1926), 220–70.

at 2nd Army HQ on 8 September. For the Reichsarchiv official history Matthes, since the deaths of Lauenstein and Bülow the only surviving senior 2nd Army officer, recovered his memory. Most of what he now said supported the contention that it was Hentsch's pessimistic impression of the 1st Army's position which was decisive in convincing the 2nd Army to withdraw.[10]

The Reichsarchiv's major elaboration on Müller-Loebnitz's original thesis was an emphasis on Hentsch's psychological condition. It said that at the beginning of the war Hentsch had already arrived at a very pessimistic appreciation of Germany's position. The Reichsarchiv contended that the impressions of retreating German columns that Hentsch gained during his trip to 1st Army HQ reinforced his already pessimistic evaluation of the strategic and operational situation. He also heard that the BEF had crossed the Marne and knew from his conversations with Bülow and Lauenstein that this would force the 2nd Army to begin its withdrawal. The Reichsarchiv contended that Hentsch wanted to pull back all five right-wing armies, which was a gross falsification of Hentsch's stated intentions.

The Reichsarchiv said that Hentsch's pessimism was fatal for the German army. On the afternoon of 9 September, just as Hentsch was ordering Kuhl to withdraw, the Germans had won the battle. The 1st Army was defeating the left wing of the French 6th Army and the left wings of the 2nd Army and the 3rd Army were crushing the right flank of the French 9th Army.[11] Further British advance would only have resulted in the BEF's destruction.

On that afternoon Kuhl and Hentsch discussed the situation, for the most part alone. Kuhl said he told Hentsch that from previous experience he knew that the British would move too slowly to have any effect on his advance against the French 6th Army. With considerable exaggeration, Kuhl said that he was attacking the French 6th Army in the flank and rear, which promised great results. In fact, he was attacking the French left frontally. His 'outflanking force' consisted of a single reserve infantry brigade, and there was no reason to believe that the French would have had any difficulty blocking this weak force and withdrawing on Paris if necessary. In any case, Hentsch still insisted that the 1st Army cover the 2nd Army's flank. When Kuhl said that he could not do that on 10 September, even if he defeated the French 6th Army, Hentsch told Kuhl to withdraw to Soissons. The Reichsarchiv said that Kuhl still resisted. Kuhl then maintained that Hentsch told him that the 2nd Army was *Schlacke*—had been reduced to cinders. This, said Kuhl,

[10] Müller-Loebnitz, *Hentsch*, 43; Reichsarchiv, *Der Weltkrieg*, iv. 240–1.
[11] Ibid. 255.

was decisive: if the 2nd Army could not fight, then the 1st Army had to retreat. The use of the term *Schlacke* has been attributed to many officers during 8 and 9 September. Whether Hentsch actually said this to Kuhl is an open question. It did give Kuhl an escape hatch—the 1st Army was not withdrawing because of its own situation, but because of the 2nd Army.

All this emphasis on Hentsch diverted attention from the 1st Army. The Reichsarchiv contended that Kuhl had arrived at a correct appreciation of the situation and on 9 September was on his way to winning a decisive victory. In fact, Kuhl did not have the intellectual flexibility necessary to fight a maneuver battle, although he would do very well later on as a trench warfare bureaucrat. He had misread the situation both at Mons and Le Cateau and had twice missed golden opportunities to destroy the BEF. On 5 September he once again misread the situation and then disobeyed orders, launching his army into a classic *Luftstoß* and thereby putting the entire campaign at risk. He then pulled III and IX Corps away from the 2nd Army flank in a questionable all-or-nothing attempt to defeat the French 6th army although it could easily retreat to Paris. Now, according to the Reichsarchiv, Bülow and Hentsch had prevented Kuhl from finally winning a great victory.

In fact, Kuhl's primary mission throughout the campaign was flank guard. Had he carried out that mission, there seemed to have been every prospect that the Germans would have been able to break the French fortress line and the first campaign would have been successfully, if unspectacularly, concluded.

MORE EXCUSES AND ACCUSATIONS

Hermann Stegemann made some of the debates raging in the German army public in his 1917 book, and the 1st Army comes off rather well.[12] He thought that the 1st Army had enveloped both British flanks at Mons and effectively wrecked the BEF, and that the success of the German advance was in large part due to the 1st Army's outflanking the French line. However, he also said that by moving south of the Marne the 1st Army completely changed the strategic situation in favor of the French. Joffre was then able to outmaneuver the German envelopment. He went on to rehabilitate the 1st Army, saying that Kluck was the hero of the Marne. (On closer inspection it is clear that what he really admired was the fighting ability of the German infantry and the epic forced marches conducted by the III and IX Corps.) There was no reason for OHL to have ordered a withdrawal, Stegemann maintained,

[12] See Ch. 1.

because the 1st Army had already beaten the French 6th Army and there was no serious pressure on the 2nd Army's right either. Stegemann said that the 2nd Army's withdrawal uncovered the 1st Army's left flank and therefore the 1st Army had to break off its victorious offensive and withdraw. The reason for the German retreat was something of a mystery—tactically, the Germans were winning. It would appear that most of Kuhl's explanations for the Marne were gaining currency in the German army.

One of the first *apologiae* published after the war was Baumgarten-Crusius' defense of the Saxon 3rd Army, *Die Marneschlacht 1914*, which appeared in 1919 (Baumgarten-Crusius said that he started writing the book in 1915).[13] Baumgarten-Crusius had the immense advantage of being able to base his work on Saxon Army archives: he was therefore not under General Staff control.[14]

The 3rd Army had initially escaped censure: indeed, Hausen had been praised for emulating Blücher at Waterloo and rushing to the rescue of his neighbors. Then the realization began to dawn that by doing so the Saxons had violated one of Schlieffen's cardinal rules and had repeatedly missed chances to break the French line and destroy entire French corps.

Baumgarten-Crusius contended that on 22 August the Sambre–Meuse battle had provided a heaven-sent opportunity for a great *Kesselschlacht*—a battle of encirclement. The French were already half-surrounded and heavily outnumbered. Baumgarten-Crusius faulted OHL and Bülow for failing to win the war here at one blow, and not the 3rd Army's inability to cross the Meuse on 23 September or to cut off the French 5th Army on 24 September.

Baumgarten-Crusius admitted that between the Meuse and the Marne the 3rd Army was opposed only by French rear guards and the army had a clear road to the French rear. Nevertheless, on 27 and 28 August the 4th Army's cries for help were urgent. The 3rd Army therefore ignored OHL instructions to advance south-west and went south-east to the 4th Army's assistance. Again an opportunity to encircle large French forces was lost. Baumgarten-Crusius' excuse was that OHL issued too few orders and the few it did give were not precise. He also said that OHL at Luxembourg was too far away to control Kluck and Bülow. More to the point, the 3rd Army had no communications problems: for example, an operations order left OHL at 0755 hours on

[13] A. Baumgarten-Crusius, *Die Marneschlacht 1914 insbesondere auf der Front der deutschen dritten Armee* (Leipzig, 1919).
[14] He was also able to see the war diary of the 2nd Army, which he said had been poorly kept and was of little historical value.

1 September and arrived at 3rd Army headquarters at 0812 hours, 17 minutes later. The 3rd Army's failure both to follow orders and thereby win a great battle was the result not of bad communications with OHL, but of Hausen's timidity.

Baumgarten-Crusius then made a serious accusation that had also clearly been circulating through the German army. He said that the 1st Army had left only one reserve corps to watch Paris and, crying tally-ho, charged off towards the Seine as all the armies raced for the *Kaiserpreis* (Emperor's Trophy). This surely is an accurate reflection of the attitude of senior German officers in the first week of September 1914. Nevertheless, it was tantamount to saying that Kluck and Kuhl had placed ambition above their duty. Baumgarten-Crusius then made up for it by maintaining that it was impossible for the 1st Army to have carried out the OHL operations order of 5 September to guard the right flank. The success of the entire operation in the west depended on the 1st Army and OHL was too far away and out of touch to realize this.

The last charge against the 3rd Army was that on 6 September it could have advanced into the open gap in the French center and completely broken the French line, with decisive strategic consequences. Instead, it missed its chance and let itself be sucked into the tactical battles of the neighboring armies. Baumgarten-Crusius' defense once again was that the cries for help from the VIII Corps on its left and the Guard Corps on the right were so insistent that the Saxon corps had no choice but to go to their assistance. He also contended that the 3rd Army was too weak to conduct a breakthrough—an obvious criticism of Moltke's transfer of the XI Corps from the 3rd Army to the east.

Baumgarten-Crusius then criticized the 1st Army for transferring the III and IX Corps from the right flank of the 2nd Army and also faulted OHL for not stopping this movement. Kluck should have left at least a corps on the 2nd Army's right: he didn't need five corps to defeat the French 6th Army. Baumgarten-Crusius said that a 'creeping rumor' ('schleichende Kriegslegende') in the German army during the war held Kluck responsible for the Marne.

At the same time, Baumgarten-Crusius said that the 2nd Army hadn't needed to withdraw, but should have stood and fought until the 1st and 3rd Armies had won their battles. On 9 September the 3rd Army was making good progress on its right flank and was finally intending to attack into the gap in the center with the 23rd Reserve Division. The 3rd Army was forced to withdraw on 9 September because the 2nd Army had pulled back.

Baumgarten-Crusius made a short and oblique mention of

Schlieffen's plan ('Schlieffensche Kriegsplan'), which resembled
Kuhl's excuses more than it did the 1905 *Denkschrift*: the intent of the
plan was to exert continual pressure on the French left and drive the
French army into Switzerland while the Germans stood on the defensive in Lorraine. The decisive battle would be fought south of the
Marne. There was no mention of specific force ratios between the right
and left wing nor of the 1st Army circumnavigating Paris.

Indirectly, Baumgarten-Crusius would also defend Hentsch, another
Saxon officer, against the 1st Army's charges that Hentsch was responsible for the Marne. He said that the principal blame for failure to win
the 1914 campaign lay with the General Staff. The French did not win
on the Marne, rather a few senior German leaders had failed to win it.
Hentsch, who was relatively junior, was not mentioned.

FIRST EVIDENCE OF THE SCHLIEFFEN PLAN

Making Hentsch and Bülow—both dead—responsible for the defeat on
the Marne solved the General Staff's immediate problem in justifying
its performance in the war. However, the question of why the General
Staff's strategy had not brought victory was sure to arise. The first indication we have of the explanation the General Staff would use—the
Schlieffen plan—is found in a letter, classified Secret, from the Chief of
the Army Historical Section, General Mertz, to Groener on 11 October
1919.[15] Mertz explained that he was sending Groener a copy of a
Denkschrift titled 'Die Entwicklung des operativen Gedankens im
Zweifrontkrieg von 1871 bis 1914' (The Development of Operational
Thought for a Two-Front War from 1871 to 1914). Mertz said that this was
to be regarded as preparatory work for the official history, and asked
for Groener's evaluation, particularly concerning the ideas of the
younger Moltke. Groener had just resigned as *Erster Generalquartiermeister* on 30 September. He had appointed Mertz to his position and
was surely aware of the work the historical section was doing. Groener
favored Mertz with his thoughts on German strategy for the entire
period, in the form of a cover letter and marginal notes to the
Denkschrift, demonstrating an intimate familiarity with the subject.
Groener was not merely passing along information, he was putting his
interpretation on the events: this was the birth of the Schlieffen plan.

Groener began by saying that he was an enthusiastic (*rückhaltslos*)

---

[15] *Nachlaß* Groener, BA-MA N46/41. I would like to thank Frau and Herr R. Erben for
their assistance in deciphering Groener's crabbed and practically illegible Standard
script notes. It is important to note that in the original document Groener's comments
on the *Denkschrift* are *typed*. The handwritten notes are excerpts from the *Denkschrift*.

supporter of Schlieffen. He said that when the question of whether or not to continue to plan for *Aufmarsch* II was raised in 1912, as the Chief of the Rail Section he argued forcefully for the 'so-called great *Westaufmarsch*'. Without further ado Groener went on to begin adding his 'Schlieffen plan' spin. He said that as of 1910 the Rail Section had been planning to transfer nine corps from the left flank to the right. Empty rolling stock was assembled along the Rhine to expedite these movements. That nine corps' worth of rolling stock was prepared to conduct massive troop movements is a significant indicator that Schlieffen's concept of using rail mobility as a force multiplier had been incorporated in German war planning. Groener's statement that the rolling stock was concentrated behind the left wing to expedite its transfer to the right is less reliable: at the start of operations the 6th and 7th Armies together only had eight corps. It is far more plausible that the rolling stock was evenly distributed behind the front to facilitate movements all along the west front or from west to east. This would be confirmed by Moltke's idea on 24 August to transfer two corps from the right wing, center, and left wing to the east. What Groener's fabrication was intended to show were the measures he contended he had taken to 'make the right wing strong'.

Groener said that in reading 'Entwicklung des operativen Gedankens' he was struck by the question as to whether Moltke was fully aware that the changes he, Moltke, had made in the war plan had muddied the clarity of the Schlieffen *Aufmarsch*. He believed that in August and early September 1914 Moltke still thought he was acting in accordance with Schlieffen's concept. Even the decision on 27 August to break the French fortress line between Toul and Epinal seemed to have been considered a Schlieffenesque operation. Groener said that he thought this to have been the 'greatest sin against the spirit of Schlieffen's ideas'. In Groener's opinion OHL believed the exaggerated reports of victories coming from the armies and therefore did not perceive the real situation and neglected Schlieffen's operational concept. The question to be considered was therefore: did Moltke lose sight of the Schlieffen plan before or during the war? Groener also asked about the purpose of 'Entwicklung des operativen Gedankens'. Was it merely to describe the decisions that had been taken, or to show that an invasion of Belgium was the precondition for victory in a two-front war?

Groener was not an admirer of the elder Moltke's war planning between 1871 and 1888. 'Entwicklung des operativen Gedankens' pointed out that in Moltke's war plans of 1879 and 1880 the French could not conquer Alsace and Lorraine until they had taken Metz and Strasbourg. Groener said that he doubted that the Germans could have held the fortresses for long. Groener's most telling argument against an *Ostaufmarsch* was that it could not be supported logistically. Given the lines of communication available at the time, wrote Groener, neither a quick nor a decisive operation could be conducted in the east. If there was a long war in the east it was to be expected that eventually the Italians would attack Austria.

Groener generally saw Schlieffen's thought moving in a slow but direct progression to the Schlieffen plan. 'Entwicklung des operativen Gedankens', however, noted that no later than the 1900/1 *Aufmarsch* Schlieffen planned to retain corps in their mobilization stations and then move them by rail to conduct surprise counterattacks against the French left flank. Groener's reaction was to finesse this discrepancy in the Schlieffen plan theory by discussing the importance of the 1899/1900 and 1900/1 *Aufmärsche* not in terms of the development of the Schlieffen plan, but in terms of the development of the operational use of rail mobility. Groener said that at this time he was the action officer for rail deployment in the west. Based on these *Aufmärsche* he began to study the tactical movement of division-sized units in *Operationsstudien* and *Kriegsspiele*. In the following years Groener said Schlieffen frequently gave the rail section such problems to work out.

Under the heading 'Denkschrift 1905' 'Entwicklung des operativen Gedankens' then jumped into the middle of one of the problem areas concerning the Schlieffen plan: the fact that the invasion of Belgium added one more enemy against Germany. The General Staff historian proposed the possibility that Schlieffen had hoped that the Belgians wouldn't fight. Groener thought this assumption unlikely, though he said that if the Belgians had more political acumen, they might have been able to preserve their neutrality.

Groener then wrote: 'When you read the Schlieffen *Denkschrift* of 1905, it's enough to make you cry for rage and shame at our stupidity in 1914. If the leadership had not memorized it, they needed only to have put this breviary for victory (*Siegesbrevier*) in their pocket and then pulled it out.'

'Entwicklung des operativen Gedankens' then hazarded an explanation as to why in the 1905 *Denkschrift* Schlieffen had not left any troops in East Prussia: Schlieffen had intended the plan for a Franco-German war, not for one involving the Entente against the Central Powers. Groener would not be diverted. Regardless of the political situation, he wrote, there was only one way to conduct the offensive against France and Britain, and that was the one chosen by Schlieffen. 'Entwicklung des operativen Gedankens' maintained that it was also possible that Schlieffen thought the Russians would not immediately attack if the Germans for their part did not deploy forces in the east, although the younger Moltke apparently did not share this conviction. Groener felt that this theory was implausible. He maintained that the essential point was that if Moltke had needed to move troops from the west to the east, these needed to be drawn from the left wing, not from the right.

'Entwicklung des operativen Gedankens' then noted that the younger Moltke had said that the war would be decided in the west. Groener took the opportunity to drive the point home again: 'a *great* victory only from a *very strong* right wing'. Groener maintained that Moltke weakened the right wing in order to protect German territory in Prussia and Alsace. This was a mistake. The further the French penetrated into Alsace and Lorraine, the farther away they moved from their railheads and the more difficult it would have been for the French to transfer forces to their left wing. Groener said that the 7th Army should have been sent to Aachen by rail. Where 'Entwicklung des operativen Gedankens' maintained that a victory in Lorraine would have assisted the right wing, Groener again disagreed. Groener also denied that there was ever any intention of encircling the French armies in Lorraine, as the General Staff historian contended.

Groener wrote that the General Staff historian assumed that Moltke wanted to win 'the most complete victory possible' in order to be able to transfer troops to the east. Groener's reaction was to ask what kind of victory that was. An 'ordinary' victory was alien to Schlieffen's operational concept.

Next came the thorny question of the ersatz divisions. 'Entwicklung des operativen Gedankens' noted that in 1912 it was planned to send them to the east. Any that were excess to requirements there might be sent to the west or used for coast defense. Since the ersatz divisions were to go to the east, the number of active and reserve divisions assigned to the east was reduced in 1912 from 13 to 9. Groener tried to ignore the ersatz division problem. He made the remarkable assertion that the ersatz divisions contributed nothing to the operational concept. The real problem was that Moltke experimented with the 1905 *Denkschrift* without adopting it wholeheartedly. He just couldn't admit that Schlieffen was right. Instead, he adopted half-measures.

The General Staff historian said that all the indicators before the war pointed to an increasing probability of a Franco-British violation of Belgian neutrality, regardless of whether Germany did so first or not. Groener agreed, but noted that the important point was who violated Belgian neutrality first. He was also critical of the attack on Liège because of the political fallout.

This document demonstrates what obstacles Groener had to overcome to establish the Schlieffen plan. The General Staff historian had clearly not come to the conclusion that the 1905 *Denkschrift* was the template for the German war plan in 1914. His intention was to find reasonable explanations for the inconsistencies in the Schlieffen plan and to reconcile it with the younger Moltke's war plan. Groener had to continually reinforce his main point: the Schlieffen plan would have worked because it kept the right wing strong, leading to a quick, decisive victory in the west. Everything else was secondary. It was, however, decided to put the project in more capable hands than those of the General Staff historian. The job of presenting the Schlieffen plan to the public was turned over to Kuhl.

REFIGHTING THE BATTLE OF LORRAINE

An essential element of the critique of Moltke's 1914 war plan was that he made the left wing too strong at the expense of the right. When Groener published *Das Testament des Grafen Schlieffen* in 1929 he went one step further and accused the Bavarian commander in Lorraine, Crown Prince Rupprecht, and his chief of staff, Krafft von Dellmensingen, of having missed an opportunity to destroy the French in Lorraine.[16] Groener almost overreached himself. It was one thing to place the blame on dead officers like Hentsch, Moltke, and Bülow. Krafft, on the other hand, was alive, alert and boiling mad. Unlike Groener, who served exclusively in staff positions, Krafft had distinguished himself as a combat leader and, as the commander of the elite *Alpenkorps*, was something of a folk hero in south Germany. Krafft wrote a pamphlet attacking Groener's conclusions.[17] The situation threatened to spin out of Groener's control when Krafft's pamphlet received a generally favorable review from Ernst Kabisch in the 25 January 1932 issue of the prestigious *Münchener Neuste Nachrichten*.[18] Kabisch himself was no minor figure, having written an important book on the war, *Streitfragen des Weltkrieges*, in 1924.[19] The argument also had a political dimension, because at the time Groener was the second man in the Brüning government, being both War and Interior Minister. Much of the dispute was carried out in private correspondence between Krafft, Kabisch, and Wolfgang Foerster, whose job was clearly to calm the waters before permanent damage was done.

In 1915 and 1916 Krafft had also written a defense of his actions in the

---

[16] W. Groener, *Das Testament des Grafen Schlieffens* (2nd edn., Berlin, 1929) 44–55.

[17] Krafft von Dellmensingen, *Kritischer Streifzug durch die Studien des Generalleutnants a. D. Wilhelm Groener über den Weltkrieg* (Munich, 1931).

[18] E. Kabisch, 'Streit um die Lothringer Schlacht', *Münchener Neuste Nachrichten*, 25 Jan. 1932.

[19] E. Kabisch, *Streitfragen des Weltkrieges* (Stuttgart, 1924).

first weeks of the war.[20] Krafft was therefore fully prepared in 1931/32 to meet Groener with facts and well thought-out arguments. In defending his decisions in August 1914, Krafft made a thorough analysis of his mission as presented in the *Aufmarschanweisungen*. Krafft's dogged adherence to the concept of the real war plan forced Groener and Foerster to the admission, at least in private correspondence, that, as Wolfgang Foerster noted in a letter to Kabisch on 30 March 1932, Groener's 'current interpretation' of the left wing's mission agreed with Krafft's own: 'obtain the time the right wing needed to conduct its offensive in Belgium and France or, if the French army conducts its main attack in Alsace and Lorraine, give the right wing time to swing to the south in support'.[21] This is a mission out of the *Generalstabsreisen West* or Beseler's *Operationsstudie*, and a poor defense of the genius of the 'Schlieffen plan'. Groener had admitted that the left wing was as important to the German war plan as the right wing and the main battle might well have been fought in Lorraine, not by outflanking the French left near Paris. Faced with competent professional criticism even Groener was forced to back away from the Schlieffen plan.

THE WENNINGER CONTROVERSY

Next, the Bavarian big guns, the Bavarian Kriegsarchiv, became involved in the battle between Krafft and Groener. This was extraordinarily dangerous for the Reichsarchiv official history. The Kriegsarchiv probably possessed all the pre-war planning documents and intelligence reports that the Reichsarchiv did except for the Schlieffen plan *Denkschrift* itself. In addition, it had its own war diaries for the first months of the war and had published an excellent official history of the Lorraine campaign. It was staffed with very capable personnel and was said to have been a disguised continuation of the Bavarian General Staff. Worse, the Kriegsarchiv staff was not a party to the Schlieffen plan project.

Moreover, the Kriegsarchiv held the reports of the Bavarian military representative in Berlin at the start of the war, Generalleutnant Karl Ritter von Wenninger, who had been killed in action during the war. Wenninger's reports not only supported Krafft's version of events, they went Krafft one better. Wenninger wrote that Moltke and Stein were considering an attack through the 'Trouée de Charmes' as early as 15 August. If true, it meant that Moltke had never seriously considered the Schlieffen plan, but was aiming at breaking the French fortress line to the south of Nancy from the very beginning of the campaign.

---

[20] *Nachlaß* Dellmensingen, Kriegsarchiv Munich.
[21] *Nachlaß* Groener, BA-MA N46/41, Blatt 204.

Most damaging, however, was Wenninger's report of 7 September 1914.[22] Wenninger was writing a summary of the operations to that point in the war. He said that the Germans had conducted the operation according to the concept of Schlieffen's plan ('Schlieffensche Operations Plan') of 1909. Indeed, it had been possible to follow the plan beyond the first battles (a remarkable accomplishment given Moltke's famous dictum that no plan survives contact with the enemy). The only glitch was that the 6th and 7th Armies had not been able to advance as far as they did in the Schlieffen concept, because the famous gap at Charmes was really no gap at all. The 6th and 7th Armies had instead encountered fortress-like field works which had been prepared in peacetime. OHL had been slow to recognize this fact. Wenninger wrote that the last page of the Schlieffen concept called for the northern and southern halves of the army to meet in the greatest Cannae in world history 'on the Catalaunian fields'.[23] This was no longer possible. OHL must now think of an expedient of its own. In a letter to the Reichsarchiv on 12 November 1932 Dommes acknowledged that Tappen had made a similar reference to the 'Catalaunian fields'. Therefore when officers referred to Schlieffen's plan before 1919, what they meant was an operation identical to Beseler's 1900 *Operationsstudie*. Groener, Kuhl, et al. had brazenly highjacked the Schlieffen plan name and attached it to the 1905 *Denkschrift*.

The Kriegsarchiv sent excerpts of Wenninger's reports to the Reichsarchiv.[24] The Reichsarchiv's reaction was characteristic: an attack on Wenninger's credibility. According to the Reichsarchiv, Wenninger could have seen neither the *Aufmarschanweisungen* or the 1905 *Denkschrift*. Wenninger was basing his reports on half-understood rumors. As proof of Wenninger's incapacity, the Reichsarchiv disingenuously noted that everyone was now aware that the Schlieffen plan

[22] Kriegsarchiv Munich, Altreg. Abt. III Bd. 5, Bay. Bevollmächtigter 18. Bericht, 7 Sept. 1914. *Nachlaß* groener BA-MA N46/41.

[23] The 'Catalaunian fields' was a reference to the battle of Châlons (actually *campi Catalauni* near Troyes) in June 451 in which Aëtius defeated the Huns. The phrase had been long in use by German officers, most of whom had a classical education in school, to mean any decisive battle. For example, the elder Moltke's operations officer, Paul Bronsart von Schellendorff, used a similar '*katalaunischen Gefilden*' phrase in a conversation on 28 August 1870 with Bismarck just before Sedan to describe the impending battle (Bronsart von Schellendorff, *Geheimes Tagebuch 1870–1871*, P. Rassow (ed.) (Bonn, 1954), 52.) A certain amount of hyperbole was involved here. Had the Germans actually been able to close the sack around the Verdun–Toul fortress complex a great many French troops would have been surrounded—the garrisons of the two great fortresses and the *Sperrforts* were not insignificant. Nevertheless, it would have been unlikely that the Germans could have caught a very large portion of the French field army in the trap.

[24] Kriegsarchiv Munich, Altreg. Abt. III Bd. 5, Akt. V C 3b 5246/32; 5472/32; 5571/32; 4610/32.

Denkschrift was written in 1905, not 1909 as Wenninger stated. The Reichsarchiv had thus added insult to injury by impugning the reputation of a highly regarded Bavarian officer who had died on the field of battle: it is evident from the internal Kriegsarchiv correspondence that the Bavarians were furious.

From Wenninger's statement the obvious conclusion would have to be that the concept for the final German war plan was composed in 1909; this plan looked like Beseler's 1900 *Operationsstudie* and Wenninger called this Schlieffen's plan. Wenninger's version is indirectly supported by the Reichsarchiv official history itself, which acknowledged that in 1909 Moltke formulated his own plan. Wenninger had said on 19 August 1914 that he had received his information on the war plan from Tappen. The Reichsarchiv therefore was forced to write Tappen twice for a clarification. On both occasions, Tappen's reply was vague and evasive.

Nevertheless, both Krafft's argument with Groener and the Wenninger controversy died out around late January 1933. It would appear that political events took precedence at this point. In any case, Nazi assumption of control (*Gleichschaltung*) would have made it impossible for the Kriegsarchiv to have pursued an independent, critical and highly controversial line. Courtesy of a genuine *deus ex machina* the Reichsarchiv had withstood the last and by far the most serious threat to the Schlieffen plan, which now became dogma.

THE REAL GERMAN WAR PLAN

Using Schlieffen's 1898 *Denkschrift*, Beseler's 1900 *Operationsstudie*, the *Generalstabsreisen West* between 1902 and 1908, and the 1905 *Kriegsspiel* we can reconstruct the manner in which both Schlieffen and the younger Moltke expected to fight the battle in the west. Both officers were acutely conscious that the German army would be outnumbered on both the east and west fronts. The intent of the *Westaufmarsch* was therefore to win the first battles and not to concoct a grand plan for a colossal Cannae-type battle of annihilation. Every German Chief of Staff also maintained that the French had the positive political goal, would have the initiative, and would therefore begin the war by attacking, probably into Lorraine. This might very well be the French main attack. Depending on the political circumstances, the French could also launch a supporting attack, or the main attack, north of Metz into the Ardennes. The first battle would therefore most likely be fought in Lorraine or in the Ardennes. The German intent was to defeat this attack as decisively as possible.

It seems clear that Schlieffen was willing to allow the French to advance well into Lorraine and Belgium. He then planned to make massive use of German rail mobility to conduct surprise counterattacks. He considered two techniques for accomplishing this. Either he would retain a large number of corps in their mobilization stations or he would transfer forces from one German wing to another. Moltke was unwilling to take the risks Schlieffen ran by allowing the French to advance so far. In the event he lacked Schlieffen's confidence that he could control either complex deployment plans (as evidenced by his decision to use just one *Aufmarschplan*) or a Schlieffen-style mobile battle. Moltke, as well as the Army commanders and Chiefs of Staff, wanted to fight much safer, set-piece linear battles.

The initial frontier battles would not end the war. If the German army won—and the Germans expected to be able to defeat the French army on the open field—then the Germans had two choices. If the Russians had penetrated deeply into East Prussia or near the borders of Posen and Silesia, then the largest possible reinforcements would be sent east for a surprise counterattack. If Prussia was secure the most likely course of action was that the Germans would continue the attack in the west. The right wing would have to cross the Meuse and swing behind the French fortress line while the German left wing fixed the French forces in place. The French field army would be forced to fight again, this time to defend the fortress line. Having won this battle, the German army would break the French fortress line by attacking it from the front and rear. This would link up the two halves of the German army. The French remnants would fall back to the plateau of Langres or the Loire. It was reasonable to expect that this campaign would be completed in about a month. The first campaign would, however, be followed by a second campaign into the interior of France.

It is therefore clear that at no time, under either Schlieffen or the younger Moltke, did the German army plan to swing the right wing to the west of Paris. The German left wing was never weak, rather it was always very strong—indeed, the left wing, not the right, might well conduct the decisive battle. The war in the west would begin with a French, not a German attack. The first campaign in the west would end with the elimination of the French fortress line, not the total annihilation of the French army. It would involve several great conventional battles, not one battle of encirclement. If the Germans did win a decisive victory, it would be the result of a counter-offensive in Lorraine or Belgium, not through an invasion of France. There was no intent to destroy the French army in one immense Cannae-battle. There never was a Schlieffen plan.

There was, however, a Schlieffen doctrine, and its characteristics are clear from Schlieffen's last exercises. The way Germany could fight outnumbered and win was to use mobility and surprise to create battles of annihilation. Mobility meant rail mobility, which meant also that the decisive battles would be fought near the German railheads, as counteroffensives against attacking French and Russian forces. Rail mobility must be used for two purposes: to attain surprise and to position large bodies of German troops where they could attack the enemy lines of retreat. Detraining would best be screened by friendly fortresses, such as Metz, Strasbourg, Thorn, or the Vistula forts. Once the German forces detrained they had to continue to be operationally and tactically mobile, for fluid battles would exploit superior German individual and unit training and officer initiative. The purpose of German counteroffensives had to be the destruction of entire enemy corps with their cadres: Germany would lose a war of attrition.

Schlieffen's doctrine, along the lines of the great 1905 *Kriegsspiel*, was not applied in the west. In fact, it can be said that Schlieffen had only one true disciple, and that was Ludendorff. Ludendorff's successes in the east in 1914 were due to the fact that all he needed to do was execute Schlieffen's war games in a live-fire environment.

The concept for the battle of Tannenberg was drawn directly from the 1894 *Generalstabsreise Ost*. The subsequent battle of the Masurian Lakes was a copy of the 1888 *Generalstabsreise Ost*, Schlieffen's first, and the 1901 *Strategische Aufgabe*. By the time Ludendorff concluded this offensive the Austrians were collapsing. Ludendorff left an absolute minimum of forces in East Prussia, then shifted the 9th Army to southern Poland—exactly as Schlieffen had planned to do in his 1894 *Aufmarsch*. The Russian attack was halted in the nick of time.

Ludendorff now went his master one better. He was convinced that his success in southern Poland would be fleeting. Sooner or later the Russian hordes would push his army back toward Posen and Silesia. Therefore, long-term preparations were made for the withdrawing German forces to conduct rail demolitions to delay the Russian advance.

The stage was now set for the *pièce de résistance*. There was no prospect of the heavily outnumbered German forces being able to conduct a static defensive against the Russian masses. Ludendorff therefore sought salvation in operational mobility. While the Russians advanced by foot through Poland, Ludendorff moved the 9th Army by rail from Silesia and offloaded it to the south of Thorn. In early November, when the Russians had reached the German border, Ludendorff struck to the south, towards Lodz, splitting the Russian 1st and 2nd Armies, and rolling up the 2nd Army's right flank. It was an operation strikingly similar in concept to Schlieffen's 1897 and 1903 *Generalstabsreisen Ost*. Falkenhayn had it in his power to reinforce this offensive with 16 newly raised divisions which were at their mobilization stations in Germany. Had he done so, he would have created the classic Schlieffenesque battle in the east. The Russian 2nd and 5th Armies could hardly have escaped, because the Germans would have been directly across their lines of retreat. The destruction of some six Russian corps would have dwarfed even Tannenberg and had a fundamental effect on the course of the war.

Instead, Falkenhayn chose to commit his new divisions into futile frontal attacks in Flanders, such as the infamous battle at Langemarck. In the east, the German troops were simply not strong enough to complete the encirclement and the Russian 2nd and 5th Armies escaped. This was the last real chance that any army had in the war to conduct a *Vernichtungsschlacht*. That Falkenhayn should have chosen such a course of action was no accident. Falkenhayn was one of those officers Schlieffen had warned about who believed in frontal attacks and attrition.

Ludendorff had put on a virtuoso display of the power of Schlieffen's doctrine. He continually shifted forces back and forth along the entire length of the German eastern border, hammering a different Russian army with every move. If he only fought one *Vernichtungsschlacht*, at Tannenberg, he nevertheless dealt the Russian armies terrific damage and stopped the Russian steamroller in its tracks. This has not been adequately appreciated. Historians have emphasized the Russian army's 1917 mutinies as though everything preceding it were a prelude to Russian collapse. In fact, the Russian army in August 1914 was strong, numerous, and full of fight. The French and British had expected that the Russian attack would be unstoppable and that this insured that the Entente would win the war in 1914. Ludendorff's campaign in the east in 1914 derailed the entire Entente war plan. The French and British were put in a perilous position. Owing to Ludendorff's victories the French received nothing like the degree of help from the Russians that they had expected. Ludendorff's economy of force operations had allowed Falkenhayn to retain the mass of the German army in the west. France and Britain would nearly bleed to death attempting to break the German fortifications in the west: in the end their armies would be saved only by American intervention.

EPILOG

In addition to Ludendorff, Schlieffen had one other great disciple: Erich von Manstein. Manstein's plan for the attack in France in 1940 was obviously inspired by exercises such as the 1903 *Generalstabsreise Ost*, in which an advancing enemy is fixed by a diversionary frontal attack and then struck in the flank by a surprise counteroffensive. All the elements of Schlieffen's doctrine were clearly present, including a careful appreciation of the enemy's most likely course of action, the use of surprise, and the willingness to take great risks. His goal was the same as Schlieffen's—to attack the enemy's line of retreat in order to fight a battle of annihilation, a *Vernichtungsschlacht*. Manstein's contribution was to marry Schlieffen's doctrine of mobile warfare at the operational level to the possibilities provided by the new Panzer divisions. He was practically the only one to do so. The French and British, for example, tried to use their tanks to supplement positional trench warfare.

Manstein's counterattack in the Ukraine in late February and early March 1943 displayed even more strongly the influence of Schlieffen's doctrine. The German situation in southern Russia at this time was catastrophic. The 6th Army had surrendered at Stalingrad. The Russian offensive had captured Kharkov and threatened to cut off Army Group A in the Kuban peninsula and Crimea. 'A flood of Russian tank, cavalry, and motorized troops was cresting southward. By 20 February Russian spearheads were within twenty miles of Dnepropetrovsk and had cut the railroad into Stalino, severing Manstein's supply lines.'[25] Manstein's reaction was pure Schlieffen. Rather than hold a static defensive position to try to stop the Russian attack frontally, Manstein counterattacked at operational depth against the Russian flank and rear, in the process destroying the Russian forces in detail. Although heavily outnumbered, Manstein rescued the German southern front and crushed the Russian offensive. He had displayed a willingness to run risks, exploit mobility, and maximize surprise in order to achieve a decisive victory which would have made Schlieffen proud.

TRUTH AND CONSEQUENCES

The Schlieffen plan is one of the principal pieces of evidence for German war guilt. Schlieffen has been cursed as the personification of German militarism and the Schlieffen plan as its embodiment. The great arrows of the Schlieffen plan slashing across the map of France are interpreted as graphic representations of German aggression.

The case against German militarism will now have to be proven without the support of the Schlieffen plan, and without the Schlieffen plan the political–military situation in 1914 looks very different. The problem facing Schlieffen and Moltke was how win the first battles while fighting outnumbered, not win the war at one stroke with an enormous

---

[25] V. J. Esposito (ed), *The West Point Atlas of American Wars* 1900–1953 (New York, 1959), ii, Map 30.

battle of annihilation. There are no longer any great arrows sweeping to the west of Paris. Far from having an aggressive war plan in 1914, the German armies initially stood on the defensive in East Prussia as well as in Lorraine. Schlieffen's intent was not to attack deeply into France, but to compensate for his inferior numbers by counterattacking, using rail mobility as a force multiplier. This meant that Schlieffen preferred to fight as close to the German railheads as possible. Moltke was implementing Schlieffen's doctrine to the best of his limited ability.

Ritter's Schlieffen plan portrayed Schlieffen as a megalomaniac who promised the swift annihilation of the entire French army. In fact, Schlieffen was too much a realist to promise quick, total victory. For every one of Schlieffen's exercises that ends in the destruction of the French army there is another in which the French win, or are merely pushed back to their fortress line. The Germans lose or draw as many battles in the east as they win. Schlieffen was also painfully aware that the German army could produce another General Steinmetz—or several—who could put everything at risk. Fighting outnumbered is no fun. In the last analysis, Schlieffen saw that the only reasonably certain way out of the German strategic dilemma was to utilize all of Germany's manpower.

At the conclusion of deployment in early August 1914 the main bodies of both the French and German armies were lined up along those countries' borders with Belgium. The common interpretation of the two war plans is that the French deployed in this manner to defend against a German attack through Belgium. In fact, the French intent was to make their own main attack into the Ardennes. The French also conducted the initial serious attack in the west in Alsace and Lorraine, while the Russians attacked into Prussia. On both fronts, the German army was on the defensive and conducted counterattacks.

The Germans used everyone in the front line: reserve corps, ersatz units, Landwehr, Landsturm, especially in the east. Although the German forces were still usually heavily outnumbered, the German counterattack in Lorraine was successful and the Germans won all the encounter battles in Belgium. This was not because of the genius of the 'Schlieffen plan' but because of German superiority at the tactical level. The subsequent German advance into the Champagne was not intended to annihilate the French army according to some master plan, but was an attempt to surround Verdun and break the French fortress line. Ludendorff fought the campaign in the east from August to December 1914 according to Schlieffen's principles, defending Germany's eastern border with strategic and operational mobility, not by lurching deeply into Poland as the elder Moltke would have done.

The entire case for German military aggression is therefore reduced to the attack on Liège. The Germans attached Liège based on their evaluation of the secret Anglo-French military agreement. While the Entente found this to be of great propaganda value, no historian maintains that it was a major cause of the war. The arguments that the attack on Liège reduced the opportunity for negotiations are disingenuous.

It has also been contended, by Craig and Kitchen amongst others, that Schlieffen wrote the 1905 *Denkschrift* for a preventive war against France. This old canard can finally be laid to rest. The Schlieffen plan was never a German war plan, and Schlieffen's exercises, particularly the great November–December 1905 *Kriegsspiel*, prove that Schlieffen intended to fight a defensive war.

Mobilization did mean war—for the French and Russians as well as the Germans—and the Russians mobilized first. The French and Russians had agreed to launch simultaneous offensives no later than the 15th day of mobilization. Failure to attack would have ruptured the Russo-French alliance, with catastrophic consequences. There is every reason to believe that the civilian leadership of all three Entente Powers, who were all intimately involved with military planning, understood this fully.

Faced with professional extinction, the General Staff decided to explain its failure in 1914 by maintaining that it had an infallible plan, which was spoiled by the actions of three dead officers, Moltke, Hentsch, and Bülow. After the Second World War historians took this explanation at face value, but used its inconsistencies to demonstrate the errors and evils of German militarism. The end result was an enormous and shaky house of cards, a victory of expediency and political theory over military analysis. This study has been an attempt to put the history of German war planning back on a firm professional military and historical foundation.

Bibliography

PRIMARY SOURCES

BAYERISCHES HAUPTSTAATSARCHIV—KRIEGSARCHIV, MUNICH

Kriegsministerium

1829/1 Bayerischer Militärbevollmächtigter.

3165: 1. Große Generalstabsreise 1903 [character sketches of participants].

4581: Umbau von Festungen, 12. März 1887; Ergänzung und Ausgestaltung der Festungen, 26. April 1887; Zur Sicherung der Festen gegen die Splitterwirkung schwerer Mörsergranaten C/83, 20. Mai 1887.

4605/2: Die Entwicklung des deutschen Festungssystems seit 1870, Geheim! n.d. [last update 1914?].

4669: Angriffsverfahren gegen Sperrforts, 25.2.1880–9.10.1911.

Generalstab

175: Sperrfort bei Manonviller, Dezember 1908.

177: Sperrfort Pont St. Vincent, März 1909.

178: Die Befestigungen bei Nancy einschl. Fort de Frouard nebst Aussenwerken, April 1909.

179: Festung Toul, 1911.

207: Veränderungen im Heerwesen Rußlands im Jahre 1905; 1906.

207: Jahresbericht Rußland 1906, 1907.

207: Veränderungen im Heerwesen Rußlands 1908.

208: Jahresbericht Rußland, 1909, 1910

208: Die Entwicklung der russischen schweren Artillerie seit dem russisch–japanischen Krieg, März 1909.

208: Veränderungen im Heerwesen Rußlands 1909, 1910, 1911.

209: Mitteilung über russische Taktik.

209: Veränderungen im Heerwesen Rußlands 1912.

209: Veränderungen im Heerwesen Rußlands 1912, Ergänzung 1. Juli 1914.

213: Narew-Linie 1909 (updated 1912).

925: Nachrichten über die militärische Lage in Frankreich: Politische Spannung 1912/1913.

925: Nachrichten über die militärische Lage in Rußland: Politische Spannung 1912/1913.

1231: Korps Generalstabsreisen, Zusammenstellung 1882–1893, Generalstabsreisen 1873, 1885, 1887, 1890, 1891, 1893, 1899, 1900, 1902, 1904, 1906, 1907, 1910, 1911, 1914.

1231: Festungsgeneralstabsreisen 1897, 1897–1899.

1231: Intendanturreise 1902.

1233: Uebungs-Reise [Generalstabsreise] 1885.
1234: 1. Große Generalstabsreise 1902.
1235: 2. Große Generalstabsreise 1902.
1236: 2. Große Generalstabsreise 1903.
1237: Schlußbesprechung [Kriegsspiel November–Dezember] 1905.
1238: Große Generalstabsreise 1906.
1239: Festungsreise Oberrhein 1903.
1240: Festungsreise Weichselbefestigungen 1904.
1241: Festungsreise Straßburg 1905
1242: Festungsreise Köln 1906.
1243: Festungsreise Mainz 1907.
1244: Festungsreise Königsberg 1908.
1245: Festungsreise Metz 1909.
1246: Festungsreise Kaiser Wilhelm II 1910.
1247: Festungsreise Marienburg 1911.
1248: Festungsreise Oberrheinbefestigungen 1912.
1249: Festungsreise Köln 1913.
1289: Festungskriegsspiel über die Position de Nancy 1905.
1293: Studie eines Durchbruches durch die Maas-Linie Toul–Verdun, K. b. Generalstab November/Dezember 1906.

Armeeoberkommando 6 (AOK 6)

Bund 1: Kriegstagebuch 2.8.14–14.3.1915.
Bund 1 Nr. 10: Die Operationen der 7. Armee vom 3.8. bis 16.9.1914.
Bund 1 Nr. 10: Auszug aus dem Kriegstagebuch des AOK 7 ab 1. August 1914.
Bund 369 Nr. 45: Aufmarschanweisungen für Oberkommando der 6. Armee 1914/1915
Bund 925: Die Kriegsbereitschaft Rußlands Februar 1914

III. bayerisches Armeekorps

Bund 9/Generalstab 180: Mittlere Maas-Forts, April 1909.
Bund 9: Aufmarschanweisung, 3. August 1914.
Bund 9: Bemerkungen zum Kaisermanöver 1911, 7. Januar 1913 [Moltke's thoughts on operations].
Bund 10: Direktive AOK 6, 16 August 1914.

Nachlaß 145 Krafft von Dellmensingen

Eine Beurteilung der Lage verfaßt in München 2–5.8.1914.
Aufmarschanweisungen 6. Armee.
Aufmarschanweisungen 7. Armee.
Kurzer Überblick über die Vorgänge beim Oberkommando der 6. Armee im August 1914 bis zur Schlacht in Lothringen am 20.8.1914.

Altregister Abteilung III

Bund 5: Akt V C 3b [Wenninger Controversy] 5246/32, 5471/32, 4610/33, 4620/33.

BUNDESARCHIV-MILITÄRARCHIV, FREIBURG IM BREISGAU

PH 3

60: 1917 General Order exonerating Hentsch
256: Aufmarsch und operativen Absichten der Franzosen. (Last updated April
  1914. AOK 4 copy.)
284: 5th Army *Aufmarschanweisungen* (English translation).
445: Die militärpolitische Lage 21.12.12.
529: Die militärpolitische Lage Deutschlands Ende November 1911.
628: Aufmarsch und operative Absichten der Franzosen.
659: 1. Große Generalstabsreise 1904.
661: 2. Große Generalstabsreise 1904.
646: Kriegsspiel November–Dezember 1905.
663: Große Generalstabsreise 1906.
664: Große Generalstabsreise 1908.

Personalakten

8/618 Wilhelm Dieckmann

Manuskripten (MSg)

131/7: Reymann, Martin. Die Entstehung des Reichsarchivs und die
  Bearbeitung des amtlichen Kriegswerkes 1914–1918.

W/10 [Reichsarchiv Working Papers]

50220: Dieckmann, Wilhelm, Der Schlieffenplan.
50221: Operationen gegen Rußland. Vortragsnotizen Mai 1905.
50222: Regenauer, Materialsammlung zur Darstellung der operativen
  Verhandlungen des Grafen Schlieffen mit Österreich–Ungarn (Wien, 8.
  Jänner 1939) [from Austrian sources].
50233: Schäfer, Der Kriegsplan für den Zweifrontenkrieg bearbeitet von
  Archivrat von Schäfer unter Benutzung der Vorarbeiten des Archivrats
  Foerster (23.1.1924).
50267: Greiner, Welche Nachrichten besaß der deutsche Generalstab über
  Mobilmachung und Aufmarsch des französischen Heeres in den Jahren
  1885–1914?
50589: Angriffsverfahren gegen die Sperrforts der mittleren Maas, last updated
  31 July 1914.
51039: Tappen's letters to Reichsarchiv concerning Battle of Marne.
51062: Moritz Freiherr von Lyckner diary.
51062: Statements concerning Hentsch by König, Köppen, Schübert, and Dr.
  Ramstedt.
51062: Hentsch's statement 2 May 1917.
51063: Moltke letter to Freytag-Loringhoven 26 June 1915.
51063: Letter Moltke to Rupprecht 10 September 1914.
51063: Inventory of after-action reports of the battle of the Marne.
51063: Oldershausen's letter to Reichsarchiv concerning French troop movements 5–6 September 1914.

51063: Plessen Diary.

51063: Statements about Marne from Generalleutnant Scheuch (Chief of Staff of War Ministry), Landrat a. D. Marx (Hentsch's driver); Major Schwantes (Admin officer in operations section); and General von Stein (Oberquartiermeister) and Hauptmann Mewes (officer in operations section).

Nachlässe

Schlieffen N43

133: Kriegsspiel November–Dezember 1905.

137: 'Schlieffen plan' handwritten notes.

138: 'Schlieffen plan' *Denkschrift.*

140: 1912 Denkschrift.

141K: 'Schlieffen plan' maps

143: Inventories.

Tappen N54

Tagebuch

Groener N137

20: excerpts from 1896 Generalstabsreise, 1898 Operationsstudie, Generalstabsreisen in 1898, 1900, both Generalstabsreisen in 1903 and 1904 and the 1905 Kriegsspiel.

20: Kriegsspiel 1897.

20: Schlußaufgabe 1907.

40: Bemerkungen zu der Arbeit von Herrn Universitätsprofessor Dr. Bredt [Groener writes that the Schlieffen plan was the actual war plan].

41: Letter to Mertz, October 1919.

41: Streit um die Lothringer Schlacht.

41: Letter to Reichsarchiv concerning war planning, 11 November 1923.

41. Groener contends the German Army had no supply problems on the Marne.

111: Schlußaufgabe 1907.

Foerster N121

35: Moltke's tactics 1905.

35: Order of Battle for Aufmarsch I 1905/06 and Aufmarsch I and II 1906/07.

35: Schlieffen's Efficiency Reports.

SÄCHSISCHES HAUPTSTAATSARCHIV—DRESDEN

KA (P)

623: Mitteilung über russische Taktik 22. März 1913.

1422: Sächsische Militärbevollmächtigter.

4517: Große Generalstabsreise 1900 [note from Sächsische Militärbevollmächtigter].

9195 Schlußaufgabe 1907.

9195. 2. Große Generalstabsreise 1902.

9195: Veränderungen im Heerwesen Rußlands 1913.

9195. Veränderungen im Heerwesen Frankreichs 1913.
9195: Dreijährigen Dienstzeit in Frankreich.
9195: 1. Große Generalstabsreise 1903 [*Schlußbesprechung* only—no maps]
9195: Schlußaufgabe 1913.
9195: Die Kriegsbereitschaft Rußlands Februar 1914.

STAATLICHES ARCHIV BADEN-WÜRTTEMBERGS—HAUPTSTAATSARCHIV
STUTTGART

M33/1 (XIII Armeekorps)
Bund 1: Die Kriegsbereitschaft Rußlands, Februar 1914.
Bund 1: Schlußaufgabe 1910.
Bund 1: Schlußaufgabe 1911.
Bund 35: Schlußaufgabe 1907.
Bund 35: Schlußaufgabe 1908.
Bund 35: Schlußaufgabe 1909.

STAATLICHES ARCHIV BADEN-WÜRTTEMBERGS—GENERALLANDESARCHIV
KARLSRUHE

Gla 456
201: 6th Army Operations Orders 13 August, 14 August, 29 August, 1 September,
    2 September 1914.
553: OHL Intelligence Summaries #2 (28 July 1914) through #12 (7 August 1914).
659: OHL Intelligence Summaries # 13 (8 August 1914) to #17 (12 August 1914),
    #19 (14 August 1914), #20 (18 August 1914) to #32 (31 August 1914), #34 (2
    September 1914) to #39 (10 September 1914).
659: OHL Operations Orders 27 August 1914, 5 September 1914.

UNITED STATES NATIONAL ARCHIVES

Papers of Wilhelm Groener N137
20: Short sections from Schlußbesprechungen of the Generalstabsreisen in
    1896, 1st 1898, 1900, 1st and 2nd 1903, 1st and 2nd 1904, Operationsstudie
    1898, Kriegsspiel November–Dezember 1905.
20: Kriegsspiel 1897.
20: Schlußaufgabe 1907.

OFFICIAL HISTORIES

BAYERISCHES KRIEGSARCHIV, *Die Bayern im großen Kriege 1914–1918* (Munich, 1923).
—— *Die Schlacht in Lothringen und in den Vogesen 1914* (2 vols., Munich, 1927–29).
Collected Diplomatic Documents Relating to the Outbreak of the European War [British
    Red Book] (London, 1915).
GENERALSTAB DES HEERES (ed.), *Die großen Generalstabsreisen—Ost—aus den Jahren
    1891–1905* (Berlin, 1938).

GENERALSTAB DES HEERES, *Die taktisch-strategische Aufgaben aus den Jahren 1891–1905* (Berlin, 1937).

Die Große Politik der Europäischen Kabinette. 1. Band: Der Frankfurter Friede und seine Nachwirkungen 1871–1877 (Berlin, 1926).

—— *3. Band: Das Bismarck'sche Bündnissystem* (Berlin, 1927).

—— *6. Band: Kriegsgefahr in Ost und West. Ausklang der Bismarckzeit* (Berlin, 1927).

—— *7. Band, 1. Der Russische Draht* (Berlin, 1927).

GROSSER GENERALSTAB, *Campaign of Germany in 1866* (English translation, London, 1872).

—— *Deutsch–Französische Krieg 1870/71* (Berlin, 1874–81). (8 vols).

—— *Moltkes Militärische Werke I Militärische Korrespondenz 2. Theil Aus den Dienstschriften des Krieges 1866* (Berlin, 1896).

—— *Moltke's Militärische Werke I Militärische Korrespondenz 3. Theil Aus den Dienstschriften des Krieges 1870* (Berlin, 1896).

—— *Moltkes Militärische Werke, I Militärische Korrespondenz 4. Theil, Aus den Dienstschriften des Jahres 1859* (Berlin, 1902).

—— *Moltkes Militärische Werke II Die Thätigkeit als Chef des Generalstabes der Armee im Frieden 1. Theil Taktische Aufgaben aus den Jahren 1858 bis 1882* (Berlin, 1892).

—— *Moltkes Militärische Werke II Die Thätigkeit als Chef des Generalstabes der Armee im Frieden 2. Theil Taktisch-strategische Aufsätze* (Berlin, 1900).

—— *Moltkes Militärische Werke II Die Thätigkeit als Chef des Generalstabes der Armee im Frieden 3. Teil Generalstabsreisen* (Berlin, 1906).

—— *Moltke in der Vorbereitung und Durchführung der Operationen.* (Kriegsgeschichtliche Einzelschriften Nr. 36 Zur Enthüllung des Moltke-Denkmals) (Berlin 1905).

MINISTÈRE DE LA GUERRE, *Les Armées francaises dans la Grande Guerre, Tome Premier, Premier Volume* (Paris, 1923).

REICHSARCHIV, *Das deutsche Feldeisenbahnwesen. 1. Die Eisenbahnen zu Kriegsbeginn* (Berlin, 1928)

—— *H. von Moltke. Ausgewählte Werke. Dritter Band. Feldherr und Staatsmann*, ed. F. von Schmerfeld (Berlin, 1925).

—— *Kriegsrüstung und Kriegswirtschaft* (Berlin, 1930).

—— *Kriegsrüstung und Kriegswirtschaft. Anlagen zum ersten Band* (Berlin, 1930).

—— *Der Weltkrieg, Band I, Die Grenzschlachten im Westen* (Berlin, 1925).

—— *Der Weltkrieg, Band II, Die Befreiung Ostpreussens* (Berlin, 1925).

—— *Der Weltkrieg, Band III, Der Marne-Feldzug. Von der Sambre bis zur Marne* (Berlin, 1926).

—— *Der Weltkrieg, Band IV, Der Marne-Feldzug. Die Schlacht* (Berlin, 1926).

SECONDARY SOURCES

ALBERTINI, LUIGI, *The Origins of the War of 1914* (3 vols., Oxford, 1952–7).

ANON., 'Militärische Rundschau', *VTfHk* 11(3) (1914) 574–83.

—— (Nr. 95), 'Zur Feldzugseröffnung im Westen im August 1914', *MW* 46 (1925), 1440–6.

—— (einem deutschen Offizier), *Die Befestigung und Vertheidigung der deutsch–russischen Grenze. Dem deutschen Volke dargestellt* (4th edn., Berlin, 1901).

—— 'Schlieffenschule', *MW* 44 (1925),1370–3.

ASCOLI, DAVID, *A Day of Battle. Mars-la-Tour 16 August 1870* (London, 1987).

ASSOCIATION VAUBAN, *Actes du Colloque Séré de Rivières* (Paris, 1999).

BAARE, HAUPTMANN, 'Taktische Fragen aus den französischen Armeemänover 1913', *VTfHk* 9(3) (1914), 390–5.

—— 'Neue taktische Anschauungen im französischen Heere', *VTfhK* 9(5) (1914), 396–418.

BAUMGARTEN-CRUSIUS, A., *Die Marneschlacht 1914 insbesondere auf der Front der deutschen dritten Armee* (Leipzig, 1919).

BECK, LUDWIG, 'West oder Ost-Offensive 1914?', in Hans Speidel (ed.), *Ludwig Beck, Studien* (Stuttgart, 1955), 139–89.

BERGHAHN, V. R., *Germany and the Approach of War* (2nd edn., London, 1993).

BERNHARDI, FRIEDRICH VON, 'Das Studium der Fridericianischen Kriege in seiner Bedeutung für die moderne Kriegskunst', *MW* 4 (1892), 165–90.

—— *Vom Heutigen Kriege* (2 vols., Berlin, 1912).

—— 'Über Millionenheere', *DR* 37 (Februar 1912), 207–13.

—— *Deutschlands Heldenkampf* (Munich, 1922).

BERNHARDT, HARRI, *Geschichte der Stadt, Festung und Garnison Köln* (Cologne and Frankfurt am Main, 1959).

BIGGE, W., *Feldmarschall Graf Moltke* (Munich, 1901).

BISKUP, KRZYSTOF, 'Russische Festungsanlagen in Polen 1815–1914', in Volker Schmidchen (ed.), *Sicherheit und Bedrohung—Schutz und Enge. Gesellschaftliche Entwicklung von Festungsstäden* (=*SF Band 6*) (Wesel, 1986), 142–8.

BOETTICHER, GENERALMAJOR FRIEDRICH VON, 'Der Lehrmeister des neuzeitlichen Krieges' in *Generalleutnant* von Cochenhausen (ed.), *Von Scharnhorst zu Schlieffen 1806–1906*, (Berlin, 1933), 249–16.

—— *Schlieffen* (Göttingen, Berlin, and Frankfurt, 1957).

BOUR, BERNHARD, 'Die Feste Kaiser Wilhelm II von 1893 bis heute', in Volker Schmidchen (ed.), *Festungsforschung als kommunale Aufgabe* (=*SF Band 5*) (Wesel, 1986), 151–66.

BRAMSCH, HAUPTMANN, 'Die französische Armee nach Durchführung der dreijährigen Dienstzeit', *VTfHk* 11 (2) (1914), 222–35.

BREDT, JOH. VIKTOR, *Die belgische Neutralität und der Schlieffensche Feldzugsplan* (Berlin, 1929).

BUCHFINK, ERNST, 'Moltke und Schlieffen', *HZ* 158 (1938), 308–22.

BUCHOLZ, ARDEN, *Hans Delbrück and the German Military Establishment* (Iowa City, 1985).

—— *Moltke, Schlieffen and Prussian War Planning* (New York, 1991).

BÜLOW, WILHELM, *Mein Bericht zur Marneschlacht* (Berlin, 1919).

CARRIAS, EUGÈNE, *La Pensée militaire française* (Sceaux, 1960).

CHURCHILL, WINSTON, *The World Crisis: The Eastern Front* (London, 1931).

—— *The World Crisis 1911–1918* (1938 abridged edn., New York, 1993).

COLLINS, D., 'The Franco-Russian Alliance and Russian Railways 1891–1914' *HJ* 16 (1973), 777–88.

CONTAMINE, HENRI, *La Revanche 1871–1914* (1957).

CRAIG, GORDON, *The Politics of the Prussian Army* (2nd rev. edn., Oxford, 1964).

—— *Germany 1866–1945* (Oxford, 1978).

DELBRÜCK, HANS, *Die Geschichte der Kriegskunst im Rahmen der politischen Geschichte* (4 vols., Berlin, 1900–20).

—— *Krieg und Politik 1914–16* (Berlin, 1918).

—— *Krieg und Politik II. Teil 1917* (Berlin, 1919).

—— *Krieg und Politik III. Teil 1918* (Berlin, 1919).

—— 'War es zu vermeiden?', *PJ* 175 (Januar bis März 1919), 127–31.

—— 'Der zu erwartende Frieden', *PJ* 175 (Januar bis März 1919), 146–50.

—— 'Die deutsche Kriegserklärung 1914 und die Einmarsch in Belgien', *PJ* 175 (Januar bis März 1919), 271–80.

—— 'Waffenstillstand und Friede', *PJ* 175 (Januar bis März 1919), 422–8.

—— 'Schuldbekenntnisse', ibid., *PJ* 176 (April bis Juni 1919), 141–52.

—— 'Die Friedensbedingungen', *PJ* 176 (April bis Juni 1919), 321–6, 472–8.

—— 'Die Verantwortungs-Frage', *PJ* 176 (April bis Juni 1919), 479–86.

—— 'Schuld und Schicksal', ibid, *PJ* 177 (Juli bis September 1919), 136–41.

—— 'Entehrungsfrieden', *PJ* 177 (Juli bis September 1919), 142–9.

—— 'War unsere Niederlage unabwendbar?', *PJ* 177 (Juli bis September 1919), 301–11.

—— 'Enthullüngen', *PJ* 177 (Juli bis September 1919), 459–71.

—— 'Erich Ludendorff. Meine Kriegserinnerungen 1914–18', *PJ* 178 (Oktober bis Dezember 1919), 83–101.

—— 'Die Tirpitz-Erinnerungen', *PJ* 178 (Oktober bis Dezember 1919), 309–25.

—— 'Abschied', *PJ* 178 (Oktober bis Dezember 1919), 369–72.

—— 'Selbstanzeige. Krieg und Politik III. Teil 1918', *PJ* 178 (Oktober bis Dezember 1919), 481–3.

—— 'Der parlamentarische Untersuchungsausschuß', *PJ* 178 (Oktober bis Dezember 1919), 542–50.

—— 'Auswärtiges', *PJ* 178 (Oktober bis Dezember 1919), 550–2.

—— 'Die deutschen Dokumente zum Kriegsausbruch / Karl Kautsky, Wie den Weltkrieg Entstand', *PJ* 179 (Januar bis März 1920), 71–100.

—— 'Falkenhayn und Ludendorff', *PJ* 180 (April bis Juni 1920), 249–81.

—— 'Geschichte', *PJ* 180 (April bis Juni 1920), 290–2.

—— 'Die strategische Grundfrage des Weltkrieges', *PJ* 183 (Januar bis März 1921), 289–308.

—— *Ludendorffs Selbstportrait* (Berlin, 1922).

—— 'Kriegsschulddiskussion mit Ausländern', *KSF* 1. (1923), 22–5.

—— 'Offener Brief an Herrn Hjalmar Brantling 12 August 1924', *KSF* 2 (1924), 362–4.

DEMETER, KARL, *Das Reichsarchiv: Tatsachen und Personen* (Frankfurt am Main, 1969).

DOBROROLSKI, SERGEI KONSTANTIN, *Die Mobilmachung der russischen Armee 1914* (Berlin, 1922).

DONAT, F. M. VON, *Die Befestigung und Vertheidigung der deutsch–französischen Grenze* (1st edn., Berlin, 1879; 4th edn., Berlin, 1894).

DUPUY, T. N., *A Genius for War: The German Army and General Staff 1807–1945* (Englewood Hills, NJ, 1977).

EARLE, EDWARD MEADE (ed.), *Makers of Modern Strategy: Military Thought from Machiavelli to Hitler* (Princeton, NJ, 1943).

ECHEVARRIA, ANTULIO J. II, 'General Staff Historian. Hugo Freiherr von Freitag-Loringhoven and the Dialectics of German Military Thought', *JMH* 60 (3) (July 1996), 471–94.

—— *After Clausewitz: German Military Thinkers Before the Great War* (Lawrence, Ks, 2000).

EGGELING, BERNHARD, *Die russische Mobilmachung und der Kriegsausbruch* (Oldenbourg and Berlin, 1919).

EINEM, GENERALOBERST VON, *Erinnerung eines Soldaten* (Leipzig, 1933).

ELLISON, HERBERT J., 'Economic Modernization in Imperial Russia: Purposes and Achievements', *JEH* 25 (4) (December 1965), 523–40.

ELZE, WALTER, *Graf Schlieffen* (Breslau, 1928).

—— *Tannenberg: Das deutsche Heer vor 1914* (Breslau, 1928).

—— *Die strategische Aufbau des Weltkrieges 1914–1918* (Breslau 1933).

ESPOSITO, VINCENT J., *A Concise History of World War I* (New York, 1964).

—— (ed.), *The West Point Atlas of American Wars 1900–1953* (2 vols., New York, 1959).

FALKENHAUSEN, GENERAL DER INFANTERIE FREIHERR VON, *Der große Krieg der Jetztzeit* (Berlin, 1909).

FALLS, CYRIL, *A Hundred Years of War 1850–1950* (New York, 1953).

FARRAR, L. L., *The Short War Illusion* (Santa Barbara, 1973).

FERGUSON, NIALL, *The Pity of War* (New York, 1999).

FISCHER, EUGEN, 'Der Sinn der russisch–französischen Militärkonventionen', *PJ* 192 (April bis Juni 1923), 65–98.

FISCHER, FRITZ, *Griff nach der Weltmacht* (Düsseldorf, 1967).

—— *Krieg der Illusionen* (Düsseldorf, 1970).

FISCHER, GÜNTHER, *Die Festung Mainz 1866–1921* (Düsseldorf, 1970).

FISCHER, G., and BOUR, B., *Die Feste Kaiser Wilhelm II / La Position de Mutzig 1893–1918* (Mutzig, 1980).

FERRON, 'Les chemins de fer allemandes et les chemins de fer français au point de vue de la concentration des armees', *JSM* (Mai 1879), 5–16; (Juillet 1879), 357–80.

—— 'Etude strategique sur la Frontière du Nord-Est', *JSM* (Janvier 1880), 49–68.

FOERSTER, FR. W., 'Zur Frage der deutschen Schuld am Weltkriege', *PJ* 178 (Oktober bis Dezember 1919), 117–34.

FÖRSTER, STIG, *Der doppelte Militärismus. Die deutsche Heeresrüstungspolitik zwischen Status-Quo-Sicherung und Aggression 1890–1913* (Stuttgart, 1985).

—— (ed.), *Moltke. Vom Kabinettskrieg zum Volkskrieg* (Bonn and Berlin, 1992).

—— 'Der deutsche Generalstab und die Illusion des kurzen Krieges, 1871–1914. Kritik eines Mythos', *MM* 54 (1995), 61–95.

FOERSTER, WOLFGANG, *Prinz Friedrich Karl von Preußen. Denkwürdigkeiten aus seinem Leben* (2 vols., Berlin, 1910).

—— *Graf Schlieffen und der Weltkrieg* (1st edn., 1921, 2nd edn., Berlin, 1925).

—— 'Der deutsche Kriegsplan', *DOBl* (16 August 1924), 209–12.

FOERSTER, WOLFGANG, 'Wollte Graf Schlieffen Holland im Kriegsfalle vergewalti-
gen?', *KSF* 3 (1) (1925), 22–7.

—— 'Die Entstehung des operativen Gedankens in Frankreich von 1871–1914',
DOB 6 (3) (1927), 93–8; 6 (4), 131–5; 6 (5), 174–6.

—— 'Schlieffen und Ludendorff', *DOBl* (25 Februar 1930), 187–91.

—— *Aus der Gedankenwerkstatt des deutschen Generalstabes* (Berlin, 1931).

—— 'Ist der deutsche Aufmarsch 1904 an die Franzosen verraten worden?', *BM*
(November 1932), 1053–67.

—— *Der strategische Aufbau des Weltkrieges 1914–1918* (Berlin, 1933).

—— 'Hat es eine Schlieffenplan-Legende gegeben?', *WR* 2 (12) (Dezember 1952),
601–5.

—— 'Das Geheimnis des Sieges. Graf Schlieffens Größe als militärischer Denker',
DSZ (26. Februar 1953), 7.

—— 'Einige Bemerkungen zu Gerhard Ritters Buch "Der Schlieffenplan" ', *WR* 2
(1957), 37–44.

FRANÇOIS, HERMANN VON, *Marneschlacht und Tannenberg* (Berlin, 1920).

—— 'Der Grenzschutz im Osten im August 1914 und seine Reibungen', *WW* 10 (6)
(1929), 341–56.

FRANTZ, GUNTHER, 'Der russische Generalstab vor dem Weltkriege über Stärke,
Aufmarsch und erste Operationen der Zentralmächte. Nach amtlichen russischen Dokumenten aus dem Frühjahr 1914', *PJ* 179 (Januar bis März
1920),101–13.

—— 'Der russische Aufmarsch gegen Deutschland in August 1914', *WW* 2 (1920),
212–22.

—— 'Rußland und der Zweifrontenkrieg', *PJ* 181 (Juli bis September 1920), 67–78.

—— *Rußlands Eintritt in den Weltkrieg. Der Ausbau der russischen Wehrmacht und ihr
Einsatz bei Kriegsbeginn* (Berlin, 1924).

—— 'Die Kriegsvorbereitungsperiode in Rußland', *KSF* 2 (1924), 89–98.

—— 'Die Entwicklung des Offensivgedankens im russischen Operationsplan',
WW 5 (4) (1924), 373–92.

—— 'Das strategische Eisenbahnnetz Rußlands', *BM* (1930), 259–80.

—— 'War 1914 Mobilmachung gleichbedeutend mit Krieg?', *BM* (1930) 632–64.

—— 'Die Wandlung des operativen Gedankens in Rußland von 1908 bis 1912',
DOB (5 Oktober 1930), 1010–13.

—— 'Die Entwicklung des Befestigungssystems in Westrußland von 1880 bis 1914',
DW 3 (18 Juni 1930), 573–6.

—— 'Wie Rußland mobil machte', *BM* (1936), 277–318.

FREYTAG-LORINGHOVEN, HUGO FREIHERR VON, *Folgerungen aus dem Weltkriege* (Berlin,
1917).

—— *Generalfeldmarschall Graf von Schlieffen: Sein Leben und die Verwertung seines geisti-
gen Erbes im Weltkriege* (Berlin, 1920).

—— *Menschen und Dinge* (Berlin, 1923).

FROBENIUS, HERMANN, *Unsere Festungen: Entwicklung des Festungswesens in Deutschland
seit Einführung der gezogenen Geschütze bis zur neusten Zeit. Band 1. Die Ausgestaltung
der Festung* (Berlin, 1912).

FULLER, J. F. D., *The Decisive Battles of the World 1772–1944* (3 vols., St Albans, 1970).

FULLER, JOSEPH V., 'The War Scare of 1875', *AHR* 24 (2) (January 1919), 196–226.

GABER, STÉPHANE, *La Lorraine fortifiée* (Metz, 1994).

GACKENHOLTZ, HERMANN, *Entscheidung in Lothringen 1914* (Berlin, 1933).

GAMBIEZ, F. and SUIRE, M., *Histoire de la Première Guerre Mondiale* (Paris, 1968).

GAYL, E. FREIHERR VON, *General von Schlichting und sein Lebenswerk* (Berlin, 1913).

GEBSATTEL, FREIHERR LUDWIG VON, *Von Nancy bis zum Champ des Romains 1914* (2nd edn., Oldenburg i. O. and Berlin, 1924).

GEMBRUCH, WERNER, 'General von Schlichting', *WW* (1960), 188–96.

GEYER, MICHAEL, 'Die Geschichte des deutschen Militärs von 1860 bis 1945: Ein Bericht über die Forschungslage', in Hans-Ulrich Wehler (ed.), *Die moderne deutsche Geschichte in der internationalen Forschung 1945–1975*, (Göttingen, 1978), 256–86.

—— *Deutsche Rüstungspolitik 1860–1980* (Frankfurt am Main, 1984).

GEYR VON SCHWEPPENBERG, LEO FREIHERR, 'Der Kriegsausbruch 1914 und der deutsche Generalstab', *WR* (1963), 150–63.

GIRAULT, RÉNE, *Emprunts russes et investissements françaises en Russe 1887–1914* (Paris, 1968).

GOERLITZ, WALTER, *The German General Staff* (New York, 1963).

GOLOVIN, N. N., *The Russian Army in World War I* (New Haven CT, 1931).

GOLTZ, COLMAR FREIHERR VON DER, *Denkwürdigkeiten* (Berlin, 1929).

GOTTBERG, OTTO VON, 'Schlieffen' *TR Unterhaltungsbeilage* Nr. 47, (26. Februar 1920), 1.

GRABAU, ALBERT, *Das Festungsproblem in Deutschland und seine Auswirkung auf die strategische Lage von 1870–1914* (Berlin, 1935).

GRAHAM, LUMLEY, 'The Russo-German Frontier in 1880', *JRUSI*, 24 (1880), 129–49.

GREENE, F. V., *Report on the Russian Army and its Campaigns in Turkey in 1877–1878* (Washington, 1879).

GRIFFITH, PADDY, *Forward into Battle: Fighting Tactics from Waterloo to the Near Future* (rev. edn., Novato, CA, 1991).

GROENER, WILHELM, 'Die Liquidation des Weltkrieges', *PJ* 180 (April bis Juni 1920), 21–31, 161–78, 305–14.

—— 'Das Kriegsgeschichtliche Werk des Reichsarchivs', *PJ* 199 (Januar bis März 1925), 47–56.

—— 'Das Testament des Grafen Schlieffen', *WW* 4 (1925), 193–217.

—— *Das Testament des Grafen Schlieffen*, (2nd edn., Berlin, 1929).

—— *Der Feldherr wider Willen* (Berlin, 1931).

GROUARD, A., *La Guerre éventuelle* (Paris, 1913).

—— *La Conduite de la Guerre jusqu'à la bataille de la Marne* (Paris, 1922).

HAEFTEN, OBERST, 'Bismarck und Moltke', *PJ* 177, (Juli bis September 1919), 85–105.

—— GENERALMAJOR, 'Der deutsche Generalstabschef in der Zeit der Spannung Juli 1914', *DOBl* 28 (24) (24 Juli 1924), 185–8.

HANKE, WILHELM VON, 'Zum Schlieffen-Plan und Moltke-Aufmarsch', *MW* 110 (2) (1925), 44–8.

HARMS, PAUL, 'Schlieffen', *BTH* 11 (1913), 1.

HAUSEN, FREIHERR M. CH. L. VON, *Erinnerungen an den Marnefeldzug 1914* (Leipzig, 1920; 2nd rev. edn., Leipzig, 1922).

HEARDER, HENRY, *Europe in the Nineteenth Century 1830–1880* (London, 1966).

HELLER, EDUARD, 'Bismarcks Stellung zur Führung des Zweifronten-Krieges'. *APG* 4.(9.) 12 (1926), 677–97.

HENNING, A., *Unsere Festungen* (Berlin, 1890).

HERMANN, MATTHIAS, *Das Reichsarchiv* (Berlin, 1993).

HERRMANN, DAVID, *The Arming of Europe and the Making of the First World War* (Princeton, 1996).

HERZFELD, HANS, *Die deutsch–französische Kriegsgefahr von 1875* (Forschungen und Darstellungen aus dem Reichsarchiv, Heft 3) (Berlin, 1922).

HERWIG, HOLGAR, *The First World War. Germany and Austria–Hungary 1914–1918* (London, 1997).

HH., 'Deutsche Flieger in der Schlacht von St. Quentin: 28. bis 30. August 1914', *WW* 4 (2) (1923), 145–53.

HOBHOM, MARTIN, 'Delbrück, Clausewitz und die Kritik des Weltkrieges', *PJ* 181 (Juli bis September 1920), 203–33.

HOENIG, FRITZ, *Die Wehrkraft Frankreichs im Jahre 1885* (Berlin, 1879).

HOFACKER, GENERALLEUTNANT, 'Zu den neusten Veröffentlichungen über den Moltke-Plan und die August-Operation 1914', *MW* (1925), 1292–3.

HOWARD, MICHAEL, *The Continental Commitment* (London, 1972).

H. SCH., 'Der Verteidigungszustand der Festung Paris in August und September 1914', *DW* (6. Juli 1929), 502–6.

—— 'Die militärischen und maritimen Abmachungen zwischen Frankreich und Rußland vor dem Weltkriege', *DW* 3 (12), (26. März 1930), 265–8.

HUGHES, DANIEL J., 'Schlichting, Schlieffen and the Prussian Theory of War', *JMH* 59 (2) (April 1995), 257–78.

IMMANUEL, FRIEDRICH, *Siege und Niederlagen im Weltkriege* (Berlin, 1919).

JANNEN, WILLIAM, JR., *The Lions of July* (Novato, CA, 1996).

JANY, C., *Geschichte der preußischen Armee* (2nd edn., 4 vols., Osnabrück, 1967).

JOFFRE, JOSEPH J. J.-C., *Mémoires 1910–1917* (2 vols., Paris, 1932).

JOLL, JAMES, *The Origins of the First World War* (2nd edn., Harlow, 1992).

JUSTROW, KARL, *Feldherr und Kriegstechnik. Studien über den Operationsplan des Grafen Schlieffen und Lehren für unseres Wehraufbau und unsere Landesverteidigung* (Oldenburg, 1933).

K., OBERST, 'Über die Folgerichtigkeit der Operationen der 7. und 6. Armee im August 1914', *DW* 3 (33) (3 September 1930), 845–7; ibid. (34) (10 September 1930), 875–6.

—— 'Nochmals über die Folgerichtigkeit der 7. und 6. Armee im August 1914', ibid. 4 (6) (11 Februar 1931), 146–7.

KABISCH, ERNST, *Streitfragen des Weltkrieges* (Stuttgart, 1924).

—— 'Die Angriffshandlungen der Feindmächte zu Beginn des Weltkrieges', *BM* (Juni 1932), 535–51.

KANIA, HANS, *Graf Schlieffen der Chef des Großen Generalstabes als Vorbereiter des Großen Krieges* (Potsdam, 1915).

KANN, RÉGINALD, *Le Plan de campagne allemand de 1914 et son exécution* (Paris, 1923).

KAULBACH, EBERHARD, 'Schlieffen. Zur Frage der Bedeutung und Wirkung seiner Arbeit', *WR* (1963), 137–49.

KEEGAN, JOHN, *The First World War* (New York, 1999).

KEIGER, JOHN F. V., *France and the Origins of the First World War* (London, 1983).

KEIM, AUGUST, 'Graf Schlieffen', *MWR* 595 (1921), 177–91.

KENNEDY, PAUL, 'The Operational Plans of the Great Powers 1880–1914: Analysis of Recent Literature', *MM* 19 (1976), 189–207.

—— (ed.), *The War Plans of the Great Powers 1880–1914* (London, 1979).

—— *The Rise of the Anglo-German Antagonism* (London, 1980).

KESSEL, EBERHARD, *Moltke* (Stuttgart, 1957).

KILIANI, EMMANUEL VON, *Graf Schlieffen* (Berlin, 1921).

—— 'Die Operationslehre des Grafen Schlieffen und ihre deutsche Gegner', *Wehrkunde* 2 (1961), 71–6; 3 (1961), 133–8.

KITCHEN, MARTIN, *A Military History of Germany* (Bloomington and London, 1975).

KIRCHHAMMER, 'Deutschlands Nordostgrenze', *Streffleur's* 20 (3–4) (1879), 229–39.

KLEMP, HAUPTMANN, 'Einsatz der Fliegerverbände auf dem westlichen Heeresflügel während der Marneoperation 1914', *DW* 1 (15) (18 April 1928), 302–3.

—— 'Lufterkundung auf dem deutschen rechten Heeresflügel während der Vormarsches zur Marne 1914', *DW* 1 (16) (25. April 1928), 323–5.

—— 'Lufterkundung auf dem rechten deutschen Heeresflügel zu Beginn der Marneschlacht 1914', *DW* 1 (17) (2. Mai 1928), 348–50.

—— 'Lufterkundung auf dem rechten Heeresflügel während des Höhepunktes der Marneschlacht 1914', *DW* 1 (18) (9. Mai 1928), 373–5.

KLOSTER, WALTER, *Der deutsche Generalstab und der Präventivkrieg-Gedanke* (Stuttgart, 1932).

KLUCK, A. VON, *Der Marsch auf Paris und die Marneschlacht 1914* (Berlin, 1920).

—— *Wanderjahre–Kriege–Gestalten* (Berlin, 1929).

KÖNIGSDORFER, GENERALMAJOR, 'Übersicht über die operative Bedeutung der Festungen in den Feldzügen des Jahres 1914', *DW* 3 (36) (24. September 1930), 925–7.

KRAFFT VON DELLMENSINGEN, KONRAD, *Die Führung des Kronprinzen Rupprecht von Bayern auf dem linken deutschen Heeresflügel bis zur Schlacht in Lothringen im August 1914* (Berlin, 1925).

—— 'Nochmals über die Folgerichtigkeit der Operationen der 7. und 6. Armee im August 1914', *DW* 3 (44) (19 November 1930), 1115–17; (45) (26. November 1930), 1142–5.

—— *Kritischer Streifzug durch die Studien des Generalleutnants a.D. Wilhelm Groener über den Weltkrieg* (Munich, 1931).

KUHL, HERMANN VON, *Der deutsche Generalstab in Vorbereitung und Durchführung des Weltkrieges* (Berlin, 1920).

—— *Der Marnefeldzug 1914* (Berlin, 1921).

—— 'Warum mißlang der Marnefeldzug 1914?', *DOBl* (21. Dezember 1920), 894–5; (21. Januar 1921), 38–9.

—— 'Beurteilung unserer Heerführer im Weltkriege', *PJ* 184 (April bis Juni 1921), 289–99.

—— 'Die Verletzung der belgischen Neutralität durch Deutschland im Jahre 1914', *DOBl* (21. Oktober 1921), 596–9.

KUHL, HERMANN VON, 'Kriegsliteratur', *DoBL* (21 Juni 1921), 355–6; (21 Juli 1921), 416–17; (21. August 1921), 475–6; (21. November 1921), 657–8; (21. Dezember 1921), 719–20.

—— 'Die französische und englische Literatur über den Weltkrieg', *WW* 3 (1921), 147–54.

—— 'Die Kriegserinnerungen des Kronprinzen', *PJ* 191 (Januar bis März 1923), 166–81.

—— 'Graf Schlieffen und der Weltkrieg', *WW* 1 (1923), 1–8.

—— 'Die Verletzung der Neutralität Belgiens', *DAZ Beiblatt Morgen Ausgabe*, 5. August 1923.

—— 'Ost oder Westaufmarsch 1914?', *KSF* 1 (1923), 73–76.

—— 'Der Telegrammwechsel zwischen Moltke und Conrad von Hötzendorf am 30. und 31. Juli 1914', *KSF* (1924), 43–7.

—— 'Graf Schlieffen's "Cannae", *MW* 109 (16) (25. Oktober 1924), 417–20.

—— 'Eine neue französische Darstellung des Krieges', *MW* 109 (17) (4 November 1924), 449–54.

—— 'Streitfragen des Weltkrieges', *MW* 109 (36) (25 März 1925), 1089–94.

—— 'Der französische und belgische Aufmarsch 1914', *MW* 39 (18 April 1925), 1185–90. [Review of Selliers de Moranville, *Du haut de la Tour du Babel*].

—— 'Generalleutnant von Mosers "Ernsthafte Plaudieren über den Weltkrieg" ', *MW* 109 (43), 1323–6.

—— *Der Weltkrieg 1914–1918* (2 vols., Berlin, 1929).

LANGDON, JOHN W., *July 1914. The Long Debate, 1918–1990* (New York and Oxford, 1991).

LANGE, SVEN, *Hans Delbrück und der 'Strategiestreit'* (Freiburg im Breisgau, 1995).

LANREZAC, CHARLES, *Le Plan de campagne français et le premier mois de la guerre* (Paris, 1920).

LEHMANN, KONRAD, 'Ermattungsstrategie—oder nicht?', *HZ* 151 (1935), 48–86.

LEINVEBER, GENERALMAJOR, 'Die Strategie Moltkes und Joffres im Marnefeldzug westlich Verdun' *Das Wissen vom Kriege (Beilage zum DOBl)* 15 (15. Juni 1927), 57–8; 16 (27. Juni 1927), 61–2; 17 (3. Juli 1927), 65; 18 (13. Juli 1927), 70–1.

—— 'Moltkes System der Aushilfen. Eine Klarstellung', *Das Wissen vom Kriege (Beilage zum DoBL)*, 26 (5. Oktober 1927), 102–3.

LENSKI, FRANZ VON, Generalleutnant, 'Der Schlieffensche Aufmarsch gegen Frankreich und seine spätere Abänderung', *Das Wissen vom Kriege (Beilage zum DoBL)*, 1 (15. Mai 1922), 1–4.

—— 'Eine Erwiderung auf die Aufsätze des Generals Leinveber "Die Strategie Moltkes und Joffres im Marnefeldzuge westlich Verduns" ', *Das Wissen vom Kriege (Beilage zum DoBL)*, 20 (3. August 1927), 77–8; 21 (10. August 1927), 82–3.

LEPPA, KONRAD, 'Schlieffen in Polen', *DW* 3 (Dezember 1930), 1167–9.

LIDDELL-HART, Sir B. H., *The Real War 1914–18* (1930).

LISS, ULRICH, 'Graf Schlieffens letztes Kriegsspiel', *WR* 15 (1965), 162–6.

Lobell's Jahresberichte über das Heer- und Kriegswesen XXXIII. Jahrgang (1906), Pelet-Narbonne, *Generalleutnant* (ed.), (Berlin, 1907).

LUDENDORFF, ERICH, *Meine Kriegserinnerungen* (Berlin, 1919).

—— *Kriegführung und Politik* (Berlin, 1922).

—— 'Der Aufmarsch 1914', *DW* 3 (32) (8. August 1926), 1–2.

—— 'Der Aufmarsch 1914', *LV* 31 (24. Dezember 1929), 1.

—— 'Der Aufmarsch 1914', *DW* (4. Februar 1930), 3–4.

—— *Mein militärischer Werdegang* (Munich, 1933).

MACDONALD, G., 'The Railways of France and Germany, considered with Reference to the Concentration of Armies on the Franco-German Frontier', *JRUSI* 24 (1880), 725–37.

McELWEE, WILLIAM, *The Art of War: Waterloo to Mons* (London, 1974).

MANTEY, OBERST, 'Betrachtungen über den deutschen Aufmarschplan', *WW* (1926), 234–50.

—— 'Die Bedeutung von Meldungen', *DW* 1 (23) (20 Juni 1928), 489–92.

—— 'Führung von oben und Selbständigkeit der Unterführer' *DW* (26. November 1930), 1139–41; (5. December 1930), 1164–6.

MARCHAND, A., *Plans de concentration de 1871 à 1914* (Paris, 1926).

MAURICE, JOHN FREDERICK, *The Balance of Military Power in Europe* (Edinburgh and London, 1888).

MAY, ERNEST R. (ed.), *Knowing One's Enemies. Intelligence Assessment before the Two World Wars* (Princeton, 1984).

MAYR, KARL, 'Kriegsplan und staatsmännische Voraussicht. Kriegsgeschichtliche Betrachtungen über die Schlieffenschule' *ZP* 14 (1925), 385–411.

MEISNER, HEINRICH OTTO, *Denkwürdigkeiten des General-Feldmarschalls Alfred Graf Waldersee* (Berlin, 1923).

MENNING, BRUCE W., *Bayonets before Bullets: The Imperial Russian Army, 1861–1914* (Bloomington, IL, and Indianapolis, IN, 1992).

METTE, SIEGFRIED, *Vom Geist deutscher Feldherren* (Berlin, 1938).

MEYER, HAUPTMANN, *Zur Frage der Landesbefestigung* (Berlin, 1898).

MICHALKA, WOLFGANG (ed.), *Der Erste Weltkrieg. Wirkung, Wahrnehmung, Analyse* (Munich, 1994).

MICHON, G., *L'Alliance franco-russe 1871–1917* (Paris, 1931).

—— *La Preparation de la guerre. La loi de trois ans 1910–1914* (Paris, 1932).

MILLER, FORREST, *Dmitri Miliutin and the Reform Era in Russia* (Charlotte, NC, 1963).

MILLER, STEVEN, *Military Strategy and the Origins of the First World War* (Princeton, 1995).

MILLET, ALLEN AND MURRAY, WILLIAMSON (eds.), *Military Effectiveness. Volume I: The First World War* (Winchester, MA, 1988).

MIQUEL, PIERRE, *La Grande Guerre* (Paris, 1983).

MOHS, HANS (ed.), *General-Feldmarschall Alfred Graf Waldersee in seinem militärischen Wirken* (2 vols., Berlin, 1929).

MOLTKE, HELMUTH VON (ELDER), 'Betrachtungen über Konzentration im Kriege', *MW* (April 1867), 187–9.

—— *The Franco-German War of 1870–71* (English trans., London, 1907).

MOLTKE, HELMUTH VON (YOUNGER), *Erinnerungen, Briefe, Dokumente 1877–1916* (Stuttgart, 1922).

MOMBAUER, ANNIKA, 'A Reluctant Military Leader? Helmuth von Moltke and the July Crisis of 1914', *WH* 6 (4) (1999), 417–46.

MOMMSEN, W. A. (ed.), *Die Nachlässe in den deutschen Archiven 'mit Ergänzungen aus anderen Beständen'. Teil 1: Verzeichnis der schriftlichen Nachlässe in den deutschen Archiven und Bibliotheken. Band 1: Schriften des Bundesarchivs 17* (Boppard am Rhein, 1971).

MONTHILET, J., *Les Institutions militaires de la France 1814–1932* (2nd edn., Paris, 1932).

MOSER, OTTO VON, *Feldzugsaufzeichnungen als Brigade-, Divisionskommandeur und als kommandierende General 1914–1918* (Stuttgart, 1920).

—— *Kurzer strategischer Überblick über den Weltkrieg 1914–1918* (Berlin, 1921).

—— *Ernsthafte Plaudieren über den Weltkrieg* (Stuttgart, 1924).

—— *Das militärisch und politisch Wichtigste vom Weltkriege* (Stuttgart, 1927).

MÜLLER, HERMANN VON, *Die Thätigkeit der deutschen Festungsartillerie bei den Belagerungen, Beschiessungen und Einschliessungen im deutsch–französischen Kriege 1870/71. Erster Band. Die Belagerung von Straßburg* (Berlin, 1898).

—— *Geschichte des Festungskrieges von 1885–1905 einschließlich der Belagerung von Port Arthur* (Berlin, 1907).

MÜLLER-LOEBNITZ, WILHELM, *Die Sendung des Oberstleutnants Hentsch* (Forschungen und Darstellungen aus dem Reichsarchiv, Band 1) (Berlin, 1922).

—— 'Französische Kritik der Marne-Schlacht', *WW* 4 (2) (1923), 82–103.

NEHBEL, GENERALLEUTNANT, 'Königsberg 1914', *DW* 3 (29) (28. Mai 1930), 492–4.

NEUMANN, HARTWIG, *Die klassische Großfestung Koblenz* (Koblenz, 1989).

OTTO, HELMUT, 'Militärische Aspekte der Außenpolitik Bismarcks (1871–1890)', *ZMG* 2 1967, 150–66.

PALÉOLOGUE, MAURICE, 'Un prélude a l'invasion de la Belgique', *RDM* 102 (8.11) (1932, vol. 5), 481–524.

PARET, PETER (ed.), *Makers of Modern Strategy from Machiavelli to the Nuclear Age* (Princeton, NJ, 1986).

PESCHKE, RUDOLF, 'Moltke als Politiker', *PJ* 158 (Oktober bis Dezember 1914), 16–35.

PFLANZE, OTTO, *Bismarck and the Development of Germany* (3 vols., Princeton, 1990).

PICQ, ARDANT DU, *Battle Studies* (English trans., Harrisburg, PA, 1946).

PORCH, DOUGLAS, *The March to the Marne: The French Army 1871–1914* (Cambridge, 1981).

RAHNE, HERMANN, *Mobilmachung* (Berlin, 1983).

RALSTON, DAVID, *The Army of the Republic: The Place of the Military in the Political Evolution of France* (Cambridge, MA, 1967).

RASSOW, PETER, *Der Plan Moltkes für den Zweifrontenkrieg* (2nd edn., Breslau, 1938).

RITTER, G., *Kritik des Weltkrieges, von einem Generalstabler* (Leipzig, 1920).

RITTER, GERHARD, 'Das Problem des Militarismus in Deutschland', *HZ* 177 (1954), 21–48.

—— *Der Schlieffenplan. Kritik eines Mythos* (Munich, 1956); English edn.: *The Schlieffen Plan: Critique of a Myth* (London, 1958).

—— *Staatskunst und Kriegshandwerk* (2 vols., Munich, 1954–68); English edn.: *The Sword and the Scepter The Problem of Militarism in Germany* (2 vols., Miami, 1969).

ROCHS, HUGO, *Schlieffen* (Berlin, 1926).

ROLF, RUDI, *Die deutsche Panzerfortifikation. Die Panzerfesten von Metz und ihre Vorgeschichte* (Osnabrück, 1991).

ROPPONEN, RISTO, *Die Kraft Rußlands: Wie beurteilte die politische und militärische Führung der europäischen Großmächte in der Zeit von 1905 bis 1914 die Kraft Rußlands?* (Helsinki, 1968).

ROQUES, OBERST, 'Die operativen Nachrichtenverbindungen der Armeen des rechten Flügels im Marnefeldzug 1914', *DW* (14. März 1928), 188–91.

ROSINSKI, HERBERT, *Die deutsche Armee* (Düsseldorf and Vienna, 1970).

ROTHENBERG, GUNTHER E., *The Army of Francis Joseph* (West Lafayette, IN, 1976).

RUDT VON COLLENBERG, FREIHERR LUDWIG, *Die deutsche Armee von 1871 bis 1914* (Berlin, 1922).

—— 'Graf Schlieffen und die Kriegsformation der deutschen Armee', *WW* 10 (1927), 605–34.

—— 'Die deutsche Heeresverstärkungen von 1871 bis 1914', *BM* (November 1930), 1043–65.

RUITH, RITTER VON, OBERST, 'Der Feldzug in Lothringen 1914', *WW* 4 (1921), 255–71; 5 (1921), 297–318.

RUPPRECHT VON BAYERN, *Mein Kriegstagebuch*, (ed) Eugen von Frauenholz (Munich, 1929).

SCHÄFER, HUGO, Oberst im österreichischen Bundesheere, 'Die militärischen Abmachungen des Dreibundes vor dem Weltkriege', *PJ* 188 (April bis Juni 1922), 203–14.

SCHÄFER, GENERALMAJOR, 'Die Operations- und Organisationspläne des Grafen Schlieffen und des französischen Generals Michel', *DW* (20. März 1929), 198–200.

SCHÄFER, OBERSTLEUTNANT THEOBALD VON, 'Der Grenzschütz in Ostpreußen 1914', *WW* 10 (1929), 504–6.

—— 'Die deutsche Mobilmachung', *BM* (August 1936), 597–639.

SCHIFF, OTTO, 'Moltke als politischer Denker', *PJ* 181 (Juni bis September 1920), 318–36.

SCHLEGEL, KLAUS, *Köln und seine preußischen Soldaten. Die Geschichte der Garnison und Festung Köln von 1814 bis 1914* (Cologne, 1979).

SCHLIEFFEN, ALFRED VON, *Cannae* (Berlin, 1925).

SCHMERFELD, F. VON, (ed.) *Die deutschen Aufmarschpläne 1871–1890* (Forschungen und Darstellungen aus dem Reichsarchiv) (Berlin, 1929).

—— 'Aus des großen Moltke geistiger Werkstatt. I. Taktische Aufgaben', *DW* (6. Februar 1929), 82–4.

SCHMIDT, RAINER F., *Die gescheiterte Allianz* (Frankfurt am Main, 1992).

SCHNIEWINDT, GENERALLEUTNANT, 'Die Nachrichtenverbindungen zwischen den Kommandobehörden während des Bewegungskrieges 1914', *WW* 3 (1929), 129–52.

SCHÖLLGEN, GREGOR (ed.), *Flucht in den Krieg? Die Außenpolitik des kaiserlichen Deutschland* (Darmstadt, 1991).

SCHÖN, J., 'Der Kriegsschauplatz zwischen dem Rhein und der Seine und die Hauptaufgaben seiner Befestigungen' in K. und k. technischen Militärkomitee (eds.) *Mitteilungen über Gegenstände des Artillerie- und Geniewesens* 35 (1904).

SCHULTE, BERND, *Die deutsche Armee 1910–1914. Zwischen Beharren und Verändern* (Düsseldorf, 1977).

—— 'Neue Dokumente zu Kriegsausbruch und Kriegsverlauf 1914' [Wenninger Reports and Diary], *MM* 25 (1979), 123–85.

SCHWEINITZ, W. VON (ed.), *Denkwürdigkeiten des Botschafters General von Schweinitz* (2 vols., Berlin, 1929).

SCHWEPPENBERG, LEO FREIHEER GEYR VON, 'Der Kriegsausbruch und der deutsche Generalstab', *WR* (1963), 151.

SEECKT, HANS VON, *Moltke. Ein Vorbild* (Berlin, 1931).

SELLIERS DU MORANVILLE, *Du haut de la Tour du Babel* (Paris, 1925).

SENFTLEBEN, E., 'Das Kriegstagebuch des Kronprinzen Rupprecht von Bayern', *DW* (20. Februar 1929), 132–3.

SHOWALTER, DENNIS, 'The Eastern Front and German Military Planning 1871–1914', *EEQ* 15 (1981), 163–80.

—— *Tannenberg, Clash of Empires* (Hamden, CT, 1991).

SNYDER, JOHN, *The Ideology of the Offensive: Military Decision-Making and the Disasters of 1914* (Ithaca, NY, and London, 1984).

STAABS, H. VON, *Aufmarsch nach zwei Fronten auf Grund der Operationspläne von 1871–1914* (Berlin, 1925).

STEGEMANN, HERMANN, *Die Geschichte des Krieges, Band I* (Stuttgart and Berlin, 1917).

STEIN, GENERAL, *Erlebnisse und Betrachtungen* (Leipzig, 1919).

STEINHAUSEN, GEORG, *Die Grundfehler des Krieges und der Generalstab* (Gotha, 1919).

STEVENSON, DAVID, *The Outbreak of the First World War. 1914 in Perspective* (London and New York, 1997).

STONE, NORMAN, 'Gerhard Ritter and the First World War', *HJ* 13 (1970), 158–71.

—— *The Eastern Front 1914–1917* (London, 1975).

STRACHAN, HEW, *European Armies and the Conduct of War* (London, 1983).

—— (ed.), *World War I. A History* (Oxford and New York, 1998).

—— *The First World War. Volume I: To Arms* (Oxford and New York, 2001).

Streffleur's XX Jahrgang (1897).

—— *XLVII (der ganzen Folge 83. Jahrgang)* (1906).

STÜRMER, M., *Das ruhelose Reich. Deutschland 1866–1918* (n.p., n.d.).

SUEVICUS, 'Beiträge zur Geschichte der Marne-Schlacht. Die Kämpfe südlich der Marne' *WW* 4 (1920), 367–83.

SZCZEPANSKI, MAX VON, 'Zur wissenschaftlichen Kritik des Weltkrieges', *PJ* 183 (Januar bis März 1921), 124–32.

—— 'Der Spuk der Ermattungsstrategie', *DW* (27. März 1929), 217–18; (4. April 1929), 237–8.

TAPPEN, GENERALLEUTNANT, *Bis zur Marne 1914* (Berlin 1920).

TAYLOR, A. J. P., *The Struggle for Mastery in Europe 1848–1918* (London, 1954).

—— *War by Timetable: How the First World War Began* (London, 1969).

TERRAINE, JOHN, *The Smoke and the Fire: Myths and Anti-Myths of War 1860–1945* (London, 1980).

TESKE, HERMANN, *Colmar Freiherr von der Goltz: Ein Kämpfer für den militärischen Fortschritt* (Göttingen, 1957).

TREBILCOCK, CLIVE, *The Industrialization of the Continental Powers 1780–1914* (London, 1981).

TUCHMANN, BARBARA, *The Guns of August* (New York, 1962).

TUNSTALL, GRAYDON A., *Planning for War against Russia and Serbia: Austro-Hungarian and German Military Strategies 1871–1914* (Highland Lakes, NJ, 1993).

TURNER, L. C. F., 'The Russian Mobilisation in 1914', *JCH* 3 (1) (January 1968), 65–88.

—— *Origins of the First World War* (London, 1970).

—— 'The Significance of the Schlieffen Plan' in Paul Kennedy, (ed), *The War Plans of the Great Powers 1880–1914* (London, 1979), 199–221.

VAN CREVELD, MARTIN, *Technology and War* (New York, 1989).

VOIGTLANDER-TETZER, GERHARD, 'Die Geschützturme der deutschen Panzerfortifikation bis zum 1. Weltkrieg', in Volker Schmidchen (ed.), *Festung, Ruine, Baudenkmal (=SF Band 3)* (Wesel, 1984), 95–114.

WALLACH, JEHUDA L., *The Dogma of the Battle of Annihilation* (Westport, CT, 1986).

WAWRO, GEOFFREY, *The Austro-Prussian War. Austria's War with Prussia and Italy in 1866* (Cambridge, 1996).

WEBER, EUGEN, *The Nationalist Revival in France, 1905–1914* (Berkeley and Los Angeles, 1959).

WEBERSTEDT, HANS, 'Moltke als Staatsmann', *Das Wissen vom Kriege (Beilage zum DOBl)*, 11 (4. Mai 1927), 41–2.

WEGNER-KORFES, S., 'Realpolitische Haltung bei Offizieren der Familien Mertz von Quirnheim, Korfes und Dieckmann', *MG* 25(3) (1986), 226–33.

WEHLER, HANS-ULRICH, *The German Empire 1871–1918* (German edn., Göttingen 1973; English trans. Providence, RI, and Oxford, 1985).

WETZELL, GEORG, GENERAL DER INFANTERIE, 'Das Kriegswerk des Reichsarchivs "Der Weltkrieg 1914/18". Kritische Betrachtungen zum 1. Band: Die Grenzschlachten im Westen', *WW* 1 (1925), 1–43; 3 (1925), 129–57.

—— 'Schlieffen-Moltke (der Jüngere)-Bülow', *MW* 109 (44) (25 Mai 1925), 1352–64.

—— 'Ein Wertvolles kriegsgeschichtliches Buch. Das Marnedrama 1914', *DW* 1 (6) (Februar 1928), 283–4; 1(24) (27. Juni 1928), 516–18.

—— 'Die Marneschlacht im September 1914', *DW* 1 (33) (5. September 1928), 709–12; 1 (34) (12. September 1928), 734–7; 1 (35) (19. September 1928), 758–61; 1 (36) (26. September 1928), 779–83.

—— 'Des Feldmarschall Grafen Moltke deutsche Aufmarschpläne 1870–1890', *DW* 1 45 (5. December 1928), 954–6; 1 (46) (12. December 1928), 969–70.

WILLIAMSON, SAMUEL R., *The Politics of Grand Strategy: Britain and France prepare for War 1904–1914* (Harvard, 1969).

WILSON, KEITH, *Decisions for War, 1914* (London, 1995).

WOLBE, EUGEN, *Alexander von Kluck* (Leipzig, 1917).

WRISBERG, GENERALMAJOR, 'Zur Beurteilung des Reichsarchivwerkes', *MW* 46 (1925), 1437–40.

ZANDER, ERNST, *Köln als befestigte Stadt und militärischer Standort* (Cologne, 1941).

ZIEKURSCH, JOHANNES, 'Ludendorffs Kriegserinnerungen', *HZ* 25.3 (121) (1920), 441–65.

ZIMMERMANN, EUGEN, 'Um Schlieffen's Plan', *SM* (März 1921), 369–84.

ZOELLNER, GENERALLEUTNANT VON, 'Schlieffens Vermächtnis', *MWR Sonderheft 4* (Januar 1938), 1–56.

ZWEHL, GENERAL, 'Die Sending des Oberstleutnants Hentsch', *DOB* 25 (11. Juni 1921), 333–5.

—— 'Vom Operationsplan des Grafen Schlieffen', *KZ* 46 (1921).

Index

Lightning Source UK Ltd.
Milton Keynes UK
UKOW04f0619110514

231430UK00001B/2/P